Edging

into the

Future

Edging into the Future

Science Fiction and Contemporary Cultural Transformation

Edited by

VERONICA HOLLINGER and

JOAN GORDON

PENN

UNIVERSITY OF PENNSYLVANIA PRESS

Philadelphia

10 9 8 7 6 5 4 3 2 1

Published by
University of Pennsylvania Press
Philadelphia, Pennsylvania 19104-4011

Library of Congress Cataloging-in-Publication Data

Edging into the future : science fiction and contemporary cultural transformation /
edited by Veronica Hollinger and Joan Gordon.
    p. cm.
   Includes bibliographical references and index.
   ISBN 0-8122-3657-2 (cloth : alk. paper)—ISBN 0-8122-1804-3 (paper : alk. paper)
   1. Science fiction, American—History and criticism. 2. Science fiction, English—
History and criticism. 3. Popular culture—United States. 4. Popular culture—Great
Britain. I. Hollinger, Veronica. II. Gordon, Joan, 1947—
PS374.S35 E37 2002
813'.0876209—dc21

                                                              2001052530

For Dede Weil

Contents

1

Introduction

Edging into the Future

VERONICA HOLLINGER
and JOAN GORDON

It has become a truth universally acknowledged that contemporary life in the West reiterates not the past but the future. In his introduction to *Interzone: The Second Anthology*, John Clute offers a succinct version of this truism when he observes that "[w]e no longer feel that we penetrate the future; futures penetrate us" (vii). Variations on this theme have been developed by cultural diagnosticians from Jean Baudrillard to Scott Bukatman and by sf writers from Bruce Sterling to Gwyneth Jones. In Jones's foreword to *Deconstructing the Starships: Science, Fiction and Reality*, she says, "[A] great deal of the future imagined by *my* generation's sf writers is actually with us." She goes on to suggest that "at this particular moment in time, reality and science fiction are moving into such close conjunction that science fiction is no longer the strange reflection and artistic elaboration of current preoccupations: the mirror and the reality have almost become one" (vii). Situated as we are well on the other side of cyberpunk—long considered to be sf's most up-to-the-minute subgenre—science fiction has come to function not only as metaphor for the present but also, and increasingly, as literal description. These days it is both fictional genre and discursive field. One of the aims of *Edging into the Future* is to examine science fiction's complex intersections with this transitory present moment.

We live our lives within a technoculture defined by communications systems that are in the process of transforming human interactions, as well as by reproductive technologies and breakthroughs in genetic engineering that are well on the way to dismantling familiar ideas about what it means to be human. Ideas and images that very recently seemed far-fetched and figurative—Baudrillard's notion of the imploding present, Donna Haraway's cyborg theory—strike us now as increasingly accurate, and the challenge for science fiction today is less to extrapolate a far future than to keep up with a permanently mutable present, to live up to its reputation as a literature of change. At the same time, the challenge for contemporary science fiction criticism and theory is to keep up with a popular genre that is itself in a state of constant flux and that is often far ahead of its critics in terms of its sociopolitical and ethical explorations. So, from this perspective, this book is an attempt to catch up to the imaginative futures being constructed in contemporary science fiction, those futures that function, in part, to shape our own present experiences in technoculture.

Edging into the Future is a collection of essays by science fiction writers and scholars that acknowledges and explores this expanded role for science fiction and that emphasizes its ongoing narration of the future/present. At the same time, the collection hopes to disrupt the potential ossification of the sf canon as it has been developed through the academic teaching and critical writing of the 1990s. The broad range of these contributions demonstrates a healthy argument about which works are central to the genre as it exists today, and about which approaches and world-views most usefully respond to our lives in technoculture; concomitantly, these essays suggest some of the intriguing directions in which sf has developed and in which it may continue to move.

If modernism, with its connotations of both the "new" and the "now," refers to a cultural movement already swiftly receding into historical distance, then postmodernism, which names our present cultural moment, has come also to include the future that has overtaken the modernist present. This moment in cultural time teeters, then, on the edge of the future, neither there, nor, though it seems impossible, here. After all, if we are no longer modern, neither are we not modern. Already moving into the future and overwhelmed by the increasingly radical transformations affecting every aspect of our lives in culture, our postmodern condition encompasses both ties to and ruptures with the past. *Edging into the Future* looks at the variety of ways in which science fiction, both as genre and as discursive field, has been deployed as a means to think about these contemporary social, cultural, political, and technological transformations, fractures, and gaps. Boundaries have become permeable: the present is past, the future is now, and the work of redefinition is compulsive and itself a defining feature of the moment. Genres, subjects, bodies, communities, and futures are all in flux.

As the essays in this collection demonstrate, science fiction is both symptomatic of this cultural disruption and an expression of our desire to situate and give a shape to the moment. As symptom, we see how sf's generic boundaries have become more and more difficult to delineate; how its conventional relationships with the real have become more and more intricate; how many of its narratives fail to keep up with the postmodern present. As expression, we see in contemporary sf one of the most accurate and sophisticated tools currently available to us in our efforts at what Fredric Jameson has termed the "vocation" of a politically aware postmodernism: "the invention and projection of a global cognitive mapping, on a social as well as a spatial scale" ("Postmodernism" 92).

The cautionary "post" in postmodern represents both our hesitation to let go of the past/present and our anxiety that we are, in fact, on the other side of irrevocable change. This moment of seemingly perpetual cultural and political crisis is represented by a bewildering assortment of postings. The present is postcolonial. It may, in fact, be posthistorical. Our theoretical strategies are poststructuralist, if not downright postcritical, while our imaginative strategies are, thanks to postprint communications technologies, postnarrative. This is, no doubt, related to the fact that we inhabit an increasingly postliterate world. We verge on both postsubjectivity and posthumanity, and, according to many depressing reports, postfeminism as well. Baudrillard has argued for a construction of America as the postutopia, while Haraway has found a powerfully political image in the figure of the postgender cyborg, inhabitant of a postnatural world. Science is not only post-Newtonian, it has long since become post-Einsteinian.

Science fiction, which has conventionally used the future to comment on the present and the alien to comment on the familiar, provides an ideal site from which to explore the liminal, the brink, the verge, the frontier, the edge, over which all these postings hover. More and more writers are turning to science fiction as a narrative discourse through which to map the metamorphoses of present reality. Whatever else it may be about, and no matter how strong the impulse toward extrapolative world-building it may demonstrate, science fiction is also always about its own present, and never more so than now, because sf too resides on the borderland of our current critical condition, addressing the futurity of our present moment.

Edging into the Future comprises thirteen essays organized into three sections. "Genre Implosion" explores the dissolution of borders between science fiction and other genres; "Imploded Subjects and Reinscripted Bodies" examines shifting definitions of bodies, genders, and sexualities; and "Reimagined Apocalypses and Exploded Communities" considers the continuation, in new forms, of sf's narrations of apocalypse and its attempts to imagine new communal identities. The future's grip upon our imaginations is an important focus in this book, since our ideas about the future affect how the present constructs actual bodies, actual genders, real-world politics, and real-world communities.

Gary K. Wolfe opens with a study of the complex generic interplay among science fiction, fantasy, and horror that aims to show how "the fantastic genres contain within themselves the seeds of their own dissolution." His detailed history of the development of science fiction as a publishing category is followed by a discussion of the kinds of generic exchanges and interchanges that have resulted in its ongoing transformation. He concludes by identifying features of postmodern "genre dissolution" in hybrid fictions such as Sheri Tepper's *Plague of Angels*, Peter Straub's *Mr. X*, and Geoff Ryman's *Was*. These ideas about transformation, exchange, and interchange are central to all the essays collected here.

The other contributions in this first section—Lance Olsen's autobiographical meditation on rock music, avant-pop fiction, and science fiction and Brooks Landon's expert-witness testimony about some of the ways in which the technologies of virtuality are currently transforming sf film—also explore genre implosion and reinvention. Olsen's "Omniphage" is an exercise in "autobiographiction" that traces the avant-pop intersections of sf and rock 'n' roll in his own fiction, in particular his novels *Tonguing the Zeitgeist*, *Time Famine*, and *Freaknest*. Olsen also provides an experimental history of the avant-pop, ranging widely through the writings of postgeneric authors such as Kathy Acker, William Gibson, Steve Aylett, and Paul Di Filippo. A self-identified work of "performative critifiction," "Omniphage" unfolds against a background of sf-inflected rock 'n' roll.

Brooks Landon's essay on "post-sf film" turns our attention from the printed page to the computer screen and offers us a concise examination of what comes after the science fiction film. Basing his speculations on developments in CGI (computer-generated imagery) and other aspects of electronic media, Landon undertakes to develop a theoretical understanding of our experience of such new media. His wide-ranging foray through a variety of high-tech science fiction sites takes in not only the computer-generated morphs of *Terminator Two* and the fictional holonovels of *Star Trek: Voyager* but also considers the new spectatorial spaces made possible by DVD and Web technologies and the new reading practices invited by hypertext.

"Imploded Subjects and Reinscripted Bodies" looks closely at some aspects of the increasingly pervasive interpenetrations of bodies and information, and of bodies and technology, and suggests some of the ways in which subjects, bodies, and genders are becoming (re)constructed and (re)defined in the context of postmodern technoculture. Jenny Wolmark's opening essay maps the territory of the posthuman subject—a hybrid and shifting techno-self composed at once of flesh, information, and technology—through a reading of post-cyberpunk film and fiction, raising questions about gender, embodiment, and politics. Framed by a combination of feminist and queer theory, Wolmark's discussion explores some of the imaginary spaces constructed for the "unstable posthuman bodies" of recent films such as *GATTACA* and *The Matrix* and recent novels such as Kathleen Ann Goonan's *Queen City Jazz*. According to Wolmark, such unstable bodies "provide an opportunity to rethink distinctions between human and inhuman, body and machine, and to question the boundaries of gender identification."

Questions about gender identification morph into questions about gendered metaphors in Brian Attebery's examination of how gendered bodies influence gendered ways of knowing. Attebery explores expressions of such "embodied knowledge" in his readings of important recent novels by Gwyneth Jones and James Morrow, in particular Jones's *White Queen* and Morrow's *Towing Jehovah*. Attebery argues that these novels self-consciously "call [our] epistemological habits into question, and they do so partly by directing attention to the gender-marked body as a basis for knowledge and judgment."

The uncertain and mutable nature of the sex/gender system as a system of (coercive) representation is the focus of Wendy Pearson's study of how the hermaphrodite body has been imaginatively constructed in recent sf novels by Melissa Scott and Stephen Leigh, as well as in sf's most celebrated attempt to think about gender, Ursula K. Le Guin's *Left Hand of Darkness*. Pearson's discussion is informed by Anne Fausto-Sterling's theoretical critique of gender as a two-term category, as well as by the life story of the nineteenth-century French hermaphrodite, Herculine Barbin. Pearson closes by suggesting that the "supplementarity" of the figure of the hermaphrodite can reveal "the extent to which seeking the truth of the individual in sex and the sexed body can only ever trap us within those very discourses from which we seek to escape."

Rob Latham's essay, "Mutant Youth," is also concerned with subjects and bodies. He examines a range of (post)cyberpunk stories and novels about near futures in which virtual reality systems make it possible for characters to transcend their physical bodies. In the context of contemporary materialist analyses of the interactions of technology and corporate capital, Latham reads Pat Cadigan's *Tea from an Empty Cup*, Marc Laidlaw's *Kalifornia*, and Richard Calder's *Cythera* as exemplary novels depicting versions of "a media-saturated, near-future youth culture dominated by VR technologies." His interest is in exploring "the complex dialectical logic" of these narratives, whose young protagonists "struggle to realize a cyborg agency latent in the estranged machineries of high-tech culture."

Roger Luckhurst's subject is rage, and its iconic figure is the cyborg assassin played with such convincingly blunt affect by Arnold Schwarzenegger in *The Terminator*. Luckhurst undertakes a cultural study of rage in America, suggesting links between contemporary states of rage and the perceived boundary threats posed by technology to the conventionally self-contained masculine subject. In the process, he explores "the contention that science fiction can become a privileged space in popular culture for examining that peculiar late twentieth-century phenomenon of 'going postal,' and that it can do so because it tends to privilege the conjunctures that determine the irruptions of rage."

Our third section, "Reimagined Apocalypses and Exploded Communities," begins with works that consider fictional constructions of, and contemporary attitudes toward, the apocalypse as the end of time and history and concludes with two considerations of science fiction's imaginative treatment of the meanings, functions, and strategies of community at this moment in our future/present. Veronica Hollinger's "Apocalypse Coma" explores some of the fictional endings and discontinuities of recent science fiction as expressions of postmodern crisis. She develops close (re)readings of William Gibson's *Neuromancer* and Douglas Coupland's *Girlfriend in a Coma* within the context of a series of influential theoretical statements about postmodernism by, among others, Donna Haraway, Jacques Derrida, and Fredric Jameson, statements that demonstrate the extent to which "the apocalypse has recurred obsessively in our cultural discourses" in the past several decades. Hollinger concludes her discussion by attempting to identify the nature of "our own particular apocalypse" as, not the end of history, but the end *within* history.

While Hollinger's essay provides a theoretical ground for exploring the postmodern apocalypse, the following two essays analyze the apocalyptic imagination from the more intimate vantage point of the individual author. Gwyneth Jones meditates on the treatment of apocalypse as "opportunity: the critical moment" in her own science fiction writing. Her visions of apocalypse are, she argues, as culture bound as the Big Bang hypothesis itself, although more self-consciously so. Drawing upon elements from Asian religions in

Divine Endurance, Western traditions in *Escape Plans*, and "the defeated margins of feminist and socialist protest in 1980s Britain" in *Kairos*, Jones maps the "apocalyptic progress" of her own fiction as it takes her "to the brink of a new creation—but no further, because it wouldn't be any fun."

Brian Stableford also reflects upon his own writing, in this case a series of six novels chronicling the future history of "emortal" posthumans. Beginning with *Inherit the Earth* and continuing through *The Omega Expedition*, Stableford's series dramatizes the lives of posthuman characters who have emerged after "an all-encompassing ecocatastrophe" and who are immune to aging and illness, although not to violence. Although Stableford's novels are fiction, not prediction, he makes it clear that—given present developments in politics and biotechnology—he means his literary vision to be read as a warning of the inevitable. "If there are two things of which we can all be absolutely certain," he writes, "one is that the ecosphere will soon go postal and the other is that the current leaseholders of Earth will all die soon."

If the apocalypse hovers over the future, what of the future/present? Joan Gordon discusses science fiction's use of the alien contact novel to explore what she describes as the "monstrous social implications of the utopian vision." Her readings of Paul Park's *Celestis* and Mary Doria Russell's *The Sparrow* and *Children of God* are informed by postcolonial criticism's examination of hegemony, decolonization, and the indigene and explore the link between utopian thinking and the cultural apocalypse of genocide. Gordon's argument is that, contrary to conventional wisdom, sf confronts the horrors of the historical Holocaust not in postholocaust (often called postapocalypse) sf, but in the alien contact novel.

Given the historical events of the past century, it may not be surprising that sf tends to downplay nationalism and the politics of ethnicity in its speculative futures. Looking closely at these issues, however, Istvan Csicsery-Ronay, Jr., raises complex questions about recent genre constructions of "collective identities." In the process, he offers a detailed critique of some of the ways in which sf "erases or displaces the future history of nations and ethnic groups." What Csicsery-Ronay identifies as a postnationalist or antinationalist stance is, he argues, based "on the political perspective of the dominant technopowers, for whom national cultural identity represents an obstacle to political-economic rationalization, the foundation upon which their hegemony is based." He concludes, as does our collection, with a question—more anxious than hopeful—about sf's capacity for (re)imagining community in the context of our future/present's conditions of technological deracination.

Questions, of course, initiate conversations, and we would like *Edging into the Future* to be read as part of an ongoing conversation among writers and critics who love to talk about science fiction. Science fiction itself is an ongoing conversation, each work responding to what has gone before, so that the whole corpus forms what Brooks Landon (*Science Fiction After 1900* 9), Brian Attebery (107–8), and others call the science fiction megatext. These essays also form another, imbricated part of that megatext. Set in motion by the act of reading, each resonates with the others in the collection and edges into its own kind of future as its readers—scholars, critics, students, fans—respond to it. Welcome to the chatroom.

Part One

Genre

Implosion

2

Evaporating Genre

Strategies of Dissolution in the

Postmodern Fantastic

GARY K. WOLFE

For the first several years of their history, the major publishers of American mass-market paperback books numbered each new title sequentially, providing what is now a fascinating chronicle of popular reading habits during the 1940s, as well as a valuable resource for tracing the evolution of what we now regard as the major market genres of popular fiction. In May 1943, Donald A. Wollheim's anthology *The Pocket Book of Science-Fiction* appeared as Pocket Book no. 214, following no. 212 (Raymond Chandler's *Farewell, My Lovely*) and no. 213 (*The Pocket Book of True Crime Stories*) in a wildly eclectic list of titles that included not only Shakespeare's *Five Great Tragedies* (no. 3) and Dale Carnegie's *How to Win Friends and Influence People* (no. 68) but also a more specialized list targeted to specific audiences. These latter volumes, which characteristically followed the proprietary title formula "The Pocket Book of ———," began with broadly generic topics such as *The Pocket Book of Verse* (no. 62) or *The Pocket Book of Short Stories* (no. 91) but soon began to include such extraliterary oddities as *The Pocket Book of Boners* (no. 110)—a collection of humorous schoolboy mistakes—*The Pocket Book of Vegetable Gardening* (no. 148), *The Pocket Book of Crossword Puzzles* (no. 210), and *The Pocket Book of Home Canning* (no. 217).

This is the context in which the first American mass-market science fiction anthology, and probably the first American commercial book to use the term *science fiction*, appeared. It seems clear that publisher Robert F. de Graff and the editors of Pocket Books—which began its mass-market publishing program in May of 1939 with a fantasy novel, James Hilton's *Lost Horizon* (following a 1938 test market edition of Pearl Buck's *Good Earth*)—were, by the mid-1940s, still tentatively groping toward defining a variety of specialized readerships. Some of these areas of interest, like mysteries and westerns, had already long since crystallized as popular genres; in fact, nearly a quarter of the first one hundred Pocket Books published were classified as "mystery and detective stories" and given a separate list in the pages of promotional material that appeared in the back of each Pocket Book. Science fiction, however, was relegated to those specialty topics, like vegetable gardening and home canning, that presumably could be covered adequately in a one-shot publication (Bantam Books, another mass-market paperback publisher that came to prominence in the 1940s, proved even more tentative in dealing with the field when it tried to market its first science fiction anthology, Judith Merril's *Shot in the Dark* [1950], as "a different kind of mystery thrill," not mentioning science fiction at all in the book's front cover copy but including in the back pages a mail-order offer for several specialty-press hardcovers, presumably as a kind of market test). Prior to the advent of Ballantine Books in 1952, according to paperback historian Kenneth C. Davis, science fiction "barely existed in book form at all. It was viewed by publishers as a sort of fringe genre that they knew or cared little about" (166).

This would seem to suggest that, as of the mid- to late 1940s, science fiction had yet to emerge as anything like an identifiable genre in terms of the rapidly expanding paperback book market—the market that, within the next two decades, would largely supplant cheap magazines as the principal medium of popular fiction. Yet, as the contents of Wollheim's anthology clearly demonstrate, science fiction had developed not only a clear identity but also a fiercely loyal readership, demonstrated by the pulp magazines that flourished in the two decades immediately preceding the rise of the paperback. Pulp fiction—which shares with paperback fiction the odd distinction of being the only narrative traditions so marginalized that they are commonly identified by the technologies of their manufacture rather than their textual content—had evolved from general-interest adventure fiction magazines around the turn of the century, and by the 1930s had developed special-interest microgenres or niche markets to a degree never seen before or since, with magazines devoted to everything from varsity football fiction and World War I aviation stories to tales of "oriental menace." Fantastic narratives were no strangers to these magazines, and one of the more enduring, *Weird Tales*, debuted in 1923 and would play a significant role in the development of the horror genre.

Science fiction, which famously entered this specialized pulp magazine market with Hugo Gernsback's *Amazing Stories* in 1926, was one of the more successful of these new pop genres, with something like thirty-five different magazine titles having been introduced by 1943, the year *The Pocket Book of Science Fiction* appeared. Why, then, would such an apparently successful genre in the pulp magazines—as well as their immediate successors, the digest-sized fiction magazines, which came to dominate the 1950s short genre fiction market—fail for over a decade to gain purchase in the burgeoning field of paperback books, with its apparently similar patterns of readership? Literary elitism alone hardly seems sufficient to account for this, despite the widely held belief among science fiction readers and writers that it has long been the most unfairly maligned of popular genres: it seems fairly clear from a perusal of the early lists of Pocket, Bantam, Avon, and other paperback publishers that marketability was a far more important concern than respectability, and it seems likely that had a sufficient number of novel-length science fiction texts been available and visible, the paperback houses would not have hesitated to try to sell them, as they would do so successfully in the following decade.

Texts and Text-Products

But what does it mean for a text to be both available and visible? In the simplest terms, an available text is one that exists as a potential candidate for book publication or for paperback reprinting. Visibility is a different problem, and one that raises crucial questions of genre identity: even though there may have been a substantial number of reasonably contemporary novel-length science fiction narratives available by the 1940s, they tended to be defined either as oddball mainstream thrillers (such as William M. Sloane's *To Walk the Night* [1937] and *The Edge of Running Water* [1939]) or as longish pulp stories or serials, with little crossover between the two. While both detective stories and westerns flourished alongside science fiction in the pulps, each also had developed as a distinct tradition within popular novels—Mary Roberts Rinehart, Agatha Christie, Rex Stout, Dashiell Hammett, and Raymond Chandler were among those in Pocket Books' stable of mystery writers, while Max Brand and Zane Grey were among the somewhat smaller number of western writers to appear. Nearly all of these writers had developed followings in the hardcover market as well, prior to their entry into the paperback world, and many hardcover publishers had clearly defined lines of mystery and western fiction. Equally important, westerns and mysteries had quickly gained purchase as important genres in the newer mass media of film and radio, arenas in which science fiction would fail to cohere as a market segment until the 1950s.

With rare exceptions, no such parallel tradition had emerged in American science fiction, despite the popularity of the scientific romances of H. G. Wells and the adventure tales of Jules Verne.[1] While scores of novels that we can now readily identify as science fiction had appeared throughout the nineteenth and early twentieth centuries, the science fiction novel persistently failed to cohere as a genre in the manner of mysteries and westerns. Interestingly enough, the allied fantastic genres of horror and fantasy seemed to follow a similar pattern: while Gothic novels and several varieties of sub-Gothic vampire stories retained popularity throughout the nineteenth century, a canon of popular horror stories failed to emerge clearly until well into the twentieth, and fantasy— though arguably the oldest narrative tradition of all—did not descend (or ascend) into pop genredom until about the same time. *Lost Horizon* may indeed have been Pocket Book no. 1, but neither its publisher nor its readers apparently saw it as an expression of an ongoing literary tradition connected with other nonrealistic texts: its popularity, both as novel and film, seemed to derive neither from its origins in utopian discourse nor from its modality of lost-world fantasy, but rather from its appeal as escapist romantic adventure in an unsettled time.

The fantastic genres as a set, then—some would say the supergenre of the fantastic[2]—remained locked into the original mode of their publication in the pulp magazines; in order for the texts to gain definition as an ongoing narrative project rather than as the contents of ephemeral periodicals, they needed to be, in effect, liberated: the texts had to be decontextualized from the text-products, which in this case were the pulp magazines. For this reason alone, the appearance of the Wollheim anthology in 1943 marks a crucial moment in the history of science fiction's developing genre identity—although this decontextualizing process would not really gain momentum until the series of large hardcover anthologies, which began to appear in the late 1940s and early 1950s from such editors as Groff Conklin (*The Best of Science Fiction* [1946]; *A Treasury of Science Fiction* [1948]; *The Big Book of Science Fiction* [1950]), Raymond Healy and Francis McComas (*Adventures in Time and Space* [1946]), and John W. Campbell, Jr. (*The Astounding Science Fiction Anthology* [1952]). These and other anthologies from the postwar period not only vitally preserved stories that had for the most part been consigned to ephemeral publications but, by finding their way into public libraries, permitted the genre to begin to coalesce as something more than the object of momentary passions of pulp readers.[3] Science fiction now had a more or less permanent set of reference texts from which to derive its lasting ideologies.

By the mid-1950s, science fiction had clearly arrived as something more than a set of text-products: in magazines, in paperback, hardcover, and specialty press books, even in film and television, science fiction had become a widely recognized and readily identifiable genre. And almost as soon as it arrived, it began to disassemble itself. Even by the late 1950s and early 1960s, there were only nominal relationships between the various media products marketed or perceived as science fiction: novels by authors as diverse as Kurt Vonnegut, Jr., and E. C. Tubb, films as different as *The Day the Earth Stood Still* and *Them!*, TV programs as various as *Tom Corbett, Space Cadet,* and *The Twilight Zone.* Unlike mysteries or westerns, each of which tended to appeal in the same ways to the same audiences, science fiction had already begun to experience a radical balkanization of its reader- and viewerships. Similarly—though not to such a dramatic degree—the horror genre would eventually grow to encompass everything from Shirley Jackson to Clive Barker, and fantasy everything from Robert E. Howard to J. R. R. Tolkien. The fantastic genres may have gained market individuation, but in a more formal narrative sense the genre markers remained radically unstable.

Narrative Formulas and Emergent Ideologies

Because of the uncertainty of these genre markers, the fantastic genres contain within themselves the seeds of their own dissolution, of a nascent set of postmodern rhetorical modes that would, over a period of several decades, begin to supplant not only the notion of genre itself but also the very foundations of the modernist barricades that had long been thought to insulate literary culture from the vernacular fiction of the pulps and other forms of noncanonical expression. Other popular genres that grew to prominence in the early twentieth century gained their followings largely through the development not only of characteristic tropes but also of conventional narrative formulas. In his landmark 1976 study of such stories, John G. Cawelti identified formulas for crime novels, the classical detective story, the hard-boiled detective story, the western, and even the "best-selling social melodrama" (Irving Wallace, Harold Robbins, etc.). Significantly, Cawelti's study included virtually no discussion of the three major fantastic genres that interest us here, and in fact it would be difficult for any critical approach based largely on narrative formula to accommodate the genres of the fantastic, which are more readily described as collective world-views than as patterns of repetitive action. In terms of the narrative geographies staked out by each of these genres, one might almost invoke analogues of the "matters" first identified by the medieval French poet Jean Bodel: the matter of science fiction is the geography of reason; of horror, the geography of anxiety; of fantasy, the geography of desire.

This is not to deny that each of these genres developed its own share of characteristic and clichéd narrative formulas—only that such formulas were never sufficient to be the defining characteristic of the genre. Science fiction, once it emerged from the cocoon of the space operas that dominated the early pulp era, began to explore its potential as a genre based as much in ideology as in story, eventually transforming itself into a dialogue and a dialectic about change that would almost inevitably lead to a blurring of its identity, as its favorite concerns and obsessions grew more congruent with the concerns and obsessions of the society at large. Horror, perversely naming itself not after narrative structures or settings or even ideas but rather after its intended emotional effect on its audience, emerged from the shadow of the Gothic to discover that its key dynamic was not a particular story pattern but an unanchored anxiety, which also came into eventual congruence with broader cultural issues. Fantasy—the oldest genre of all, but one whose principal pulp identity had been largely confined to sword-and-sorcery tales—did not really develop a clear market identity until fairly late in the paperback revolution (following the enormously successful American paperback editions of J. R. R. Tolkien's *Lord of the Rings*) but quickly moved to catch up with its sister genres in the process of dissolving its own borders, as its authors began to discover that the Tolkien quest formula was but one expression of the genre's potential and not a totalizing definition of it.

By the late stages of the pulp era (a decade or so later in terms of fantasy), the writers and readers of these genres had developed easily recognizable protocols and even consensus literary histories, all based in a kind of populist canon developed through common reading and in some cases through that proto-Internet of cons, hectographed fanzines, and magazine letter columns collectively known as fandom. The contents of these informal canons were often fascinating; while the texts included were not always popular or even widely available, they came to represent emergent ideologies that defined the genre in terms of both its market and its texts. Each genre's readers came to identify a central ideological linchpin—Robert A. Heinlein in the case of science fiction, Howard Phillips Lovecraft in the case of horror, J. R. R. Tolkien in the case of fantasy—and to a great extent the dialectic of the relevant genre seemed to define itself in recapitulation of, or reaction against, the world-views of these central figures.[4] And in each field the dialectic seemed to offer two possible routes for later writers: either expansion of the discourse to the edges of genre and beyond or collapsing of the discourse into an increasingly crabbed and narrow set of self-referential texts. Both kinds of results tend to promote the dissolution of the original genre—the one by integration with other modes of fiction, the other by implosion—and both are abundantly in evidence in each genre today.

Science Fiction and the Colonization of Genre

Unlike horror, which built upon a longstanding Gothic tradition and almost abruptly emerged as a blockbuster market genre in the 1970s, and unlike fantasy, which could lay a persuasive claim to being the dominant mode of narrative for most of human history, science fiction, despite its healthy legacy throughout the nineteenth century, was essentially a *designed* genre after 1926, the year in which Hugo Gernsback launched *Amazing Stories*—a set of available markets to which writers would conform rather than a tradition of narrative that would eventually find its markets. This inevitably placed serious constraints upon the ability of writers to expand the boundaries of the genre, and the field is rife with tales like that told by Daniel Keyes, author of "Flowers for Algernon" (1959), about the insistence of editor Horace Gold that he tack a "happy ending" onto the tragic story in order to make it more acceptable to the readership of *Galaxy Science Fiction* (Keyes 111). Because of the limitations of the market, the obtuseness of editors, the decline of the magazines, the growth of the bestseller mentality among publishers, and the incursion of paraliterary offshoots of the genre such as movies, TV, and game novelizations, science fiction writers periodically publish essays mourning the recent or imminent death of the field (such essays appear only a little less frequently among horror writers and fantasy writers). What these essays are really mourning, upon closer inspection, is the declining health of that self-invented genre. They tend to offer little evidence that science fiction is actually disappearing—only that its consensus core is evaporating. Writers from "outside"—Doris Lessing, Marge Piercy, Paul Theroux, John Updike—freely appropriate its resources,[5] while the notion of a common readership with a common reading background—once defined by the magazines and later by the paperback book publishers with regular science fiction lines—grows increasingly shaky.

Writers have begun to respond to this circumstance in a variety of ways, developing strategies for writing science fiction without writing in *the genre* of science fiction. One strategy is essentially to colonize another genre, using the tropes of science fiction as instrumentalities for moving the narrative into a different mode altogether. The time-travel theme, for example, has often served as a convenient mechanism for constructing science fiction narratives that at the same time appropriate the protocols of historical fiction. A fictional group of time-traveling historians in twenty-first-century Oxford has provided Connie Willis with an angle of approach for several richly detailed historical fictions set in venues as diverse as London during the Blitz ("Fire Watch" [1982]), a fourteenth-century village suffering from the Plague (*Doomsday Book* [1992]), or the 1889 Oxfordshire of Jerome K. Jerome (*To Say Nothing of the Dog* [1998]). An earlier novel, *Lincoln's Dreams* (1982), uses a kind of crosstime psychic connection to move the narrative into the era of the American Civil War. In each case, despite the science fictional frame, the main narrative is constructed around the historical setting, which is the centerpiece of the novel and its *raison d'être*. Jack Dann, another writer with strong science fiction roots, moved even more directly into the realm of historical fiction with his novel *Memory Cathedral: A Secret History of Leonardo da Vinci* (1995), which retains a claim to a science fiction identity through a speculative passage involving da Vinci's "lost" years, and the Civil War novel *The Silent* (1998), whose connection to science fiction genre materials is even more vestigial.

Another genre that science fiction writers have with some regularity been attempting to colonize is that of the suspense thriller. Here the dissolution of genre boundaries is more subtle, since the imaginative material and narrative conventions of science fiction may be retained, while the plot, structure, and tone are borrowed from a mode of paranoid pursuit melodrama pioneered in espionage novels from John Buchan to Robert Ludlum. Initially, the novelists who seemed most successful—at least commercially—in effecting this merger were those whose starting point was the thriller rather than the science fiction tale: Robin Cook, Michael Crichton, and Peter Benchley are among the most prominent examples, with Crichton having based nearly his entire career on science fiction conceits. Occasionally, professional science fiction writers have ventured with some success into this arena (Frank Robinson's *The Power* [1956]; D. F. Jones's *Colossus* [1966]), but for the most part the very intellectual challenges that traditionally define an effective technological science fiction story seem to militate against the largely anti-intellectual (or at least antiscientist), technologically ambivalent tone of the paranoid thriller. This may be a rare case where the most visible barriers separating two related genres lie in ideologies of power rather than in narrative mechanisms. Nevertheless, science fiction writers fairly consistently try to bridge the gap, sometimes very successfully (as with Greg Bear's 1999 novel, *Darwin's Radio*, which freely uses the multiple viewpoints and globe-hopping locations of thriller fiction but offers a solidly imagined evolutionary speculation as its thematic center), more often with mixed results (such as Ben Bova's *Death Dream* [1994] or Wil McCarthy's *Murder in the Solid State* [1996]).

The science fiction writer who has most consistently tried to expand into the thriller market is Gregory Benford, one of the premier hard sf writers of the last three decades, whose most famous novel, *Timescape* (1980), was praised for its realistic depiction of academic scientists at work in the 1960s, as well as its ingenious plot involving crosstime communication. In 1985, Benford published *Artifact*, an archaeological thriller involving the discovery of an ancient Minoan artifact that seems to contain some sort of extraterrestrial singularity which, if released, could have catastrophic effects. Despite the sophisticated physics that goes into the explanation of the artifact (some of which is shifted to an appendix at the back of the novel), this central science fictional device is for the most part relegated to the role of a maguffin (to use Alfred Hitchcock's term for an object whose sole purpose is to motivate characters) in what is primarily a novel of international political intrigue and adventure. Later, Benford adopted the pseudonym "Sterling Blake" for his thriller *Chiller* (1993), a Robin Cook–style suspense novel involving cryonics. In 1997, Benford returned to this field under his own name with *Cosm*, which was essentially driven by a simple chase-and-pursuit plot, despite another ingenious device at its center, drawn solidly from theoretical physics (a chromelike sphere accidentally created in a uranium nuclei experiment turns out to be a window into a newly created microuniverse—the "Cosm" of the title). But the novel is the result of two genres virtually laid one on top of the other, with the Cosm itself serving as, on the one hand, an inventive and evocative *novum* in the most traditional science fiction sense and, on the other, a thriller-maguffin like the artifact in *Artifact*. As in *Artifact*, Benford offers an afterword arguing for the plausibility of the physics involved, but for the purposes of the thriller aspect of the novel, the Cosm is for the most part merely a very strange object that might explode, like a smuggled atomic bomb or a vial of deadly viruses.

Benford's most successful foray in transforming science fictional materials into the materials of the commercial thriller is the novel *Eater*, published in early 2000. *Eater* seems almost a deliberate exercise in genre dissolution. It begins as an astronomical puzzle but in rapid succession turns into a first-contact tale, a world-threatening disaster epic, a tragic romance, a space adventure, and an ontological fable that returns to one of Benford's favorite science fiction themes—the relation of organic to artificial intelligences in the universe. Benjamin Knowlton is an astrophysicist at the Mauna Kea Observatory and husband of an ex-astronaut who is suffering from terminal cancer. When a young colleague presents him with evidence of a highly anomalous astronomical arti-fact—a repeating gamma ray burster—he is initially skeptical but is hesitant to discourage the enthusiasm of a younger, more idealistic scientist. The young scientist's measurements hold up, however, and the mysterious object—which has many of the characteristics of a black hole—is not only real but is headed rapidly toward Earth. The object, which comes to be known as "Eater of All Things" because of its tendency, like a black hole, to consume objects in its path, proves to be intelligent—apparently the remnant of an ancient civilization, which, faced with doom at the hands of the black hole, downloaded itself into the singularity's magnetic fields and has been cruising the universe ever since, collecting samples from various civilizations. Now it demands the uploaded minds of several hundred humans—whom it identifies by name—to add to the collection, and to underline the seriousness of its demands it burns a huge swath across eastern North America, including the Washington, D.C., area. The scientists—who must contend with paranoid government bureaucracies as well as the all-powerful and possibly deranged alien—face the Abraham-like dilemma of whether to offer up the sacrifices. The dying astronaut volunteers to have her consciousness uploaded into a space vehicle, in the hopes that she can at least do some damage to the seemingly invincible alien. Not surprisingly, there is an Achilles' heel waiting to be discovered, and while Benford's version of it is more sophisticated and intelligent than most, the novel's final chapters carry echoes of more formulaic works, including such pop films as *Independence Day*, *Contact*, and *Armageddon*.

Eater works so well as a science fiction novel that it might seem perverse to cite it in the context of novels that test the boundaries of genre or that contribute to the dissolution of their source genre. But the solid science fiction narrative at its core is repeatedly diluted by echoes of other genres—not only the thriller but the epic disaster novel (which Benford had visited before with his 1980 *Shiva Descending*, coauthored with William Rotsler), the academic novel, and the mainstream novel of science, which Benford had effectively blended with a sci-ence fictional conceit in his classic *Timescape*. Still, the novel must be counted as a more successful hybrid of science fiction and the thriller than some prominent examples of the reverse—novels by thriller writers seeking to exploit science fictional plots—such as James Patterson's *Where the Wind Blows* (1998) or Michael Crichton's *Timeline* (1999), both of which cavalierly violate the terms of their science fiction rationales in order to expediently deliver the next chapter-ending cliffhanger.

Science Fiction/Science Fantasy/Fantasy

The most obvious candidate of all for science fiction's imperialist impulses is the sister genre of fantasy. The most important of the fantasy pulp magazines,

Unknown, was founded by John W. Campbell, Jr., largely as a venue for fantastic stories that did not meet his rather narrow technological criteria for *Astounding Science Fiction*, even though many of these stories came from regular *Astounding* contributors. But Campbell's materialistic bias tended to influence these writers toward a more rigid brand of fantasy that had much in common with science fiction. *Unknown*'s authors included Henry Kuttner, L. Sprague de Camp, Eric Frank Russell, L. Ron Hubbard, Jack Williamson, Theodore Sturgeon, and even Robert A. Heinlein, and their characteristic approach to fantasy was to treat it as a kind of alternative science, with its own rigorous and internally consistent rules and a minimum of mythological supernaturalism. On several occasions, a fantasy template would be introduced and developed only to be resolved as, for example, the work of aliens interfering in human affairs. This was the central conceit of Eric Frank Russell's Fortean novel, *Sinister Barrier*, the lead story in the first issue of *Unknown* in March 1939, which to some extent set the tone for the skeptical approach to fantasy that would characterize much of the magazine's fiction.[6] "They" (1940), for example, one of Heinlein's three contributions to the magazine, presents a classically paranoid vision of a world the protagonist believes to be constructed entirely for his own benefit, only to reveal in the closing paragraphs that the Dr. Hayward to whom he has been revealing his suspicions is in fact a strange creature called "the Glaroon" and is indeed supervising every aspect of his life as though it were a scientific experiment or military observation. Heinlein stops short of explaining in science fictional terms who or what the Glaroon is and what its motives are, but only this withheld explanation would seem to qualify the tale as fantasy. (Later, of course, Philip K. Dick would virtually make a career out of paranoid visions of reality resolved into science fictional scenarios, and later still, films such as *The Truman Show* would exploit this fantasy in pop-media terms.)[7]

"Rationalized fantasy" of one sort or another has been a common enough device over the years to earn no less than three definitions in John Clute and John Grant's *Encyclopedia of Fantasy* (1997): works in which such fantasy elements as magic are given quasi-scientific rules, *Unknown*-style; works in which the fantasy elements are explained away altogether; and works in which fantasy elements are transmuted into sf tropes—elves or witches turning out to be mutants with psychic powers, for example, or the dragons of Anne McCaffrey's Pern novels revealed as the product of genetic engineering (801–2). This sort of device has been commonly used to rationalize aspects of supernatural horror as well, with trumped-up biomedical "explanations" for vampirism so common as to have generated a small but persistent narrative tradition of their own, from Richard Matheson's *I Am Legend* (1954) to Tim Powers's *Stress of Her Regard* (1989) and Dan Simmons's *Children of the Night* (1992). Works set in what appears to be a fantasy landscape but is in fact a science fictional world are even more common, and this kind of hybridization—sometimes called "science fantasy," in one of that term's various incarnations—has provided the template for some of the most powerful ongoing narrative traditions in either field, the romantic epic set in such a distant world that connections to our own are nearly unrecognizable, such as Jack Vance's *Dying Earth* (1950) and its most important heir, Gene Wolfe's four-volume Book of the New Sun series (1980–83).[8] All these examples are what Mark W. Tiedemann calls "seed stories," which would eventually give rise to the more radical genre mixing of writers such as Jonathan Lethem, Jonathan Carroll, and Michael Swanwick.

Such narratively complex genre mixing, in which the narrative is not necessarily resolved according to the protocols of either fantasy or science fiction, is somewhat less common than rationalized fantasy. Some earlier experiments in this area were little more than crude tricks of marketing, such as Piers Anthony's Apprentice Adept series, which began with *Split Infinity* (1980) and generated a roomful of sequels. Anthony's gimmick involved a protagonist who moves between the science fiction world of Proton and the fantasy world of Phaze, both portrayed in terms of the most generic clichés of the genre, with the narrative shifting between worlds at convenient points like a juggling act. A much more provocative novel published the same year as *Split Infinity* is the British novelist Ian Watson's *Gardens of Delight*, which ingeniously provides a science fiction rationale for what appears to be a purely spiritual landscape in the tradition of David Lindsay, in this case a planet whose exotic landscape and inhabitants seem to be a living realization of Hieronymus Bosch's famous apocalyptic painting, *The Garden of Earthly Delights*. (It is also worth noting that 1980 saw the publication of *The Shadow of the Torturer*, the first volume of Gene Wolfe's Book of the New Sun series.)

A writer who has made something of a career out of conflating genre protocols is Sheri S. Tepper, whose first published novels, the True Game series (1983–84), followed the pattern of science fantasy by introducing fantasy tropes into what was essentially a science fiction environment. Her 1991 novel, *Beauty*, combines elements of fairy tale, historical fiction, science fiction, and genre fantasy; in later works she has deliberately played with genre expectations. *A Plague of Angels* (1993) is one of her more successful novels in this regard, aggressively challenging the commonly held assumptions that one cannot mix spaceships and robots with dragons and ogres or place high-tech cities in medieval fairy-tale landscapes. Like Gene Wolfe, Tepper uses sf concepts to generate what appears to be a fantasy environment and then gradually reveals the science fictional underpinnings so that the novel appears to shift genre in midstream. Science fantasy of this type is so easy to do badly ("Good heavens! The oracle is a *computer*!") that when it works it is especially impressive—a way of asserting, as does the most effective postgenre writing, that the author and not the genre is in control of the material. But *A Plague of Angels* plays with this issue of authorial control in ways unusual even for this unusual genre.

The novel calls attention to its own textuality at once: a young girl named

Orphan lives in an "archetypal village" where everyone fulfills a traditional fairy-tale role—hero, oracle, miser, and so on. Furthermore, the characters *know* that it is an archetypal village and refer to it as such in the text. So do other characters, such as a farm boy named Abasio, who sets out, hobbitlike, to have an adventure and ends up in the violent and seedy city of Fantis. Dominated by youth gangs and plagued by drug abuse and immune deficiency diseases, Fantis reveals that this world is neither as innocent nor as pastoral as it seems. By the time we learn that the "witch" Ellel is seeking to dominate the world with the aid of an army of androids and weapons she hopes to retrieve from a long-abandoned space station, the reader confidently assumes that the setting is a disguised sf environment, the novel a variety of rationalized fantasy. But then Tepper introduces talking animals. Much of the appeal of *A Plague of Angels* comes from learning how and why this world came to be; much also comes from watching Tepper adroitly fit new pieces into her puzzle as the narrative progresses. As we watch Abasio and Orphan grow from childhood to adulthood, we learn that neither are they quite who they seem to be, nor is the world they inhabit. This rich background gives rise to a plot that on its surface is the simplest of fairy tales: the wicked witch pursuing the innocent orphan for nefarious purposes, while the farmer's son helps her evade capture and gradually enlists the aid of whole armies of allies, each with different strengths. The concluding epic battle fits the traditions of both heroic fantasy and heroic science fiction, but even then we are still receiving significant revelations about this world, the place of humans in it, and the relationship of the novel itself to the genres it critiques.

Horror and Fantasy

While the main focus of my discussion has been strategies of dissolution in science fiction, a couple of key recent examples of such authorial strategies in fantasy and horror must also be mentioned. Peter Straub and Stephen King's 1984 collaboration, *The Talisman*, for example—the bestselling work of fiction for that year, according to *Publishers Weekly*—surprised many horror readers by borrowing its basic structure from the fantasy quest romance and scattering throughout the narrative allusions to writers from Mark Twain and L. Frank Baum to J. R. R. Tolkien and even John Gardner. Described by Bill Sheehan as "an eccentric hybrid of a book that is frequently vital and moving, and occasionally attenuated and overlong" (148), the novel may well have confused critics and reviewers with its refusal to abide by the largely self-referential traditions of horror fiction and with its implicit assertion that the membranes separating the fantastic genres from each other, and from external literary traditions, are highly permeable.

Straub had been testing the borders between mainstream and genre fiction since his earliest successes; his first major bestseller, the 1979 *Ghost Story*, with its studied allusions to Hawthorne, James, and Stephen Crane, its leapfrogging chronology, and its multiple viewpoints, was an effort, he told Stephen King, to do "something which would be *very* literary, and at the same time take on every kind of ghost situation I could think of" (King 251). It was, in effect, Straub's first concerted effort to deconstruct the genre from within, and in less than a decade Straub had begun the series of interlinked "Blue Rose" stories and novels that retained the sometimes gruesome tone of his earlier supernatural fiction in nonsupernatural narrative modes that borrowed far more freely from traditions of the crime novel (*Koko* [1988]; *Mystery* [1990]; *The Throat* [1993]) and the fairy tale ("The Juniper Tree" [1985]; "Ashputtle" [1994]) than from the traditions of genre horror. *The Throat*, it might be argued, is a genuine postgenre work, a horror novel that lacks not only supernatural horror but also explicit horror scenes of any sort. By this point, Straub's authority and popularity were such that he continued to be honored for fantasy and horror even with works clearly more closely allied with crime fiction, if not with an even more diffuse American Gothic tradition (*Koko* won the World Fantasy Award in 1989 and *The Throat* a Bram Stoker Award in 1993).

Mr. X (1999), heralded as Straub's return to the realm of the supernatural, proved in its own way to be equally subversive of genre conventions. There is plenty of traditional horror in *Mr. X*, including a substantial subplot involving Lovecraft and his Cthulhu mythos, but there are also many elements that look beyond the conventions of genre, not the least of which is Straub's choosing to make his protagonist and his family black (without directly asserting this) and to use jazz performance as a fairly complex central metaphor. *Mr. X* is essentially a doppelgänger tale, and the main doppelgänger belongs to the narrator, Ned Dunstan, a software programmer drawn back to his hometown of Edgerton, Illinois, because of forebodings about his mother, Star, a sometime jazz singer who has maintained a close relationship with Ned despite having given him up to foster parents. Since childhood, Ned has experienced lapses of consciousness on his birthday, sometimes seeming to be transported to another time and place. More recently, he is occasionally mistaken for someone else—the classic doppelgänger plot point—and thus finds himself accused of murder before he has been in Edgerton for long. Ned becomes involved with a number of local characters—various aunts and uncles, an assistant district attorney named Ashley, who is investigating a powerful local developer named Stewart Hatch, a secretive landlady named Helen Janette, and most importantly Hatch's wife, Laurie, and her son, Cobbie. In keeping with the shadow-figure motif, most of these characters are not quite who they seem to be, and even the town of Edgerton itself seems to have a dual identity, with its oddly out-of-place street names like Fish, Button, Treacle, and Wax, its Brazen Head Hotel, and its ominous Veal Yard. Ned's own family history is even more mysterious, dating back at least to eighteenth-century Providence, where a long-abandoned family mansion came to be known as "the Shunned House" (allusions to Lovecraft permeate the novel). While in Edgerton, Ned discovers that his father of record is not his real father, a man named Edward Rinehart, and that a twin brother had apparently disappeared shortly after birth.

Rinehart—the Mr. X of the title—provides the novel's second narrative voice, and unlike Ned, he *knows* he is in a horror story, largely one of his own creation. Obsessed with Lovecraft's Cthulhu mythos, which he regards as a kind of divine revelation, Rinehart is one of Straub's most chilling creations—a sadistic murderer with supernatural psychic powers, self-styled Lord of Crime, and bad horror story writer in the Lovecraft tradition. He is, in effect, a creature made of genre. Rinehart's story provides a grotesque mirror image of Ned's: their respective youthful experiences at college and a military academy are pointedly juxtaposed, and Rinehart's contemptuous hatred of Star is as central a motivation as Ned's tacit devotion to her. It hardly comes as a surprise that Rinehart's mission in Edgerton is to destroy Ned. But Ned's own supernatural powers, together with those of his shadowy brother, Robert, are sufficient to set the stage for an epic confrontation.

Despite several scenes of gruesome murder, a deliberate evocation of Lovecraft's paranoid world-view, and a protagonist who seems, science fictionlike, to be able to time travel, *Mr. X* is a complex novel that engages in an active and often witty critique of the horror genre while staking an authoritative claim to being part of it. Lovecraft, for example, functions partly as an emblem of horror's chronic looniness and partly as an inside joke for genre readers. But such allusions are crucial to the texture of the narrative, which—like much of Straub's work—strives to add multiple tonalities to a genre best known for one-note performances: the tragic and often treacherous family relationships, the detailed and richly textured portrait of the small southern Illinois town of Edgerton, the persistent infusion of music into the narrative at both dramatic and structural levels, combine to give the novel a density of layers within which the conventions of genre horror are subsumed as merely another narrative resource. If *The Throat* moved purely into postgenre territory by forsaking both supernaturalism and graphic terror, *Mr. X* proves to be even more subversive by returning to the matter of horror and refusing to let it dictate the terms of the novel.

In the fantasy genre, a novel that similarly sets out to confront directly the question of genre identity is Geoff Ryman's 1992 *Was* (British title *Was . . .*), described by its author as the work of a "fantasy writer who fell in love with realism." *Was* is set in a version of the American Midwest that seems strongly influenced by such naturalist writers as Hamlin Garland and Frank Norris and on the surface offers few of the solaces of traditional fantasy—despite the fact that it was nominated for the World Fantasy Award in 1993.

The novel's central conceit is that the Dorothy Gale (Gael in Ryman's novel) of L. Frank Baum's *Oz* books was an actual orphan in turn-of-the-century Kansas, sent with her dog, Toto, to live with her cruel Auntie Em and Uncle Henry and haunted by the memory of her brief happy earlier childhood in St. Louis, before her father disappeared and her mother died of diphtheria. Dorothy comes to think of her idealized past as a place called Was. Sexually abused by Uncle Henry, she becomes a behavior problem in school, until a visiting substitute teacher takes an interest in her and asks her to write about her life and the land of Was. The substitute teacher is, of course, Baum himself, who goes on to appropriate large segments of Dorothy's tale into his famous novel. This narrative alternates with two other narratives, one involving the childhood of the actress Judy Garland and the other concerning a contemporary actor dying of AIDS who, in conversations with his therapist, becomes obsessed with the idea that Dorothy was real.

By an unlikely but fortuitous coincidence, the therapist who is working with the actor had been a teenage student holding a summer job at a mental hospital in Kansas decades earlier when, during the first network television broadcast of the 1939 film *The Wizard of Oz*, in November 1956, one of the hospital's oldest inmates began hysterically claiming that the movie had stolen her life: she was, of course, the aged Dorothy, driven to madness by a long life of disappointment and sexual exploitation and given to rambling on about a place called Was, and how you can't get there from Is. This key scene, which briefly unites the three plot lines of the narrative, is extremely powerful and lovely, but it is not fantasy. Nor is most of the rest of the novel, except perhaps for two brief episodes: one involving the runaway Dorothy's mystical encounter with a white buffalo and the other, at the very end, when the dying actor seems to disappear while searching for Dorothy. At the thematic center of the novel is, of course, the great fantasy *The Wizard of Oz* itself, and much of the novel can be read as an extended meditation on the spiritual power of fantasy, but the novel is very nearly an antifantasy in its mode of presentation—as though Dorothy were the invention of Thomas Hardy rather than of Baum.

Interestingly, the novel's contrasting landscapes echo the traditional contrast between realistic and fantasy worlds in Baum's novel: the bleak, gray Kansas of the real Dorothy is not dissimilar from the equally monochromatic Kansas in the opening chapter of *The Wizard of Oz*, while Dorothy's remembered childhood in Was is an obvious analog of Oz itself. Other fantasy worlds populate the novel in subtler ways: the unreal Hollywood life of Judy Garland contrasted with her own childhood, the false Oz of the movie set, the promise of a broader world, which briefly seems held out to Dorothy by the attractive substitute teacher Baum, even the world beyond AIDS that haunts the young actor, who comes to conflate it with the myth of Dorothy. Structurally, many of the elements of classic fantasy are present in the novel—the youthful protagonist, the magical tutelary figure, the quest, the secondary world—but they are consistently undercut by the intrusion of realism, by reminders that, in Dorothy's words, you can't get there from Is. Ryman is an author who in other works has deliberately tested the boundaries of genre, shifting between politically charged realism, fantasy, and science fiction often in the same work, but in *Was* he seems to be out to explode the notion of genre altogether.

Genre Implosion

"Fantasy is evaporating." At the risk of unseemly self-quotation, this is a sentence I found myself writing a few years ago in a review of the annual anthology *The Year's Best Fantasy and Horror*, edited by Ellen Datlow and Terri Windling. I meant to suggest not that the genre was in a state of collapse but quite the opposite: that it had grown so diverse and ubiquitous that it seemed a central part of the fabric of contemporary culture—infiltrating other genres, the literary mainstream, otherwise conventional movies and TV programs, commercial art and advertising, music, theater, design, even pop ontology, as people showing no other outward signs of religious practice proclaim belief in angels, while Goths, Wiccans, Druids, Vampires, and Elves have their own Websites and, in some cases, their own nightclubs and conventions. Fantasy, in other words, was in the air, like a mist. I could have said much the same thing about science fiction, and to a more limited extent about horror, which of the three major fantastic genres seems still to be struggling for identity. The writers who contribute to the evaporation of genre, who destabilize it by undermining our expectations and appropriating materials at will, their fiction shaped by individual vision rather than the conventions of fictive traditions, are the same writers who continually revitalize genre: a healthy genre, a healthy literature, is one at risk, whose boundaries grow uncertain and whose foundations get wobbly.

The authors discussed here are only the tip of a very large and imposing iceberg, and several more and lengthier essays could be devoted to those writers who, in the last decade or so, have moved even farther along the postgenre path than some of those discussed here—Jonathan Lethem, Jonathan Carroll, Paul Auster, Paul di Filippo, Stepan Chapman, and Elizabeth Hand, to name only a few.[9]

But there is another aspect to the destabilization of genre that is far less sanguine. While on one end of the spectrum are writers who strive to liberate genre materials from genre constraints, and in the vast center are authors who work with varying degrees of contentment within a genre, testing its possibilities without contesting its terms, there are at the other end writers for whom genre seems to be its own reference point, if not very nearly the whole of the literary universe. For every Peter Straub or Stephen King, the horror genre is populated by dozens of writers of fatally limited ambition, content—even eager—to recycle familiar tropes and effects in increasingly crabbed and self-referential works that appear in tiny-circulation magazines or as evanescent paperbacks, their apparent goal not to enter into dialogue with earlier horror writers but simply to echo them: a kind of literary karaoke. Much the same is true of many current fantasy trilogists and series authors, with their endless redactions of Tolkien or with bloated noveloids whose settings, characters, and narrative rules are predetermined by the game or software franchise that issues the contract. Science fiction writers who periodically proclaim the impending death of that genre cite as major culprits the flood of novelizations and franchises based on properties such as *Star Trek*, *Star Wars*, or *The X-Files*, which, it is claimed, divert the skills of talented novelists from their own work and crowd more imaginatively challenging science fiction off the bookstore shelves.[10] Publishing executives, drawn increasingly from the financial and marketing ranks of parent conglomerates, supposedly look only at prior sales records and presold formula markets, further driving out fictions at the edges.

In fact, there is at most limited evidence that any genre has been halted in its creative tracks by commercial franchises and corporate bottom lines; one might even argue that, as we saw at the beginning of this essay, popular genres owe at least a portion of their origins and growth to just such marketing decisions, albeit in a more primitive economy. But it is demonstrable that certain kinds of books, such as short-story collections and experimental fictions, have increasingly shifted toward smaller, independent publishers.[11] Of greater concern than simple commercialism is the increasing self-referentiality of many genre texts, a narrowing of horizons that eventually leads to an accelerating inward spiral, resulting in a kind of genre implosion or collapse—virtually the opposite of the volatility represented by the more innovative and adventurous writers, which has been my primary focus here. Something very close to this happened in the horror field in the early 1990s, with designated mass-market imprints folding under the weight of too many novels that looked far too much like each other or like replications of a handful of source texts. Genre implosion does not necessarily lead to the disappearance of a given genre or even to a weakening of its market viability, but it can lead to atrophy and to a limited, self-contained readership, as happened with the western novel after a half-century of dominance, with the series romance after a decade in which it grew to account for startling percentages of total paperbacks sold, and with the classical English-village murder mystery, which essentially devolved into a kind of puzzle recreation for a limited circle of devotees.

The fantastic genres, by virtue of the kinds of instability that I have attempted to delineate here in a very preliminary form, would seem to be less vulnerable to such genre-wide implosions—perhaps better able to sustain the depredations of formula abuse and rampant commercialization, but hardly immune to the damage from these forces. One can readily visualize a scenario in which science fiction, fantasy, and horror continue to evolve into postgenre modes of narrative discourse while leaving behind pools of comparatively degraded self-referential formula fictions. Already, it has become problematical to discuss in any meaningful way a "genre" that includes both Peter Straub's *The Throat* and teenage slasher movies, both the novels of Sheri Tepper and *Star Wars* novelizations, both Sean Stewart and Robert Jordan. In fact, the term *genre* itself has become almost too slippery to be useful: in one sense, it simply refers to market categories; in another, it refers to a set of literary and narrative conventions; in yet another, to a collection of texts with perceived commonalities of affect and world-view. To some extent, these problems affect all genres: John Le Carré has never quite nestled comfortably within the conventions of the espionage thriller, nor has P. D. James or Scott Turow fit easily into the mystery genre. But the fantastic genres in particular seem evolutionary by their very nature: science fiction must accommodate the shifting and often counterintuitive visions of reality that science itself reflects; horror must accommodate the constantly shifting sources of the anxiety that it seeks to exploit; fantasy must adapt to the dreams of a world no longer governed by the conventionalized desires of pastoral idealism. In the end, these are the genres that at their best, by the very terms of the imaginative processes involved, transcend genre. They are narrative modes that have already leaked into the atmosphere, that have escaped their own worst debilitations, that have survived.

3

Omniphage

Rock 'n' Roll and Avant-Pop Science Fiction

LANCE OLSEN

1. When I'm Sixty-Four; or, Speculative Autobiographiction

... will you still feed me ...

I want to begin by going out on a limb and suggesting—only half face-
tiously—that the first rock album you buy as a kid often functions at some
deep-structure as an act of speculative autobiography.

It functions, in other words, as a species of science fiction.

The first rock album you buy manifests sf's allegedly predictive role by
hinting at something about your future: about, perhaps, your tastes to come,
certain aesthetic and psychological predilections you possess that not infre-
quently will shadow you in one guise or another for the rest of your life. There
is a reason, in other words, that you buy the first album you buy, something essentially you in that choice that will visit you again and again in later years
and may even begin to feel like what you think about when you think about
such notions as stable identity (poststructuralist problematics notwithstand-
ing), about being the same person at sixty-four as you were at sixteen ("you"
perhaps being too strong a word).

Even as you entertain such thoughts, of course, part of you also understands that you are *not* the same person at sixty-four as at sixteen, biologically
or psychologically speaking, not really, neither at a cellular nor at a cognitive
level. A part of you intuits an unnervingly Heraclitean perspective on personality and personality's historicity. Or, to put it slightly differently, part of you understands that the real lesson of science fiction is not about the Newtonian
knowability of the future but about how the future will always remain un-
knowable, how it will always remain that Heisenbergian shimmer we will
never get right until we live it—until, that is, it dissolves into something it is
not: the present.

A thought, needless to say, that never stops the doubting subject from con-
templating the future, constructing narratives that help her or him think about
tomorrow in ways that link it in a comprehensible necklace of cause-and-effect
events with today and yesterday.

2. A Day in the Life; or, Suburban Nostalgic Teenage Blues

Somebody spoke and I went into a dream ...

My own narrative, which I more often than not believe is close to what happened, or what might have happened, or in any case what should have happened, goes something like this.

Bruce Encke, a tall skinny guy with thyroidal eyes and a horse chin, was my
best friend in grade school and junior high in my leafy bland hometown of

River Edge, New Jersey, twenty minutes away from the George Washington Bridge and Manhattan.

One of Bruce's two older sisters, Ginny, had a complex network of boyfriends I could never quite untangle, and somehow—though I don't quite recall how this came about—Bruce and I found ourselves in one of said boyfriend's rooms after school on a late summer day in 1967.

Maybe we were supposed to meet Ginny and him.

Maybe we were doing something we weren't supposed to be doing.

At any rate, I was eleven and Bruce was twelve and what I remember most about that afternoon was how the bright white sunshine flooded the bright white room while Bruce rifled through Ginny's boyfriend's record collection because he wanted me to hear this new album he thought was just the coolest thing in the world.

I remember him raising it from a batch of other records. I remember its red back cover busy with black lyrics and how that cover caught the light. I remember lying among overstuffed pillows on Ginny's boyfriend's couch, listening to it with my eyes closed.

And I remember how, listening to it, my body understood Bruce was right.

It really *was* the coolest thing in the world.

It was called *Sgt. Pepper's Lonely Hearts Club Band* and it had come out on June 2 and I had never heard anything like it before and I believe something in me altered for good during the roughly forty minutes it took me to hear it the first time.

Sometime down the road, somewhere in the future, when I was somebody else, biologically and psychologically speaking, I'd come to discover that much the same thing holds true for the aficionado's experience of certain science fiction texts: there is something of the secret handshake to that instant, something electric and momentous when you come across something fresh and quick in the field that someone has just passed on to you, or told you about, or that you just read about in some essay or review or online chat space.

Sometime down the road, when I was somebody else, I'd come to write an essay ("essay" perhaps being too strong a word), *this* essay, the one you are now reading, it turns out, about science fiction's appropriation and manipulation of rock 'n' roll.

And sometime down the road, somewhere in the future, I'd come to learn The Lore associated with that album.

I'd come to learn, that is, that producer George Martin and the Beatles created it over the course of 129 days in that famous Studio Two on Abbey Road, and that while they had spent 585 minutes recording the Beatles's first album, *Please Please Me,* it took them 700 hours to do *Sgt. Pepper.*

That the thirteen songs on it were recorded, not in the order that they finally appeared, but in the order of the thirteen sections that currently constitute the piece you are now reading.

Sometime down the road, somewhere in the future, I'd also come to learn some of the ludic brilliance that went into the thing—how, for instance, Lennon insisted that Martin attach a couple of seconds of mischievous fifteen-kilocycle tone to the end of "A Day in the Life" in order to annoy any dogs that happened to be in the neighborhood, or how the group recorded several seconds of hebephrenic babble (which sounds like *never do see any other way*, though I'm not really sure, even now, if that's what it really says—"really" perhaps etc.) and then stuck it in the runout groove so that people who bought the record but didn't have an autoreturn on their stereo would suddenly hear this caffeinated twaddle looping just when they thought the album was over.

But what absolutely blew me away as I lay among those overstuffed pillows on Ginny's boyfriend's couch was how that record was finally all about aesthetic possibility.

There was, first off, Peter Blake's incredibly self-reflexive cover littered with simulacra of Poe, Brando, Stockhausen, Wilde, and Marx (not to mention, interestingly enough, given my current obsessions, three sf writers: H. G. Wells, Aldous Huxley, and proto-avant-popster William Burroughs), among many other cultural icons, including a tidy gray-suited 1964 simulation of the Beatles supplied by Madame Tussaud's standing directly to the left of the flesh-and-blood 1967 version wearing lime green, electric pink, sky blue, and redcoat red pop military-marching-band regalia.

That cover pointed to a certain density, a certain richness in the project that was borne out again and again by the music itself. Here was a real-time group, after all, that had created an unconsciously Baudrillardian concept album about a nonexistent group (with Ringo as the lead singer, "Billy Shears," no less) that seemed to be playing live before an audience that was in fact simply generated with Martin's help in the London studio. And here was a record that took chance after proto-avant-pop (more on which soon) chance with form and content. There were McCartney's orchestral tune-up noises and audience murmurs on the title track, Lennon's surreal lyrics for "Lucy in the Sky with Diamonds," the warped carnival sounds on "Being for the Benefit of Mr. Kite!," Harrison's world-music dreamtime sitar on "Within You Without You," and various cut-and-splice and reverse-track procedures, not to mention the intricate development of "A Day in the Life" and that awe-inspiringly resonant final chord thrumming for what seemed like forever at the song's conclusion, which suggested to me through its force and abrupt appearance a key (yes) sf trope: the detonation of a nuclear bomb that brings to startling conclusion this day in the life of London (with distant echoes of that great final montage in *Fail Safe* [1964]) that the album as a whole has been about all along: the laughter, the youth angst, the sad departures, the circus, the meter maid, the love, the loneliness, the sex, the spirituality, the generation gap, the drugs, the various social registers, all amounting to an Eliotic pastiche that does not so much do the *police* in different voices as contemporary urban reality itself.

3. Sgt. Pepper's Lonely Hearts Club Band; or, Critifiction as Concept Album

We hope you will enjoy the show . . .

Naturally, my allegedly predictive, allegedly speculative narrative is remarkable precisely to the extent that it is so unremarkable.

It is remarkable precisely to the extent, that is, that it resembles so many narratives recited by so many members of the generations born after World War II, during the era when the idea of the teenager was invented.

While the piece you are now reading is shaped by the belief that "the best histories are . . . personal histories, informed by the author's own experiences and passions" (11), as Robert Miklitsch reminds us that Robert Palmer reminds us with regard to all rock 'n' roll criticism, it also strikes me that we regularly seem to experience those personal histories as communal, even ritualistic, phenomena. Not only can everyone who was conscious in 1963 tell you where they were and what they were doing when they first heard JFK had been assassinated (I was seven, in case you're interested, home from school for lunch, watching *Rocky and Bullwinkle* cartoons), but they can also tell you where they were and what they were doing when they first heard this particular rock song or that particular rock album.

Despite the fact that so many of those songs and albums sound strangely uninteresting in retrospect, blur into each other, pale, gray away in one's ever more socially and temporally mediated imagination (not unlike those first sf B-films you saw or space operas you read as a kid), at the moment one initially hears or reads them they stand out in such shocking relief that they come to function down the road as nothing less than temporal mappings of one's desires, losses, and self-definitions—the instants that finally go into constructing the narrative(s) one comes to think of as one's life ("one's life" perhaps etc.).

Moreover, those sounds tend to be tied up in profound if convoluted and even quasi-Proustian ways with that very tangible, very tactile part of rock 'n' roll: the smell of the vinyl and the plastic wrapping of a new record as you tear into it in your bedroom the second you return home from the mall, or how you spend hours studying the details of your favorite cover and lyrics for illumination, or the feel of that safe, hermetically sealed space of your car as you cruise town ("as almost any Chuck Berry song attests," Miklitsch underscores, "'classic' rock 'n' roll is frequently about auto-mobility" [51]), playing those albums on the cassette or 8-track or listening to cuts off the radio, as if this time they might reveal something to you they hadn't already revealed to you a hundred times before.

And they do.

That's the extraordinary thing: they always do.

* * *

In much the same way, while I can't remember exactly where I was when I first encountered William Gibson's *Neuromancer* shortly after it appeared in 1984, I remember distinctly the jolt of wonder and admiration I felt realizing I'd never read anything like it before.

Its focus on amped-up language, metalogic imagery, MTV-ized speed, film-noir sensibility, full-bore channel-surfing narratology, clear awareness of pop culture (*my* pop culture, with allusions to everything from Steely Dan to Sylvia Plath), and thoughtful speculation on the technosphere (especially information systems) was another Sgt.-Pepperization for me.

No doubt there were myriad literary antecedents to *Neuromancer* and what came to be known as cyberpunk, from Alfred Bester's dark, gritty corporate universe in *The Demolished Man* (1953) and Anthony Burgess's protopunk near-future edge dwellers in *A Clockwork Orange* (1962) to John Brunner's investigation of future shock, computerized existence, and the necessity of adapting to rapid social change in *The Shockwave Rider* (1975), but somehow that isn't what I found myself thinking about as I read Gibson.

Rather, what I found myself thinking about was how he was doing to science fiction novels in 1984 exactly what *Sgt. Pepper* had done to rock music back in 1967, which is my point ("point" perhaps etc.).

He was elbowing the genre awake, making permeable its definitional membrane.

He was showing me that art could exist in ways I had not imagined—not, despite the misleading musical metaphor housed within the word "cyberpunk," in a stripping down of narrative to its raw three-chord basics, but in an elaborate building up of narrative into a techno-arabesque structure that combined various avant-aesthetics with a sophisticated understanding, appropriation, and reconfiguration of pop and alternative thematics and formalistics.

And I remember it occurring to me at the same time that *Neuromancer* (along with a small constellation of texts that would come to harmonize well with it in my mind) thus could not have existed in the manner it had (any more than this piece you are now reading could have existed in the manner it does) without the existence of rock 'n' roll.

4. Good Morning, Good Morning; or, The Reinvention of Writing

Everyone you see is full of life.

Just as modern painters had to reinvent painting because of the discovery of photography, Donald Barthelme once mentioned parenthetically in a symposium on fiction (26), so modern and postmodern writers have had to reinvent writing because of the discovery of film.[1]

Something along the same lines likewise seems to have held true in the second half of the twentieth century with respect to rock 'n' roll. Several generations of postmodern writers—including but not limited to the Beats, the cyberpunks, and those associated with the avant-pop—have sometimes consciously and sometimes unconsciously responded to rock's ubiquitous presence in our culture by reinventing poetry and fiction, including science fiction. I do not necessarily mean to suggest a direct line of influence between rock and literature, but rather a gradually tighter and more rapid looping where the latter comes to condition the former just as the former comes to pervade the latter. At its most obvious, this reinvention is a reply to rock's transgressive attitude—an attitude, as Larry McCaffery argues,

> of defiance toward cultural and aesthetic norms; an attitude of distrust towards rationalist language and all other forms of discourse required by legal, political, and consumer capitalism, but which ultimately have the effect of distorting the individual's sense of him-or-herself as an individual and as a body made of flesh; (therefore) an attitude that artists need not only to *disrupt* the usual modes of communication but to find a means of self-expression that is more "authentic," less tied to abstractions, more tied to the senses and emotions; an attitude that extremities of content and aesthetics are valuable and interesting in and of themselves (they produce bodily and emotional responses that are powerful and hence undeniably "real") and valuable, too, because such art fundamentally questions the assumptions of "normative art" (and of the culture which produces this). ("Cutting Up" 289)

In the fall of 1956, the year I was born—two years after Elvis Presley laid down "That's All Right" at Sam Phillips's Memphis Recording Service and exactly ten years before the Beatles entered Studio Two on Abbey Road—City Lights published Allen Ginsberg's *Howl*. Jack Kerouac's *On the Road* appeared the following year, and William Burroughs's weirdly science fictional *Naked Lunch* followed in 1959.

From one angle, this literary troika would become emblematic of the first generation to internalize rock's benzedrined, incantational rhythms, its emotional intensity and roughness, its sexual and pharmaceutical excess, and its revolutionary political awareness. Tracing back through an avant-garde lineage to Baudelaire's bleak studies of urban fringe dwellers and an aesthetics of the shocking—even of the ugly—both rock (think of Kurt Cobain, Jimi Hendrix, Janis Joplin, Keith Moon, Jim Morrison, Iggy Pop, Henry Rollins, Patti Smith, Sid Vicious) and the Beats highlighted the role of the artist as alien, criminal, and prophet while underwriting a creative act that championed honesty, spontaneity, and radical formal innovation. Such a transgressive, rock-inspired attitude evinced itself throughout fiction and poetry in the late twentieth century (think of Ai, Imamu Amiri Baraka, Steve Erickson, Eurudice, Lauren Fairbanks, Lawrence Ferlinghetti, Darius James, Doug Rice, Ed Sanders, William T. Voll-mann), but it did so nowhere more than in the dystopic sf cityscapes and the outsiders, body-modified punks, and enraged anarchists that inhabit them in such cybernoir novels and story collections as J. G. Ballard's *Crash* (1973), Bruce Sterling's *Artificial Kid* (1980), *Mirrorshades: The Cyberpunk Anthology* (1986), George Alec Effinger's *When Gravity Fails* (1986), Pat Cadigan's *Mindplayers* (1987), Jack Womack's *Ambient* (1987), Misha's *Red Spider White Web* (1990), John Shirley's *New Noir* (1993), and Ian McDonald's *Terminal Café* (1994).

If thematically the reinvention of poetry and fiction (perhaps especially sci-ence fiction) was in some measure a reply to rock's transgressive attitude, then structurally it was a reply to the idea of aesthetic piracy—of what Raymond Fe-derman calls *pla(y)giarism* (51). After all, rock is nothing if not a radically appro-priative art form. Its roots commingle country and western, blues, jazz, and Southern gospel, literally enacting Roland Barthes's poststructuralist con-tention that every text is "a multi-dimensional space in which a variety of writ-ings, none of them original, blend and clash," "a tissue of quotations drawn from the innumerable centres of culture" ("Death of the Author"146). Rock is a music without borders or autonomy which, as Steven Connor argues, embraces a "congenital impurity of means and nature" (207), a potent icon of which is Public Enemy's song "Fight the Power," whose first ten seconds contain no fewer than seventeen samples (Dettmar B4).

Or, of course, to return to what for me is the iconic alpha, *Sgt. Pepper's Lonely Hearts Club Band*, which blends early rock 'n' roll amalgams with full or-chestral compositions, Indian instruments and rhythms, circus and beer-hall motifs, 1940s crooning, and even the aural equivalent of Burroughsian cutups via samples of barnyard-animal squawks and snorts and segments of back-tracking human voices and strange phantasmagoric instrumental riffs on a number of songs, each of which almost seamlessly bleeds into the next.

I am reminded of another iconic image of this impulse, too, a science fictional one: the Oakland Bay Bridge in Gibson's *Virtual Light* (1993) and *All Tomorrow's Parties* (1999). Abandoned by the city after a megalithic earthquake, slowly taken over by the homeless, and currently the topic of research by a young Japanese scholar named Yamasaki, the construction has become a patch-work of dwellings from bars to tattoo parlors, sushi shops to ragtag shelters, which "had occurred piecemeal, to no set plan, employing every imaginable technique and material. The result was something amorphous, startlingly or-ganic" (*Virtual Light* 62).

The Oakland Bay Bridge that inhabits the landscape of Gibson's imagina-tion is a work—like rock 'n' roll and, I want to argue, like a particular avant-pop shading of sf—of *bricolage* fabricated haphazardly from the material one finds among the metaphoric aisles of the millennial cultural hypermart.

5. Being for the Benefit of Mr. Kite! or, Omniphagic Dreams

Lastly through a hogshead of real fire!

Before going much further, I should point out what many readers of this piece probably already intuit: that I am using the term *science fiction* in its widest, most inclusive sense.

In other words, I have the greatest interest in those texts that not only evidence sf's obsession with technology, speculation, and future-oriented thinking but that also conceive of themselves, like Gibson's bridge, as more than those fairly limited component parts.

It is surely the case that my generation is not only one of the first to be raised on rock 'n' roll and its visual peer, TV, but also one of the first to be raised on literary and cultural theory inside and outside of the university, and if one takes Barthes's familiar notion of intertextuality seriously, it soon becomes difficult to limit the fiction one writes by means of traditional marketing categories (Sword and Sorcery, Science Fiction, Thriller, Pornography, Detective, and so forth) and ever easier to conceive of it as an oceanic discursive zone where at certain points of concentration many texts, genres, and literary and cultural and theoretical influences come together in nourishing, heterogeneous ways in a complex conversation that transcends such reductive notions as border, package, and containment implied by those marketing categories.

I have the greatest interest in those postgeneric texts, in a phrase, that are not even quite sure how to conceptualize themselves—and which delight in that uncertainty, despite the small sales such an amphibious narratological nature tends to augur.

The sort of fiction I am describing has obvious affinities with what Sterling labeled *slipstream* in his influential 1989 essay, "Catscan 5: Slipstream," which originally appeared in *Science Fiction Eye*. There he writes that contemporary sf "is a lot like the contemporary Soviet Union; the sprawling possessor of a dream that failed. Science fiction's official dogma, which almost everybody ignores, is based on attitudes toward science and technology which are bankrupt and increasingly divorced from any kind of reality. 'Hard-SF,' the genre's ideological core, is a joke today; in terms of the social realities of high-tech post-industrialism, it's about as relevant as hard-Leninism" (quoted from Website version).

Consequently, he proceeds, "many of the best new sf writers seem openly ashamed of their backward Skiffy nationality." In place of this market-driven variety of science fiction, Sterling offers antimarket slipstream (giving examples in a postscript list that mentions, among many others, John Barth's *Giles Goat-Boy* [1966], Gabriel García Márquez's *One Hundred Years of Solitude* [1967], Robert Coover's *Public Burning* [1977], D. M. Thomas's *White Hotel* [1981], and

Walker Percy's *Thanatos Syndrome* [1987]), which, he asserts, is less category or genre than it is a mode of writing "which has set its face against consensus reality. It is fantastic, surreal sometimes, speculative on occasion, but not rigorously so." Unlike traditional hard-sf, it is not concerned with systematic extrapolation or strict adherence to scientific fact: "instead, this is a kind of writing which simply makes you feel very strange; the way that living in the late twentieth century makes you feel, if you are a person of a certain sensibility" (quoted from Website version).

The equivalent, one might offer, of an indie label in the recording industry, slipstream functions, according to Sterling, "outside the cozy infrastructure of genre magazines, specialized genre criticism, and the authorial esprit-de-corps of a common genre cause." It explores, among other techniques, "infinite regress, *trompe-l'oeil* effects, metalepsis, sharp violations of viewpoint limits, bizarrely blasé reactions to horrifically unnatural events . . . all the way out to concrete poetry and the deliberate use of gibberish. Think M. C. Escher, and you have a graphic equivalent." Moreover, it possesses what I think of as an omniphagic impulse, a garbage-disposal imagination that eats, metabolizes, and transforms everything it touches: "history, journalism, official statements, advertising copy . . . all of these are grist for the slipstream mill, and are disrespectfully treated not as 'real-life facts' but as 'stuff,' raw material for collage work. Slipstream tends, not to 'create' new worlds, but to *quote* them, chop them up out of context, and turn them against themselves."

I wrote about much the same subset of fiction in *Ellipse of Uncertainty* (1987), in which I argued that writers as diverse as Franz Kafka, Jorge Luis Borges, Alain Robbe-Grillet, Samuel Beckett, Carlos Fuentes, Thomas Pynchon, Gabriel García Márquez, and J. M. Coetzee worked within an antinarrative belt that I called *postmodern fantasy* and that I argued was the literary equivalent of deconstruction in that it challenged all we once took for granted about language and experience. So I respond deeply to many of the traits Sterling limns in his discussion of so-called slipstream work: its drive to disrupt notions of consensus reality, its messy sense of surrealism and speculation, its intent to generate a sense of disorientation in the reader that mimics a larger sociohistorical sense of having come unstuck in a subjectivist postmodern pluriverse, its employment of various radical narrative techniques to bring about that sense of disorientation, its self-reflexive thrust to quote rather than to create, its aesthetic of the textual collage, and its satisfaction with (even its *need for*) existing outside the mainstream—whether that mainstream be the conventional realm of science fiction ("science fiction" perhaps etc.) or of domestic realism.

Within the last ten or so years I have become increasingly engaged with a subset of that subset: with those texts closer in tone and texture to, say, *The Public Burning* than to *The White Hotel* or *One Hundred Years of Solitude*—those texts (perhaps *Gravity's Rainbow* [1973], a speculative hallucination, can serve as an emblem for the ones I mean) that not only bring ontology, epistemology, and narratology into question in captivating, omniphagic ways but also display an opulent knowledge of contemporary culture and theory, chiefly (though not exclusively) media culture and theory, while investigating that terrain in a language that at some level seeks to embrace the carnivalesque energy and abandon of rock 'n' roll.

I am speaking, of course, of what came to be referred to during the early 1990s as the avant-pop.

6. Fixing a Hole; or, An Avant-Popology

> And it really doesn't matter if I'm wrong
> I'm right
> Where I belong I'm right
> Where I belong.

In "Avant-Pop: Still Life After Yesterday's Crash," his 1995 manifesto-like introduction to *After Yesterday's Crash*, McCaffery asserts that "the biggest challenge facing contemporary American artists is no longer a matter of trying to figure out how to halt or deflect the progress of the [Yeatsian] beast [of apocalyptic change], but of learning how to coexist with it. For the beast is *already here*, having checked in a few years ahead of its originally scheduled arrival time, accompanied by its most recent live-in lover and caretaker, Hyperconsumer Capitalism" (xii).

Framing his discussion in terms of Fredric Jameson's argument in "Postmodernism, or the Cultural Logic of Late Capitalism" (1984), McCaffery theorizes that "pop culture has not only displaced nature and 'colonized' the physical space of nearly every country on the earth, but (just as important) it has also begun to colonize even those inner, subjective realms that nearly everyone once believed were inviolable, such as people's memories, sexual desires, their unconsciousness" (xiii). We thus enter the topography of "a multidimensional *hyperreality* of television lands, media 'jungles,' and information 'highways'" (xiv) in which printbound fiction of any sort—in particular that which aims to attack these very cultural centers—seems at best ill equipped to persist. If this is the case, McCaffery asks, then what mode of authentically subversive art can survive, respond to this set of historical circumstances in a positive, meaningful way, engage with and subvert the amorphous and ubiquitous forces whose desire is to commodify aesthetic subversion itself?

For McCaffery, at least one answer is the avant-pop, a term that conflates an obsessive interest in pop culture with the avant-garde's mutinous mutant spirit.

McCaffery appropriated the appellation from the 1986 Lester Bowie jazz album by the same title that itself features appropriations and reconfigurations of such classic rock songs as "Blueberry Hill" and "Oh, What a Night." These ideas of appropriation and reconfiguration form the essential aesthetic strategy for such avant-pop authors as Philip K. Dick, Chuck Palahniuk, and Don Webb, who "share a fascination with mass culture and the determination to find a means of entering and exploring the belly of the beast without getting permanently swallowed or becoming mere extensions of its operations" ("Avant-Pop" xvi). They consciously absorb and commandeer pop-cultural artifacts from comix to science fiction novels, B-films to TV shows, which supply "citizens of postindustrial nations with the key images, character and narrative archetypes, metaphors, and points of reference and allusion that help us establish our sense of who we are" (xviii), in order to turn the self-perpetuating mechanisms of these hyperconsumer capitalist products in upon themselves, dismantle them, demythologize them, reveal their inner workings, and, perhaps, even make them ours while probing tentative means to (if only briefly) transcend them.

Art consequently regains its subversive power, not by shunning the Debordian society of the spectacle in which it finds itself, nor by attempting to seal itself off from that society in some aesthetically antiseptic room, but rather by pirating and deconstructing the spectacle from within.

7. Lovely Rita; or, The Science-Fictionization of Rock 'n' Roll

When it gets dark I tow your heart away.

Rock 'n' roll appropriates many sf thematics and formalistics through a multitude of avant-pop operations. As long ago as 1969 David Bowie, inspired by the July Apollo moon mission, wrote "Space Oddity" about an astronaut who loses contact with Earth and drifts toward deep space, thereby metaphorizing teen alienation and existential angst through a stock sf trope—a trope, one should note, that Elton John himself appropriated and transformed three years later in "Rocket Man" (1972). Bowie's avant-pop persona, Ziggy Stardust, explores transgender concerns in a dark sf universe while his *Diamond Dogs* (1974) album, like the more recent work of Marilyn Manson, an avant-pop postcyberpunk incarnation of Alice Cooper, forms the antithesis of *Sgt. Pepper*'s exuberant psychedelic affirmation: a concept album focused on a postapocalyptic near-future cityscape where "fleas the size of rats sucked on rats the size of cats and ten thousand peoploids split into small tribes coveting the highest of the sterile skyscrapers." Bands like Devo, with its hyperironic Devolutionary Oath and lack of affect, artists like Laurie Anderson, with her heavily digitally manipulated voice and borrowings from Burroughs ("Language Is a Virus" [1987]) and other more general sf topoi ("O Superman" [1987]), and even a number of current rock genres (techno, jungle, trip-hop, and so on), foreground the cybernetic. While some bands write straight tributes to specific sf authors and texts (Sonic Youth, to cite one example, bases "The Sprawl" on their *Daydream Nation* [1988] album on the world of Gibson's pivotal novel), Michael Jackson's forever morphing body unconsciously becomes an sf trope itself, and artists like Scott Weiland (with his 1998 homage to Jane Fonda in the B-film *Barbarella* [1968]), Aqua, and Gwar self-consciously manipulate sf tropes to camp comic effect.

8. Lucy in the Sky with Diamonds; or, The Rock 'n' Rollization of SF Subject Matter

The girl with kaleidoscope eyes . . .

What I want to concentrate on here, however, is the opposite avant-pop strategy—sf's appropriation and manipulation of rock 'n' roll—first at the more obvious stratum of subject matter, then at several less obvious strata of structural mechanics and linguistic intensity.

I am thinking, in the first instance, of quite well-known, fairly mainstream sf novels such as Gibson's *Idoru* (1996), which feature stock types from rock 'n' roll in fairly stock sf situations. In Gibson's case, these include Chia McKenzie, a fourteen-year-old fan of the Seattle band Lo/Rez, and Rez himself, who has decided to marry Rei Toei, a virtual superstar adored in Japan, and a series of chases right out of last season's summer action film. But I am also thinking of perhaps much-less-well-known novels that skirt the edges of sf while often consciously swerving into the territory of other genres and traditions for material, texture, and even narrative framework. One brief example will need to suffice here: Paul Di Filippo's *Ciphers* (1997).

Ciphers is a sprawling, ribald, crazed encyclopedic novel. It focuses on Cyril Prothero, a fragile-minded Pynchonesque schlemiel (his name recalls Tyrone Slothrop's from *Gravity's Rainbow*) and (despite ten years of higher education) a clerk at Planet Records in Boston. One afternoon in the early 1990s he comes across a zincless-middled penny minted in Arizona, and then a barcode on a CD that invades his body with a flood of unwanted information when he touches it, only to return home to find his lover, a black woman named Ruby Tuesday, suddenly vanished. The chapters involving his search for her alternate with those involving various other quests and spoofy-if-nebulous conspiracies encompassing snake goddesses, secret gnostic sects, genome mapping, miscellaneous cosmic synchronies, government control and manipulation of mind-expanding drugs, a virus that leads those infected to spiritual enlightenment, and a mysterious international conglomerate called Wu Labs run by a mysterious three-thousand-year-plus-old man in pursuit of immortality and omniscience.

Behind these complex plots and subplots exists a metacommentary on the history of rock 'n' roll. *Ciphers* is rich with facts and fictions about its development, analyses of its lyrics, allusions to its greatest hits, and, above all, its transgressive and appropriative spirit—as well as containing forty-one pages of double-columned footnotes on the musical and myriad other references in the text, from James Brown and Beck to the Sex Pistols and ZZ Top. Behind these runs a secondary river of literary and filmic allusions to and parodies of everything and everybody from *The Wizard of Oz* (1939) to *Ulysses* (1922) (Boston is Di Filippo's Dublin), Borges to porno films, Gurney Norman's almost forgotten countercultural classic, *Divine Right's Trip* (1971), to Sterling and Gibson's *Difference Engine* (1991), mock autobiography to multicultural mythologies, cartoons to screenplays. Look at the first four lines of the novel for a microcosm of its textual logic:

Am I live or am I Memorex?
Soup or spark?
Patient Zero, or just a patient zero?
Or maybe a Nowhere Man. (13)

The first announces the novel's dominant thematics: how our televisual and digi-popular culture of distraction has moved from outside to inside, colonizing our cellular complex. The second alludes to the nascent years of molecular biology when scientists still questioned whether a nerve impulse crossed from synapse to synapse chemically (soup) or electrically (spark), thereby raising the problematics of consciousness, which the rest of the novel addresses. In addition to shadowing AIDS, the third flags the author as a linguistic punster while introducing the critique of language and meaning on which Cyril (and, behind him, Di Filippo) will obsess for the next 541 densely packed pages. The fourth ignites the metacommentary on rock 'n' roll, citing in particular the Beatles and raising the investigation of selfhood-as-cipher.

Di Filippo's text, in other words, becomes the very tissue of quotations Barthes describes in his seminal essay, a ribofunk[2] metafiction that delights in the act of multilayered telling.

No wonder, then, that it is subtitled "A Post-Shannon Rock 'n' Roll Mystery, Composed Partially by Sampling, Splicing, Channeling, and Reverse Transcription"[3]—or, put more simply, messing with the narrative genome.

9. Getting Better; or, The Rock 'n' Rollization of SF Structure and Language

You gave me the word . . .

That impulse toward sampling (which, needless to say, played such a large role in *Sgt. Pepper*) trails back in sf at least to the novels of William Burroughs (whose likeness, as I have mentioned, appears prominently on that album's busy cover) and his cut-up technique, discovered in Paris in 1959 through painter Brion Gysin. Influenced heavily by the dadaists and surrealists, especially Tristan Tzara, Burroughs literally scissored passages composed by himself and other writers and then pasted them back together in an aleatoric procedure in order to generate new texts. This mechanical method of juxtaposition formed the structural principle of his Nova Trilogy—*The Soft Machine* (1961), *The Ticket That Exploded* (1962), and *Nova Express* (1964)—which gives birth to an avant-pop sf mythology for our Age of Uncertainty involving a group of space aliens called the Nova Mob who come to earth seeking control over humans by assuming the form of a virus that invades them and addicts them to media images, drugs, sex, and the pursuit of power.

If Burroughs frequently employed sampling on a local linguistic level in order to short-circuit rationalist language, thereby disrupting what he thought of as the dominant culture's Reality Studio, then Kathy Acker (who, by the way, was always closely allied to the alternative rock scene, in 1996 even collaborating with the Mekons on their album *Pussy, King of the Pirates,* based on her novel by the same title, and then touring with them) frequently employed sampling on the larger level of plot in order to rewrite and re-right key stories of Western culture (by, most famously, Cervantes, Dickens, and Robert Louis Stevenson), thereby disrupting what she thought of as the dominant culture's patriarchal tyranny of narrative construction. In her avant-pop appropriation and reconfiguration of the sf genre, *Empire of the Senseless* (1988), the story of Abhor (part robot, part black woman) and Thivai set in a postapocalyptic near-future United States, Europe, and the Middle East, where anarchists and other outsiders have taken over the streets, Acker rethinks not only central passages from *The Adventures of Huckleberry Finn* (1884) and the quest myth generally but also, as Brian McHale has documented, two key passages from Gibson's *Neuromancer* (Case and Molly's break-in at Sense/Net and Finn's story of the fence killed for crossing the Tessier-Ashpool clan) as well as the general cyberpunk ambience of Gibson's novel and various occasional details (Gibson's Artificial Intelligence becomes Acker's American Intelligence, for instance, his Panther Moderns becomes her Moderns, his Wintermute becomes her Winter). But while McHale argues that such an approach here is "pointless," simply "blank parody" that has "no discernible purpose apart from that of producing the 'sampling' effect itself" (234), it seems clear to me that it represents on the contrary one of the few instances where Acker *isn't* deconstructing, or merely sampling to sample, but rather quoting and manipulating as a kind of tribute to Gibson's cyberpunk text, with whose portrayal of the socially and economically marginalized, dystopic worldview, investigation into the limits of the human, and critique of commodified and digitized flesh she felt a special aesthetico-philosophic rapport.

A sense of MTV-ized velocity, information density, and jump-cut surreality enters the very sentence rhythms of many avant-pop sf texts, from, again, Burroughs's experiments in the late 1950s and early 1960s through the hyperfic- tions in Mark Leyner's collection *My Cousin, My Gastroenterologist* (1990), where one regularly encounters the hyperbolic caricature of an entire cyberpunk sf story in the space of a few sentences, to, more recently, Steve Aylett's *Slaughtermatic* (1998), the caustic narrative—reminiscent in its high-energy tone, cynical-chic vision, cartoon-noir atmosphere, and hallucinogenic vigor of Jeff Noon's avant-pop sf cult classic *Vurt* (1993)—of a botched bank robbery in the English rust-belt city of Beerlight that launches a time-travel plot that may in truth be part of a larger virtual-reality game. Its prologue begins like this:

Beerlight was a blown circuit, where to kill a man was less a murder than a mannerism. Every major landmark was a pincushion of snipers. Cop tanks navigated a graffiti-rashed riot of needle bars, oil-scabbed neon and diced rubble. Fragile laws were shattered without effort or intent and the cops considered false arrest a moral duty. Integrity was no more than a fierce dream. Crime was the new and only art form. The authorities portrayed shock and outrage but never described what it was they had been expecting. Anyone trying to adapt was persecuted. One woman had given birth to a bulletproof child. Other denizens were bomb zombies, pocketing grenades and wandering gaunt and vacant for days before winding down and pulling the pins on themselves. There was no beach under the sidewalk. (N.p.)

The insistence on metaphor, non sequitur, breathless staccato rhythm, jerky point of view, data compression, and abrupt emergence of dream-reality into an already enormously dystopic narrative signals, as it were, a "criminal" art form that violates conventional narratology and epistemology in the same way that crime itself violates the once-conventional world of Beerlight—a city whose name is yet another distant comic echo of Gibson's Straylight, the shadowy high-orbit Tessier-Ashpool core of Freeside where irrationality rules and all fences are down.

And, it goes without saying, in the same way that Elvis's pelvis and then the Beatles's mop-tops or, later, the mods' guitar smashing and then The Doors's uncensored lyrics on *The Ed Sullivan Show*, or, later still, the punks' body modification and then rap's aesthetics of machismo brutality signal a "criminal" art form that violates conventional musical and social contracts.

It's the stuff, in other words, your parents will always hate.

10. She's Leaving Home; or, Hey, Hey, We're the Monkees

We gave her everything money could buy . . .

A few months after listening to *Sgt. Pepper* with my eyes closed among those overstuffed pillows on Ginny's boyfriend's couch, I had another musical revelation: I met the tunes and TV show of the Monkees—through, I should mention, another friend, Michael Pardo, a neighbor who lived two houses behind me and who in 1970 (the year the Beatles broke up for good and about two years before I began playing keyboards for a very bad, very enjoyable local band) would drop LSD, walk out to the middle of the George Washington Bridge, climb over the railing, and jump to his probably unintentional dream-reality death.

The Monkees, it didn't take anyone long to figure out, were a kind of corporate merchandising machine designed to look, sound, and act like the Beatles. They soon taught me something much less sanguine about rock 'n' roll's heart: that hyperconsumer capitalism is all about absorbing the innovative like some pod monster from a bad 1950s sf film, commodifying it, and recirculating it as the radical-made-safe flavor of the month. Hence the dark emblem of the fairly recent Northwest grunge phenomenon, itself a late outrider of punk (itself a quickly commodified musical fashion), which became media-fied and spawned a slew of corporate-generated clones seemingly within seconds of its appearance.

In other words, the whole idea of extremity in rock 'n' roll easily tips over into marketing gimmickry, or, as Connor suggests, "what seems to have happened is that the cycle of inclusion, in which new forms and energies are incorporated, tamed, and recycled as commodities, has accelerated unimaginably, to the point where authentic 'originality' and commercial 'exploitation' are hard to distinguish" (206).

The consequence is a kind of flattening out, a heterogeneous neutralization of serious intent in the face of commodified desire. Suddenly the Beatles's anthem "Revolution" on *Hey Jude* (1970) becomes the score for a Nike commercial and Fleetwood Mac morph into cheerleaders for Bill Clinton. Charlie Manson tries out for the Monkees, Marilyn Manson names himself after Charlie, and neo-Nazi bands appropriate rock 'n' roll conventions for their own creepy ends. It is increasingly difficult to tell, that is, what exists within quotation marks and what does not, where self-aware irony stops and unconscious self-parody begins—which leads us into the theoretical precinct of Baudrillard, who argues in "The Precession of Simulacra" (1983), an essay that influenced me profoundly when I first came across it in graduate school seventeen years ago, that at the millennial edge "reality" has dissolved into the simulation of reality, one media-generated image mirroring only other media-generated images.

Infinitely.

11. Within You Without You; or, Tonguing the Zeitgeist

> . . . and the people
> Who gain the world and lose their soul . . .

Such understanding leads into the deeply conflicted region of rock 'n' roll that has obsessed me for the last decade or so and helped reconstitute my own fiction in the four sf novels following my first, *Live from Earth* (1991), a gentle, fairly conventional magical realist one about a woman's love affair with her dead husband.[4]

Since then, I have increasingly conceptualized my own criticism as a mode of speculative fiction, my own speculative fiction as a mode of criticism. If the former provides me with an intellectual territory in which to explore the need to construct cosmos out of chaos, the latter provides me with a seriously ludic region in which to think about theory from, as it were, some Möbius-strip perspective. My criticism, then, speaks from within my sf, my sf from within my criticism (as in the essay you are now etc.; "essay" perhaps etc.). Both—let's call each a variety of *critifiction*, following Raymond Federman's coinage nearly a quarter of a century ago—both amount in the final analysis to acts of self-portraiture, ways of documenting what matters to me at various life instants, what texts catch my attention, what cultural outcroppings, what I care or cared about and why.

"Science fiction," Samuel R. Delany once wrote in a lovely line, "is a tool to help you think" (*Starboard Wine* 34), yet the opposite has also held true for me: criticism has become a tool to help me feel—which, I imagine, is no more than to affirm yet again (if in different words) that the lamina between various genres, various approaches to knowledge and thus to the world, have begun eroding into an addling if engrossing state of ambidextrousness.

It is fair to say that long before *Live from Earth* appeared I knew I wanted to go somewhere very different for my next book—to create, as it were, a companion piece, the dark negative of *Live from Earth*'s sweetness and light (the reason, I'm sure, is a long story with a long history, involving among other things my father's death by cancer, my own entry into academentia, my increasing interest in a global ecosystem that had gone rotten in the teeth, and a number of other passing strange happenings)—and so I set about writing what would become, through the vicissitudes of the publishing world, my third novel, *Burnt*, to which I will return on the next cut.

As a kid I didn't read a lot of science fiction, I should admit, except in the form of awful comic books, though I saw tons of sf films (especially those fabulous sf B-films from the 1950s and 1960s) and TV series (*Twilight Zone*, *Outer Limits*, and *Star Trek* are still among my very favorites). As a graduate student my reading took me elsewhere as well: into theories of postmodernity, at the time a bewilderingly fresh and tantalizing topic (this was, remember, the late 1970s and early 1980s), and into the lineage of the avant-garde, the alternative, and the transgressive in American and European fiction. But during the late 1980s my fascination with sf was rekindled and broadened with a vengeance through my introduction to cyberpunk in general and, needless to say, *Neuromancer* in particular—as well as through my reading of Baudrillard and my discussions with people like McCaffery about texts that a number of us had begun referring to in our criticism and manifestoes as examples of the avant-pop.

It was in this context that I started *Tonguing the Zeitgeist* (1994)—mostly for creative sport, really, mostly just to see if I could do sf, mostly just to show some sf texts I cared, though I had gone fairly far in the direction of convincing myself (the games we writers play with ourselves, etc. . . .) that it would never, ever see print because it was just too damn weird. I deliberately pirated science fiction protocols (specifically cyberpunk ones) in order to defamiliarize the present pluriverse through a fictive glass darkly. For my core plot, I cribbed the Faust myth, centering things around a young rockstar wannabe, Ben Tendo (a name, like most in my novels, that waves over the heads of my characters to Pynchon, one of my megalithic literary heroes), who cuts a deal with a large music corporation in order to become famous. Ben asks himself how much he would be willing to give up to become the latest marketing fad, and the answer turns out to be everything, absolutely everything: the music corporation rebuilds him from the ground up, you see, reshaping his body, his gender ("gender" perhaps etc.), and his voice to make him salable for a few weeks while alive, then assassinates him so that his entertainment stock spikes shortly and lucratively before being replaced by the next manufactured skin-job goods.

(Look at how this sounds too simple by half.)

(By three-fourths.)

Thematically, then, I was primarily concerned with investigating the commodification of desire, the question of authenticity, and the relationship of the body to selfhood. Structurally, I wanted to probe the notion of genre appropriation, quoting heavily not only from cyberpunk but also from various thrillers, Acker, Burroughs, the Horatio Alger myth, the dystopic novel, the essential rock 'n' roll narrative of sudden success followed by physical and mental dissipation, and through a series of disruptive techniques (rapid scene displacements, abrupt point-of-view shifts, hallucinogenic narratological zones that stutter between dream world and real world, the latter perhaps etc.) that tended to draw attention to the reading process itself, the textuality of the text, the constructedness of the construction at hand. Tonally, I was interested in generating a playfulness that was lacking in the straight-faced, even somber sf of early Gibson, Lewis Shiner, and Richard Kadrey, though often evident in spades in much avant-pop sf (Di Filippo, Leyner, Neal Stephenson).

What I wanted to do linguistically was not only sample lyrics and mimic musical forms like rap, punk, and heavy metal but also charge my sentences with a kind of manic density that in some way competed with as well as commented upon and critiqued the hyperactivity of the late-stage capitalist entertainment industry, thereby echoing at least in part the sonic domain of rock 'n' roll. (It goes almost—but not quite—without saying that I've always been a sucker for amazing language. If you're a writer and can't say that, in my opinion, then why not just make movies or write for the daily papers?) For a quick sense of what I mean, listen to the following passage. It appears in the novel's overture and limns a near-future rock concert at the Royal Albert Hall. The concert will go very wrong in a matter of paragraphs, but right now everything is lightshow and vigor. I've chosen the thing pretty much at random, though I hope it makes my point:

Twenty-five meters above the stage the holounit unfolds marvelous forms and applause lurches through the hall.

A beautiful naked woman with dark red hair and pale freckled skin, sixteen meters tall, the mad Pre-Raphaelite dream of a haunted Rossetti, floats over the crush. Two delicate batwings, blanched flesh and cartilage, extend from her shoulders. She lifts her right hand, opens the palm in which blinks a crystal blue eye, surveys her surroundings.

The eye closes. Her palm folds. Lowering her head, hair spreading over her shoulders like wind, she curls into herself, rotates, loses age and size, dissolves into a fetus, becomes a plant with short parrot-green stems and swollen wet flowers shaped like the plum-colored lips of a vagina. These separate slowly and release a swarm of tiny transparent fish with blueblack wings and scarlet hearts pumping rapidly in their chest cavities. Thousands of tiny orange bubbles swell from their gills. They morph into copper snakes, purple geckos, angels with monkey faces, transparent fish again, and then a young man in an olivesheen business suit and derby sitting in the lotus position under a banyan tree.

He is speaking to a naked tanned boy with white hair and four arms who sits across from him, also in the lotus position.

"The black box represents the small secret moments, a sense of peace, a sense of wonder," he says. (10-11)

We're back, at least in my mind, of course, to an act of Sgt.-Pepperization—an attempt on my part, that is, to elicit in others the thrill I first felt lying among those overstuffed pillows on Ginny's boyfriend's couch, eyes closed, listening to that extraordinary music. If textured prose is usually described as "painterly," I wanted to find a linguistic and syntactic analogue for some kind of televisual, high-definition word experience, a kind of cartoon jell of saturated hues, Dolby sound for your eyes, while foregrounding with every image precisely the idea of Image itself, the semiotics of stimulation and simulation.

Whether or not I succeeded is, I'm sure, not for me to say, but the truth ("truth" perhaps etc.) remains that I found myself having such a good time that somewhere in the midst of working on *Tonguing the Zeitgeist* the concept of an extended antitrilogy planted itself in my brainstem: a series of novels (in this case three) that inhabited the same world and time, more or less, though shared neither the same protagonists nor the main plotlines (though secondary characters from some novels would appear as primary characters in others, and vice versa, subplots in earlier ones grow to elephantiasized proportions in later ones). This move wasn't so much the perhaps obvious homage to the tradition of novelistic sf and fantasy series, whose predictability and marketing savvy simply didn't appeal to me, but rather to William Faulkner's Yoknapatawpha County, a fictional space that looks epistemologically and ontologically steady upon first reading, yet upon closer examination shapeshifts subtly, contradicts itself in barely discernible ways (a character in one novel is described as being a certain age and weight, for instance, yet in another he is anachronistically twenty years older and anasurfeitly a hundred pounds heavier), generating a sense of existential instability that ultimately gives rise to queries associated with what I think of as Quantum Mechanics Narrativity.

If *Tonguing the Zeitgeist* is set primarily in the Northwest and Britain, then *Time Famine* (1996), the novel that followed two years later, is set in the Northwest and in the cardinal geography of hyperconsumer capitalism: the Southwest (think Las Vegas, think L.A.—only to maybe the twentieth power). *Time Famine*'s temporal focus is split between the middle of the twenty-first century and the middle of the nineteenth, and its bifurcated plot centers around a new type of theme park that makes spectacular entertainment from various historical atrocities, including various ugly wars and even uglier concentration camps (a metaphor that thereby replaces rock 'n' roll here as the site of comodification). The nuclear reactor powering BelsenLand, one of said theme parks, melts down during an earthquake, releasing a cloud of radiation that causes those who come into contact with it to experience, not physical sickness, but intense memories that are not their own. One of my protagonists—"Uly," short for "Ulysses"—experiences recollections associated with and apparently journeys back to the Donner Party, that ill-fated emigrant group that set out from Independence, Missouri, in April 1846, only to become bogged down in the snowy Sierra Nevada that winter and resort to cannibalism in order to survive until the rescue expeditions could reach its members the next spring.

Time Famine thus not only appropriates and modifies the time-travel plot (for me H. G. Wells's *Time Machine* [1895] is one of the most perfect sf novellas ever written) but also engages with the literature of the New West, wondering precisely how far imperialist America has traveled over the course of the last century and a half (not, it almost—but not quite—goes without saying, very). In my mind, the Donner Party is emblematic, consequently, not so much of the pioneer spirit as it is of the deep structure of the American soul ("soul" perhaps etc.), which D. H. Lawrence famously defines in his essay on James Fenimore Cooper as "hard, isolate, stoic, and a killer" (73). Behind my retelling of that story is a retelling of one of the most disturbing literary explorations of commodification I have ever read, *Heart of Darkness* (1900), with short umber ivory hunter Kurtz at its humid pith. If commodification has moved from the external world in Joseph Conrad's novella into the flesh in *Tonguing the Zeitgeist*, then in *Time Famine* it has moved from the flesh into our very recollections (which, of course, are no longer ours . . . or no longer exactly ours)—into, in other words, our very dendritic circuitry—in the person of another of my protagonists there, Krystal, who inexplicably (she is nowhere near BelsenLand's radioactive swath, you see) begins to experience bizarre visions involving strange surgeries, space probes, and transgendered perceptions of the world ("world" perhaps etc.).

What she never learns is that she is a living, breathing experiment. Nanobots have been injected along her optic nerve during routine cosmetic surgery, made their way into her brain, and colonized her cerebral cortex. This actuality doesn't fully resolve itself into focus until the final pages of *Freaknest* (2000), the third panel in my antitrilogic triptych, set in a Dickensian future-London of 2023. There, the inevitable happens: shortly after nanotechnology becomes available to the upper echelon of a burgeoning technocracy, black-market nanodrugs start appearing on the streets. Instead of being designed by your standard dealers, however, it turns out they are designed by the govern-corp (governments then being run by CEOs rather than such antiquated figure-heads as presidents and prime ministers) to surreptitiously rewire the brains of would-be deviants, and they are tested on (among others) a group of parentless children locked in a block of flats just across the street from Harrod's hyper-mart.

What I tried to accomplish in *Freaknest* was partly to confiscate and recon-figure the narrative of the feral boy and girl, which I have always found capti-vating (especially the versions, such as the history of Kaspar Hauser, that have some basis in fact and suggest something profound about the nature of educa-tion and language acquisition), and partly to confiscate and reconfigure the ro-mantic myth of the child as a locus of Rousseauian innocence, goodness, and hope. Beyond that, I wanted to investigate the thematic terrain of bioethics con-cerning human experimentation, the relationship of identity and memory, ageism (the marginalized elderly in this society eat their young), and the in-evitability of a rising nanocracy (along with many of my other deep-rooted fixa-tions, including questions of where the human ends and the machine begins, body modification *in extremis*, various encroaching environmental catastro-phes, etc.). Metaphorically, as the title suggests, I wanted to explore how at the launch of a new millennium many people were beginning to feel like teratoids in the global commodity exchange. Freaks, needless to say, are just like us, only more so.

By this stage of the game, however, we seem to have drifted pretty far afield from rock 'n' roll and this essay's alleged essence.

But not really.

Or perhaps not exactly.

You see, the deep structures of both *Time Famine* and *Freaknest* are profoundly influenced by rock 'n' roll, especially in the embodiment of MTV's speed and televisual delirium, and both novels attempt to capture on the page a number of MTV's signature effects, among which are its use of nonlinear (one could even say hypertextual, rhizomatic, and certainly irrational—not, one might be inclined to argue, unlike the piece you are now reading) narrative, split screen, unusual angles and cropping, rapid cuts, stop action, slo-mo, hypnotic repetition, breakneck point-of-view switches, information thickness, and, once again, once again, when all is said and done, a garbage-disposal imagination.

12. With a Little Help from My Friends; or, Eco-Fiction

I get by with a little help from my friends . . .

Which, in a very roundabout way, pilots me back to the harbor of my second novel, published as my third, *Burnt* (1996).

My editor at Available Press/Ballantine, who was hoping for a sweetness-and-light tonal sequel to *Live from Earth*, took one look at this new manuscript back in the early 1990s and said, forget it. It was way too stylistically flashy and psychologically dark for him. Why? Well, it's a speculative fiction about a professor of popular culture who (probably, depending on one's point of view) kills one of his students because of that student's bad prose style, and, while it doesn't foreground rock 'n' roll in its plot any more than *Time Famine* or *Freaknest* does, rock 'n' roll and the Baudrillardian theory of simulation are very much on the mind of its author, Lance Olsen, as well as its protagonist, whose name is Murphy Porter.

(Look at that: I'm back again as a definite noun.)

Talking to a friend of his about the loss of reality at the *fin-de-millennium* as they stroll across the campus at Central Kentucky University, where he teaches, Murphy, for instance, mentions a supposedly "live" album by Twisted Sister, saying:

"See, the band performs in a stadium packed with eighty-thousand fans. But the fans don't see the real band. Instead they see the video image of the 'band' playing on a gigantic screen behind the band, which itself is a compilation of carefully designed media images of what a heavy metal group should be. In other words the fans see an edited aestheticized experience of a replica of a rock 'n' roll band. Nor do they hear the real band. They hear noises produced by a complicated series of sound mixes, samplings and lip syncs. . . . Only it turns out they like the unreal so much . . . that they run out to buy the album of this replicated event—a gesture which is itself a replica of a gesture generated

by advertising to create the replica of desire where it didn't exist in the first place. But the album isn't a recording of the replicated event the fans attended in, say, Philadelphia, but of a 'live' replicated performance they didn't attend in, say, Atlanta, which nonetheless is enough like the replicated event they attended in Philadelphia to convince them it isn't replicated. Only it isn't really a recording of the replicated event in Atlanta either, since the band went back into the studio after the fact and dubbed over the 'original' songs, themselves not original, in order to make them sound better than the originals, which, of course, weren't original to begin with." (53)

Three quick points about this passage.

First, it isn't mine.

Or it isn't exactly mine.

("Mine" perhaps etc.)

Rather, it's an appropriation and transformation of a passage—or, more precisely, a series of passages (151-54)—from the first edition of Connor's *Postmodernist Culture*, where he discusses the nature of postmodern performance in light of theories by, among others, Gilles Deleuze, Jacques Derrida, Walter Benjamin, and, needless to say, Jean Baudrillard, whose perspective Connor briefly assumes.

Second, my appropriation of Connor's appropriation functions synecdochially for the novel as a whole, which I conceive of as an *eco-fiction*—that is, as a text (a critifictional intertext, really) that both concerns itself with various kinds of pollution (environmental, psychological, ethical, linguistic, e.g.) *and* recycles various genres (murder mystery, academic satire, love affair, speculative fiction, e.g.) to create the literary equivalent of a collage (in a similar way that, say, a song like "A Day in the Life" or "Being for the Benefit of Mr. Kite!" on *Sgt. Pepper* etc.).

Third, while surely such a novel falls outside the marketing pale of mainstream sf (its manuscript was the one that led me out of said pale into the smaller, more luminous universe of the micropress, the equivalent in U.S. publishing of the indie label), it nonetheless appropriates a number of sf tropes (alien abduction, alien invasion, alternate-universe construction, e.g.) while alluding to a number of those fabulous sf B-films (*Frankenstein* [1931], *Donovan's Brain* [1953], etc.), which I teethed on as a kid, narratologically speaking, and to a number of amphibious texts that don't really want to think of themselves as either generic surf or turf (think Kurt Vonnegut, Douglas Adams, Don DeLillo), which I discovered early on and which in some nearly shamanistic way entered the bedrock (no pun intended) of my consciousness during my teens and twenties.

I could go on, it turns out.

I could go on and on.

Once you get an author talking about his favorite subject, it looks like, there's simply no shutting him up.

Nonetheless . . .

13. Sgt. Pepper's Lonely Hearts Club Band (Reprise); or, Möbius Aesthetics

We hope you have enjoyed the show . . .

I want to finish by offering several possible abbreviated conclusions ("conclusions" perhaps etc.) that might supplement the by-now I hope obvious (and hence unnecessary) one about the interconnectivity of rock 'n' roll, the avant-pop, and science fiction, particularly though by no means exclusively in my own work.

One such conclusion might involve a restatement of Brian McHale's assertion that over the course of the last thirty years or so science fiction—or, closer to the point, at least a single self-reflexive subset of science fiction—has become increasingly postmodernized while postmodern fiction has become increasingly science-fictionized. This, according to McHale, is a function of each genre's becoming gradually more aware of the other since the post–New Wave 1970s. By the 1980s, McHale continues, we discover "a feedback loop" blossoming between the two: "That is, we find postmodernist texts absorbing materials from SF texts that have already been 'postmodernized' to some degree through contact with mainstream postmodernist poetics. Reciprocally, we find SF texts that incorporate models drawn from postmodernist fiction that has already been 'science-fictionized' to some degree through its contact with SF poetics. Thus certain elements can be identified as having cycled from SF to mainstream postmodernism and back to SF again, or in the opposite direction, from mainstream fiction to SF and back to mainstream again" ("POSTcyberMODERN-punkISM" 228–29).

It almost—but not quite—goes without saying that the current situation strikes me as a lot less crisp, definitionally speaking, than the slightly easy binary McHale employs. While facets of postmodernism may indeed have become commodified (fashion trends, art movements, haute cuisine, etc.) in our late-stage capitalist culture of excess, I remain apprehensive about talking about a "mainstream" postmodernist poetics, since it seems to me that at the very core of postmodern consciousness is an always ongoing struggle to trouble and subvert such restrictive hegemonic concepts—even while maintaining an awareness that that always ongoing struggle is ultimately doomed to defeat again (and again and again) through hyperconsumerism's own omniphagic impulse.

Also, the *either-or* metaphor of a feedback loop assumes two discrete entities to begin with—a supposition that, as McHale himself admits, has not held firm for more than a quarter of a century (if it ever really did) except, perhaps, on the shelves of bookstores and in the minds of marketing executives and literary critics. Perhaps a more apt metaphor might be instead the *both-and* Möbius strip, since presently notions such as *inside* and *outside*, *here* and *there*, *this* and *that*, a thing called *science fiction* and a thing called *postmodern fiction*, seem inaccurate and unhelpful in the extreme, barely more than uneasy modernist attempts to describe and thus circumscribe a state of affairs that is anything but settled, comfortably differentiated, effortlessly canvassed and considered.

Consequently, I would reiterate that what we are witnessing outside limited market-driven domains is a willful amalgamation and bafflement of manifold genres on the part of many writers who no longer conceive of themselves as primarily creators of either postmodern or science fiction texts. Rather, my sense is that they conceive of themselves simply as narratologically and theoretically savvy composers uninterested in limiting the scope of their efforts by engaging in the manufacture of prim "mainstream" contracts between writer and reader. These authors' goal (think of Don Webb, Hal Jaffe, Lidia Yuknavitch), then, has less to do with finding publication through the normal and often normative New York channels (although they are not necessarily averse to doing so, as recent fictions by Jonathan Lethem, David Foster Wallace, and Steve Erickson confirm) than it does with attempting to capture felt experience at the millennial edge—a multidimensional, televisual, discontinuous experience that cannot easily be limned by conventional narrative modes.

If we are thus witnessing the proliferation of a postgenre composition (as in the piece you are now etc.) that has begun to question the need for discussing such apparently singular species as *science fiction* and *postmodernism*, we are also witnessing the proliferation of a postcritical writing (as in the etc.) that has begun to question the need for discriminating between such apparently singular species as *theory* and *fiction*. We are witnessing—and have been for the last thirty or forty years outside of science fiction studies (which, it nearly goes without saying, is finally, and none too soon, edging into the future itself)—what Connor discusses as the slow "collapse of criticism into its object" (227). Roland Barthes, Hélène Cixous, Derrida, Federman, Ihab Hassan, Dick Hebdige, Steven Pfohl, Ronald Sukenick, Steven Shaviro, and Gregory Ulmer, to name the first ten who come to mind, have been investigating in various performative critifictions ways to erase the artificial distinction between primary and secondary texts, asserting by example that all texts are in fact secondary ones, linguistic and generic collages, bits of *bricolage*. In other words, these writers have attempted to efface, or at least deeply and richly complicate, the accepted difference between a privileged discourse written by those who believe that they can somehow step back from what it is they are discussing and attain with respect to it something like an elite position of metacommentarial Newtonian objectivity, on the one hand, and, on the other, some subordinate discourse that can be intellectually colonized, written *about* without actually being engaged *with*, written through, or changed by the very act of said writing.

What I hope I have suggested through the mildly impish form of this piece is another beginning of another beginning (which has been beginning at least since Plato's critifictional utopian narrative) of thinking ourselves into a realm of speculative (let's call it Heisenbergian) autobiographiction. While such undertakings have, as I say, occurred outside the gates of what we once thought of as the science-fiction-studies compound on an increasingly wide scale, inside those now-deteriorating gates very few performative critifictionists come to mind—Brooks Landon (in his contribution to the future-of-narrative issue of *ParaDoxa*), Istvan Csicsery-Ronay, Jr.'s contribution to Larry McCaffery's *Storming the Reality Studio*), Samuel R. Delany (in the last collaged pages of *Dhalgren*), Donna Haraway (in "A Manifesto for Cyborgs: Science, Technology, and Socialist Feminism in the 1980s"), and a few others.

Yet that's precisely what I'd like to close by opening up: the potential for post-New Wave postcriticism(s) among the para-sites we used to call sf that will blur, interrupt, question, subvert, recontextualize, personalize, deconstruct, and plain mess up.

All, naturally, with that old rock 'n' roll spirit.

Thereby enriching our experience of writing, it almost—but not quite—goes without saying.

Of writing and, of course, living.

Because that's where I imagine things will start getting *really, really* interesting.

4

Synthespians, Virtual Humans, and Hypermedia

Emerging Contours of Post-SF Film

BROOKS LANDON

"Do you carry video equipment and computer equipment?"

"Yes, we do."

"OK, there's something, I'm not exactly sure what it is—some kind of interactive computerized laser video player or interactive digital video software or something—but it enables you to take any movie and insert Arnold Schwarzenegger as the actor in the lead role. . . ."

"Yes, we have what you're talking about, but you're a little confused about it. We have the equipment here: the computer, the digital video image synthesizing unit, the software—all that—we have that in the store. You tell us what you want—which films you want Schwarzenegger inserted into and we do it do it right here for you."

"So you do it—I don't need to buy the equipment?"

"Oh no no no, we do it right here. As a matter of fact, you can even fax your order in and we'll deliver the Schwarzeneggerized videos to your home."

"Oh cool! Can I order some now?"

"Sure."

"OK. I'd like *My Fair Lady* with Arnold Schwarzenegger as Professor Henry Higgins, *Amadeus* with Arnold Schwarzenegger as Salieri instead of F. Murray Abraham, *The Diary of Anne Frank* with Arnold Schwarzenegger as Anne Frank, *West Side Story* with Arnold Schwarzenegger as Tony, *It's a Wonderful Life* with Arnold Schwarzenegger instead of Jimmy Stewart, *Gandhi* with Arnold Schwarzenegger instead of Ben Kingsley, *Bird* with Arnold Schwarzenegger as Charlie Parker instead of Forest Whitaker. . . . [C]an you do documentaries?"

"Sure."

"There's a documentary called *Imagine* about John Lennon. Could you fix it so that it's Arnold Schwarzenegger instead of Lennon?"

"No problem."

"So it'll be Schwarzenegger playing with the Beatles on Ed Sullivan and Schwarzenegger doing those peace things in bed with Yoko Ono and everything?"

"Yes, ma'am. Our equipment is state of the art."

"OK, and one last one . . . how about *Rain Man*?"

"Would you like Arnold Schwarzenegger as the autistic brother or the Tom Cruise character?"

"Could you do it so he's both, sort of like Patty Duke did as Patty/Cathy in 'The Patty Duke Show'?"

"We can, yes . . . that may be a little more expensive, though." (Mark Leyner, *Et Tu, Babe* 50–51)

In the above scene from *Et Tu, Babe*, a cyberpunkish avant-pop romp through most of the playing fields of postmodern culture, Mark Leyner explores the hilarious prospect of video-editing technology that would allow the substitution of a digital simulacrum of a "new" actor for one who had "originally" starred in a released commercial film. "Schwarzeneggerization" is the name Leyner gives to this process, since the semblance of his novel envisions video customers wanting to make such a substitution only for the image of Arnold. I'm not sure how unlikely Leyner thought this prospect in 1992 when *Et Tu, Babe* was first published, but there is an instructive irony in the fact that now, only a decade later, such a process of digital substitution is almost within reach not only of Pixar or ILM or Digital Domain or dozens of other large SFX shops but also of independent CGI (computer-generated imagery) artists running Macs or Pentium PCs. Indeed, the idea of substituting a digital or virtual or "silicentric" actor for a "carbon-based" or "wetware" actor in commercial film is now so accepted a practice (as opposed to prospect) that "synthespians" is a trademarked term for virtual actors, and the legal issues raised by the use of such virtual actors have been the subject of an article in the *New York Law Journal* (Beard). The list of people who have been digitally simulated in or inserted into commercial films and TV advertisements already includes Bill Clinton, Marilyn Monroe, Fred Astaire, John Wayne, Ed Sullivan, Elvis Presley, and George Burns. President Clinton's comments about possible life on Mars, originally made in a speech given in the White House Rose Garden, have been famously reset and inserted into a scene in *Contact* (1997), a CGI Virtual Bill has been seen on MTV, and a virtual Jay Leno greets visitors to Leno's Website.

Even more ironically, Arnold Schwarzenegger is himself one of a growing number of Hollywood actors (one company advertises that it has scanned over seventy) who have gone "under the beam," getting laser scanned to create a data set that can then be used to manipulate the image of the actor (Parisi, "New Hollywood" 2). So far, Schwarzenegger and other actors including Jim Carrey, Kate Mulgrew, Michelle Pfeiffer, Denzel Washington, and both Gillian Anderson and David Duchovny have just had their heads scanned, but Cyberware's or Cyber F/X's full-body scanners will soon make what we might call "full-blown Schwarzeneggerization" a very real option. And, while a swirl of conflicting rumors makes more than vague speculation impossible, James Cameron is known to have at least considered using a Digital Domain virtual actor as the villain in a film project titled "Avatar." Even if "Avatar"—as now seems likely—is never made, Cameron's other possible post-*Titanic* film projects, including an IMAX 3D film about Mars, all seem likely to take the use of CGI to radically new levels. Indeed, we already have had dueling CGI movies, as Pacific Data Image's *Antz* competed in 1998 with Disney's *A Bug's Life* for audiences attracted by hyperreal computer animation.

My purpose in citing Leyner's Schwarzeneggerizing scene in *Et Tu, Babe*, however, is not to point out that very similar technology now exists but to ask whether such a technology, one that could produce a Schwarzeneggerized *Gandhi* or *Rain Man*, would in fact create new movies we might think of as science fiction. My initial answer, based on arguments I developed in *The Aesthetics of Ambivalence: Rethinking Science Fiction Film in the Age of Electronic (Re)Production* (1992), is—of course—yes. Such an answer rests on considering sf film in largely affective terms—asking what the film does to or for its audience—rather than on focusing exclusively, or even primarily, on the film's narrative, the sf story it purports to present. My focus on the affective impact of sf film in turn calls for our adding the concept of "science fiction seeing" to our longstanding but only loosely codified sense of "science fiction thinking" (*Aesthetics of Ambivalence* 94–99). A secondary response, however, based on the cascade of developments in CGI and other aspects of electronic film, including the advent of commercially released digital movies, is to ask whether the Schwarzeneggerization scenario can still be understood as sf film. And here my answer is no, based on my growing belief that we are entering an era of multimedia post-sf film that must be completely reconceptualized and retheorized, both in terms of the diegetic nature of this new medium and in terms of its new relationships with its audiences. (What I am referring to as post-sf film might actually be thought of as *ultra-sf film* or *hyper-sf film*, suggesting that it is *more* than we are used to in sf film, but I will stick with the post-sf film rubric to retain the critical valence associated with those other noteworthy "posts," such as postmodernism, poststructuralism, and the posthuman.) Here I will suggest through ten propositions some of the lines or contours along which this new medium seems to be developing. First, however, I need to rehearse the assumptions about sf film that have led to these propositions.

I wrote *The Aesthetics of Ambivalence* to counter what I saw as the mistaken central assumption of most science fiction film criticism—that science fiction film and science fiction literature sprang from the same roots and pursued the same goals. Somewhat whimsically following the utopian call made by Vachel Lindsay in his 1916 *The Art of the Moving Picture* for an essentially non-narrative cinema understood primarily in terms of space and spectacle and motion, and drawing heavily upon the work of Vivian Sobchack, Annette Michelson, Garrett Stewart, J. P. Telotte, Scott Bukatman, and Tom Gunning, I called for a new understanding of science fiction film based on three main arguments. The first was that science fiction literature and science fiction film actually arose from quite different traditions and assumptions and pursue quite different goals. While science fiction literature privileged narrative concerns, I argued, science fiction film not only did not privilege the narratives of its ostensible written sources and/or inspirations but instead offered in place of narrative the attraction of cinematographic technology—spectacles of production largely associated with "trickery," special effects, *trucage*. Accordingly, my second argument was that the history and theory of science fiction film should privilege the concept of spectacle and the meaning of special effects over narrative, recognizing that the story of science fiction film was not limited to the diegetic world of the film's story. And my third argument was that the future of science fiction film would be itself ever more science fictional, that the production of science fiction film/media was becoming an activity so imbricated in new technology that it would raise the kinds of speculative issues traditionally explored in written sf narratives.

Developments in sf film, digital technology, and science fiction film scholarship since my book appeared in 1992 have convinced me even more strongly of the utility of and necessity for these arguments, particularly as CD-ROM and DVD technology and the World Wide Web have provided exciting new sites for the multimedia exploration of science fiction thinking. My goal in this essay is to outline some of the distinguishing characteristics of post-sf film. Each of these aspects either involves the recognition of new technological phenomena or calls for recognizing the need for new critical approaches to these phenomena. I will try to organize my suggestions around ten propositions, but these propositions inevitably deal with subjects that overlap and cut across categories.

   1. *Post-sf film requires a film-specific and non-narrative-centered critical approach that we might call post-sf film criticism.* Post-sf film criticism both reconceptualizes earlier sf film and directs our attention to the developing contours of post-sf film in the final years of the twentieth century and the early years of the twenty-first. It now seems safe to claim that during the 1990s there was a clear shift from diegetic to spectatorial focus within the critical discourses of sf film. Vivian Sobchack's *Screening Space: The American Science Fiction Film* (1987) was instrumental in promoting this reorientation. Later, essays collected in the Spring 1998 *Film Theory and the Digital Image* special issue of *Iris* and Annette Kuhn's 1999 *Alien Zone II: The Spaces of Science Fiction Cinema* suggested the extent to which spectators and spectacle now command a prominent place—if not center stage—in our understanding of sf film. Kuhn signals this shift at the beginning of her introduction to the section on "Cultural Spaces" in *Alien Zone II* when she notes that, "while science-fiction films may certainly tell stories, narrative content and structure per se are rarely their most significant features" (11), a condition she later proposes we might address with a "phenomenological metapsychology of cinema" that would "open up new ways of understanding cinema's, in particular science-fiction cinema's, singular capacity to offer the spectator all-encompassing visual, kinetic and affective experiences" (222). Similarly, Scott Bukatman has suggested the need "to restore a balance between the ideological critiques of representation (and narrative) which have long dominated cinema studies, and a phenomenological approach that acknowledges that, as Steven Shaviro puts it, 'Cinema is at once a form of perception and material perceived, a new way of encountering reality and a part of the reality thereby discovered'" (Bukatman, "Ultimate Trip" 77). Or, as Shaviro also explains this crucial proposition, "Cinematic images are not representations, but events" (41).

   In one sense, this important trajectory that is redirecting sf film scholarship from a primary focus on the diegetic world of the film to its affective/phenomenological impact and implications can be thought of as fulfilling a dialogue initiated by Annette Michelson in her famous 1969 essay, "Bodies in Space: Film as 'Carnal Knowledge,'" in which she explored the phenomenal impact of *2001: A Space Odyssey* (1968). Michelson's brilliant challenge to understand the genius of Kubrick's film in terms of its nondiegetic or extradiegetic impact continues to inspire this dialogue, most recently giving rise to Garrett Stewart's meditation on what Michelson meant, precisely, when she referred to *2001* as an "epiphany." If there is also now a phenomenon we might call post-sf film criticism, and I believe there clearly is, its muse is Annette Michelson.

2. At the heart of post-sf film are the digital technologies of electronic cinema. The production of science fiction film/media has become so imbricated in new technologies that it has become a science fiction narrative in its own right, not just a more sensational vehicle for presenting sf narratives. The inexorable shift of film in general and sf film in particular away from its celluloid past and toward its electronic future calls our attention to a fundamental material change in the nature of post-sf film—a material change not without phenomenological consequences for the viewing of these films. "The very concept of science-fiction cinema," Annette Kuhn emphasizes, "is undergoing transformation at every level, from the metapsychological to the institutional to the economic" (*Alien Zone II* 6).

Even if I am not granted the non-narrative-centered revisionist history I proposed in *The Aesthetics of Ambivalence* for the first hundred or so years of sf film, recent technological developments argue strongly for the proposition that current and coming sf films have passed a boundary that not only justifies but demands that they be reconceptualized as significantly different from earlier sf films. It is this break I would recognize by invoking the term *post-sf film*, a "film" that is increasingly characterized not as film at all but as electronic cinema. And while the question of whether all electronic cinema can be thought of as sf remains debatable, what seems indisputable is that almost all "sf films" are now markedly electronic.

In an important article in *Film Quarterly*, Stephen Prince details why electronic cinema necessarily calls for a reexamination of the ontological status of cinematic representation. Noting ways in which CGI challenges us to rethink concepts of realism based on photography, Prince argues in "True Lies: Perceptual Realism, Digital Images, and Film Theory" that "digital imaging operates according to a different ontology than do indexical photographs" (27). He then proposes a theory of "perceptual realism" that particularly addresses the phenomenological challenge of the highly realistic "unreal" computer graphic images that are one of the most obvious features of post-sf film. What Prince discusses as the "perceptual realism" of digital film also contributes to ontological confusion at the level of genre, as post-sf film further blurs the already fuzzy distinctions between fantasy and science fiction and, increasingly, between animation and live action. Animated features such as *Titan A.E.* (2000) increasingly combine "traditional" computer animation with CGI, to the effect that the animated feature becomes realistic or even hyperrealistic in some scenes. Meanwhile, "live action" feature films such as *X-Men* (2000) increasingly use CGI to present otherwise fantastic "impossible" scenes. And CGI films such as *Stuart Little* (2000) present audiences with "realistic" images that previously could only have been achieved through cartoon animation.

More important, we must remember that concerns with the "realism" of CGI assume that verisimilitude is the ultimate value, while computer graphics frequently sacrifice verisimilitude for a highly artificial hyperreal look. While the desire for realism in CGI imagery surely accounts for some of its use, the singular unreality or hyperreality of computer-generated images has become, as much as or more than realism, a goal of filmmakers. One example of this phenomenon would be the early 1990s Pacific Arts Video's demo tape, *State of the Art Computer Animation*, which featured the striking "Chromosaurus," a realistic computer generation of loping dinosaurs, whose "skin" had been texture-mapped into highly reflective chrome. This understanding that CGI imagery must be acknowledged for its intrinsic aesthetic qualities has been succinctly explained by Michele Pierson:

Much of the computer generated imagery that found popularity with audiences in the early-to-mid-1990s represents the refinement, not of a realist aesthetic that takes the cinematographic image as its point of reference, but of a hyperreal electronic aesthetic that takes the cinematographic image as its point of departure. For all its ability to produce stunningly plausible objects—solid, textured, light-refracting bodies—computer generated special effects during this period also showed a marked preference for imagery displaying the kind of visual properties that can only be achieved in the hyperreal electronic realm of computer generation. Too bright and shiny by far, the hyper-chrominance and supra-luminosity characteristic of CGI effects in this period imbued the digital artifact with a special visual significance. This significance was augmented by a style of arts-and-effects direction that, by bracketing the computer generated object off from the temporal and narrative flow of the action, offered it to the contemplative gaze of cinema audiences. (37)

It should be noted that the ontological implications of the transition from photochemical film to digital electronic cinema may be even more sweeping for film theory than for discussions of sf film. In a series of important articles and in his *Between Film and Screen: Modernism's Photo Synthesis*, Garrett Stewart has explored (and decried) the "capitulation" of film to digital technology.

The fact that there has been a major shift in our perception of what is or is not real seems clear, as does the fact that such a shift is ontologically significant. In later propositions, I will also suggest more concrete ways in which electronic cinema employs new distribution and promotion practices that encourage fans to extend the diegetic world of the film to other imaginative constructs, thus expanding the audience for, as well as changing the nature of, post-sf film.

3. *Digital SFX/CGI technologies function in post-sf film in ways not closely tied to advancing an sf narrative.* Distinguished by digital special effects that usually call attention to themselves in ways that slow or interrupt the film's narrative, electronic sf cinema has both a different ontological status and a different affective impact on its audiences. Annette Michelson, Vivian Sobchack, Garrett Stewart, and Scott Bukatman have all noted ways in which effects sequences interrupt narrative flow, variously calling attention to themselves as spectacle, as self-reflexive focus on film technology, and even as liberatory counternarratives. *Hollow Man* (2000), one of the most recent examples of what might be called post-sf film, and possibly the most pronounced, presents its electronic special

effects not only as the main attraction of the film but literally as its main character, causing actor Kevin Bacon to quip that he had become a special effect. Much the same could be said of *X-Men*, whose foregrounding of special effects led *New Yorker* film critic David Denby to note that film seems to have passed into a new phase of what might be called "visual rapture," a phenomenon he ties to special effects that dramatize metamorphosis (86–87). With this observation, Denby moves into post-sf film critical territory already provocatively explored by Sobchack and Bukatman. Sobchack's *Screening Space* could only respond to the harbingers of electronic cinema, the first generation of films to make heavy use of electronic digital effects—films such as *Tron* (1982) and *The Last Starfighter* (1984)—but her characterization of the transformation of the "wonderfully functional" in SFX technology into the "functionally wonderful" pointed the way toward the interrogation of sf film in terms of the affective impact and implications of its digital sequences. "Indeed," Sobchack concluded, "now the primary sign-function of sf special effects seems to be precisely to connote 'joyful intensities,' 'euphoria,' and the 'sublime'" (*Screening Space* 283).

Building on Sobchack's work, Scott Bukatman has recently offered in a BFI Modern Classics book an intriguing study of *Blade Runner* (1982), one as concerned with its euphoric or utopic special effects and kinetic aspects as with its discursive narrative. He has more explicitly explored the idea of "the formal rhythm and logic" of special effects in an essay that suggests that special effects in general, and digital special effects in particular, may actually perform "an idea of utopia." As he explains, "The special effects sequences of science fiction cinema are not literally utopian—neither are they, in fact, non-narrative, antirational, or transgressive. Instead, they articulate, as an embodied knowledge, a utopian discourse of possibility—they present the possibility of utopia, not its realization. They show us what utopia might feel like" ("Ultimate Trip" 92).

CGI special effects may also be thought of as utopic in a second sense tied to the dream of their being able to be produced at home, using readily accessible and relatively inexpensive computer hardware and software. Michele Pierson has provocatively considered this utopic production dream in her *Postmodern Culture* essay, "Welcome to Basementwood: Computer Generated Special Effects and *Wired* Magazine."

4. *Digital SFX and CGI technologies that emphasize morphing are central to post-sf film.* David Denby's perception is that the key to what he calls the "visual rapture" of new cinema rests on special-effects technologies that foreground metamorphosis. In this sense, change, perhaps the concept most crucial to the understanding of science fiction thinking, becomes equally crucial for the understanding of post-sf film. A metonymic and emblematic sign of a fundamental change in sf film is the phenomenon of morphing, the transformation of one image into another, which has become perhaps the salient visual phenomenon associated with state-of-the-art special effects technology. In post-sf film, "metamorphosis" becomes instantiated in the digital technologies of "morph-

ing." "If the nineteenth century dreamed of cinema," observes Scott Bukatman, "then the twentieth has been dreaming of morphing," explaining that in its articulation and condensation of philosophical positions, desires, and anxieties, morphing "enacts many of the contradictory impulses of contemporary culture" ("Morphing" 225). If postmodern culture is thought of as the culture of the "easy edit" where everything is subject to transformative editing through one technology or another, then morphing becomes a particularly powerful emblem of this culture.

The cultural importance of morphing is the subject of a recent collection of essays assembled by Vivian Sobchack. Sobchack's introduction to *Meta-Morphing: Visual Transformation and the Culture of Quick-Change* starts with this double-edged claim:

Amid myriad forms and articulations of computer-graphic representation, there is certainly something particular about the "morph" that compels our contemporary attention. Against the ground of (and sometimes grounding) the photo-realisms of film and television, its effortless shape-shifting, its confusions of the animate and inanimate, its curiously static movement, its queerly hermetic liquidity, its homogenizing consumption of others and otherness, are uncanny—uncanny not only in the sense of being strange and unfamiliar but also in the sense of being strangely familiar. Indeed, one could argue that at this historical moment and in our particularly digitally driven American context, the morph fascinates us not only because of its physical impossibility and strangeness but also because its process and figuration seem less an illusionist practice than both a presentational mode and an allegory of late capitalist "realism." (xi)

In arguing in her essay "'At the Still Point of the Turning World'" that the morph "is at once science fictional and realistic," Sobchack offers a specific locus in post-sf film for the application of Stephen Prince's concept of "perceptual realism" (152). Post-sf film specifically threatens to disrupt traditional categories of "the realistic" and "the fantastic" which have structured so much previous discussion of sf film. Taking Sobchack's emblematization of the morph one step farther, Kevin Fisher suggests that the battle between the two generations of Terminators in *Terminator 2* (1991) offers a self-reflexive and ontologically charged emblem of the state of morphing within film technology, and in so doing he offers us a useful emblem for the discontinuity of post-sf film:

The two rival Terminators not only represent the forces of good and evil but also structurally allegorize the tension between the analog-machinic and the digital within technologies of representation. Specifically, the T-1000 embodies the transcendence of the digital over the limitations of the analog cinematic apparatus. Both terminators are copies—simulacra—but each emerges as a very different species of representation. The original terminator is a copy of a human being, but the T-1000 is a copier: a shape-shifter. By similar comparison, the photographic cinema photochemically and mechanically represents objects of which it becomes a fixed copy, whereas the digital represents pixels, which can be made to copy anything. (119–20)

In fact, morphing is perhaps the key to understanding the phenomenon of post-sf film because the concept applies so well to spectatorial practices both within and without the diegetic world of post-sf films. As my seventh and ninth propositions will suggest, the morphing of images within this new medium is attended by the morphing of the medium itself as it inexorably morphs into other media characterized by more immersive and interactive spectatorial experience.

5. *Post-sf film extends sf film's production and distribution matrix to new spectatorial spaces made possible by DVD and Web technologies.* Every studio-released film and most independent films now include promotional Websites as part of their distribution strategy. Indeed, the ingeniously multifaceted Web campaign preceding the release of Spielberg's *A.I.* (2001) suggests that the Web is being used to construct a context in which the film shown in theaters can be given an entirely new durational life with many of its features available to the public long before and long after its release. These Websites (which are themselves frequently impressively animated and highly interactive) generally feature theater and TV trailers for the film, sound tracks from or about the film, biographical information about and interviews with actors and major production staff, promotional stills from the movie, "behind-the-scenes" features on special effects technology and other production phenomena, tie-in merchandise for sale, and, increasingly, some form of interactive game based upon or related to the diegetic world of the film. DVD releases of contemporary films tend to include all of the above plus more related material, including story boards, outtakes, extended (sometimes scene-by-scene) commentary on the film by its director or major actors, and a range of other metafilmic features. The look and feel of both promotional Websites and DVD framing apparatus almost always derive from and extend the diegetic world of the film—supporting the illusion that the "world" of the film can be extended to include the viewer in ways beyond simply serving as a spectator. For example, the Website for *X-Men* divides links into those pertaining to "the movie" and those pertaining to "the experience." To participate in "the experience," Website visitors are challenged to take the "entrance exam" for Dr. Xavier's School for Gifted Youngsters. Fifteen questions or requests for information follow (when I somewhat randomly responded to these fifteen items, my application was "rejected").

I call attention to the experiential phenomenon of the Websites for post-sf film as yet another indication of the way in which, as Lauren Rabinovitz puts it, "cinema's status as a certain kind of institution organized around moviegoing requires redefinition not only because of cinema's entrance into the domestic realm vis-à-vis the accelerated availability of a range of video and computer appliances but because of cinema's computer-aided expansion into the public sphere as well" (4). I would further note that, apart from specific Website features such as games or interactive options that promote imaginative extension of the diegetic world of the sf film, these Websites isolate special effects sequences and production technologies, further focusing spectatorial attention on these films as windows onto new cinema technologies more than as narratives.

6. *Post-sf film is also characterized by new spectatorial spaces constructed and organized on the Web by fans.* Even for marginal or protoelectronic cinema such as the *Star Wars* films, the *Alien* films, and *Blade Runner*, the electronic venue of the World Wide Web has provided new spectatorial space in which fans can extend and elaborate sf films, in much the same way as print previously supported the extension of the *Star Trek* universe into Kirk/Spock narratives. In part following the lead of Henry Jenkins, Will Brooker has recently called attention to this fan-driven extension of "official" film narratives in his "Internet Fandom and the Continuing Narratives of *Star Wars, Blade Runner* and *Alien,*" one of the essays in Annette Kuhn's *Alien Zone II.* Considering Webrings (Websites literally linked in a common enterprise) connecting fans of three highly popular narrative universes, Brooker characterizes these Websites as "a democratic arena within which distinctions between 'professional' and 'amateur' productions are eroded, and the 'official' site for a film will not automatically be afforded more status than a good fan site—if, indeed, either can be recognized as such" (55). Participatory and interactive features also abound on these fan Websites, notes Brooker, who concludes that these sites exploit the identification of Web technology with technologies within the diegetic world of these sf films "to transform reading and viewing into writing and participating. You are no longer simply a fan of *Blade Runner*: you are part of the world of *Blade Runner* or even a blade runner yourself" (60). By inviting such immersion in the story space or diegetic world of an sf film, these sites suggest to me another way in which sf has ridden technology into a post-sf film future.

7. *Post-sf film suggests a new reciprocal relationship between electronic games and narrative cinema; likewise, post-sf film may call for the redrawing of distinctions between cinema and hypertext.* Official Websites for recent sf films such as *The Matrix* (1999), *Mission to Mars* (2000), and *Hollow Man* feature games linked to the diegetic world of each film's narrative, thus presenting the less-well-known other side of the phenomenon of computer games that have been made into films: on the Web, feature films are routinely turned into games. *Tron* and *The Last Starfighter* incorporated computer games into their narratives, but *Super Mario Brothers* (1993), *Mortal Kombat* (1997), and *Wing Commander* (1999) are films whose narratives have been entirely extrapolated from popular computer games. Prerelease buzz predicted that *Final Fantasy* would take CGI to stunning new effects when it appeared in 2001; *Lara Croft: Tomb Raider* and *Dungeons and Dragons* were also released in that same year. Disney has spun off multiple games in multiple formats from *Toy Story* (1995), *Toy Story 2* (1999), *A Bug's Life* (1998), and *Dinosaur* (2000). *Alien Resurrection* (1997) has also spawned a popular computer game, further extending the "immersive and interactive experi-

ence" offered on the film's Website. The obvious point here is that post-sf films and computer games increasingly share imaging technologies, making the distinctions between the diegetic worlds of each medium less and less clear.

Indeed, an even larger challenge to medium boundaries is at work here, as computer games and discursive hypertexts more and more share navigational and interactive practices, blurring distinctions among hypermedia texts, computer games, and post-sf film (interactive rides such as the "Race for Atlantis" ride at Caesar's Palace or Universal's "Amazing Adventures of Spiderman" complicate this picture even further). Responding to the phenomenal popularity of *Myst*, Ruggero Eugeni has recently argued that a multimedia hypertext or fictional hypermedium such as *Myst* creates a consistent immersive diegetic world that might better be understood through film theory than through literary theory. And, as I have elsewhere argued, hypermedia productions such as David Blair's Waxweb combine and blur distinctions between film and hypermedia (Landon, "Diegetic or Digital?" 44–47).

8. Post-sf film utilizes new distribution technologies that make possible widespread viewing on the Web of short and experimental sf features for which there had previously been only limited distribution possibilities. Just as videotape technology has revolutionized film study by making readily available films that had been either unavailable or extremely difficult to see, the World Wide Web is now making readily available computer animation shorts and independent sf features that previously were unlikely to find any widespread distribution. Computer animation that a few years ago could only be found on compendium CGI demo videotapes can now be directly accessed on the Web, allowing CGI artists to display their computer animations and SFX sequences independent of framing narratives. Now special effects shops such as Pixar, ILM, Digital Domain, PDI/Dreamworks, and Alias/Wavefront post online demos of their own work, winners of computer graphic animation contests, and other examples of CGI. Stunning computer animation shorts such as Chris Landreth's *Bingo* are now available online, as are striking CGI demos from *Final Fantasy*.

CGI projects that may never come to fruition as theatrical releases are accessible on the Web, introducing us to collaborative animation projects such as "*The Prometheus Factor* Project" or to Curtis Davis's twenty-minute 3D project, *Atlantis Falling*. As a result, if we think of post-sf film in terms of its offering a new cinema of digital attractions, those attractions, frequently divorced from conventional narrative and conventional commercial film length, are now widely available on the Web. Perhaps most interesting is that the SciFi Channel devotes part of its Website to independent short features, making them available for viewing at its "Exposure: The Future of Science Fiction Film" Website. Representative of the experimental films to be found on SciFi's Exposure site is *Replica*, a 3:39-minute computer animation and video combination by Violet Suk and Martin Koch in which a shapeshifter eludes chasing security forces by adopting a series of new identities. A link on the Exposure screen featuring *Replica* then takes a viewer to Suk's and Koch's impressively animated CGI Website, where other examples of their work can be seen, including their director's reel featuring a montage of their special effects.

9. *Post-sf film utilizes new production practices that more closely parallel those of sf literature; conversely, Web technologies make possible interactive collaborations not possible in either traditional sf film or sf literature.* Ursula K. Le Guin once described how she wrote her celebrated cloning short story, "Nine Lives," explaining that "[i]t all took place in the dark, in silence, by groping" ("Nine Lives" 205). Her comment highlights what has until recently been another very significant difference between sf literature and sf film: most sf literature is created by individuals "in the dark, in silence, by groping," while almost all sf film is manufactured by production teams, each responsible for one part or aspect of the overall film. Developments in digital cinema, however, may actually be more and more in the process of erasing this distinction, as digital technology can increasingly be controlled by a single artist. In a recent *Wired* interview, George Lucas specifically invoked the comparison between writing and filmmaking but concluded that new technologies were allowing him to bridge that gap: "Instead of making film into a sequential assembly-line process where one person does one thing, takes it, and turns it over to the next person, I'm turning it more into the process of a painter or sculptor. You work on it for a bit, then you stand back and look at it and add some more onto it, then stand back and look at it and add some more. You basically end up layering the whole thing. Filmmaking by layering means you write, and direct, and edit all at once. It's much more like what you do when you write a story" (Kelly and Parisi 2).

What is so striking about Lucas's view of the future of filmmaking from the very top of the "New Hollywood" production hierarchy is that it is almost exactly mirrored by the view of independent moviemakers at the bottom or on the margins of that hierarchy. For example, the ubiquitous Scott Billups, a self-styled outlaw digital-effects artist, has called attention to the same phenomenon cited by Lucas, concluding, "It's getting back to the single person, the author, who has an idea and can go with it" (Parisi, "Outlaw" 2). In this respect it grows ever more possible for sf film to be made, not only through a process much more similar to that which produces sf literature, but for the two endeavors to be guided by much more similar teleologies. And, just as digital technology gives a kind of creative control to the sf filmmaker previously reserved for sf writers, that same digital technology more and more affords multiform and multimedia options to the sf writer that were previously reserved for sf filmmakers (see Pierson).

Indeed, one possible future for sf film would collide the parallel worlds of sf writing and sf film in the "holonovel" of virtual reality considered by Janet H. Murray in *Hamlet on the Holodeck: The Future of Narrative in Cyberspace.* Invoking the idea of the "holodeck" made familiar on *Star Trek: The Next Generation* and its spin-offs, *Deep Space Nine* and *Voyager*, Murray calls attention to an episode of *Voyager* in which Captain Janeway uses a holosuite to insert herself into a three-dimensional computer-driven sensorium that instantiates the semblance of a Victorian world very reminiscent of Charlotte Brontë's *Jane Eyre*. Captain Janeway assumes the role of governess "Lucy Davenport" in this semblance, and Murray simply dubs the resulting holonovel *Lucy Davenport*, characterizing it as a "universal fantasy machine, open to individual programming: a vision of the computer as a kind of storytelling genie in the lamp" (13–17).

Murray labels *Lucy Davenport* a "multiform narrative," a label that conveniently lets us sidestep the question of whether a holonovel would actually be an example of sf writing or of sf film, combining as it would salient characteristics from both traditions. Of course, what we have available to us at the beginning of the twenty-first century is not quite the sensorium of the holodeck, but it is the new space of hypermedia, where hypertexted narratives can be realized with multimedia. Hypermedia sf experiences that suggest future areas for development are game/narratives such as *Myst*, interactive Websites such as Diana Slattery's *Glide* Project, Erik Loyer's *Chroma*, and even marginally graphically driven hyperfictions such as Shelley Jackson's *Patchwork Girl*. Distinctions among the current forms of hypermedia should not obscure the fact noted by N. Katherine Hayles that they all require cyborg reading or viewing practices. Hayles limits her explanation to hypertexts, but it applies equally to all interactive hypermedia and to viewing or playing as well as to reading: "Because electronic hypertexts are written and read in distributed cognitive environments, the reader necessarily is constructed as a cyborg, spliced into an integrated circuit with one or more intelligent machines. To be positioned as a cyborg is inevitably in some sense to become a cyborg, so electronic hypertexts, regardless of their content, tend toward cyborg subjectivity" (Hayles, "Flickering Connectivities"). In this sense, it is important to note that the technologies of post-sf film implicate viewers/spectators in the very technosphere that sf film so long sought to depict.

10. *Post-sf film is perhaps most intensely science fictional in its development of synthespians and in their "evolution" into virtual humans.* "Synthespians" is a term probably destined to have the short shelf life of "scientifiction." The appearance of the CGI character Jar Jar Binks in *Star Wars: The Phantom Empire* (1999) marked yet another stage in the use of synthespians in starring roles in post-sf film, where they already represent a technology that has doubly surpassed original expectations. While numerous Hollywood discussions still center on the degree of realism that can or cannot be achieved by synthespians, it has become clear that these CGI figures now function as a realization of technological prowess as much as or more than as a representation of human beings. In a world that has already produced a Jar Jar Binks, Leyner's "Schwarzeneggerization" process seems not much of a stretch.

Moreover, uses for these computer-generated actors already extend beyond the boundaries of sf film, suggesting a fast-approaching degree of synthetic agency for synthespians or virtual humans that should itself be thought of as a science fictional phenomenon. As I have suggested in previous propositions, the CGI technology that makes synthespians possible does not just allow them to substitute for human stars but also makes the fact that they are substituting for human stars one of the distinguishing affective features of post-sf film. Jar Jar Binks, after all, is not a CGI character because his role called for morphing or SFX sequences that would have been beyond human capability; Jar Jar Binks is a synthespian because Lucasfilms/ILM wanted to see whether a synthespian could be given a starring role in a major film. That Binks annoyed many critics and viewers has been widely noted, but the annoyance came from his characterization rather than from his computer-generated status, almost certainly making him a harbinger of more CGI figures in the upcoming *Star Wars* episodes. Vivian Sobchack argues that digital phenomena such as synthespians have already served "to disrupt the spectator's traditional modes of identification with central human characters and to displace them onto posthuman dramatizations of technological jouissance" (*Meta-Morphing* xix–xx).

Roger Warren Beebe links the increasing importance of morphing synthespians to the great popular and financial success of essentially characterless films such as the *Jurassic Park* series and the *Toy Story* series. Beebe argues that we now can see an emerging aesthetic of posthuman cinema, in which blockbuster CGI-heavy films "need not be either a star vehicle or even a narrative centered on the plights and adventures of a single human subject" (171–72).

An even more telling development in synthespian capability is that the entertainment-centered term *synthespian* no longer adequately covers the range of applications for this technology, a range now better suggested by the term *virtual humans*. Unlike a synthespian programmed for a single completely predictable role, virtual humans are being constructed to interact realistically and in real time with other entities either human or virtual. Murray's *Lucy Davenport* holonovel, for example, would depend on the interaction of such virtual humans with the human character performed by Janeway. This means that researchers are striving to create simulated people with lifelike behaviors. The range of commercial and military applications for such simulated people is easy to imagine, and it is almost inescapable that virtual humans will play key roles in the next stage of human-computer interface. Bruce Sterling has already suggested that some of the ostensibly unintended applications of this simulated agency will be the creation of service-providing "mooks," who, apart from being useful search engines and screening programs, will also make perfect criminal accomplices and pornography actors ("Lifelike Characters").

Best known of the current virtual-human researchers is Nadia Thalman, whose "Virtual Marilyn" project at Miralab strives to give a computer-generated Marilyn Monroe realistic behaviors as well as a realistic look, but efforts to develop virtual human agency are now widespread. That research and commercial applications already exist for virtual humans suggests in turn that the new technologies of what I call post-sf film may themselves be blending back into the new digital realities of the twenty-first century. The synthespian / virtual human phenomenon offers one of the most dramatic pieces of evidence for my longstanding contention that the situation of sf film has become as deserving a topic for interrogation as have been the semblances of its films. Virtual humans are but one digital aspect of the way that post-sf film performs or embodies science fictional thinking.

As opposed to being merely a new wrinkle in the presentation of science fiction stories, post-sf film has morphed into the apotheosis of a science fiction story. Taken individually or collectively, the individual propositions I have offered here boil down to the simple but thrilling argument that post-sf film has already become a technology on the way to somewhere else.

Part Two

Imploded Subjects and Reinscripted Bodies

5

Staying with the Body

Narratives of the Posthuman in Contemporary

Science Fiction

JENNY WOLMARK

The erosion of the boundaries between human and machine and between organic and inorganic has given rise to general anxieties about the instability of the subject, and the body has become the focus for many of these anxieties. The determining social and cultural context for the representation of posthuman bodies is, arguably, provided by current developments in information technology and artificial intelligence,[1] and much contemporary science fiction has responded to these developments by focusing on the interface between the body and technology. In the case of influential cyberpunk narratives such as William Gibson's *Mona Lisa Overdrive* (1988) and Bruce Sterling's *Schismatrix* (1985), for example, the interface is the means by which the body is transcended, and the "disappearing body" has become an ironic, and indeed iconic, form of posthuman embodiment. It is, however, a form of embodiment in which the idea of the "natural" body is left unchallenged, allowing the unstable subject to be restored to a unitary wholeness that excludes difference of any kind.

I suggest in this essay that science fiction narratives also provide other fantasies about the interpenetration of information and flesh, competing fantasies that deconstruct the unspoken assumptions about the normative body on which the restoration of the unitary subject depends. The hegemonic status of normative, heterosexual bodies, through which these assumptions are sustained, can be challenged by means of a narrative reading that combines the insights of queer and feminist theory. Such a reading is significant, firstly, for the way in which it emphasizes the subversive and radical nature of bodies and identities that are differential, hybrid, and potentially monstrous, and, secondly, because it articulates possibilities for different forms of embodiment. Differently embodied subjects are central to the three sf narratives that I discuss in this essay: the science fiction films *GATTACA* (1997) and *The Matrix* (1999) and Kathleen Ann Goonan's sf novel, *Queen City Jazz* (1994). I argue that a queered feminist reading of the narratives not only reveals the presence of incoherent bodies that are defined by their difference but also opens up the discourses of the posthuman body for critical interrogation. The posthuman subjects in these narratives are obstinately, if strangely, embodied, and as such they redefine the nature of the interface between technology and the body. As the boundaries between human and machine and self and other are destabilized, ambiguity and difference are redefined to become signifiers of an inclusive posthuman embodiment.

* * *

Contemporary science fiction has become increasingly concerned with the relationship of the body to technology, although an interest in the intimate relations between science and the body is not a new preoccupation in sf. As Mary Ann Doane has pointed out, science fiction as a genre "frequently envisages a new, revised body as a direct outcome of the advance of science" (163). Cyberpunk, for example, depicts the new and revised bodies that have emerged from the imaginative engagement of sf with information and virtual technologies, and, as Scott Bukatman has noted in his discussion of postmodern science fiction, the "sustained inscription of a spectacular discourse of the body in cyberpunk is conspicuous and remarkable" (*Terminal Identity* 296). This discourse of the body marks the emergence of the posthuman subject, and the nature of such a subject is, appropriately, under great debate. While predominantly masculinist cyberpunk narratives recognized the startling possibilities of the erosion of the boundaries between human and machine, the disembodied posthuman subject in cyberspace nevertheless retained its unitary identity, thus failing to dislodge what Anne Balsamo describes as "the obsessive reinscription of dualistic gender identity in the interactions between material bodies and technological devices" (162). Donna Haraway's conceptualization of the posthuman subject as a cyborg, however, rejects these dualisms, as well as the prescriptive and normative posthuman subjectivity that is sustained by them. She argues that the multiple entanglements of the body with technology facilitate a denaturalization of the relationship between the body and cultural identity, which in turn destabilizes the "structure and modes of reproduction of Western identity, of nature and culture, of mirror and eye, slave and master, body and mind" ("A Manifesto for Cyborgs" 199).

The posthuman subject can, then, be envisaged within a frame of reference that enables bodies to escape categorization in terms of familiar binaries. If bodies are thought of in terms of their "pliability or plasticity," as Elizabeth Grosz suggests, rather than in terms of their fixed characteristics, then their difference makes them "other than themselves, other than their 'nature,' their functions and identities" (209). Rather than functioning as an exclusionary category, difference becomes integral to embodied subjectivity; thus the posthuman is prevented from being associated with the kind of "body loathing" that Mark Dery identifies as a characteristic of cyberculture and that he defines as "a combination of mistrust and contempt for the cumbersome flesh that acts as a drag coefficient in technological environments" (235). One instance of the form that such body loathing might take can be found in Arthur Kroker and Michael A. Weinstein's *Data Trash* (1994), a critical account of the "virtual" class's view that the "wired body is perfect," because it is "the (technoid) life-form that finally cracks its way out of the dead shell of human culture" (1). While such a view appears to be offering a form of embodiment appropriate to the contemporary environment, this version of the cyborg body remains technologically determined, subjected to, rather than being a subject in, technology. The formulation of the cyborg as a "(technoid) life-form" underestimates the possibility that the material body—inscribed by the historical, social, and cultural practices and representations within which and by which it is constituted—has a productive and inscriptive capacity of its own. Wired or not, culturally constituted bodies are not only individually experiencing and living bodies, they are also gendered bodies and, in their specificity, they define their environments as much as they are defined by them.

The defining environment for the contemporary technologized body is that of information, so any discussion of embodiment in a posthuman context must inevitably address the complex and shifting relationship between information technology and the body. In *How We Became Posthuman*, Katherine Hayles traces the history of "how information lost its body, that is, how it came to be conceptualized as an entity separate from the material forms in which it is thought to be embedded" (2). She argues that it is precisely the centrality of disembodiment in information technology that has been instrumental in producing problematic definitions of the posthuman in cyberculture. Hayles outlines the way in which developments within cybernetics produced a conception of information as a "disembodied medium" (50), which in turn facilitated a conception of the human as a "set of informational processes" (4). In what she calls the "computational universe," bodies can be thought of as being both interpenetrated by and reduced to information: humans and machines are linked through the view that "the essential function for both intelligent machines and humans is processing information" (239). Hayles draws a parallel between the discorporation of the body in cybernetics and another set of developments within poststructuralist theory, in which the body is constituted as a text, a surface that is "written on," or inscribed by, the structures through which social, cultural, and political power is both disseminated and maintained. The problem to which Hayles is drawing attention is that of abstraction, since both poststructuralist theory and information theory are founded on a generalized disembodiment that entails a loss of social, cultural, and sexual specificity. Information has meaning, however, only in a social and cultural context, just as bodies have meaning only in the particular social and cultural circumstances of which they are a product and which they simultaneously help to produce. Both bodies and information, therefore, are contingent and unpredictable; as a result, posthuman embodiment may be expected to take some surprising forms.

In these circumstances, Mark Dery may be right to suggest that "[w]e don't know what to make of ourselves precisely because we are, more than ever before, able to *remake* ourselves" (*Escape Velocity* 233). The posthuman subject, no longer sustained by the idea of a fixed and unified self, appears to be marked by instability. The provisional and contested nature of such a subject allows for a greater flexibility in thinking about gender in the context of shifting sets of relations between human and machine, the natural and the unnatural. It also allows for another set of relations to be taken into account when considering the posthuman subject, described by Judith Butler as the "matrix of gender relations" (7). As Butler explains it, this matrix provides the framework within which the subject is gendered, and it enables the founding process by which the "girl is 'girled,'" as well as the constant reiteration of that original naming or interpellation. The process of "girling" can be thought of as performative in the sense that it is both "the setting of a boundary, and also the repeated inculcation of [the heterosexual] norm" (8). Further, such interpellations of gender normativity have a coercive and regulatory aspect since they "contribute to that field of discourse and power that orchestrates, delimits, and sustains that which qualifies as 'the human.' We see this most clearly in the examples of those abjected beings who do not appear properly gendered; it is their very humanness that comes into question" (8).

In this way, the matrix of gender relations operates in a regulatory fashion to enable gender to define and delimit the "human" by means of exclusion; those who are excluded are not only marked as different but are also denied legitimacy because of it. At the same time, however, that which is defined as fully human depends absolutely on the inadequately gendered and the not fully human for its own legitimacy. Consequently, the abject and the incompletely human always return to disrupt and destabilize the regulatory and performative norms of gender. Even as they are denied legitimacy, these disruptive bodies are a persistent, if haunting, presence as they challenge those "ideals of femininity and masculinity" that are "almost always related to the idealization of the heterosexual bond" (232). As Butler points out, embodied individuals can never entirely live up to these idealizations; they can merely approximate to them. Embodied individuals diverge from, and negotiate with, those idealizations, and as they do so, they inevitably generate changes in the way gender is both represented and lived within the contemporary social and cultural context. What is needed, then, is a critical perspective from which those changes and their material consequences can be understood.

Since contemporary sf is replete with contradictory fantasies of the body, it can make a significant contribution to the development of such a perspective. Even as science fiction narratives celebrate the erosion of the body's boundaries, they also reveal considerable anxiety about the emergence of what Dery has described as increasingly indeterminate "engineered monsters" (231). The new forms of embodiment that are envisaged in sf's fantasies of the technologized body are emergent and incomplete; as a consequence, they are often disruptive, even monstrous. The differently embodied subjects in sf narratives have the capacity to destabilize the matrix of gender relations even while being fully implicated in it, which suggests that monstrosity can become, as Judith Halberstam puts it, "almost a queer category that defines the subject as at least partially monstrous" (27). My understanding of *queer* in this context, which influences my subsequent use of the term, is that it interrogates the limits imposed by "proper" gender identification and enables the articulation of a critical position from which to rethink definitions of identity. The "entanglement of self and other in monstrosity" (Halberstam 20) opens up possibilities for a reconceptualization of the self in terms that are both nonhierarchical and

inclusive of difference, as well as being grounded in the actualities of embodiment in the material world of social relations.

Those who are defined as monstrous are, however, pushed to the margins
of visibility, and in order to bring them properly into focus and to problematize
the category of the human, I propose to adopt a tentative reading strategy
based on what Veronica Hollinger has described as "queering feminist critical
reading" ("(Re)reading Queerly" 23). She argues that, although sf is described
as the literature of cognitive estrangement, and despite the increasing involvement of feminist writers and critics, the genre has failed to defamiliarize heterosexual gender norms. Instead, sf remains embedded in the gendered network
of social and sexual relations by which it is produced, and that it also reproduces. A theoretical framework that incorporates the insights of queer theory
into a feminist critical reading might reveal the "heterosexual presumption" (6),
to use Tania Modleski's phrase, that underlies much sf; it might also facilitate
alternative ways of thinking and writing about gender, difference, and the construction of the posthuman body. Since both queer theory and feminism are
concerned to question the binarisms of gender norms and the hegemonic status
of heterosexuality, they share much common ground as analytical perspectives.

The representation of the posthuman body, in science fiction and other cultural narratives, as technologized and often monstrous allows the body consistently to exceed its designation as natural, organic, or even human. The
binarisms through which control over the body is enforced are weakened, en-
abling a differently embodied human subject to become increasingly open to a
whole series of other connections, some of which are virtual. The implications
of this for the way in which identity is constructed are interesting, particularly
in the context of Karen Cadora's suggestion that "the blurring of human-ma-
chine-animal and reality-fantasy means that there is no identity that is essentially or uniquely 'human'" (370). This suggests a form of embodiment that,
because it is based on contingency, accepts the permeability of boundaries between self and other, the human and the inhuman. The complex and dynamic
interactions between the embodied posthuman subject and its material circumstances thus require other ways of representing the "human," perhaps as the
"promising monsters" invoked by Donna Haraway and found repeatedly in
the imaginative and imaginary spaces of sf narratives.[2] In the three narratives
under discussion in this chapter, posthuman bodies persistently destabilize
Modleski's "heterosexual presumption" and open up opportunities for exploring the ways in which bodies are marked by differences of all kinds. Such unstable posthuman bodies provide an opportunity to rethink distinctions
between human and inhuman, body and machine, and to question the boundaries of gender identification. This argument will be explored further in relation
to each of the three narratives under discussion, in which bodies are not what
they seem.

* * *

The cool, designer world evoked in *GATTACA* is set in the "not too distant future," a narrative device that ensures that audiences identify the main themes of the film as emerging from contemporary issues. Biotechnology is a key source of anxiety in the narrative, the main theme of which is ostensibly the perilous and ultimately repressive possibilities of genetic manipulation.[3] In this dystopic near future, genetic modification has resulted in a society divided along genetic lines into "Valids," those whose genetic potential has been optimized, and "In-valids," those who have not been genetically modified and improved. The narrative presents a rigidly structured social and physical environment within which social identity, and therefore gender identity, is determined by genetic identity. In-valids, also referred to as "degenerates," are excluded from the privileges available to Valids, and they have become a new underclass, existing at the margins of society. The central character in the film, Vincent, is an In-valid who was conceived as a "faith child," in other words, without any genetic manipulation to maximize his potential, leaving him entirely subject to the vagaries of his genetic inheritance. Vincent's ambition is to become an astronaut, but as a result of the inherited genetic "faults" of short-sightedness and a potentially fatal heart condition, he is automatically denied entry to the requisite training and education programs. As an In-valid, he is clearly not made of the "right stuff." Vincent's solution is to find a Valid who is willing to let Vincent pay for the use of his validated identity in order to gain entry into the space-training program at the Gattaca Corporation.

The narrative portrays a highly regulated environment in which style and uniformity are predominant and in which "the only remaining pleasures seem to be well-tailored suits, lounge jazz and sleek monumentalist architecture," as Jonathan Romney puts it (49). In this genetically determined world, symbolized by the Gattaca Corporation, identity is confirmed by means of repeated genetic sampling. In order to maintain his identity as Jerome, the Valid whose identity he has acquired, Vincent has to submit samples of Jerome's blood and urine for daily testing. He also has to rid himself scrupulously of any evidence of his own identity as Vincent, so all bodily detritus such as skin scales or hair has to be removed. The title sequence of the film shows this process in grotesque detail, with highly magnified images of gigantic nail cuttings, blizzards of skin scales as they fall, and false fingertips being painstakingly glued on. These images suggest an unruly and monstrous body that has to be subjected to stringent control if its difference is to be disguised. The narrative concentration on the mundane bodily processes by means of which Vincent divests himself of one identity and remakes himself in another indicates that, as Elizabeth Grosz puts it, "the stability of the unified body image, even in the so-called normal subject, is always precarious" (43). The narrative constantly recalls the invalid nature of

Vincent's body, which constitutes his "real" identity as an In-valid; in doing so, it also reveals the performative actions through which identity is constructed and reconstructed in social and cultural space. Thus, when Vincent fears that he has been found out as his "real" image is flashed on computer screens through-out Gattaca, Jerome reassures him, correctly, that nobody sees him as "Vincent"; rather, he is seen only in terms of his acquired identity as "Jerome."

Despite the repeated representation of constructed and controlled bodies, the narrative reveals an equal preoccupation with unruly bodies that resist all attempts at control and whose identities are destabilized by difference. Vincent disrupts his own identity as an In-valid by exceeding it, because he combines his own differences with Jerome's genetic markers in the same desiring body to reach another form of embodiment. In terms of the narrative, this enables him finally to become an astronaut. Similarly, Jerome's identity as a Valid is disrupted because he has crippled himself in an attempted suicide provoked by his own perception of himself as failing to live up to the idealized image of a Valid. Despite being coded as Valid, his imperfectability is literally inscribed on his body. Even the director of the space program, played with suitable irony by Gore Vidal, is revealed as a man who has been driven to excess and murder because of the threatened cancellation of a vital space launch. The murder causes a police investigation that Vincent fears will reveal his identity, but the attempts of the chief investigator to "police" the unruly bodies in the narrative are irrevocably flawed because he conceals from everyone that he is Vincent's Valid brother, Anton.

Above all, the relationship between Vincent and Jerome is central to the undermining of normativity in the narrative. The relationship that Vincent has with Irene, a co-worker from Gattaca, remains largely peripheral to the intimate and intense relationship between Jerome and Vincent. As Jerome gives Vincent both his bodily fluids and his identity, the sexual undercurrents are made clear in Jerome's references to the fact that he is "loaning" or "renting" his body, implying as well that he is prostituting himself for money. Vincent, in turn, is paying for the privilege of acquiring Jerome's body—or at least his bodily fluids—even if desire for his body is displaced onto the genetic coding contained in the bodily samples. Jerome is integral to, and increasingly seduced by, Vincent's ambition to go into space, and thus he becomes complicit in Vincent's desire. This is consummated symbolically at the conclusion of the film: Vincent achieves his ambition to go into space, and Jerome immolates himself in the furnace after leaving enough bodily fluids to last Vincent a lifetime, thus finally giving his body to Vincent. Symbolically, he also leaves Vincent a lock of his hair, a gesture that conflates the genetic with the romantic and that confirms the possibility of a queered feminist reading of the film. In such a reading, it could be argued that Vincent is defined as a posthuman subject because he has acquired a double coding, as both Valid and In-valid, as both "human" and only partially human—thus he is potentially monstrous. The limits of cultural constructions of the human and of gender identity are revealed as binaries collapse, and Vincent provides both a narrative and a theoretical position from which to explore embodied difference. In contrast, Jerome's coding as Valid, which renders him incapable of exceeding either the physical or the psychic limits of normativity, ultimately results in self-destruction and narrative erasure. Embodiment, then, is not shown to converge around uniformity and sameness in the narrative, and despite its dystopian gloss, the narrative ultimately comes down in favor of a more utopian view of difference and of what being "human" might entail.

* * *

A queered feminist reading of *The Matrix* reveals the presence of yet more indeterminate and unruly bodies that challenge exclusionary definitions of the human. The narrative explores the destabilization of identity and the emergence of the posthuman subject by means of the collapse of the real into the virtual. The Matrix is the construction of an artificial intelligence that has taken control of all forms of organic life and "farms" humans for their essential bodily fluids in order to sustain itself. Presumably in order to reduce the likelihood of mass psychosis, it has created the Matrix, a virtual environment in which humans live out disembodied, virtual lives. The narrative abounds in self-conscious references to the erosion of boundaries between reality and virtuality, from the use of Jean Baudrillard's *Simulacra and Simulation* as a visual prop to the description of the world of the Matrix as a "computer generated dream world" that is "more real than the real." In the virtual environment of the Matrix, organic and artificial life forms are set in opposition to one another and embodiment has become irrelevant; all humans are constituted as marginal, abjected beings that are categorized as monstrous by the AI. The sentient programs that the Matrix has created to police its borders describe humans as a "plague," a "disease," or a "virus," for which the Matrix itself is the only cure. The savagely disparaging terms used to describe embodied human subjects in the disembodied information environment of the Matrix are a clear echo of the homophobic terms used in our own reality to define, and therefore to exclude, difference of any kind. Since the story revolves around the drive to overcome the marginality of humanity, however, the narrative actually functions in opposition to those exclusions. The frame of reference that is established by the narrative, in which the human is defined as the monstrous, ultimately subverts the film's attempts either to reinvent the human in normative terms—most familiarly as heterosexual, white, and male—or to reinscribe cultural narratives of gender. Indeed, the limits and definitions of "proper" bodies are constantly questioned as bodies move between the real and the virtual worlds.

A small group of aberrant humans who have escaped the confines of their virtual existences becomes the focus of the narrative action. Led by Morpheus, they move between the real and the virtual, attempting to find "The One" who they believe will provoke the collapse of the Matrix and return humanity to the real. The film defines these posthuman subjects of the Matrix in terms of the increasingly unstable borders between the real and the virtual and creates a narrative space within which possibilities for a differently embodied virtuality can be articulated, however tentatively. Within this space, definitions of gender identity are treated with a certain amount of ironic playfulness. The characters of both Trinity and Neo are knowingly presented as being at odds with cultural constructions of femininity and masculinity, particularly in the exaggerated forms in which such constructions are familiarly reproduced in big-budget action films. Keanu Reeves, playing the part of Neo, lacks the spectacular body that audiences have come to expect of a male action hero,[4] a role that is more overtly taken by the female character Trinity. The initial appearance of these characters in the narrative further problematizes the performative aspects of gender identity, as the opening sequence of the film establishes Trinity in action-hero mode, whereas the character of Neo is introduced by a soft focus close-up that emphasizes the androgynous attraction of Reeves's face. Even as Reeves appears to grow into the role of action hero during the course of the film, this role is played out against the initial framework for his character established at the beginning of the film, and it remains less than convincing.

In a striking parallel to GATTACA, the expression of heterosexual desire in The Matrix remains largely tangential in the narrative. Trinity's attraction to Neo functions, for the most part, as a plot device, so that narrative attention remains almost entirely focused on the intense desire for Neo that is expressed by Morpheus throughout the film. Despite the veneer of religious symbolism in the repeated references to Neo as "The One," Morpheus signally fails to take on the role of acolyte. His fascination with Neo is evident throughout the film, from the tender care he gives Neo's newly birthed body to the suggestive "come hither" gesture he makes in the virtual kung-fu sequence. Throughout, Morpheus is insistent that Neo is The One, and since the narrative consistently denies the mystical possibilities of this reference, its meaning can instead be attached to desire. When, therefore, Neo is described as being "not too bright" at one point in the narrative, this becomes a deeply ironic comment on his lack of self-awareness. The narrative provides a symbolic opportunity for both the realization and the reciprocation of desire, however, for when Morpheus is captured by the sentient programs, Neo leads his rescue from the Matrix. At this point, Neo finally enters into the role of The One, not as a form of transcendence, but as an indication that he has rejected the normative and regulatory fictions—of the real and of gender—that have been imposed by the Matrix. This is signaled visually by the slow-motion moment in which their bodies are joined in an embrace, as Neo leaps into space to save Morpheus from falling to his death. As The One, Neo can now become both a desired and a desiring body; he can, as Morpheus says, tell the difference between "knowing the path and walking the path." Neo's call at the end of the film for a world without either "rules and controls" or "borders and boundaries" reinforces his transgression of the boundaries of both narrative expectations and gendered normativity.

The relationship between the body and cultural identity is persistently denaturalized in a narrative that enacts the pleasure to be gained from inhabiting the borders between the real and the virtual. Although the transgressive possibilities inherent in such a border existence are never fully realized in the film, neither are they entirely eradicated, for as Yvonne Tasker has argued, "popular film affirms gendered identities at the same time as it mobilizes identifications and desires which undermine the stabilities of such categories" (5). Thus, although the narrative does not offer a sustained deconstruction of gender categories, it has been partially successful in creating a narrative space within which orthodoxies of gender inscription are at least treated ironically, despite its definition as a conventional action film. The coercive encoding of the body as information imposed by the Matrix results in the construction of an entire network of regulatory controls, the hegemonic constructions of which are challenged by those humans who can move between the virtual and the real. These differently embodied subjects are, by definition, transgressive, since they exist in opposition to, and at the margins of, hegemonic cultural constructions of gendered humans. In the narrative they have become hybrids, or cyberforms,[5] of a particularly threatening kind, perceived as monstrous by virtue of the fact that they are embodied subjects that cross boundaries and borders and inhabit a fluid rather than a fixed space. In a queered feminist reading of the film, these embodied cyberforms can be regarded as inhabiting a narrative space that is akin to the "paradoxical space" proposed by Gillian Rose, which "straddles the spaces of representation and unrepresentability" and as such can "acknowledge the possibility of radical difference" (154).[6] This is a space in which alternative forms of embodiment for an evolving posthuman condition can be imagined. The interaction between information systems and embodied subjects in such a space produces a shift in the conceptual framework within which normative constructions of gender take place, contributing to a mapping of what Grosz refers to as the "trajectories of becoming" (210). Exceeding its own generic limitations, then, the narrative of *The Matrix* offers an ultimately openended view of what embodied existence on the borders of the real and the virtual might be like. From this perspective, identity can be understood as provisional, contingent, and multiple.

* * *

Differently embodied subjects on "trajectories of becoming" are central to Kathleen Ann Goonan's *Queen City Jazz*, and here the complex and multidimensional overlap between information technologies and biotechnologies provides the context within which subject formation takes place. The novel depicts a future in which the interface between bodies and matter has been irrevocably changed by genetic engineering and nanotechnology, and those hierarchies of being that sustain the distinction between self and other, human and inhuman, the natural and the unnatural, can no longer be sustained. The posthuman subjects of the novel evolve in a context in which, as Sadie Plant describes it, "[d]istinctions between the human, the natural and the artificial are scrambled, and whatever was once said to belong to each of them finds a new basis on which to connect in the dispersed and connective processes which link them all" (213). The erosion of these distinctions increases the potential for the emergence of a dynamic, if incoherent, posthuman embodiment that is based on hybridity and unpredictability. Judith Halberstam and Ira Livingston argue in *Posthuman Bodies* that "technology makes the body queer, fragments it, frames it, cuts it, transforms desire" (16). In other words, technology denaturalizes bodies and makes them monstrous, and as such they can interrogate the limits of hegemonic cultural constructions of self and other and thus undermine hierarchies of gender identity. Bodies and their environments are queered by technology to emerge as hybrid forms that enable difference to be rearticulated and embodied as transgressive. As they move betwixt and between unstable definitions of the human, the natural, and the artificial, the hybrid and monstrous subjects in Goonan's narrative struggle to articulate new forms of subjectivity appropriate to their precarious bodies and unstable environments.

The narrative of *Queen City Jazz* is set some time after the collapse of a golden age of nanotechnology. The nanotech revolution had initially been brought about by a "hitherto undetected quasar at the center of our galaxy" (318), which eventually blocked the radio transmission of all information, and nanotech provided an alternative form of transmission. The revolutionary aspect of this technology was that it recognized that information technology could be applied to DNA, as well as to all forms of communication, and the totality of existence came to be thought of as—or reduced to—information. As one of the characters explains, "The whole world became dependent on this new system that they thought up, the Flower Cities. Nan. Changing the human body itself to receive messages so that everything else would change" (162). Cities that were "seeded" by nanotech became "enlivened" and self-aware entities, the inhabitants of which were genetically enhanced to interface directly with the city, which then provided for all their needs in a seemingly perfect symbiosis described through the metaphor of a beehive. Thus, cities and inhabitants became organic hybrid forms, eroding the already tenuous distinctions between the human, the natural, and the artificial. Goonan's novel suggests that the most problematic aspect of the notion of hybridity is that, as the borders between the organic and the inorganic become permeable, human agency can no longer be thought of as either dominant or controlling.

Queen City Jazz explores the repositioning of the human in relation to its environment, where that environment is regarded as a complex, evolving, and intelligent system. The narrative provides an appropriate framework for the emergence of newly constituted posthuman subjects, by depicting a world in which the Cities have already collapsed, along with their economic and political infrastructures, as control over the technology proved impossible to sustain. In the present time of the narrative, the remains of the technology are regarded with both fear and superstition, as are those who have been changed by the technology. Sporadic outbreaks of uncontrolled "nanoplagues," described as "plagues of thought, and plagues that destroy very specific forms of matter" (233), keep alive fear of "contagion" in those who have not already been transformed by the technology. Those people who have been infected and "changed" by nanotechnology are regarded with both horror and fascination by the unchanged, and these "plaguers" are marginalized as both monstrous and abject.

The tension between emergent and new forms of embodiment, and hegemonic discourses of normativity, is explored in the narrative primarily through the symbiotic relationship that exists between the main character, Verity, and the "Queen City" of Cincinnati. Verity has been brought up in a Shaker community that has isolated itself from other scattered communities because its fear of the failed technology is so profound. She is increasingly defined by her sense of difference, however, as she is insistently drawn to the collapsing nanotech city of Cincinnati, despite her fear of the technology and of those who are coded as monstrous once they are infected. The reason for her sense of difference becomes clear once she is in the city, where she discovers herself to be a bioengineered repository for the memories of Abe Durancy, the instigator of the nanotech revolution. She is a genetic construct who has been preprogrammed, as have identical others before her, to interface with Durancy's memories, and with the city itself, in an attempt to find a solution to the failure of the technology. Verity is, thus, the unnatural offspring of the city itself, and as such she is a hybrid form emerging into an environment within which distinctions between organic and inorganic, human and machine, are fatally undermined. The queering of her body by technology destabilizes essentialist notions of the "natural" body at the level of both conception and reproduction, and her hybridity thus challenges hegemonic constructions of "proper" bodies.

With the information that has been coded into her DNA, Verity has complete access to Durancy's memories, including those of his boyhood, which she describes as "Not her and yet her deepest self, this mischievous boy whose memories controlled her" (310). The memories reveal a desire for dominance and control that is entirely inappropriate in the context of an enlivened entity such as the city. As Katherine Hayles argues, "Mastery through the exercise of autonomous will is merely the story consciousness tells itself to explain results that actually come about through chaotic dynamics and emergent structures" (*Posthuman* 288). While Durancy's memories may provide the information that is needed to reprogram the city, they only have meaning in the context of Verity's embodied interaction with the city. Using his memories, Verity accesses all the information stored in the city, acknowledging as she does so that the city itself "was an *entity* now; it could *know* and *understand*" (255). In other words, rather than the application of "autonomous will," it is Verity's recognition of the city as a self-organizing and intelligent system, an emergent structure, that enables her to intervene in its failing programming.

As the narrative progresses, Durancy's memories, Verity's memories, and those of the enlivened city become increasingly integrated, until the distinctions among them are eroded. Agency can no longer be thought of as resting with any one of them but has become dispersed. Verity's complex and hybrid embodiment, then, exceeds not only the distinction between technology and nature but also the limits both of heterosexual reproduction and of gender identity. Her body has been queered by technology in the sense that it has become an unnatural body, drawing attention to the way in which the normative is reinforced by its definition as "natural." She is an "inappropriate/d other," to quote Haraway, existing in a critical and deconstructive relationship with normativity.[7] As a technological offspring of the city, she, like the city, can be thought of as a self-organizing system within which information is embodied and which establishes new connections between the human and the nonhuman. *Queen City Jazz* suggests that a posthuman subjectivity, embodied by Verity, is evolving rather than fully formed, and as such it is dependent on new connections and alliances being forged between the organic and the technological. The unstable parameters and contradictory discourses of the posthuman body, by refusing the limits imposed by binary definitions of the "human," are integral to any definition of a posthuman subjectivity.

* * *

To summarize, posthuman embodiment does not entail the unproblematic replication of "natural" bodies, and, as a consequence, those discourses of the body that sustain a universal and unitary self are undermined. As distinctions between the human and the mechanical, the organic and the inorganic, are eroded, the hierarchy of difference within which narratives of exclusion are re-iterated has become increasingly unstable. The impact of these various instabil-ities on science fiction narratives has not necessarily been either immediate or obvious, however, which has been taken as an indication of the generic limita-tions of sf's ability to make critical interventions into contemporary debates about the posthuman subject. In a symposium on posthuman science fiction at the 1999 World Science Fiction Convention, Helen Merrick argued persuasively that much posthuman sf "fails to map the increasingly complex intersections and interrelations of technoscience, culture and society that contextualize any formulation of subjectivity and what the human is" (97). I would suggest that, in fact, these "complex intersections and interrelations" are already, and in-evitably, mapped onto unstable posthuman bodies. What is needed, therefore, is a mode of critical reading—a queered feminist reading—in which the com-plex and contradictory nature of such bodies is interrogated, in order to under-stand more fully the consequences of this mapping for the emerging posthuman subject. Even though widely divergent definitions of the posthu-man indicate that it is, as yet, an uncertain and contradictory category, the value of such a category is that it contests the limits imposed on definitions of the "human" by hegemonic cultural constructions of gendered identity. The queered feminist readings of the sf narratives in this essay argue for the pres-ence of unpredictable posthuman bodies and emergent and dispersed posthu-man subjectivities that redefine the human in terms of difference. Above all, to read these from a queered feminist perspective is to discover posthuman bodies that, as Nina Lykke and Rosi Braidotti put it, are "new, alternative and some-what scary figurations of our present concerns" (248).

6

"But Aren't Those Just . . . You Know, Metaphors?"

Postmodern Figuration in the Science Fiction of

James Morrow and Gwyneth Jones

BRIAN ATTEBERY

Embodied Knowledge

The two-mile-long corpse of God is found floating in the Atlantic Ocean. Alien scam artists invade earth. These are the premises—Hollywood would call them high concepts—that launch two major fictional projects of the 1990s: James Morrow's Godhead Trilogy and Gwyneth Jones's Aleutian Trilogy. In each instance, the wildly inventive concept is only the entry into a series of encounters that dramatize issues central to both science fiction and postmodernism. As if mustered into the armies of Baudrillard, Lacan, and Foucault, Jones's and Morrow's characters strive and suffer on behalf of sign systems, textualized identities, and the master narratives through which they and we interpret the world. Both series call such epistemological habits into question, and they do so partly by directing attention to the gender-marked body as a basis for knowledge and judgment.

Many commentators have noted the close relationship between sf and postmodern literature. The works of Thomas Pynchon, William Burroughs, and Russell Hoban are informed by sf tropes, while writers such as William Gibson, J. G. Ballard, and Philip K. Dick have emerged from the sf community to be embraced by critical fashion. The very theories that attempt to account for postmodern sensibility are couched in science fictional terms. Fredric Jameson's *hyperspace* uses an interdimensional metaphor to describe the contradictory locales of postmodern architecture (*Postmodernism* 43–44); Brian McHale draws on sf narratives like *Gravity's Rainbow* to characterize the impossibly blended *zones* of contemporary fiction (*Postmodernist Fiction* 45); Jean Baudrillard's *simulacra* reverse the relationship between model and imitation to turn postmodern humans into mimics of themselves ("Simulacra and Science Fiction" 309); and Donna Haraway's half-mechanical *cyborgs* take the place of myths about natural roles for women and men ("A Cyborg Manifesto"149). At the turn of the twenty-first century, these writers imply, we live in a realm familiar from sci-fi movies and popular fiction—the experience of daily life is closer to *Flash Gordon* and Philip Dick's "We Can Remember It for You Wholesale" (1965) than to the worlds of historical account or realistic fiction.

All the above terms designate constructed or virtual realities; all imply that reality itself is an artifact of the ways we represent it. The great insight of cultural critics such as Jean-François Lyotard is that we acquire much of our understanding of the world in the form of stories passed on by culture: these are master narratives that authorize society's institutions without having to be justified by experience (Bukatman, *Terminal Identity* 106–7). Some of these master narratives may be, in essence, fictions about science. Hence sf itself, as a mechanism for generating signs for things that do not exist, is a useful metaphor for the postmodern critic who wishes to prove such a preferentiality to be the condition of all signs. We cannot know; there is nothing to know; our illusion of knowing is all there is—such is the position of the most extreme postmodern theorists.

With their reality slippages and affectless apocalypses, Burroughs, Ballard, and Dick might almost have written expressly to illustrate the theory—had they not preceded it. It is no wonder that these are among the "usual suspects" of postmodern sf criticism, discussed at length by Baudrillard, Jameson, Scott Bukatman, and contributors to the special issue of *Science Fiction Studies, Science Fiction and Postmodernism* (18 [November 1991]), many of whom followed Baudrillard in using Ballard's novel *Crash* (1973) as a test case.

The interrogation of master narratives, however, including the scientific megatext, can lead to other places than Ballardian crash sites. Among many postmodernisms, some varieties attempt to find a middle ground between blind faith in traditional epistemologies and absolute rejection of objectivity. This middle way usually involves acknowledging the shaping power of the spectator's perspective while still looking for ways to test observations and theories against an external reality. Writers working along these lines treat our lenses on the world—perception, language, and scientific methodology—as neither transparent nor opaque. They see the observer's cultural biases and physical limitations not as bars to knowledge but as determiners of its form. Hence they come closer to the spirit of contemporary science than do novelists who use *chaos* or *uncertainty* as if they meant emptiness and unknowability.

Both Gwyneth Jones and James Morrow dramatize the importance of perspective in their sf. In her Aleutian novels, for instance, Jones invokes the scientific spirit with a thought experiment about aliens whose physical similarity to human beings leads to chaotic mutual misunderstanding and thence to new discoveries. In his Godhead trilogy, Morrow writes about scientific spirituality: the physicist's quest for a grand unifying theory converges with the metaphysician's quest for a glimpse into the (implicitly embodied) mind of God. Both writers investigate the way understanding and communication are grounded in physical being—we learn the universe by mapping it onto our own bodies. The only language available for communicating our discoveries is colored, as Evelyn Fox Keller and others have pointed out, by social relations such as gender difference. Hence, the universe we perceive and describe depends on who *we* are and what shapes our bodies may take.

The Dead Father

In Morrow's *Towing Jehovah* (1994) and its sequels, the body in question is human, male, alarmingly solid, embarrassingly equipped. This particular body is divine: it is that which, in Western religious narrative, made not only humans but the universe in its own image. It is also dead. The death of the prototype leaves human beings and all of physical reality in the condition of Baudrillardian simulacra—imitations of nothing. Hence, characters throughout the three volumes are in search of some new source of measure and meaning to replace the one provided, in the Christian master narrative, by the bodily image of a divine father.

The divine corpse does not appear on stage at the beginning of the book. Instead, the archangel Raphael manifests himself to Captain Anthony Van Horne in an inverted annunciation. Raphael, like the other angels, is dying, his feathers falling out and his halo fading. Echoes of the divine somatotype, the angels are more slowly sharing its fate. "Our mutual Creator has passed away," the angel tells Van Horne (7), and he is to usher the body out of the world. Van Horne is to be returned to command of the supertanker *Carpco Valparaíso* and commissioned by the Vatican to haul the body to a secret ice cavern in the Arctic.

Van Horne is a reasonable choice for the task, because he is already towing a supertanker-sized load of guilt after the *Valparaíso* was involved in a devastating oil spill. An Ahab in search of redemption rather than revenge, Captain Van Horne regains his ship and acquires a crew that is a Melvillean microcosm of American society. Among the diverse crew members, two become major viewpoint characters sharing the narrative with Van Horne: the Vatican's representative, Father Thomas Ockham, and the rescued castaway, Cassie Fowler.

Both are scientists. Fowler is a biologist who had been retracing her hero Charles Darwin's voyage when her ship, the *Beagle II*, was shipwrecked (perhaps in a spiteful last Act of God). Rescued by the *Valparaíso*, she is appalled when she discovers what sort of voyage she has shipped onto: "this damn body is *exactly* what the patriarchy has been waiting for—evidence that the world was created by the male chauvinist bully of the Old Testament" (100). The existence of the divine corpse undercuts not only her secular viewpoint but also her feminism.

Ockham's beliefs are less disturbed by the discovery, though one would think the death of God would throw some kinks into the faith even of a proverbial Jesuit. Ockham is a physicist as well as a priest affiliated with the Society of Jesus, and he has made a successful career out of combining both pursuits. He is the author of such books as *Superstrings and Salvation* and *The Mechanics of Grace*, "his revolutionary reconciliation of post-Newtonian physics with the Eucharist" (22).

For Ockham, the *corpus dei* represents the ultimate truth he has been seeking, the answer to the questions of both science and faith. On getting his first glimpse, from footward, of the supine body of God, he comments that "it's rather poetic, seeing the toes first. The word has special meaning in my field. T-O-E: Theory of Everything" (80). Those toes, "a series of tall, rounded forms, all aspiring to heaven" (79), hold the secrets of the universe. Like Moses getting a peek at God's nether parts, Ockham looks to the toes for insights hitherto withheld. His desire for scientific knowledge is bound together with his need to comprehend God in human terms:

> "At the moment, we've got TOE equations that work on the submicroscopic level, but nothing that"—his voice splintered—"handles gravity too. It's so horrible."
> "Not having a TOE?"
> "Not having a heavenly father." (80)

God's TOE, like the rest of the divine body, can be known only by reference to its humbler earthly type, the priest's own male form—which is why priests are traditionally male. Science is, in theory, less wedded to its symbol system than is the priesthood; still, images of male sexuality are embedded in traditional ways of describing the universe and the observer's relation to it (Keller 34). This habit carries over from science to science fiction, where descriptions of the penetration of space and the seeding of worlds can become positively torrid. For instance, the scientist's exploratory ray in a story from the 1930s can be seen "slowly but surely pushing its sputtering way down to the surface below, moving and thrusting like a shaft of solid fire through the strange black shroud which obstructed its progress like a solid thing" (Edwards 52). The more invisible the male body becomes within physics and religion, the more omnipresently it manifests itself in the language and culture of both endeavors.

Towing Jehovah's elaborate metaphoric system brings together the divine corpse, the paternal body that lurks in language, and the repressed desires of the male priest and theorist. In doing so, the novel only reinforces longstanding linkages within the cultures of both professions. Physics has always been a quasi-priestly calling, argues Margaret Wertheim in her book *Pythagoras's Trousers*, dealing as it does with "our conception of the universe, and of how we humans might function within it" (6). For this very reason, the field of physics has been, of all scientific endeavors, most resistant to incursion by women. It is, says Wertheim, "the Catholic Church of science" (9). Its inner circle consists of those who fit the priestly image—male but pure, that is, sexually noncompetitive and free of womanly taint. The pocket protector is the scientific equivalent of the clerical collar.

Ockham is authorized to seek out God's TOE by the fact that his own body corresponds feature by feature with the body of the deity. The angel Raphael explains to Van Horne:

> "Religion's become too abstract of late. God as spirit, light, love—forget that neo-Platonic twaddle. God's a Person, Anthony. He made you in His own image, Genesis 1:26. He has a nose, Genesis 8:20. Buttocks, Exodus 33:23. He gets excrement on His feet,

Deuteronomy 23:14."
    Van Horne objects: "But aren't those just . . . ?"
    "What?"
    "You know. Metaphors."
    Raphael answers: "Everything's a metaphor." (12)

Everything, though, is not just any kind of metaphor. These are metaphors that impose the human body upon the universe. Like the demolished giant Ymir of Norse myth—whose skull becomes the sky, his blood the seas, his bones the rocks, and so on—the apotheosized male body is figuratively strewn across the cosmos.

Language: Where the Bodies Are Buried

It is easy to see how mythological narratives, whether Norse or Christian, might involve various sorts of figurative linkages between, say, one's own parents and the forces of creation, or the mystical center of the universe and one's navel. Less obviously, though, the language of science is likewise irreducibly metaphoric. In a series of individual studies and collaborations, linguist George Lakoff and philosopher Mark Johnson have made a compelling case for metaphor as the basis for all thought and communication, including scientific discourse—though metaphor, in their analysis, does not imply the arbitrariness that Lyotard and others ascribe to master narratives.

Johnson's *Body in the Mind* (1987) offers, as an example, the many kinds of bodily experience implicated in an apparently abstract scientific term like *equilibrium*. This concept grows from humble beginnings: "First and foremost, balancing is something we *do*. The baby stands, wobbles, and drops to the floor. It tries again, and again, and again, until a new world opens up—the world of the balanced erect posture" (74). Our childish balancing act is reinforced by other physical sensations: "There is too much acid in the stomach, the hands are too cold, the head is too hot, the bladder is distended, the sinuses are swollen, the mouth is dry" (75). Feeling ourselves to be "out of balance," we respond by adding warmth, emptying or replenishing fluids, and so on until equilibrium is restored. Such bodily experiences form the ground, the schema, upon which we build our understanding of other sorts of balance: visual symmetry, the principle of the fulcrum, ecological systems, psychological stability, mathematical equations, and the scales of justice (82–90). Somewhere inside the scientist who senses the patternedness of each of these systems is the memory of a toddler struggling to stay upright.

Any given metaphor encourages some sorts of investigations while making other observations seem irrelevant or meaningless. A revealing example cited by N. Katherine Hayles is the history of the idea of entropy. In the nineteenth century, the term *entropy* invoked a whole set of cultural attitudes regarding the maintenance of order within the British Empire. "To Kelvin and his fellow thermodynamicists," says Hayles, "entropy represented the tendency of the universe to run down, despite the best efforts of British rectitude to prevent it from doing so" (*Chaos Bound* 40). The loss of energy from a higher to a lower state suggested a similar leakage of dynamism within the British state as it poured itself into the more chaotic systems of the colonies. Only after the borders of Empire were breached did new metaphors suggest themselves, including the understanding of entropy as the increase, rather than the loss, of information.

Morrow's novels can be read as reenacting precisely this metaphoric shift. In *Towing Jehovah*, the death of God reverberates through society and the cosmos as both threaten to run down. Entropy as both physical fact and social symbol is figured forth in the bodies of God's emissaries, the archangels, who seem to be falling to bits throughout the story. Having lost their progenitor and prototype, they drop feathers, fade, and finally disintegrate into disorder and death: "the archangel's eyes liquefied, his hands melted, and his torso disintegrated like the Tower of Babel crumbling beneath God's withering breath" (360). Like the phallic tower of the Babylonian empire, the universe itself threatens to collapse without its masculine principles of order and uprightness. Only in Morrow's sequels, as characters begin to learn to live with uncertainty and social chaos, do pockets of organization begin to form around new, less rigid, understandings of self and universe.

(Re)vive la Différence

The metaphoric linkage Hayles describes, between universe and empire, suggests that there is an underlying schema in which the body politic is equated with the individual body—of a man. Loss of energy, loss of heat, loss of firmness are the consequences of contact with women, according to the belief systems held by many men. Entropy threatens not only civil order but also the integrity of the male body. To overturn this view of entropy required not only a different choice of metaphor but also a reconfiguring of gender. Entropy's threat to masculine order and integrity might not seem so dangerous to a society figured as feminine.

Generally, we can ignore differences in the metaphorized bodies that pervade language. We can speak, especially in scientific contexts, as if these represented "the body" rather than individual bodies. Just because I am, say, six-foot-three and you are a hair under five feet does not mean our experiences of verticality are not translatable. You speak of the temperature rising; I comment that the stock market is up; we each translate the other's comment into our own frame of reference and are satisfied that we understand one another.

One difference that is rarely insignificant, however, is the difference be-tween male and female, especially as that difference is caught up in various cul-tural systems. For example, male bodies have traditionally been equated with strength, integrity, and the spark of the divine, and female bodies with animal nature and original sin. It is not any old "the body" that feels threatened by femininity, any more than it is "the body" that emerges from pain with a new-born baby in its arms.

Though Lakoff and Johnson generally do speak as if the gender of the metaphorized body were irrelevant, Johnson, in his discussion of the concept of force, chooses a particularly gender-charged example. Drawn from a set of in-terviews with men on the topic of rape, the testimony of one man includes a number of comparisons all growing out of the metaphoric schema that Johnson calls "PHYSICAL APPEARANCE IS A PHYSICAL FORCE":

. . . she's *giving off* very feminine, sexy *vibes.*
. . . I'm supposed to stand there and *take it.*
. . . the woman has *forced me* to turn off my feelings and *react* . . .
. . . they have *power over* me just by their presence.
Just the fact that they can come up to me, and just *melt me.* . . . (7)

This metaphoric system serves as the basis for a sequence of inferences, from "A WOMAN IS RESPONSIBLE FOR THE FORCE SHE EXERTS ON MEN" to what amounts to a rationalization for rape, "ONLY AN INJURY IN LIKE MEASURE AND OF LIKE KIND CAN REDRESS THE IMBALANCE OF JUSTICE" (8–9).

Thus, both *balance* and *force* can be invoked metaphorically to justify male violence against women. Can the use of either term, then, be completely gen-der-neutral, even in a discussion of the amount of rocket fuel needed to balance the force of gravity? Or is the pull of the earth likely to stir memories of mater-nal constraint or unrelieved desire, while the rocket becomes the escaping or ejaculating male?

Literalizing Metaphors

All this load of uneasy, aggressive, overweening masculinity, which is usu-ally allowed to imprint itself invisibly on language and thought, is given form and substance in Morrow's God. The floating corpse, accordingly, is the figure of a figure. It stands for metaphoric schemata that preside over physics as well as philosophy. The exploration of the corpse's nooks and crannies—the peaks of its nose and chin, the broad plain of its chest, the intricacies of its inner ear—

these are investigations into the ur-form of both man and universe. In exploring God's body, Ockham and the others metaphorically venture out into the cosmos. Everything they find, however, is at the same time already familiar, for it is themselves figured large.

The metaphor does not, however, figure forth their feminine selves. The body projected across nature, culture, and psyche is, as Cassie Fowler bemoans, "the gender the universe fully endorsed. Womankind was a mere shadow of the prototype" (90). This lesson is hammered home with the first "truly unnerving sight" of God's genitals (115): "the more Thomas thought about it, the more inevitable the appendage became. A God without a penis would be a *limited* God, a God to whom some possibility had been closed, hence not God at all. In a way it was rather noble of Him to have endorsed this most controversial of organs. Inevitably, Thomas thought of Paul's beautiful First Letter to the Corinthians: 'And those members of the body which we think to be less honorable, upon these we bestow more abundant honor . . .'"(116; ellipses in original).

The quotation from Corinthians is yet another metaphor turned back on itself, reliteralized, by Morrow. There is no name for this rhetorical figure, the metaphor driven relentlessly back toward concrete literality, but its effect is not so much to erase the figuration as to compound it: metaphor squared. As its use here indicates, the taboo is simply the other face (or some other part) of the sacred. We perceive the holy as well as the forbidden through reference to corporeal experiences, even—or especially—erotic experiences. Both aspects of the divine are given shape through metaphor: man-shape.

In the course of the novel, it becomes clear that there is no way to evade God's body, nor even to destroy it. Van Horne, Ockham, and even Fowler become reconciled to the idea that the only way to cope with the body is to take charge of it. They complete their quest in the face of a fully staged (in the theatrical as well as the military sense) air and sea attack. Furthermore, Ockham decides it is not enough to put God in cold storage, hiding the fact of his demise. The world should be informed, the body put on view, in order that humanity be forced out of its childhood, as, Ockham believes, God has intended all along.

This decision corresponds with Morrow's storytelling technique: forcing that which is implicit into plain sight, taking metaphor more literally even than biblical literalists do. There is no way to get outside the metaphor, implies Morrow; one can only work one's way through it to some sense of a reality beyond. It is this literalizing technique that differentiates Morrow's novel from metafictional fables like Donald Barthelme's *Dead Father* (1975), J. G. Ballard's "Drowned Giant" (1964), and Gabriel García Márquez's "Handsomest Drowned Man in the World" (1971), all of which echo Morrow's central image (though Morrow mentions that he was not aware of any of them when he began writing the novel) (Delany, "*Paradoxa* Interview" 138–39). As F. Brett Cox points out, it is Morrow's consistent working out of the material implications of the metaphor—his insistence on "the brute facticity of the corpse," to quote Cox quoting Morrow—that makes his work readable as science fiction as well as postmodern parable (Cox 20).

The next two novels of the trilogy project further into the future the results of making the world aware of God's death. In *Blameless in Abaddon* (1996), the body, now hooked up to life support and serving as central attraction in a fundamentalist Christian theme park, becomes the object of a courtroom battle that combines an exploration of the problem of evil with a debate over medical intervention in a case of probable braindeath. By the third volume, *The Eternal Footman* (1999), the body has disintegrated, but God's skull orbits the earth, a gigantic *memento mori* in the sky. In these two books, as the humor grows more mordant and the irony more wrenching, the emphasis shifts from epistemology to ethics and the relationship between art and faith.

The later novels, however, continue to explore the role of metaphor in thought and belief. They demonstrate how substantial an image can be, even while solid matter is revealed to be something less than real. *Towing Jehovah* and its sequels suggest that the best way to comprehend the power of metaphor is to look directly at the male body writ large across the cosmos, to see how we use it to maintain the illusion that science's quirks and quarks constitute a substantial commonsense reality. We are stuck with God the Father's body, one way or another; though we can transform its image through art, through reason, and through compassion, we cannot transcend it.

Other Bodies, Other Minds

Gwyneth Jones, in *White Queen* (1991) and its sequels, however, proposes another tactic: to try looking through an alternative set of metaphoric lenses. Repositioning one's viewpoint even slightly might lead to new formulations of fundamental principles. Like Morrow, Jones investigates what Mark Johnson calls "the body in the mind." Unlike him, she explores the possibility that there might be other sorts of minds incorporating other shapes of bodies.

The two rival metaphoric schemata in Jones's novels might be expressed, in Lakoff and Johnson's notation, as "THE WORLD IS AN EXTENSION OF MYSELF" versus "DIFFERENT IS ALIEN." The former metaphoric system corresponds roughly to the one Morrow has investigated: we make sense of the universe by mapping it onto our own bodies. In the latter system, the primary difference that serves as source domain is gender. Taking off from bodily differences and the social distinctions that arise from them, Jones generates alternative ways of seeing self, other, communication, and universe. The Aleutians (as her aliens choose to call themselves) of her novels inhabit a different universe from ours because theirs is figured forth in terms not only of a different body shape but also of a different set of differences. There are masculine Aleutians and feminine ones, for instance, yet the distinction has nothing to do with reproduction or divergence from a divine prototype and everything to do with desire and the presentation of self. Whose body, then, is enthroned in Aleutian scientific paradigms?

Ironically, it is the Aleutians who see the universe in terms of sameness, while the "DIFFERENT IS ALIEN" paradigm governs the reactions of most of Earth's natives. Humans see only the Aleutians' difference from themselves, while the aliens find nothing alien about us. Both perspectives lead to major misunderstandings and social disasters, but both are, at some level, truths about the nature of reality.

The landing of the Aleutians unsettles every aspect of human culture. Like an invasion of French theorists landing on the American shore, they call into question the most commonsense assumptions about both social relations and physical being. What is a parent and what is a child? Where does the self end and the other begin? What is desire? How do we distinguish between humans and their technological products? Conventional answers to these questions are thrown into doubt by the existence of the aliens.

Different Differences

Revising deeply ingrained cultural patterns requires more than simply reinserting women into narratives. One way to reshuffle the cards is to postulate a different set of gender differences, setting up contrasting identities that seem to correspond to, but are ultimately noncongruent with, those we take for granted. Gwyneth Jones performs just such a set of transformations on gender symbolism, with the ultimate effect of displacing the masculine from its privileged position in epistemology. Let's pretend, says the first of her Aleutian novels, that there are people who do not know sexual difference. Without sexual reproduction, they must have some other mechanism for reshuffling genes, so let's suppose that each one carries a multiplicity of genotypes, only one of which is expressed in the individual. It is as if all the recessive genes each of us carries made up a separate potential person to which one might give birth— only multiplied millions of times over. Each Aleutian individual resides, *in potentio*, within the genetic memory of every other and might be reborn at any time, to any parent. So there are not only no males and females among the Aleutians, there are no family lines either, no patriarchal lines of kinship and inheritance. All are family. No one is Other. All are Self.

Jones goes even farther to blur the boundaries between individual Aleutians. Using as a model the airborne chemical signals called pheromones, she imagines an even broader channel of chemical communication. The Aleutians give off insect-sized lumps of themselves, capable of carrying information about complex emotional states and even specific memories. These "wanderers" fill the air and crawl over the skin; they can be emitted deliberately as a record of important events; they can be ingested and "read" by others; and they can even make their way back into the common gene pool to make permanent alterations in the blueprint of oneself stored there.

Furthermore, the people of Aleutia share this genetic link with the other life forms in their world. Indeed, many or all of these other organisms were made to order, generated from their own bodies to serve as food sources or tools. It is a world of commensals, an ecosystem that is truly, as the etymology indicates, an *oikos*, a big household.

All this is very strange, very alien, very Other. Yet everything the Aleutians do is familiar. They eat, sleep, defecate, make love, make war, make jokes, make discoveries, bargain, commit fraud, argue, and write poems. They even divide themselves into genders, according to temperamental patterns: "Feminine people, according to the lore of Atha's kind, are the people who'd rather work through the night in the dark than call someone who can fix the light. The kind of people who chatter when they're exhausted and go to sleep when they're happy. The kind of people who can't live without being needed but refuse to need anything from anyone. Masculine people, on the other hand, can never leave well enough alone, break things by way of improving them, will do absolutely anything for a kiss and a kind word . . ." (123; ellipses in original). For the Aleutians, gender is something between a parlor game and a cult, like astrology. What sign are you: feminine or masculine? One fascinating trace to follow throughout the three books is the use of personal pronouns among the aliens: *he*s can unexpectedly morph into *she*s, and Aleutians will, with arrogant assurance, assign gender to humans without regard to biological sex.

When Aleutians meet Earthlings, they are constitutionally and culturally predisposed to see sameness. It is all they know: extensions of self. In contrast, people of Earth are predisposed to see difference, because they have always seen themselves as either/or. "People will tell you duality was invented by a chap called René Descartes," comments one human character in *White Queen*, and continues: "It's nonsense, we were always like it. We have our persistent fantasies that everything is one, man. But our experience has never borne that out, never. I look at you, you look at me. Something passes from my eyes to yours: Well, that can't happen, because the space between is 'empty.' No action at a distance. That's our predicament. We are alone. Even when we speak or touch each other separation remains what we believe in, it's our default state" (181).

And so the people of Earth expect alien visitors to be absolutely alien: mysterious, inexplicable, anything but folks like us. Ecological disasters and wars having set up conditions for a worldwide cargo cult, when strange beings from space announce themselves, most humans are ready to roll over and play dead for them. Because we habitually turn alternatives into hierarchies, the aliens must be either inferior or superior to ourselves, and the fact that they and not we have initiated contact indicates that they must be top dogs. They are the conquistadors, we the Incas; they are the masculine to our feminine.

In reality, the Aleutians are a trading expedition that has got itself a little lost. They assume that the people of Earth are basically funny-looking Aleutians, and they view Earth itself as an untidy version of the homeworld. One of the Aleutians notes this familiarity as he studies an earthly leaf: "He laid his own hand next to the hand of a fallen leaf. Even to the stubby fifth leaflet the shape was an echo, an echo of home; an echo of self. To give and to receive the Self makes open palms. He shook hands with the fallen leaf, wondering what tiny faraway contact the local people felt" (19–20).

What a disappointment, he thinks (being a poet—none of the others are much bothered): "I came to find the new, but there is nothing new. There is only the WorldSelf, perceiving itself. Any shelter out of which I look is that of my own body. Any leaf is my hand. I cannot escape; I can never leave home" (20).

A leaf is a hand; the self is the world—so metaphor allows the Aleutians to construct the universe in their own image. In this they are not so different from humans after all. They are enough like us to project an idealized version of the self onto another individual, turning that one into the Beloved. This particular application of metaphor—the lover as twin, as soul mate, as second self—turns the meeting of Aleutian and human into tragicomedy when the poet falls in love with Johnny Guglioli, with repercussions that cascade through two cultures and three books.

For Johnny, a disgraced journalist, the aliens represent a great story, a scoop, a chance to redeem himself. His meeting with the poet is the first real contact between the races and, like all subsequent interactions, is a mixture of misperceptions and surprisingly easy connections. Johnny sees the Aleutian poet Agnès sometimes as "the creature" and sometimes as "the alien girl" (56). The variation indicates his complex response to "her": fear, eagerness, disorientation, desire, alarm at his own apparent ability to speak telepathically with Agnès.

"How do you make me understand you?" he asks. "Have you learned my language or am I—uh—doing my own translation somehow?" Agnès is puzzled by his puzzlement: "This is my language. Surely Common Tongue is the same everywhere?" (58).

Each is writing the script of their conversations as s/he goes along, revising to fit unexpected responses, seeking familiar scenarios within which to place the encounter. For Johnny it is by turns the science fictional First Contact, the

Exclusive Interview, the Mental Invasion by a Super-Being. For the alien it is Initiating a Bargain, Trading Half-Truths, and ultimately, the Aleutian romantic ideal of Truechild Finding Trueparent, the meeting of two incarnations of the same person. Even though their scenarios fail to match up, there is no way to approach the other without a script. No unmediated perception can occur when perception itself is the medium that divides. As Agnès muses, "The eye attached to the word-filled mind finds it extremely difficult to come to any image 'empty': simply to see. The farther a human artist strays from representation, the more literary a picture becomes, not less. Agnès did not struggle with the paradox. She called this a poem" (59).

Agnès, now calling himself Clavel, fills his own mind with love poems and sees those instead of the "real" Johnny. In Aleutian cultural terms, this is a perfectly appropriate way to carry on a relationship. If Johnny were an Aleutian, the "Johnny" imagined by Agnès/Clavel would grow out of shared genetic memories and would be continually corrected by chemical communion. If the individual were to depart greatly from the mental image, it would be as much Johnny's duty to shape himself to the image as Clavel's to readjust it.

Body Language

The Aleutians believe themselves to be telepathic because of a combination of shared genes, chemical signals, close attention to body language, and lifetimes of common experience recorded and studied as part of Aleutian religion. These together constitute the Common Tongue mentioned by Clavel, a form of communication so effective that the majority of Aleutians do not speak in any other way. In Common Tongue, the body functions not as metaphor but as a continual presence. Only "signifiers"—poets like Clavel—bother with the disembodied "formal language."

Perhaps it is Clavel's "word-filled mind" that leads him astray in dealing with Johnny. The Johnny he is in love with is sign, not referent, not the complex and conflicted human being. The gap between the two turns Clavel's lovemaking into an act of rape. Afterward, he is baffled by Johnny's rage and revulsion, which are tied into Johnny's sense of his own signification as *Johnny*, as *human being*, and especially as *man*. He asks Johnny's human lover Braemar Wilson, "Are you a woman? I thought I knew what that meant, so far as it matters. But the worst thing was I tried to *treat him like a woman*. What does that mean?" (211).

One thing it means is to treat the Other as less integrated, less rational, more chaotic than oneself. This narrative does not allow us to identify either side, Aleutian or human, feminine or masculine, as the disorderly Other. In Jones's fictional world, as in recent mathematical theory, chaos is the product of too much information. Each species is bombarded with information about the other. As the characters try to assimilate that information to what they know, or think they know, about their own species, the chaos thickens. Eventually, though, Johnny and Clavel act as the "strange attractors" that reorganize the chaotic system.

The tiny perturbations that mark Clavel's relationship with Johnny hardly appear on the map of general Aleutian-human interaction. Most people don't know who Johnny is. Clavel is not the Aleutian leader, the "poet-princess" that the humans take him for. Their misadventure makes scarcely a ripple in the larger story of Aleutian conquest. One peculiar feature of chaotic systems, however, is their effect on differences of scale. A tiny alteration can, under the right conditions, create completely disproportionate effects. This is the famous Butterfly Effect: within the system of chaotic interactions that produce weather, the flap of a butterfly's wings in one part of the globe might trigger a hurricane far away.

Just so, Johnny and Clavel's failed mating dance continues to ripple through both worlds, a tiny spot of turbulence that redefines the whole system. They are the apparently insignificant points around which the whole figure revolves. There is no obvious reason why Johnny should find himself involved in the anti-Aleutian conspiracy called White Queen, why he and Braemar Wilson should be the ones to get the secret of instantaneous travel from an eccentric scientist named Peenemünde Buonarotti, why this act should thereby get Johnny killed in an attempt to destroy the Aleutian shipworld. How does Clavel's attempt to assuage his guilt by cloning Johnny in an Aleutian body lead, in *North Wind* (1994), to the rediscovery of that same Buonarotti device? When Clavel remakes himself into a human woman in *Phoenix Café* (1997; rev. 1998), who would expect that Clavel/Catherine should be instrumental in making Buonarotti's invention accessible to humans as well as Aleutians? Why Johnny? Why Clavel? Why this butterfly and not that?

But perhaps their little flap is unique, after all. Other humans learn to control their use of Common Tongue, but only Johnny experiences it as the Aleutians do, as a direct meeting of minds. Something passes between Johnny and Clavel, however imperfectly, and each is transformed by the exchange. This transformation is the "fixed point" of symmetry that "allows coupling to take place between different levels" in a chaotic system (Hayles, *Chaos Bound* 156). It is the tiny ripple that pulls the whole system into a new state of equilibrium. Braemar Wilson notes, "Everything that we are not they are, everything that we can't do they can. But the join is not completely sealed, a tiny trickle breathes through. Aleutia lives on the edge of our possibilities" (*White Queen* 290) .

Johnny and Clavel are not the same individual, as Clavel thinks. But there is symmetry between them, which Clavel's act of signification transforms into similarity. In the course of the three books, Johnny reappears in an Aleutian body, after which Clavel has himself reincarnated as a quasi-human woman. Neither is, by this time, truly Aleutian or human, nor recognizably masculine or feminine. Clavel's poem about the identity of self and other, leaf and hand, has come true: his metaphor remakes two worlds.

The Aleutian novels not only incorporate imagery from the science of chaos, but they also enact the broader cultural reorganization that made possible the paradigm shift of chaos theory. These books are informed throughout by postmodern notions about language, psychology, and history. In her essay "Aliens in the Fourth Dimension," Jones confesses that in her invention of the Aleutians' chemical communication, a "soup of shared presence," she was reinventing "the unconscious in the version proposed by Lacan, the unspoken plenum of experience that is implicit in all human discourse" (in *Deconstructing the Starships* 118). Lacan and Derrida even make cameo appearances in *Phoenix Café* as two of "those structuralists, post-structuralists, semioticists of the precontact so forgotten now" but whose "influence on Buonarotti has never been properly realized" (228).

Colonizing No-Man's-Land

Science fiction, a form that relies on both human interest and scientific curiosity, is uniquely suited to helping us realize the influence of Lacan on Buonarotti, or more precisely, of culture and the imagined self on scientific paradigms. Science fiction exists, as Jones says in her essay "Fools: The Neuroscience of Cyberspace," on "the boundary area between our knowledge of the world out there, our science and its technologies, and the reports we have from the inner world of subjective experience: ideology, interpretation, metaphor, myth" (in *Deconstructing the Starships* 76).

The genre does not always live up to its potential, though. Not all contemporary sf writers take advantage, as do Jones and Morrow, of postmodern methods of critique. All too often writers take a current paradigm for granted, using it as a backdrop to hang behind the conventionalized actions of their scientist heroes.

Taking a scientific model for granted is possible, however, only if one already has a place within the paradigm. Just as the scientist tends to identify with the object of study, the typical science fiction writer identifies with the scientists he is writing about, the clerics of the Church of Physics described by Margaret Wertheim. But Gwyneth Jones does not resemble those priestly scientists. It is a church that by tradition excludes her and those like her. In return, she feels free to cast a skeptical eye on the paradigm—as she says in the title of her collection of critical essays, to deconstruct the starships.

Finding herself omitted on account of her sex from the master narrative of

science, Jones has looked for other silenced, excluded, Othered categories, including the native peoples of all the continents except Europe. Her Aleutians
are composites of many such groups: "I planned to give my alien conquerors
the characteristics, all the supposed deficiencies, that Europeans came to see in
their subject races in darkest Africa and the mystic East—'animal' nature, irrationality, intuition; mechanical incompetence, indifference to time, helpless
aversion to theory and measurement: and I planned to have them win the territorial battle this time" ("Aliens in the Fourth Dimension" 110). These are also,
she points out, precisely the characteristics men ascribe to women. Accordingly, "I often awarded my Aleutians quirks of taste and opinion belonging to
one uniquely different middle-aged, middle-class, leftish Englishwoman. And I
was entertained to find them hailed by US critics as 'the most convincingly *alien*
beings to grace science fiction in years'" (111).

The strangeness of the Aleutians, then, is strange only by Western male
standards. Their interconnectedness, their silence, their willingness to pretend
to be what they are taken for—all these are part of what Jones sees as the condition of subjugated peoples of all sorts, including women. Even the peculiar
physiology of the Aleutians can be seen as a metaphor for femaleness in a male-
defined culture. I mentioned above, as an instance of the similarity between
Aleutians and humans, the fact that they defecate. In fact, the Aleutians like to
imagine that they don't—they have adjusted their diet to produce a minimal
amount of insubstantial waste, which they then cope with by wearing dispos-
able pads. "I made this up," says Jones, "because I liked the image of the alien
arriving and saying '*Quickly, take me somewhere I can buy some sanitary pads . . .'*"
(114; ellipses in original).

A male writer (Morrow, perhaps) might be able to invent such an image.
But it is highly unlikely, as unlikely as the prospect of a male writer describing
a form of selfhood that is not contained within one's skin, a self that cannot possibly be violated by penetration of the body the way Johnny Guglioli feels he
has been violated. It is this sense of the boundaried and therefore violable self
that must be overcome, within the story, before humans can use the Buonarotti
device and travel freely through the cosmos. The imagined world must change
before science can follow. Nothing new can be uttered until there is a language
to say it in and a self capable of speaking it.

Like Morrow, Jones stops short of turning science into a language game.
The Aleutians may describe the universe and the self in terms wildly unlike
ours. They may assume that telepathy is possible, gender a joke, and permanent
death merely a curious local legend. They subject their scientific accounts, however, to the same verification we do. They have discovered the same universal
speed limit that Einstein described (the Buonarotti device enables consciousness, not matter, to cross the cosmos faster than light).

Just because "everything is a metaphor" doesn't mean that one can choose any old metaphor one wishes. According to Jones in her introduction to *Deconstructing the Starships*, the "science" part of *science fiction* means "that whatever phenomenon or speculation is treated in the fiction, there is a claim that it is going to be studied to some extent scientifically—that is objectively, rigorously; in a controlled environment" (4).

Still, within those limitations, the science fiction writer can conduct any sort of thought experiment her (borrowed, adapted, figurative, reliteralized) language allows her to imagine. Morrow, in the third volume of his trilogy, has characters meeting their death-bringing Doppelgängers. Only after each character begins to adopt the perspective of this demonic Other, who is also a shadow self, can she join in constructing a new, rationally spiritual (or spiritually rational), post-Jehovan world. Jones's experiment involves aliens who are not women but whose differentness—and sameness—can stand metaphorically for the differences between the genders. She imagines a meeting between aliens and humans that results in chaos and then shows how that chaos transforms information into new patterns of meaning, including the liberating Buonarotti device.

Both Jones and Morrow play postmodern skepticism and gender-bound scientific paradigms against each other to generate fables about the emergence of new, self-critical, and self-revealing forms of knowledge. As those forms of knowledge emerge, according to both writers, they will result in futures—or at least fictions about the future—that are funny, disturbing, dangerous, chaotically complex, and enriched by all the sorts of alienness that human beings can generate.

7

Sex/uality and the Figure of the Hermaphrodite in Science Fiction;

or, The Revenge of Herculine Barbin

WENDY PEARSON

Introduction: In the Shadow of the Supplement

In Melissa Scott's *Shadow Man* (1995), the human race has reached a point, courtesy of the mutagenic effects of the drugs that make space travel possible, where the five sexes—which John Money, the primary proponent of early surgical intervention on intersex babies, defines as impossible, unnatural, and, at best, the unrestrained imaginings of rampant social constructionists—have become the human norm.[1] In Scott's science fictional world, unlike John Money's, the idea of five sexes has come to be as natural to most people as is the predominant sexual binarism of male and female to us. The comparison between the fictitious world of *Shadow Man* and the "real" world of Dr. Money is deliberate: no one researching the issue of hermaphroditism—or, more properly, intersexuality—can avoid Money's work or his and his colleagues' extraordinary effect on the lives of thousands of intersex people.[2]

Beyond this, it is primarily Money's approach to the intersexed that is under attack in Anne Fausto-Sterling's article "The Five Sexes: Why Male and Female Are Not Enough" (1993), one of the first major critical works to suggest that early surgical intervention on the non-consenting bodies of intersexed babies is both ethically inappropriate and constrained by a medical discourse of sexual dimorphism.[3] Fausto-Sterling argues that this medical discourse is engendered not by the "facts" of human biology but by the particular ideologies of medical practice; it operates under the aegis of three hundred–plus years of Western epistemological naturalization of the two-sex concept.[4] Scott cites precisely this article by Fausto-Sterling when she discusses the genesis of *Shadow Man* on her Website:

I can trace the origin of this book directly to an article by Anne Fausto-Sterling . . . [which] discusses both the biological dimensions of intersexuality and its implications for our own society. . . . Current medical practice is to surgically assign the child to the most likely sex, and to do it as early as possible to spare the child the trauma of being neither male nor female; one of Fausto-Sterling's more interesting arguments was to point out the studies from before the development of effective surgical techniques that suggest that at least some functional hermaphrodites . . . adapted quite comfortably to their sexually diverse bodies. ("Shadow Man")

In "The Five Sexes," Fausto-Sterling points out that the "normal" sex schema of male and female leave both intersex babies and their parents in a nebulous and indeterminate realm, well outside of the sociocultural and commercial discourses that normally surround the neonate ("It's a girl!" on everything pink). Instead, she suggests that we adopt a classificatory schema of five sexes, with "man" and "woman" at the extremes, the "herm" (or "true" hermaphrodite) in the middle, and the two categories of "ferm" (female pseudohermaphrodite, in medical parlance) and "merm" (male pseudohermaphrodite) in the intermediate positions.[5] In *Shadow Man*, Scott takes Fausto-Sterling's proposed five-sex schema and uses "that 'what if' to discuss the ways in which identity, gender, and sexuality intersect to shape individuals," as well as to examine more "nebulous philosophical speculations—are the social manifestations of gender related to physiology, and if so, how?" ("Shadow Man"). *Shadow Man* begins with the premise that five sexes have become the normal sex schema for humans and examines the conflict that would result if some humans rejected the biological "fact" of five sexes in favor of a sexual dimorphism that would—in this future—be clearly at odds with the biological evidence. As Scott says, "[T]he conflict between a culture that accepts five physical sexes and a culture that accepts only two provide[s] an excellent mirror for a lot of the debates over sex, gender, gender roles, and sexuality that are currently disturbing our own society" ("Shadow Man").

Scott explains the sexual/genital biology of humans in the future in terms familiar to her readers not, in all likelihood, from biology (as for example, the three varieties of hermaphrodites distinguished by Edwin Klebs in 1876 and extended into a schematic revisioning of sexual categories by Fausto-Sterling) but rather from what are probably the most famous twentieth-century works of sexology, Alfred Kinsey's twin reports on sexual behavior in humans.[6] One of the best-known features of Kinsey's work is his revisioning of the model of homosexuality and heterosexuality as binary oppositions; instead, Kinsey situated homosexuality and heterosexuality on a continuum, where only a small percentage of humans operate exclusively at either end and most are reported as exhibiting some degree of bisexuality. Scott's adoption of a somewhat similar schema, in which biological sex seems to occur along a continuum, incorporates some elements of familiarity that serve to ease the reader's cognitive dissonance on encountering what appears to be such a radically discontinuous depiction of the sexually embodied nature of humanity.[7] Some reviewers of the novel have commented precisely on the difficulty of conceptualizing such an unfamiliar sex/gender schema, as well as on the inevitable problem that English does not contain a gender-neutral pronoun for people,[8] much less pronouns for three additional sexes. Scott solves the linguistic problem by pressing into use three Old English consonants in order to create three new sets of pronouns: "ðe," "þe," and "ȝe."

In *Shadow Man*, the normal sex schema of humans appears as a sort of continuum with five points: female, fem, herm, mem, male. Of the two narrators, the first, Warreven, is a herm born and living on Hara, a planet settled before the mutagenic effects of hyperlumin (a drug that makes space travel possible) were discovered. Having lost contact with the rest of human space, Harans have been isolated from the sociological and psychological convulsions that resulted in the Concord planets coming to terms with the biological fact of five sexes. They have evolved a concomitant organization of human sexuality that admits nine different sexual orientations—a sexual schema that is more rigid than it at first seems. On Hara, by contrast, humanity is still divided into "male" and "female," and the roughly 25 percent of Harans with intermediate genitalia, the people known as the "oddbodied," are forced into the social and sexual roles of one or the other of the two recognized genders. There is some latitude, however, as the reader discovers that Warreven, who is officially "male," could have married Tendlathe, the son of the Most Important Man, had "he" been willing to accept a female gender assignment, a change purely legal and cultural, rather than surgical. Warreven and Tendlathe argue repeatedly over Warreven's commitment, not only to his hermaphroditism and his sexual desire for men (homosexuality is scorned by the Harans, who name homosexuals "wryabed"), but also to forcing political and cultural change on Hara that would bring the planet in line with the Concord in recognizing the reality of the five sexes. What is clearest in these arguments is that sex is very much a discursive construct, something Tendlathe actually understands more intuitively than does Warreven, as evidenced by Tendlathe's insistence that "[w]e need to be very careful that we understand the difference between fact and truth" (29).

One of the more interesting facets of the way in which Scott mobilizes the figure of the hermaphrodite in *Shadow Man* is that she doesn't appear to be offering the reader a choice between Hara and the Concord. Each of these societies seems to be deeply problematic in the ways in which it constructs sex, gender, and sexuality; the main difference is that the Concord is a significantly more tolerant and livable society for the people who on Hara are called oddbodied or wryabed. While Hara's rigidity about sex and gender is fairly obvious, since it most clearly reproduces both our own prejudices and our dominant cultural discourses, the Concord's sexual ideology is almost as essentialist in its own right. One of the problems between the Concord and Hara lies in the area known as "trade," a form of prostitution in which Concord visitors pay either in money or in favors for the sexual services of Hara's indigenous population. The indigenes, both "normal" and odd-bodied, are playing so far outside the rules of their own society that they willingly indulge sexual desires that are not acceptable within the Concord; while these desires are never clearly specified in the novel, they appear to consist of anything that steps outside of a person's declared sexual orientation and/or gender role. On Hara, a straight man can have sex with a hermaphrodite, or even just play a passive role with a woman. When another Haran, a man, warns Warreven away from Alex, the Concord man he is playing trade with, claiming that Alex is "[o]ff-world gay—that means he wants another man, not a *halving* like you," Warreven responds with a rush of fury "at the name, at the exclusion, at the whole incomprehensible system of off-world sexuality, with its finicking distinctions that were no distinctions at all, as far as he could see" (91). Warreven thinks that Alex is *"still trade, and what trade wants, what they come here for, is sex with us outside that system"* (91; emphasis in original).

Part of the novel's tension, in fact, resides not only in the cultural and political clash between Hara and the Concord—between Tendlathe and the traditionalists and Warreven and the modernists—but also on the personal level between the two narrators, the hermaphroditic Haran and the Concord male Tatian. Warreven is very attracted to Tatian, and Tatian's own narration seems, largely, to confirm that attraction. Tatian is straight, however; he justifies the attraction he feels towards Warreven in terms of the latter's occasional resemblance to an old female lover, even to the point of denying that his physical arousal means anything other than nostalgia and sexual deprivation. Thus, he short-circuits any possibility of a sexual relationship between himself and Warreven.

Tatian demonstrates very neatly the Foucauldian understanding of sexuality as a regulatory system within which, even more effectively than the externally applied system of law and custom (which has not, after all, stopped Warreven on Hara), the individual disciplines him- or herself. Tatian effectively censors his own sexuality in terms of what he sees as "adult" and what seems to him adolescent or childish—*"Adults don't change their minds"* (114; emphasis in original), he thinks, when he discover his Concord ex-lover Prane Am with a Haran mem. Moreover, Am's reluctance to admit that she is di,[9] not straight, emphasizes the possibility that Concord society's recognition of nine sexual orientations does not necessarily mean that all of these orientations carry the same social valence. In fact, the glossary's comment that omni (being sexually interested in people of all genders) is "[c]onsidered somewhat disreputable, or at best indecisive" (311) suggests that some sexual orientations are valued more than others. Is Prane Am simply unwilling to admit that she made a mistake or does straight perhaps have a greater degree of social acceptability than di?

The essentialism and gender-role rigidity of the Concord system is emphasized in the novel's ending, when Warreven goes into voluntary exile after Tendlathe mobilizes the conservative elements of Haran society against the odd-bodied and the modernists. Warreven's reasoning is a clear reaction to a life spent in the sexually dichotomous culture of Hara: "'It's what I said, we don't have a word for revolution or a word for herm, and I'm supposed to invent both of them. I've been a man all my life—yesterday, I was still a man. Now I'm a herm, and I don't know what that means, except that half my own people say it's not really human. How in all the hells can I lead anybody to anything when I don't know what I'm asking them to become?'" (304). When Tatian objects that Warreven was always a herm, Warreven replies, "As long as no one said it, it—I—didn't exist" (304). The discursive construction of sex and gender is what is real in Haran society, as both sex and gender are only imperfectly embodied in Haran physiology, just as they are in Concord physiology. But Hara, unlike the Concord, must change, suggesting a future that is both more fluid and more dangerous than either the stability of the Concord or the xenophobic conservatism of Hara.

Gender essentialism casts a long shadow in *Shadow Man*. Tatian can understand Warreven's decision to go off-planet only in terms of gender: "To stay was a man's solution, in the stereotypes he had grown up with, to stay and fight. Maybe Warreven's way, the herm's way, to retreat to try again, would work better, this time, in this place" (305). Many of Tatian's observations about people reinforce the valence of sexual stereotyping in Concord culture: men fight, women are passive, herms, mems, and fems all have their own particular characteristics, to such an extent that one wonders if one of the attractions of "trade" isn't perhaps the simple ability to step outside the boundaries of these cultural stereotypes, to be passive as a man or active as a woman or aggressive as a herm or otherwise to indulge in a whole range of behaviors, both sexual and nonsexual, that are denied to one by the prevalence of sex-linked gender discourses in the Concord.

It is "the herm's way" in *Shadow Man*, in fact, the very existence of people like Warreven (whether that existence can be spoken of or not), that reveals what is missing in both Concord and Haran cultures. Hermaphroditism—and Warreven in particular—functions as a Derridean supplement, revealing what was lacking all along in the sex/gender systems of both cultures. Considered natural, true, and whole, these systems are deconstructed by the very presence of the hermaphrodite him/herself. Like Rousseau's conception of Nature, sex itself, that most apparently natural of all human attributes, "*should* be self-sufficient" (Derrida, *Grammatology* 145). More than anything else, the hermaphrodite, supplementing the apparent "plenitude" of male and female taken together in a two-sex system, "adds only to replace. It intervenes or insinuates itself *in-the-place-of*; if it fills, it is as if one fills a void. If it represents and makes an image, it is by the anterior default of a presence. . . . As substitute, it is not simply added to the positivity of a presence, it produces no relief, its place is assigned in the structure by the mark of an emptiness" (145). On Hara, as in contemporary Western cultures, the supplementarity of intersexuality deconstructs the very system of sex itself, provoking extremes of defensiveness that are manifested most strongly in the desire to excise that which is definitionally, as well as physically, excessive.[10] For the Concord, it is the very unaligned nature of Haran sex/uality, centered on the figure of the hermaphrodite, that reveals the partiality and incommensurability of the Concord's own attempt to regulate and contain the sexed and sexual body, regardless of whether it has two apparent sexes or five.

True Sex: Adam and Eve Meet Herculine Barbin

On July 21,1860, a correspondent for the *Indépendant de la Charente-Inférieure* published an account of the sudden appearance of a twenty-one-year-old schoolmistress "dressed as a man" (qtd. in Foucault, *Barbin* 145). Having drawn out the townspeople's astonishment, the journalist finally explained: "It is a matter here of one of those deceptive sexual appearances, which only certain anatomical peculiarities can explain. Medical books contain more than one example of them. The error is even more prolonged because a pious and modest upbringing keeps you in the most horrible ignorance. One day some chance circumstance gives rise in your mind to doubt; an appeal is made to medical science; the error is recognized; and a court delivers a judgment that rectifies your birth record on the civil status registers" (qtd. in ibid. 146)

It is, as our anonymous journalist concludes, "a very simple story" (146). Unfortunately for Adélaide Herculine Barbin, the situation was not, indeed, a very simple story. Her very proper Catholic conscience and her fear of what discovery might do both to herself and the young woman she loved convinced Barbin to set into motion the very situation that she most feared. Camille, as she was most commonly known, then entered into a miserable existence as Abel Barbin. Fitfully employed, impoverished, embittered and—most of all—utterly isolated by her condition, Barbin committed suicide in February 1868.

Hermaphrodites were not an unknown phenomenon at this time, nor was it unheard of that someone brought up as one sex might somehow be revealed or reveal themselves to be another. Medical and scientific accounts of sexual anomalies can also be found in current literature, as for example the work of John Money, whose influence on the medical treatment of "sex errors" has already been discussed. One striking feature of Money's work is the specific nomenclature he gives to sexual differentiation in the fetus, when he claims that "[d]evelopmental sexual endocrinology is the branch of science from which the Adam/Eve principle is derived" (25). Neither properly Adam nor Eve, intersex babies must, in Money's schema, be surgically reassigned to become one or the other.

Money's construction of "the Adam/Eve principle" and his insistence that phylogeny presupposes two perfectly differentiated sexes is quite clearly— although, obviously, unconsciously so—in line with the argument that Michel Foucault makes in his introduction to *Herculine Barbin*. Foucault argues that the contemporary obsession with an irrefrangibly dichotomous division between "the sexes," the binary gulf between "male" and "female," is no longer capable of admitting an intermediate space for those whose sex does not meet medico-cultural specifications. He suggests that the medical preoccupation with the re-shaping of both the sexed body and the equally sexed psyche is very much a modern phenomenon. Prior to the nineteenth century, Foucault says, "it was quite simply agreed that hermaphrodites had two [sexes]" (Introduction vii). A more recent study of the relationship between sex and the body by Thomas Laqueur clarifies Foucault's point. In the past, Laqueur says, "[m]aleness and femaleness did not reside in anything particular. Thus for hermaphrodites the question was not 'what sex they are *really*,' but to which gender the architecture of their bodies most readily lent itself. The concern of magistrates was less with corporeal reality—with what we would call sex—than with maintaining clear social boundaries, maintaining the categories of gender" (135; emphasis in original).

Foucault's argument about hermaphrodites, of a piece with his overall argument about the ways in which the body became the site of surveillance, regulation, and discipline, presupposes a movement from a premodern ideology of the primacy of social gender over the corporeal structures of the actual body to a modern insistence that everybody "was to have his or her primary, profound, determined and determining sexual identity; as for the elements of the other sex, they could only be accidental, superficial or even quite simply illusory" (Introduction viii).

On the one hand, then, we have contemporary biological science, represented at both its most articulate and its most regulatory by Money; on the other, we have Foucault's analysis of the body as *the* site of regulation, the place where the workings of discourse are most particular and most obvious. We also have the testimony of members of the various Intersex Societies, the "hermaphrodites" themselves, and—arguably—of a small number of medical professionals who have come to oppose the practice of early surgical intervention.[11] Academic intersex writer Morgan Holmes points out in particular the contradictory scientific discourses at work in the medical construction of hermaphrodites or intersexuals, where the "scientific basis" of determining biological sex—that is the genetic information embedded in the forty-sixth chromosome—is ignored in favor of a discourse of "penile insufficiency," "enlarged clitorises," "sexual errors," and (never to be forgotten) the Adam/Eve principle. Holmes notes, furthermore, the way in which the medicalization of the hermaphrodite's body as "sick" has concomitantly worked to uphold that other medicalized discourse of "sex errors" and sickness, the division of human sexuality into heterosexual and homosexual (94–97).

A significant part of the emphasis on discovering the "true sex," whether of the body or the psyche, has related to the assumption that biological sex properly regulates the sexual desires of the body (or psyche). This assumption returns us to the difficulties Holmes delineates of deciphering whether the intersexual's body is sexually "normal," with the effect that the medical establishment has, by and large, prioritized heterosexuality over fertility. As Bernice Hausman points out, contemporary medical practitioners have consistently chosen to assign their patients to a specific sex based on the likelihood of a heterosexual outcome, even where the patient was or would have been fertile in the "opposite" sex and without surgical intervention (97–100).

Supplementing Eden: Adam and Eve and St/eve

Contemporary self-appointed guardians of the community against the threat of homosexuality are in the habit of chanting the slogan, "Adam and Eve, not Adam and Steve." As the title to this section of my chapter indicates, the hermaphrodite represents, just as much as the homosexual, the potential reappropriation of this slogan on behalf of a more diverse and gender-fluid society. In Stephen Leigh's *Dark Water's Embrace* (1998), preserving the community from the disruptive threats of both perversion and hermaphroditism is very much to the point. *Dark Water's Embrace* tells the tale of the descendants of a party of explorers who inadvertently become a colony when an accident disables their orbiting ship and kills most of their crewmates. Alone on the planet they have named Mictlan, save for the bones of a long-dead indigenous race, the humans struggle to survive, despite the harsh conditions, the danger of attack by large animals known as "grumblers," and an ever-decreasing rate of viable live births. The novel begins with the discovery of a Miccail body preserved in a peat bog; when Anaïs, the younger of the colony's two doctors, examines the body she discovers that the long-dead indigene was a hermaphrodite. Anaïs's discovery prompts the ship's computer, who alone knows Anaïs's true nature, to remark, "Now there's serendipity for you, eh?" (10). From this point on, the novel tells two interconnected stories: the story of the human colony's attempt to survive its declining birthrate and of Anaïs's personal attempt to survive when she is exiled from the colony because of what its members perceive as her lesbianism and sexual abnormality; and the story of the dead Miccail, Kai, and his self-sacrificial attempt to preserve his race and culture from extinction.

Dark Water's Embrace combines several levels of narrative: voice recordings by Anaïs, Elio (Anaïs's male lover), and Máire (her female lover); third-person narrative from the perspectives of other colonists; journal entries by Gabriela Rusack, the first person among the initial colonists to be shunned for lesbianism and the only one with a serious interest in the Miccail; and finally the first-person narrative of KaiSa, telling a story that happened long before the arrival of the humans.

Inevitably, given her hermaphroditic biology and her attraction to both women and men, Anaïs is discovered by the other colonists and shunned. Anaïs's major enemy is Dominic, the patriarch of Elio's clan, who blames Anaïs for the death in childbirth of his granddaughter, Ochiba, whom Anaïs had loved. Because one of the primary concerns of the colony is the production of babies, seen as an absolute necessity for the colony's survival, the colonists have devised a sexual system in which fertile women can take any of the males as lovers and heterosexual promiscuity is the rule. Even though the conception rate is low and most sexual acts are thus about pleasure and desire, rather than procreation, the colonists' ideology equates heterosexual sex with reproduction and forbids all supposedly nonreproductive sex, including all forms of homosexuality. When Anaïs is exiled, her lovers, Elio and Máire, leave with her, retracing Gabriela's route during her own exile as best they can in the hope of finding out more about the vanished Miccail, whose fate Anaïs believes to be closely linked to what is happening to the humans in the colony. Perhaps inevitably, it turns out that the large quasi-marsupials that the humans have named grumblers are not nonsentient beasts at all, but the last remnants of the indigenous population of the planet. Anaïs forges a link with one of the grumblers, an old male she names Silverback, eventually discovering both their true nature and the cause of their decline, which the reader already knows to some extent from the parallel story of Kai.

The Miccail have long ago degenerated from their former numbers and state of civilization as a result of a campaign by a male and female Miccail couple, DekTe and CaraTa, to control the Sa, the hermaphrodites, who have previously had a sacred role as peripatetic partners to male and female Miccail couples. The Sa will join a couple long enough to ensure conception; Kai, like all the Sa, believes it is ker sacred duty to share ker reproductive powers among the Miccail, regardless of the strength of attachment ke might feel to any given couple. Believing the Sa to have too much power, particularly over reproduction, DekTe and CaraTa fight to consolidate power in their own hands, to capture a Sa for their own particular breeding purposes, and to amalgamate the various tribes into one larger group. The Sa refuse to give up what they see as their sacred role in aiding Miccail reproduction; they know that babies conceived without Sa intervention are sickly, are prone to genetic defects, and include very minimal numbers of hermaphrodites. When the Sa are faced with inevitable defeat, they commit suicide en masse, with the result that the remaining Miccail have to rely on the occasional accidental Sa birth in order to facilitate reproduction. Leigh explains the peculiarities of Miccail biology and reproduction by providing the Sa with a role in cleansing and strengthening semen produced by the male that would otherwise be affected by the very high rate of mutation on Mictlan, and then transmitting that semen to the female.

Anaïs appears to be the first human born with this ability, although another hermaphroditic baby is born just before she is sent into exile. Inevitably, given the fear and hatred that can be incited in humans by sexual difference, many of the colonists, especially Dominic, blame Anaïs for the baby's condition, as if her presence at the delivery is somehow responsible for the infant's intersexuality. In fact, Dominic blames Anaïs not only for Ochiba's death but also for the falling birthrate, the high incidence of infant mortality, and a variety of other evils, all of which he can show statistically to have increased since Anaïs reached adolescence. And yet Anaïs's shunning is a blessing in disguise for the human colony, because it is only when the three exiles befriend a grumbler family and help deliver a breech birth, which turns out to be a hermaphroditic infant, that they realize the underlying biology of Mictlan/grumbler reproduction—and its potential repercussions for humans. Shortly after the birth of the baby Sa, Máire also discovers that she is pregnant. At first, Elio doesn't understand, having never had sex directly with Máire, that he is in any way involved in the conception of her child, but between the information in Gabriela's journals and the example of the grumblers, Anaïs has figured out the process involved in the creation of a child with three parents. In Miccail (and eventually in Mictlan-human) sexual biology, the hermaphrodite is not only an intermediate sex but an absolutely necessary one. The trio take the news of their discovery back to the other colonists, but, unable to defeat the intransigent and violent prejudice of Dominic and his followers, they are eventually forced to leave and set up a mixed encampment of humans and grumblers. Their reproductive success lures the less bigoted among the humans, and the novel ends with the assurance of a possible future on Mictlan for both Miccail and humans. As Anaïs says, "We are all learning, slowly, a different sexual dance" (324).

Like *Shadow Man*, *Dark Water's Embrace* pits a group of people who are genitally and sexually different against a conservative and bigoted enemy; also like Scott, Leigh explains the new biology of both his human and his Miccail characters via the mechanism of mutation, mutations that in this case are intrinsic to the ecology of the planet, rather than to the effects of drugs like hyperlumin. In both novels, a major part of the issue is tolerance for the different and an examination of the intransigent and irrational nature of bigotry itself. Dominic, like Tendlathe, puts his own ideological commitments ahead of both compassion and common sense. In the implicit comparison of Dominic with the power-hungry DekTe and his mate, CaraTa, who engineer the downfall of the Miccail, Leigh suggests that Dominic's bigotry is at least in part the simple will to power that cannot bear to see its own desires and beliefs brooked in any way and that, despite mobilizing discourses of survival for ideological purposes, it actually works to the detriment of the race. Where Leigh's novel differs most clearly from Scott's, however, at least in terms of its mobilization of the figure of the hermaphrodite, is in its assignation of an essential (in both senses) reproductive role to the intersexed body. In this case, the Sa and the human hermaphrodites function as a supplement to a system that is revealed as being hopelessly incomplete in even the most literal and biological sense. Male and female form no sort of natural plenitude on Mictlan, leaving the reader questioning whether the apparent plenitude of the two-sex system—the naturalness of male and female and of reproductive heterosexuality as the equally naturalized sexual expression of maleness and femaleness—does not also need supplementation, of whatever form it might take, in the so-called real world.

Leigh's concentration on the hermaphrodite's necessary role in the new re-productive schema also suggests the possibility that readers may reject the nov-el's plea for tolerance of the sexually and genitally different, except where those differences are directly linked to the reproductive survival of the race. Because of its focus on the survival both of a race that has faced near extinction and of an almost doomed colony, *Dark Water's Embrace* can do little to obviously decouple the link between sex and reproduction. Indeed, it is only Gabriela's presence, via her journals, that reminds the reader that sexual difference should be toler-ated and even—dare I say it?—celebrated for its own sake. Unlike the her-maphroditic Anaïs, Gabriela is a genuine lesbian, the *rezu* that dominates Dominic's paranoid fantasies about the sexual behaviors of others, and her fa-milial and intellectual linkage to the exiled trio is the novel's primary reminder that sex is not and never has been simply about reproduction. Despite its some-what less obviously deconstructive stance, the novel continues to replay the riff in my section title: Adam and Eve and St/eve can only be a very different ver-sion of the story of life in the Garden of Eden.

(Getting to) the Bottom of Sex

Where Hara and the Concord have five sexes and Mictlan has three, the most famous of all sf stories about hermaphrodites is set on a planet that has only one. Like the natives of Paul Park's *Celestis* (1995) or the aliens of Gwyneth Jones's Aleutian Trilogy (1991–98), the inhabitants of the planet Gethen are all hermaphrodites. Ursula Le Guin's *Left Hand of Darkness* (1969) uses the culture clash between a one-sexed version of humanity and a two-sexed version to re-veal the constructed nature of all sex/gender systems. Through the device of the naive visitor, the Ekumenical representative from Terra, Genly Ai, Le Guin sets out to consider "what, besides purely physiological form and function, truly differentiates men and women. Are there real differences in temperament, capacity, talent, psychic processes, etc.? If so, what are they?" ("Is Gender Nec-essary?" 163). To make this experiment, Le Guin contrasts the reactions of the "conventional, indeed rather stuffy, young man from Earth" (163) with the Gethenians, for whom hermaphroditism is normal; it is Genly's permanent masculinity that is alien and, indeed, in the context of Gethenian culture(s), per-verse. As the Ekumen's envoy to the recently (re)discovered planet, Genly ar-rives on Gethen already aware of the first observers' reports of the peculiarities of Gethenian sexual biology: sexually neuter most of any given month, Gethe-nians experience a monthly estrus during which they can become either male or female. Unless pregnant, the Gethenian reverts to the neutral state once estrus is over. Genly's peculiar position as the lone Terran observer provides the pri-mary narrative; it is, however, supplemented both by Gethenian myths and sto-ries and by the journals of the Gethenian, Estraven, who rescues and ultimately comes to love Genly. The dual perspective allows the reader to see the Getheni-ans both as they see themselves and as they seem to Genly, whose initial gaze is deeply stereotyping, confused, and resentful. At one point Estraven asks, "Do [women] differ much from your sex in mind behavior? Are they like a different species?" Genly stumbles with his reply, vacillating between yes and no, and concludes finally that he doesn't know if women are inferior and that he can't really tell Estraven what women are like. "You don't know," Genly says. "In a sense, women are more alien to me than you are. With you I share one sex, any-how" (*Left Hand* 234–35).

Almost all of Le Guin's novel is directed toward the possibility of express-ing a nonlinear mode of thinking, in this case most directly linked to Taoism, which would replace the Manichean and Cartesian dualisms that have ruled over Western epistemology for so long and that have perhaps found their deep-est, most intractable expression in the two-sex system that commands almost all of the contemporary world. *"Light is the left hand of darkness / and darkness the right hand of light"* (233). Thus the true hermaphroditism of the Gethenians can be understood in two ways, both as a commentary on contemporary Western gender ideology and as an epistemological—if not biological—alternative to the sexual dualisms in which we are enmeshed. The Gethenians have no "true sex" and are not ruled by its tyrannies; their sexual biology does not, no matter how much Genly attempts to read into their behavior, reveal the truth of their personhood. They are psychologically opaque to Genly, who has learned, like the reader, "that it is in the area of sex that we must search for the most secret and profound truths about the individual, that it is there that we can best dis-cover what he is and what determines him" (Foucault, Introduction x). The Gethenians are, as Genly only slowly comes to understand, fully human in ways that the reader, mired in apparent biological dimorphisms of all sorts,[12] can only hope or fear to become.

These are perhaps the two most striking points that the novel makes for the contemporary reader: first, that the two-sex system makes men and women alien to each other; second, that after Le Guin has eliminated physiological sex-ual differences from the Gethenians, her stated goal—"to find out what was left [as] [w]hatever was left would be, presumably, simply human" ("Gender" 163–64)—in fact leaves the reader with a species that is apparently intractably alien by virtue of its absolute humanity. That is, what is "simply human" is the alien in the novel. Genly's eventual growth into sympathy with the alien leaves him less than, or perhaps more than, human, utterly alienated from his own people. Thus, when the rest of Genly's fellow Envoys descend to the planet, they no longer know him and he sees them as "a troupe of great, strange ani-mals, of two different species; great apes with intelligent eyes, all of them in rut, in kemmer" (*Left Hand* 296).

Le Guin's choice of language in *Left Hand* perhaps inadvertently reinforces these points. Genly Ai and his cohorts, regardless of whether they are Terran, like Genly, or Hainish or Cetian or from some other Ekumenical planet, are referred to as "human," whereas they refer to the inhabitants of Winter as Gethenians. Gethenians, operating from the opposite assumptions about what is human, refer to Genly Ai as "the Alien" and regard him, given his permanent state of masculinity, which to them equates to a permanent state of estrus, as "a pervert." It is only Estraven, of all the characters in the novel, who from the very beginning sees the common humanity between Terran and Gethenian. Of course, given that Le Guin's Hainish stories presuppose a common history in which all humanoid species are far-scattered descendants of the ancient Hainish, it is highly unlikely that, in the context of Le Guin's Hainish oeuvre, the hermaphroditic Gethenians are truly an alien species. They are, at most, our distant cousins. Moreover, the report of the first Investigator, Ong Tot Oppong, carefully reproduced within the novel, suggests that the Gethenians "were an experiment" (*Left Hand* 89). Furthermore, Le Guin uses the context of Oppong's suggestion to situate the Gethenians firmly as human, in the Ekumenical sense, by comparing them to us: "now that there is evidence to indicate that the Terran Colony was an experiment, the planting of one Hainish Normal group on a world with its own proto-hominid autochthones, the possibility cannot be ignored. Human genetic manipulation was certainly practiced by the Colonizers" (*Left Hand* 89). What is most truly alien, then, in *The Left Hand of Darkness*, is our own epistemologies; it is not who we are nor how we are constructed sexually or biologically that makes us alien to each other, but rather the naturalized ideological bases of our assumptions about what it means to be human.

By contrast with Genly, who takes a long time to see the true humanity of Gethenians, rather than the peculiarly stereoscopic effects of his early attempts at "self-consciously seeing a Gethenian first as a man, then as a woman, forcing him into those categories so irrelevant to his nature and so essential to my own" (12), Estraven sees Genly Ai's humanity from the first moment of contact: "I first sought him out in Ehrenrang, a long time ago it seems now; hearing talk of 'an Alien' I asked his name, and heard for answer a cry of pain from a human throat across the night" (229). It takes Genly a great deal longer. In fact, it is only when they are alone on the Ice, escaping across the top of the world, that Genly learns to see Estraven as human: "And I saw then again, and for good, what I had always been afraid to see, and had pretended not to see in him: that he was a woman as well as a man. . . . Until then I had rejected him, refused him his own reality. He had been quite right to say that he, the only person on Gethen who trusted me, was the only Gethenian I distrusted. For he was the only one who had entirely accepted me as a human being: who had liked me personally and given me entire personal loyalty: and who therefore had demanded of me an equal degree of recognition, of acceptance" (248).

This meeting on the Ice is, of course, the crux of the novel. The relationship between Genly and Estraven while Estraven is in kemmer has drawn a great deal of critical attention, including the accusation that the novel is basically homophobic because it does not explore the sexual attraction between the two "men."[13] Of course, Estraven is not a man, despite the difficulties raised by Le Guin's use of the male pronoun to refer to Gethenians. This is an issue that has been dealt with elsewhere at length and that Le Guin herself admits was a mistake ("Is Gender Necessary? Redux"). Beyond this, however, lies another question of interpretation: does the reader want a sexual relationship—or a flat refusal of one—between Genly and Estraven because it is in sex that we have come to understand what is True? Not, as Genly says at the beginning of the novel, as a matter of the imagination, but rather as the matter of the body.[14] As Foucault notes, with a certain irony, in his introduction to *Herculine Barbin*: "we also admit that it is in the area of sex that we must search for the most secret and profound truths about the individual, that it is there that we can best discover what he is and what determines him. And if it was believed for centuries that it was necessary to hide sexual matters because they were shameful, we now know that it is sex itself which hides the most secret parts of the individual: the structure of his fantasies, the roots of his ego, the forms of his relationship to reality. At the bottom of sex, there is truth" (x–xi).

At the bottom of sex, there is truth: when Genly realizes the "truth" of Estraven's sexual nature, at that precise moment when they do not have sex, he offers to teach Estraven the art of mindspeech, a form of paraverbal communication in which, among other things, lying is impossible. But sex, as Foucault insistently reminds us, is only discursively—or perhaps, in this context, we should say as "a matter of the imagination"—the Truth, and mindspeech in fact does no more to reveal "the most secret parts of the individual" between Genly and Estraven than does Genly's belated understanding of the reality of Estraven's sex, his hermaphroditism. Genly tells us that "that intimacy of mind established between us was a bond, indeed, but an obscure and austere one, not so much admitting further light (as I had expected it to) as showing the extent of the darkness" (255).

The Left Hand of Darkness is perhaps the most complex—and also perhaps the most inconsistent—of these three novels in its handling of the matter of the hermaphrodite. The latter may in part be because Scott and Leigh have learned from Le Guin's mistakes, particularly in the matter of pronouns; it is also, no doubt, because the general understanding of hermaphroditism or intersexuality has changed over the quarter of a century that separates *Left Hand* from the other two novels. Yet in all three of these novels, what the figure of the hermaphrodite most clearly reveals is the inherent lack in the discourses that equate sex with the truth of the individual, the discourses that would have us believe, as Foucault tells us we do, that we will find truth at the bottom of sex. The hermaphrodite thus functions, in literature and perhaps also in life, as the supplement that deconstructs the fiction that sex, as we understand it, is natural and whole in itself: the supplement both adds and replaces, and the very contradiction inherent in the supposition that one can both add to what is already full and replace what is already irreplaceable reveals the deconstructive nature of the supplement, whatever it may be. The supplementarity of the hermaphrodite thus undermines the plenitude and naturalness of all of those discourses that would find the truth of the individual—or, come to that, of the species—in sex, and that assume that our contemporary sexual epistemologies spring from Nature, from the truth of the body itself. Only in *Dark Water's Embrace* does hermaphroditism appear to offer a cure for the problems caused by the sexual system; even there, however, that cure takes place only at the most literal level and cannot be transferred metonymically into a strategy for dealing with the real world. If the figure of the hermaphrodite seems, at times, to offer a utopian potential, it is not so much in the literal and physical possibilities offered by the intersexed body (even through surgery or genetic engineering) but rather because the supplementarity of the figure reveals to us the extent to which seeking the truth of the individual in sex and the sexed body can only ever trap us within those very discourses from which we seek to escape. The figure of the hermaphrodite offers us, at last, the possibility of learning to see in other ways, of recognizing that truth is perhaps a matter of the imagination, not of sex.

8

Mutant Youth

Posthuman Fantasies and High-Tech Consumption

in 1990s Science Fiction

ROB LATHAM

Pat Cadigan's 1986 short story "Pretty Boy Crossover" explores a near future in which one of the central fantasies of posthumanist theory has been realized: the wholesale "uploading" of consciousness in the form of a digital
simulacrum. But rather than replacing the living body with a robotic apparatus
into which this duplicate mind is transcribed, as Hans Moravec has famously
advocated, Cadigan constructs a scenario in which the translated self subsists
entirely as "sentient information" in a vast database—the body is dispensed
with entirely. In Cadigan's treatment, young people are the ideal guinea pigs
for this radical makeover, since those over twenty-five have proven unable to
"blossom and adapt . . . to their new medium"; indeed, the corporation that
promotes uploading pitches it in terms of its prospective clients' yearning for a
utopia of perpetual youth: "Never have to age, to be sick, to lose touch. You
spent most of your life young, why learn how to be old?" (137). The technical
process itself has been pioneered specifically within the domain of popular
youth culture, with the data constructs functioning as celebrities in entertainment media as well as serving as fashion trend-setters.

In effect, Cadigan's uploaded teens realize the cyborg-youth fantasies pro-
mulgated by popular cyberpunk organs such as *Mondo 2000*—a magazine that,
according to its co-editor R. U. Sirius (a.k.a. Ken Goffman), speaks for a cutting-edge cadre of "mutant youth" (14) who subsist "in images and data per-
mutated and projected across planetary distances with extra planetary—
satellite-assisted—technologies" (16). The glossy coffee-table "User's Guide"
distilled from the journal's pages aggressively promotes a series of posthumanist possibilities in the form of a supplemental "Mondo Shopping Mall" listing a
host of intellectual, cultural, and pharmaceutical resources under headings
ranging from "Bio/Cybernetics" and "DNA Music" to "Revolutionary Mutations" and "Virtual Sex." The shopping-mall metaphor is quite self-consciously
deployed because, according to Sirius, "commerce is the ocean information
swims in" (16); unapologetically libertarian, *Mondo 2000* evokes and huckster-
izes an elect audience of posthuman youth consumers, cyberbeings of undying
pubescence, with an unquenchable appetite for commodified prostheses, given
to restlessly cruising the electronic mallworlds of information.

Vivian Sobchack, in an excellent essay, has indicted the magazine's confla-
tion of utopian aspiration and advertising hype, arguing that its pervasive tone
of "optimistic cynicism" merely serves to advance, "under the guise of pop-
ulism, . . . a romantic, swashbuckling, irresponsible individualism" that pack-
ages teen rebellion for corporate purposes ("New Age" 18). While *Mondo 2000's*
vision appeals, according to Sobchack, to a pseudo-hip corps of "New Age Mutant Ninja Hackers," she traces as well the journal's oddly ambivalent attitude
toward the prosthetic enhancements it so avidly chronicles. In its giddy dreams
of bodily transcendence through high-tech consumption, *Mondo 2000* seems to
express—and perhaps to articulate among its readers—a "contradictory desire
which is, at one and the same time, both utopian and dystopian, self-preserva-

tional and self-exterminating" (22). For all its celebratory rhetoric, the magazine's posthuman vision bears with it a pronounced dark side, an anxiety that the vast potential of high technology may actually prove predatory rather than empowering.

"Pretty Boy Crossover" brings this dark side of posthumanist fantasy more fully into the open. The story involves an attempt, by a group of sinister corporate agents, to persuade a sixteen-year-old "Pretty Boy"—the story's unnamed protagonist—to join his former friend Bobby on "a whole new plane of reality" (135). This plot plays out in a chic urban nightclub filled with various subcultural types, such as "Mohawks" and "Rudeboys," but it is the Pretty Boy contingent in particular who find themselves targeted for uploading, since their heartbreaking physical beauty makes them powerfully effective spokespersons for the process. Cadigan's Pretty Boy feels the draw of this attraction himself when Bobby, now a famous video star at the club, calls out to him from a huge screen above the dance floor: "It's beautiful in here. The dreams can be as real as you want them to be" (132). Later, after the corporate agents arrange a private meeting between them, Bobby reminds his friend that uploaded life is the apotheosis of every Pretty Boy fantasy, since it preserves forever the bloom of youth that the subculture's members narcissistically worship in themselves.

For his part, the protagonist already knows this all too well. Earlier, upon entering the club, he had mused that, in two or three years, his own beauty would have faded just enough for the bouncer at the door to deny him admission; the only alternative seems to be the "endless hot season, endless youth" offered by the "Pretty Boy Heaven" of living information. At the same time, he considers this "a failing in himself, that he likes being Pretty and chased" (130); moreover, he suspects that the putative boon of uploaded existence—heightened sensation, expanded consciousness—is a mere delusion circulated by the corporation to disguise the fact that this new life form involves an epochal loss of the deep pleasures of embodied experience. The corporation, in effect, is using the compelling ideology of high-tech consumption literally to consume its youthful prey, playing upon the Pretty Boys' desire to "get [themselves] remixed in the extended dance version" (132) to transform them into information commodities immured in a meaningless dreamworld. That this supposedly wondrous change actually amounts to a terrible privation is indicated by the resonant acronym the corporation uses to identify the promised end state: "S-A-D," or "Self-Aware Data" (136). Indeed, the underlying tone of the story is deeply elegiac, as Cadigan's Pretty Boy mourns not merely his own ebbing youth but, more importantly, the arrogant self-absorption that has led Bobby to desert his friends in favor of a simulated immortality. At the end, he flees the club, reveling in his fleshly capacity to feel the winter chill and resolutely determined to protect this fragile shell from the essentially cannibalistic schemes of the corporation.

Standing behind this principled renunciation of a computerized false paradise is the signal example of Case's rejection, in William Gibson's novel *Neuromancer* (1984), of a simulated eternity of bliss with his dead lover, Linda Lee. This basic narrative set-up—a flawed protagonist's ironically noble rejection of the seductive pull of cybernetic transmutation—provides the classic temptation scene in the cyberpunk bible, and resistance to such quasi-satanic enticement stands as a character's (and writer's) affirmation that, even amid a world fallen into hyperreality, the primal verities of the embodied self endure and must be obeyed. In particular, what Cadigan's protagonist resists is the self-objectifying vanity with which the corporation baits its hook, the Pretty Boy's irrepressible fascination for "the clubs, the admiration, the lust of strangers for his personal magic" (137). This narcissistic appeal, converging as it does with the strategies of high-tech consumption, functions as the screen for a predatory system that seeks nothing less than the conscription and consequent erasure of embodied experience. In classic "if this goes on" fashion, the story extrapolates the ethicopolitical implications of the posthumanist promotion of virtual reality technologies, suggesting that full-body perceptual immersion in an artificial environment is only a short step away from disposal of the body altogether.

Virtual Reality systems that use head-mounted displays, data gloves, body-suits, and other sense-simulating apparatuses tend, as Michael Heim has pointed out, to produce a condition in which "the primary body giv[es] way to the priority of a cyberbody. . . . The user undergoes a high-powered interiorization of a virtual environment but in the process loses self-awareness" (72). N. Katherine Hayles, in a brilliant analysis, has shown how this technological "disappearance" of the body was authorized by foundational assumptions of cybernetics discourse, such as Norbert Wiener's famous claim that the human person, being only a complex pattern of information, could conceivably be de-materialized and transmitted as an electronic signal. While Wiener had assumed that "a hypothetical receiving instrument could re-embody these messages in appropriate matter, capable of continuing the processes already in the body and mind"—a thought experiment he refers to explicitly as science fiction (Wiener 96)—Cadigan dispenses with the need for a specifically physical embodiment, reconstituting her Pretty Boys exclusively within a digital domain. In short, she takes the visions of VR experts a step farther: if the "basic job of cyberspace technology, besides simulating a world, is to supply a tight feedback loop between patron [human user] and puppet [data construct], to give the patron the illusion of being literally embodied by the puppet," as Randal Walser has argued (35), then Cadigan assumes a loop so immediate and intense that the puppet essentially *becomes* the patron, whose continued existence is no longer required.

While of course the body cannot be so readily conjured away (and, in fact, VR systems have had great trouble simulating some forms of sensory input, such as the tactile or olfactory),[1] Cadigan's story may be read as a warning against what Arthur Kroker has called the "will to virtuality" that underwrites the fantasies of disembodiment circulating within contemporary cyberculture (*Data Trash* 5). Indeed, Kroker's description of the psychosocial implications of VR technologies sounds like an analytic gloss on "Pretty Boy Crossover": "A cold and antiseptic world of technologically constituted power where virtual experience means the sudden shutting down of a whole range of human experiences. . . . [T]he body floats away from itself, and in that universe of digital impulses finally alienates itself from its own life functions." According to Kroker, this epochal alienation merely brings to fruition the cyborg interface between postwar consumers and the machineries of electronic culture, climaxing a "libidinal descent into this sea of liquid media populated by organs without bodies . . . where our bodies migrate daily, and especially nightly, to be processed and re-sequenced" (*Spasm* 41–42).

Unsurprisingly, Kroker identifies Jean Baudrillard, with his theories of simulation and the social hegemony of the "code," as the major prophet of VR experience, a mantle Baudrillard himself has taken up in an essay entitled "The Virtual Illusion." In characteristically provocative fashion, Baudrillard claims that the elaborate apparatus of VR is entirely unnecessary, since the social realm we occupy is already a simulation through and through: "We don't need digital gloves or a digital suit. As we are, we are moving around in the world as in a synthesized image" (97). His argument in this essay builds on his earlier studies of telematic culture, such as "The Ecstasy of Communication," which had claimed that "as soon as behavior is crystallized on certain screens and operational terminals, what's left appears only as a large useless body, deserted and condemned" (129). In Baudrillard's analysis, television has already, through its integration of viewers/consumers into a matrix of information whose coded processes usurp their autonomous will and prescribe their deepest desires, accomplished much of what virtual reality seems to portend for Cadigan. This enwebbing code has transformed human subjects into functional extensions of the networked grid conceived as a vast social automaton, a factory of consumption. The disembodied, cybernautical "telepresence" of VR, then, is just a microcosm of the larger processes of disappearance that have marked contemporary consumer culture—the cynical, irreversible, profit-driven "translation of all our acts, of all historical events, of all material substance and energy into pure information" ("Virtual Illusion" 101).

For Baudrillard this is of course quite baleful (if also quite fascinating), and I think he has overstated his case. But his extravagant claims do point to a key problem in the deployment of VR technologies in a capitalist context—namely, their unusually puissant ability to objectify subjectivity. In the words of Tim McFadden, "If human connection to cyberspace with everydaylike qualities of experience becomes widespread, then the interface that provides the experience—say, a cyberdeck—becomes a quantifiable metric of human experience as well as a commodity. *Experience will become a substance and a commodity*" (337;

emphasis in original). The apparent capacity of VR to replace the spontaneity of direct perception with a pliable synthetic duplicate, mediated by computer interfaces, thus lends itself to applications that shape and funnel consciousness into commodified dreamworlds. These artificial realms, if they do not entirely usurp human autonomy as Baudrillard suggests, function to deepen what Stuart and Elizabeth Ewen have called the "channels of desire" that link consumers with commodity culture; the result involves a quasi-automation of preference patterns and decision-making processes, allowing for more efficient corporate targeting and exploitation of markets. As Sean Cubitt has observed, "[N]etworked subjectivity, from the standpoint of the market, has no desires, needs or goals other than to respond to market choices, and to feed back, through them, into corporate information flows" (132).

What this shows is that the promise of high technology—in this case, its achievement of "networked subjectivity," a collective nexus foretokening powerful new forms of interactive sociality[2]—always bears, under capitalism, the shadow of domination. But, *contra* Baudrillard, this domination is not a necessary outcome of the technology itself but rather a deformation of the progressive possibilities latent in the apparatus, whose cyborg energies have been turned, vampirically, against the consumers who generate and sustain them. In this context, an argument that Cubitt makes about remote satellite sensing can fruitfully be adapted to grasp the social logic of virtual reality: while this new technology offers an unparalleled global extension of human vision, "the actual form that that perception takes is overdetermined by a social order which, while capable of innovation on a massive scale, is constantly forced to drag it down to highly specific goals. . . . The truth of its findings can only be validated by success assessed according to criteria which inhere only in the present of corporate capital. The success criterion asserts the continuing validity of the present's unequal and impoverished social order into the future" (56–57).

The challenge for critics is to arraign this system in the name of the technology's buried but real utopian potential, though Cubitt—following the views of Theodor Adorno and Ernst Bloch—believes that "the point of this emergent future is that it cannot be defined, described or delimited. To give utopia a content is to deny its freedom, its autonomy from the purposes of the present." All we can know is that this radical prosthetic expansion of the human sensorium deserves to be judged by "a yardstick of values distinct from the goal-oriented future of remote sensing operated as a mimetic-speculative management of the future" (56-57). Likewise, the ludic cyborg powers that VR seems to bestow on its users must be liberated from the narrowly instrumental, profit-driven applications to which it has so far been subordinated, even if we cannot determine in advance the specific future its unleashed capacity may construct. The alternative is acquiescence to a system in which every machinic amplification of consumer agency involves a further ramification of hegemonic control.

It is precisely this difficult dialectical vision that cyberpunk science fic-

tion—especially those texts that project the future development of VR technologies—manages to capture and express. While cyberpunk texts do not
shrink from envisioning the most scathingly dystopian uses to which these systems may be put by a regnant consumer capitalism, they also suggest, if at
times only vaguely and haltingly, a higher calling implicit in their structure and
operation. For example, cyberpunk excels at critiquing the invidious reification
of subjectivity that VR allows, spawning a series of extrapolations (along the
lines of Cadigan's concept of "Self-Aware Data") that depict the commodified
simulation of human functions, from the "wetware personae" of Michael
Swanwick's *Vacuum Flowers* (1987) to the "franchise personalities" of Norman
Spinrad's *Little Heroes* (1987) to the plug-in "moddies" of George Alec Effinger's
When Gravity Fails (1986). Perhaps the most famous of such instances is
Neuromancer's "data construct," Dixie Flatline, the software duplicate of a crafty
hacker whose knowledge and skills are now copyrighted corporate property.
As David Brande remarks, "his very existence . . . has been thoroughly and
explicitly commodified—reduced to a principle of exchange, of pure iteration
and reiteration. Dixie is the refined and abstracted 'free' laborer, the 'embodiment' of the logic of alienation" (95). Yet, once Dixie has been liberated from the
corporation's vaults by Case and his hacker allies, his know-how is turned
against capitalist authority, helping to free an Artificial Intelligence from arbitrary corporate constraints placed on its development; released into cyberspace,
this entity's future evolution remains unclear in the novel, but according to
Case, at least "it'll *change* something" (260). This obscure yet insistent utopian
aspiration, inscribed in the otherwise enchained products of information technology, suggests that VR's pernicious objectification of experience is balanced
by a dormant transformative energy awaiting its momentous mobilization.

This potential for subversion of the authorized meanings and uses of VR
technology is generally crystallized, throughout the cyberpunk canon, in ambivalent figures of mutant youth. Usually these pubescent cyborgs are the stories' heroes—for example, the footloose hacker street punks in Cadigan's novel
Synners (1991), John Shirley's rock-and-roll anarchists in his Song Called Youth
trilogy (1987–90), Bruce Sterling's *Artificial Kid* (1980)—but at times their inability fully to command their evolving powers makes them into semivillains: for
example, Gibson's shadowy silicon intelligences coming to dawning self-
awareness in his "cyberspace" novels (1984–88) or the wildly out-of-control
teen-machines in the films *Akira* (1987) and *Tetsuo: The Iron Man* (1991). For all
their differences, these various figures share a number of important characteristics: they are enabled by institutional forms of power—sometimes being directly created or employed by state or corporate interests—while at the same
time functioning as wild-card agents with some (often inscrutable) degree of
autonomy; they are marked as pugnacious if not militant generational rebels,
allied with advances in technology that their cynical forebears are attempting

either to impede or to coopt; and their intimate prosthetic relation with machines and data interfaces, which permits brilliant flights of technosocial improvisation, bears with it a deep unease, since this cyborg capacity is obscurely
complicit with the predatory system they seek to resist. The inchoate but irresistible urge to free the utopian potential of these mutant-youth figures forms
the underlying narrative impetus in a number of recent cyberpunk texts.

Three novels in particular—Pat Cadigan's *Tea from an Empty Cup* (1998),
Marc Laidlaw's *Kalifornia* (1993), and Richard Calder's *Cythera* (1998)—brilliantly extrapolate this narrative template specifically in the context of a media-
saturated, near-future youth culture dominated by VR technologies. Cadigan's
novel adopts an initially less radical premise than her earlier short story, es-
chewing the possibility of literal disembodiment in favor of an investigation
of the psychosocial effects of conventional VR systems using helmet displays
and "hotsuits." Called here Artificial Reality (or AR), the technology is wildly
popular, spawning an entire entertainment industry in which consumers pay to
rent equipment in AR parlors, where they lie immersed in vivid computer-
game scenarios. The plot follows two dovetailing strands, as a young woman
namedYuki Harami searches through the AR landscape of "post-Apocalyptic
Noo Yawk Sitty" for her vanished friend Tom Iguchi while police detective
Dore Konstantin enters the same simulation to investigate the death of an AR
user who may in fact be the luckless Tom. This young victim, found dead in
an AR booth with his throat cut, joins several other recently deceased users
who seem to have succumbed to "Gameplayers' stigmata" (40)—a supposedly
mythical "disease" in which the patron's immobilized body manifests the
same wounds inflicted on its online avatar. Thus, following the example of
Neuromancer and Neal Stephenson's 1992 novel, *Snow Crash*, *Tea from an Empty
Cup* depicts a situation in which events in cyberspace can be dangerous and
even fatal to the real-world self.

This threat derives from the "intense authenticity" (96) of the simulated experience: "There was no such thing as a minor sensation in AR; every feeling
was realized in a way that was utterly complete, no aspect neglected. Because it
was customized, measured out to order for your senses alone" (173–74). There
are even rumors of the existence of a "Climax Envelope" for simulated sexual
exchanges, in which the hotsuit "mirrored the wearer's own nerves," thus indi-
vidualizing the encounter in an intimate and powerful way (65). The standard-
issue gear alone can generate overwhelmingly convincing experiences: enthusiastic players of an AR "module" called *Gang Wars*, for example, have to be
strapped down for fear that they will "go native" and, in their flailing about,
damage the equipment (38). Both Yuki and Konstantin are relative newcomers
to AR "netgaming," and each finds herself stunned by its compelling sensual
immediacy. Yuki gasps to "feel the nerve endings closest to the surface of her
fingers responding to the stimuli, absorbing it all greedily and demanding

more" (134), while Konstantin, trapped in a street riot, is beaten to the point where the simulated pain, conveyed through "the jazzy high-res authenticity of the 'suit,'" seems to go "deeper, all the way down to the level where what remained of the reptile senses sorted real from unreal" (206).

The rhetoric of avarice and violence in these passages is linked, in Cadigan's treatment, both to the commercialized objectification of perception and motor reflex that AR achieves and to the enveloping presence of capitalist imperatives in its allegedly leisure-time scenarios. Not only is the user charged for online time consumed, but numerous special features—such as the ability to morph the shape of one's puppet—are available for additional surcharges; the incessant promotional blather of software icons hawking these various options prompts Yuki at one point to remark that "[e]very other word out of anyone's mouth has something to do with billable rates" (108). Indeed, not only do users interact with personified sales pitches that cannot initially be distinguished from puppets controlled by living patrons, but they can even be recruited by advertisers to serve as icons themselves if their puppets are deemed sufficiently engaging and fashionable. Besides aspiring to this spurious "immortality" as walking talking advertisements, hardcore users also yearn to interact with the netgaming "elite," patrons who operate at advanced levels owing to their ability to pay higher rates and who occasionally deign to permit lower-level players access to their chic, exclusive simulations. These acts of miraculous largesse mirror the plot of "Pretty Boy Crossover," in which a favored few are elected to be "VIP[s] at some worthless club that isn't even real, doing things that aren't real with people who aren't real, getting some status that isn't real" (136)—as Yuki scathingly puts it.

Ironically, this online hierarchy merely reproduces the real-world class system from which so many of AR's users seek to escape. In her investigation, Konstantin encounters numerous AR addicts trapped in "the same kinds of no-brainer file and data upkeep jobs," sorry microserfs living in "urban hives" (85) for whom AR is both an anodyne to the numbing tedium of their everyday lives and a longed-for chance to see themselves as being "in the game with the name and the fame" (92). These sad-sack losers make easy marks for various kinds of online ripoffs, falling prey again and again to the "Shopper's Credo" that "[a]nything worth paying for is worth over-paying for" (163). In Tom's case, he falls prey to something more sinister—a "vampiric sequence" in which a shadowy, feral entity attacks him and drinks his blood (53-54), leading to his instantaneous real-world demise. In context, this brutal act of vampirism may be read, symbolically, as the exploitative animus of the commercial system to which his leisure has been fanatically devoted; as Yuki observes, Tom was one of those users who "would rather pursue a nonexistent Grail through an imaginary world than try to sustain a real life in a real place" (112–13) and for whom the ideal job would be "AR tester. . . . Like the sort of thing you dreamed about when you were a kid, consumer tester for Toyz U Krave, or whatever the company was called" (133). It would seem, considering Tom's dire fate, that the toys he craved craved him as well.

Given this systematic colonization of Artificial Reality by the norms of a predatory capitalism, one might assume that the deep conviction on the part of avid netplayers that "*AR is humanity's true destiny*" (83; emphasis in original) merely bespeaks the hypnotic effects of a regime that has reified their senses and thus dominates their desires. The whispered fascination of users' quest for the "Out Door" in AR scenarios—"Out. *Out.* Over the rainbow, Never-Never Land, where you go and you'll stay," as one fan dreamily remarks (87; emphasis in original)—might register no more than the programmed pleasure of locating hidden "subroutines" in the games' design, thus gaining the specious rank of an expert player. One icon admits as much to Konstantin, claiming that its job, when speaking of "the mythical Out Door," is "to stimulate a little thrill here and there, play to their curiosities and their fondest wishes and desires" (187). Yet even this huckster's rhetoric acknowledges a utopian dimension to the lure, a sense of the transformative potential built into the technology, despite its currently impoverished commercial form. Overcoming her initial skepticism, Konstantin begins to experience the emotional pull of this obscure promise herself, finally deciding that AR "really was bigger than it looked from *out there*, and it wasn't just what they—whoever 'they' were supposed to be—wanted you to believe, it was truer than most people imagined. Because most people seemed to imagine only amusement parks like post-Apocalyptic Noo Yawk Sitty and if that was all they wanted, you couldn't make them want more" (235; emphasis in original). Thus, a failure of popular imagination joins hands with the cynical regime of commodified entertainment culture to hobble the true potential of an extraordinary technology, to turn its prosthetic empowerments to vampiric ends.

The utopian appeal of AR is focused, in the story, in the person—or, rather, the puppet—of Body Sativa, a mysterious online celebrity whose richly playful name suggests both a "higher" form of embodiment (in the pun on cannabis) and veritably godlike enlightenment (in the pun on Bodhisattva). When Yuki finally does meet up with this elusive guru—on an accelerated AR plane accessed via a unique "cocktail" of adrenalin and designer drugs—she is told that the media corporations' plans for Artificial Reality are in the process of being radically subverted: "It doesn't matter what they intended, anyway. Something else is happening, something they didn't bargain for" (217). While Cadigan's resolution of this plot strand is ultimately disappointing and even a little silly—Body Sativa turns out to be the ghost of Yuki's long-dead grandmother, whose brain had been used experimentally to map out the neural pathways of the hotsuit and who has now undertaken to re-create online the lost ethnic paradise of "Old Japan"—her thematic treatment of the dialectical contrast between dystopian and utopian applications of virtual reality is brilliantly rendered.

Specifically, this contrast plays out in two variant strategies by which AR patrons are subjected to remote control manipulation via their online puppets. The dystopian strategy has been pioneered by the "whoremaster" Joy Flower, a creepy media star with a predilection for youthful cyberflesh who has discovered a way to commandeer the avatars of her devoted "Joy's Boyz" in order to directly access and steer their perceptions. Her use of this technique suggests, in context, a decadent sadomasochistic game in which the patron's immobile body is "invaded, penetrated, and permeated by some force that intended to *use* you, from the inside out" (238; emphasis in original). Once online, Yuki finds herself subjected to this literally skin-crawling control, "as if she herself . . . were somebody else's clothing" (179) to be donned and discarded; when she feels her virtual body respond to Joy Flower's distant signal, it is as if someone were "[m]olesting her gross motor movements" (141). In contrast with this debasing surrender of agency, Body Sativa's puppeteering of Yuki seems not a loss but an amplification of self, "as if someone else were sharing the suit with her by some remote access . . . a demonstration of skill and grace, control and cooperation" (219). Conveying a powerful message that "you don't have to do it alone" (231), the experience suggests that the fabled Out Door may actually be "a Door In for something else entirely . . . something strange and new and, before now, completely unknown, and then everything would change" (247). Just as *Neuromancer*'s freeing of the AI seemed to foretoken the purging reformation of a corrupted cyberspace, so the appearance of this collective prosthetic agency promises a redemption of virtual reality from its degraded (and degrading) capitalist form, a redemption that holds out hope for the utopian transformation of reality itself.

When Tom Iguchi's hotsuit is stripped off his dead body after his final traumatic immersion in AR, inscribed on his skin is "a dense pattern of lines and shapes . . . from the wires and sensors in the 'suit," leading Konstantin to muse that "[t]hey'll start calling that the latest thing in nervous systems. . . . They'll give it a jumped-up name, like neo-exo-nervous system, and they'll say it's generated by hotsuit wear, every line and shape having a counterpart on the opposite side of the skin barrier" (36; emphasis in original). This momentary idle fantasy becomes the narrative reality of Marc Laidlaw's novel *Kalifornia*, in which VR technology, rather than being externally worn, is literally sewn into the body in the form of a network of artificial nerves. These "polynerves" or "livewires" permit their owners to access media broadcasts in their own heads, experiences that fill their senses and stimulate response in the same way that immersive VR does. Most folks' systems are set to "Receive Only," but it is also possible to be a "Sender," transmitting one's direct perceptions as signals across the media "wireways" for the pleasure of others. This new sort of "live" programming is, in fact, the main form of mass entertainment in this high-tech near-future world.

The main characters are members of the Figueroa family, a popular celebrity household along the lines of the Bradys and the Partridges—the difference being that this group is really kin and their show a combination of sitcom and TV verité. Actually, when the novel opens, the program has been off the wires for several years, the only family member with an active career being daughter Poppy, who now stars in her own spin-off, a suspense melodrama. In order to boost ratings, Poppy is persuaded to give birth "live" to the first infant born with wires, its implants inserted while still in the womb. Like Lucy Ricardo's famous TV pregnancy, this one is a hit, but the chase scenario in which the birth occurs is so chaotic that it results in the child's being mysteriously kidnapped. Determined to recover her baby, Poppy pursues a series of clues that reveal her own director-producer had conspired in the grab, but before she can inform the authorities, she is struck down by a speeding truck and sent into a coma. Meanwhile, her kid brother, nineteen-year-old Sandy, undertakes his own quest for the baby—named Calafia in honor of the imminent bicentennial of California's statehood—which leads him into contact with a shadowy cult who, he soon discovers, has stolen the child in the conviction that her unique status as a livewire birth marks her as the incarnation of Kali, the Hindu goddess of destruction.

If this initial summary makes the novel sound like a wacky satire, it is. Most of the humor focuses on Sandy's situation as a former teen idol who has settled down into a typical West Coast lifestyle of surfing, smoking dope, and watching TV—or, in this case, riding the wires, "his body channels switch[ing] at random" (26). Like everyone else in this hyperreal future, Sandy's nervous system is awash in "a polluted ether of advertising and you-are-there game shows. Bad media lurked in his polynerves like an Alzheimer's prion, waiting to crystallize" (26). Entertainment culture has literally invaded consumers' cells, as they find themselves directly interpellated into commercials and, during comedy programs, can feel their "diaphragm[s] convulsing with canned laughter" (27). The vampiric aspects of this process are revealed by a hallucinatory ad for "Dr. Batori's Magical Youth Formula"—a potion of ersatz blood applied to the skin, following the therapeutic method of the infamous Countess Elizabeth Batori (often seen as a prototype for the literary and cinematic vampire).

The main difference between Sandy and other media consumers is that he alone is likely, during his wireway wanderings, to stumble into the objectified points of view of his own family members as they struggle with some vaguely comical crisis or another in repeats of the *Figueroa Show*. *Kalifornia* thus takes Cadigan's vision of reified subjectivity one step farther: in Sandy's case, not only has his life been systematically commodified, but it is even sold back to him as late-night reruns. Moreover, Sandy's budding livewired sexuality was an intense focus of teeny-bopper lust, such that he "couldn't so much as scratch his crotch without exciting legions of horny teenage wire-hoppers" (35–36). The night he lost his virginity, for example, his partner, secretly wired to Send, broadcast the experience; afterwards, the fanzines were "full of lush, overblown, almost worshipful descriptions of the act. SUPERSEX WITH THE SAND-MAN! It was recorded and duplicated and traded among the teenie fans while Sandy went crazy with embarrassment" (40). Now the boy finds himself both alienated from his former showbiz-mediated life—which "had been a string of situations dreamed up by a board of 'creative consultants' and then enlarged upon and improvised by his family"—and yearning still for that lost audience connection, for the golden time before "the wires went dead and everyone thought of [him] forever in that frozen zone of rerun adolescence" (30–31).

To return to the plot, the Daughters of Kali who have stolen Calafia arrange to have a complex prosthetic shell constructed for her by the Celestial Mechanics, another obscure sect of hardware tinkerers who "felt that much practical knowledge had been lost through disuse" (153). Owing their "allegiance to the future, to the developing machine," the Mechanics believe technology to be "a tremendous force for democracy someday, after the bumps and kinks are ironed out" (155-56). To this end, they have built the multiarmed metal-and-plastic prosthesis, as part of their commitment to fabricate "special bodies . . . that would help us travel through the social realm . . . carry us safely and humanely. . . . Machines that allowed us to be real human beings" (157). Unfortunately, once the Daughters of Kali acquire the intricate exoskeleton, they set off a chain of events that turns the entire machine culture to inhuman uses. This all begins when they install the baby Calafia in the driver's seat, from which position the budding prodigy—who has, thanks to the accelerating impetus of her inborn wires, already begun to speak and think—declares herself the goddess Kalifornia and determines to take over the world.

Because Kali's infant brain is "part polymatter, like the nerves" (183), she is able—like Joy Flower and Body Sativa in Cadigan's novel—to enter telepathically into the livewired nervous systems of others and manipulate them directly, a process Kali refers to as "wearing people" (169). She exercises this power first on her uncle, Sandy, turning him into a kind of zombie that "banged around the room unsteadily, walking into walls" (186); soon, by accessing the database of a corporate security firm, she has mobilized a phalanx of well-armed drones who become her personal bodyguards. Controlling this seemingly omnipotent child becomes a challenge for several factions in the novel, all of whom see her as "a potent tool. She has the body of a child, yes, but she has the powers of a goddess and the heart of a network executive" (183–84); through her, it should be possible to fulfill a totalitarian dream implicit in the capitalist consumer system: not merely to influence, but actually to command, the audience's every action. As Kali extends her growing mastery through the networked livewires, "waking up inside of everyone," she begins to feel "as if someone were waking up and looking around inside of *her*" (217). Suddenly, she finds her powers usurped by this intruder and her consciousness shunted off into a VR playground from which she can find no exit.

This mysterious plotter, it turns out, is the redoubtable Thaxter H. J. Half-jest, the Reverend Governor of California, a figure who, until this point, had seemed merely an amiable political hack. Halfjest is the first continuously "live" politician, always "open to the opinions of his audience, occasionally re-versing the flow to look in on their lives and listen to their opinions. This was the perpetual promise of the wires: the simultaneous involvement of all citi-zens" (38). In fact, however, the setup is a sham, the governor merely providing the masses with an illusion of collective participation; his real goals are consid-erably more sinister, as becomes clear when he hijacks Kali's souped-up ner-vous system in order to found "a horrible regime—something beyond tyranny or fascism—unimaginably worse than anything the world had seen before" (229). While Laidlaw's conclusion of his story is, as in Cadigan's novel, disap-pointing—the comatose Poppy, alerted to her daughter's plight by maternal telepathy (a natural connection contrasted with the ersatz empathy of the wires), joins Sandy to defeat Halfjest's maniacal plot—his treatment nonethe-less amounts to a potent allegory of the cyborg powers inherent in high-tech consumption and the way they have been perverted, under capitalism, into predatory tools to be used against consumers themselves.

Indeed, the central image of the book—a prosthetically empowered child literally installed at the center of a vast machinic network, whose enhanced ca-pacities foreshadow momentous new forms of collective life—provides a com-pelling crystallization of the utopian implications of youth consumption. Though the novel ultimately arranges a neo-Luddite resolution—Sandy has his wires surgically removed, and the mass audience, after the foiling of Halfjest's schemes, reverts to less threatening media such as television—there are mo-ments when the utopian possibilities latent in cyborg youth, in the vision of "a small child at the heart of the enormous cold contraption" (237), are stirringly evoked. The technodemocratic world-view of the Celestial Mechanics, for ex-ample, includes a prophetic belief in a future sociality radically cleansed and transformed by tutelary machines: "Who knows what interpersonal realms we might have entered by then: strange places we can hardly picture now" (158). Moreover, despite its retro affirmation of natural bonds, the story's climax, with Poppy saving Calafia from her VR imprisonment, reveals the redemptive po-tential of technological networks, as every interconnected viewer, "every last wired soul, received a mother's comfort. . . . And like Kali many of them wept when they heard that everything would be all right" (238).

This consoling maternal message humanizes an apparatus that, until now, had been given over exclusively to vampiric exploitation under the cynical guise of entertainment and consumerist pleasure. Yet this false paradise of "Li-bidopolis" (a term coined by one of the novel's characters as an alternative

name for the media-saturated hyperreality of California) contains within its
manifold false promises an irrepressible utopian yearning—as all consumers,
for one brief moment, recognize their implicit bond of kinship, "switching on
all at once, innumerable combinations creating a new personality, a thing different and greater than any of them" alone (228). It is this sort of ambiguous affirmation of cyborg potential, in the context of a consumer youth culture
deformed by a logic of vampirism, at which cyberpunk, I think uniquely among
contemporary discourses, excels.

Richard Calder's *Cythera* builds upon Cadigan's and Laidlaw's yearning
utopian animus in a richly imaginative way. Set in roughly the same future history as his earlier Dead trilogy,[3] *Cythera*'s plot is enormously complicated, but
at its heart lies the quest for the eponymous wonderland, a dreamy site that
represents the longed-for fusion of "Earth Prime" (a.k.a. our mundane world)
and "Earth2," "that world encoded within the shimmering, atomic structures of
magazine covers, advertisement hoardings, movie flyposters, the screens of
TVs, VCs, and PCs: another universe, a hyperuniverse that interpenetrated our
own" (30). This "interpenetration" is more than mere metaphor: the basic speculative thrust of *Cythera* is that crossover traffic has become literally possible.
Celebrity "eidolons" can be translated, by their fetishizing fans, into lumines-
cent flesh, while these fans can aspire—through the wonders of nanotechnolog-
ically augmented VR machines with "uploading" capacities—to achieve
resurrection in the "new flesh" of simulated being. This crossover traffic passes
through "The Wound," a dimensional gateway that teen hackers secretly access
to disport with their favorite simulacral superstars, sentient information systems spontaneously hatched from the multiplied images of fleshly celebrities.
Yet this intercourse is constrained both by a diurnal cycle—the Wound opens
only at night, while by day the eidolons slumber in cyberspatial "coffins"—and
by a grim authoritarianism that vigorously polices adolescent leisure, seeking
to shield teen consumers from "possession" by the vampiric eidolons.

Calder brilliantly projects a future in which claims to protect young people
from consumerist fantasy actually rationalize an "undeclared war against children" (21), whose desires, entwined with commodity culture, terrify their parents. This "Great Fear" of "a child's autonomy and all it represents: the ungovernable tide of the imagination" (65) has spawned a sinister regime of surrogate "stepfathers," puritanical robotic guardians who unceasingly monitor
teenagers' consumption practices, searching for signs of emerging obsession,
for kids "corrupted by too much [Net] surfing, too many violent *anime*" (11). In-
corrigible cases are packed off to dreary concentration camps, such as the deso-
late "Boys Town" in the wastes of Antarctica, to be "deprogrammed." Meanwhile, an underground subculture of "ghost karaokes" has sprung up to service teen runaways' Earth2 fixations, offering safe havens where eidolons and
their fans can freely mingle. Yet these assignations are achingly fleeting, always

under threat from the lurking "Censors" and their "world of surveillance, of prohibition, of cheated desire" (53). Thus has arisen the dream of Cythera, "a place where the real and the artificial became indistinguishable" (15), which offers the promise of overcoming the painful dualism between quotidian life and ideal image in a higher "dialectic[al] . . . synthesis" (15); there, youth and eidolon can coexist beyond the grasp of a "hypercapitalist" regime that seeks to divide them and to profit from this division.

Calder effectively demonstrates the hypocrisy of patriarchal capitalism's mobilization of teens as consumers: while this conscription ensures profits for the culture industries responsible for producing the glittering pleasures of the "fibersphere," it also provokes moralistic attacks by religious and "family values" advocates, who demonize the adolescent as *"Nature's great libertine . . . mad with the limitless presumption of desire"* (84; emphasis in original). A surreptitiously seductive economic appeal to children might have been acceptable, but when personified commodities literally lust after youthful consumers, luring them into "dildonic" liaisons at interactive online sites and in decadent VR parlors, then something has to be done to preserve their threatened innocence. Specifically, the Censors sponsor an International Data Subliminal Interdiction Commission, whose goal is to "cauterize" the Wound, shutting down the crossover passage that links teens and eidolons in a dangerous complicity. In short, youthful consumers must be forcibly divided from the commodities they have subjectified with their own animating desires, maintained in a state of separation lest, together, the two conspire to disrupt the cozy reign of hypercapitalists and stepfathers alike.

The utopian impulse to overcome this division suggests a more or less explicit project of consumer revolt, in which the alienated desire objectified in Earth2's eidolons is expropriated from the media elite and restored to its rightful owners. Standing opposed to this radical reintegration are not only the prim Censors, with their fanatical clampdown on adolescent fantasy, but adult consumers as well, whose dreamy eroticization of a reified "youth"—expressed in their eagerness to "buy back the innocence they had never had" through the purchase of "the magic fetishes by which entry to childhood's kingdom might be reattained" (26)—underwrites the division in the first place. Significantly, teens who have been successfully deprogrammed, their haunting eidolons exorcised and their desires channeled into dutifully repressed practices of consumption, are referred to as being "dispossessed," thus suggesting the confiscation and containment of their very subjectivity. By contrast, those who resist this process, rebelling against the "rules of desire" (21) in order to reclaim "the empowering child of the autonomous imagination" (67), are treated as implacable threats to social order.

Calder's rapturous invocation of young consumers as incipient revolutionaries is crystallized in two major subplots. First, there is the "Children's Crusade," a desperate march on Europe's high-fashion citadels by impoverished hordes of literally dispossessed youth aching to share in the seeming boon of the capitalist fibersphere. Yet this assault, while it points up the class-based limits of consumerist affluence, does not really threaten the exploitative logic of consumption, since these "dead-end kids" (56) seek only to join in the vacuous fun, to enter the beckoning mallworld of "insubstantial glitter that, in the end, neither would nor could give them anything" (25). In the words of a teen activist who fruitlessly attempts to deflect the Crusade's energies into more critical directions, "their struggle was but a war for hamburgers and coke, for the homogeneity of the globalized media, for a mass cultural haemorrhaging that would leave them as vampires, the living dead" (230).

By contrast, those who gather to form the "Army of Revolutionary Flesh" conceive their mission in a more radical way—as a utopian redemption of the historical project of high-tech consumption. Yes, these teens know that they have grown addicted to images, that they are the potential puppets of a global elite, that the price of entertaining crossover fantasies is to be cursed with a seemingly unquenchable longing linked ultimately to the profiteering imperatives of hyperconsumerism—"the little dream machines that twiddled the knobs and switches of my consciousness" (17), as one of them puts it. The emptiness of this consumerist false paradise, which lures only to trap and disappoint, is emphasized by the grasping ambitions of the "gynoid" Kito, who vends fleshly fantasy to image-addicted consumers in order to build her own vain empire: "Consumer demand!" she opines. "The only constant in our sick, sick world!" (141) Yet the response of the "revolutionary fleshers" is not a peremptory rejection of the cynical blandishments of consumption but rather a determined quest to transform its false promises into the wished-for domain of Cythera, where the "consuming ache" (272) will at last be soothed and the "Wound" dividing Earth Prime and Earth2 finally healed.

While the specific reality of Cythera is never fully assayed, its lyrical evocation as a "land of masques and bergomasques, of enchantment, of moonlight, calm, sad, and beautiful, where life was a perpetual *fête galante*" (172) suggests a redemptive realm of youthful play freed from both the tyrannical surveillance of the Censors and the exploitative aims of the Toymakers, a world where children reclaim "the power adults exercise so arbitrarily over their bodies and minds" (242). Indeed, Cythera functions in the text as a galvanizing fantasy of young people's epochal emancipation:

I seem to hear voices, children's voices carrying over the hard, crystallized ground as if over a sea that extends beyond this universe's horizons. What do you want children? I ask. We want to go home, they say. We want to go home to Cythera. Then leave behind your wicked stepfathers and stepmothers, leave your families and your treacherous friends, leave them all: seek out the place where you were before you were born, even if it means traveling to the stars, the countless archipelagos of the stars, to find your dream island, your home, your Cythera. (305–6)

In this yearning fantasy of militant autonomy, the novel at times evokes the evangelical fervor associated with the "Children's Liberation" movement of the 1960s and 1970s, where various programmatic agendas for youthful autonomy and self-government were explicitly advanced.[4] And indeed, Calder does seem to suggest that adolescents' peremptory if inchoate resistance to authority deserves to be seen as the bellwether of social revolution, the psychic bedrock on which utopia can be erected. The problem with this age-based construction of his future power struggle—adult exploiters versus teenage resistance fighters—is that it occludes their mutual implication in a "consuming youth" system: the adults spellbound by a dreamily fetishized vision of "youth" are as exploited, in the last analysis, as the literally youthful consumers themselves.

Despite this occasional tendency simply to reduce economic relations to generational ones, Calder's work brilliantly captures the complex dialectical logic in which every prosthetic empowerment of consumers both enmeshes them further in a predatory system and promises an amplification of their collective desire and will. Like Cadigan's and Laidlaw's, Calder's mutant-youth characters struggle to realize a cyborg agency latent in the estranged machineries of high-tech culture—an agency that popular posthumanist fantasies also articulate, even in their most distorted and commodified forms. While the work of these cyberpunk authors only gestures at the transformed future implicit in the dynamics of this struggle, it nonetheless, in the emotional force of its utopian longing, serves to articulate a demand that capitalist consumption incessantly mobilizes but that it can never truly fulfill.

9

"Going Postal"

Rage, Science Fiction, and the Ends of the

American Subject

ROGER LUCKHURST

"Going Postal"

In her short story "Speech Sounds" (1983), Octavia Butler sketches a vision of a disintegrated Los Angeles, the superstructure of the state gone, a dwindling population scavenging among the ruins. This social collapse comes in the wake of a degenerative disorder of the body: a virus has attacked the linguistic centers of the brain, rendering some speechless, others without the ability to read or write, but all subject to eruptive rages at their aphasic and agraphic dysfunctions. "He could read, she realized belatedly. . . . Abruptly, she hated him. She held herself still, staring at him, almost seeing his blood. But her rage crested and ebbed" (98–99). This remnant of culture is conceived along the lines of Walter Ong's conception of violence in primary oral cultures. These, Ong claims, "commonly manifest their schizoid tendencies by extreme external confusion, leading often to violent action, including mutilation of the self and of others. This behavior is frequent enough to have given rise to special terms to designate it: the old-time Scandinavian warrior going 'berserk'; the southeast Asian person running 'amok'" (69).

The same rage is evident, in different terminology, in Jack Womack's *Random Acts of Senseless Violence* (1993), another dystopian vision of the near future. *Random Acts* tracks the rapid descent of an New York Upper West Side girl into the argot and violence of street gangs, as financial collapse, civil disorder, and military occupation distend the old social boundaries of the city. The end of civil restraint is marked by a threat articulated through the ubiquitous slang term "going post office":

"I'm not like that" I said. "Like what?" "Going post office" I said. "What's meant?" "Like people who work at the post office go crazy and kill everybody they work with" I said. "Understood" Iz said. "I'm really not like that" I told her. "Must be a part of you like that otherwise it wouldn't show." (159)

One of the gang, it is said, "don't just go post office, she GPO" (126), becoming a "full-time letter carrier" (160) in the no-go zones of the city. Lola, daughter of a university teacher and a screenwriter, has her relatively privileged life stripped away in an America degenerating into ungovernable anarchy. Lola's descent is figured as a move from the secure white enclaves of lower Manhattan into the zones of the socially excluded. Her mother, an English professor on Prozac, proves unable to adapt. Her father collapses under the economics of slave labor in the new job market, cowed by his perpetually enraged boss. Lola shows increasing signs of "decontrol" (158). After her father's death, she "mindlose total," and her exorbitant rage drives her to murder. There is no ritualistic containment for this "berserking." The act of going "general post office" (251) can only be marked by Lola ending her diary, exiting language and any

discernible selfhood. "*It* rages *me*" (231; emphasis added), the construction lat-
terly runs: "When I eye myself mirrored I don't see me anymore" (241). Rage
distends language and liquidates the subject.[1] Welcome to the American future.

Womack's phrase picks up on that American-slang condensation of rage
states, "going postal." The phrase neatly condenses a number of resonances in
American culture. In 1997, there were 856 workplace homicides in America.
Most deaths were a result of armed robbery, but it is employee violence—the
scenario of the dutiful worker suddenly erupting into a violent rage directed at
co-workers—that has come to fascinate the popular imagination. This violence
acquired the "postal" tag after the foundational postal worker incident in 1986,
when Patrick Henry Sherrill responded to a long series of reprimands and sus-
pensions from his supervisors by shooting fourteen people dead and wounding
six, finally turning the gun on himself. Thomas McIlvane's rampage in Royal
Oak, Michigan, in November 1991 secured "going postal" in the modern American lexicon. The lengthy process of arbitrating his dismissal was seen to have
fueled his violent temper, recorded in verbal and physical threats for over a
year before his final spree. The case prompted a highly critical House of Repre-
sentatives report, *A Post Office Tragedy*, released in June 1992. The sequence of
postal murders now promises its own "true crime" subgenre: twenty incidents
since 1983 are recorded in Don Lasseter's 1997 book, *Going Postal: Madness and
Mass Murder in America's Post Office*—complete, the blurb adds, "WITH 12 PAGES
OF SHOCKING PHOTOGRAPHS!"

The Postmaster General of the United States Postal Service launched the
Commission on a Safe and Secure Workplace in October 1998 to counteract negative perceptions of the service. The USPS authorities are unlikely to prevent
the accretions of popular culture around the notion of "going postal," however:
its resonances are too rich. Aside from true-crime collections, anecdotes and
news stories about violence by or connected to postal workers are enthusiastically archived on the internet in "The Disgruntled Postal Worker Zone."[2] Links
from this site take you to discussions of the computer game *Postal*, the low-budget film *Postal Worker*, and a comic, *Pete the P.O'd Postal Worker*. Urban folklore
surrounding postal violence has intersected with the allure of the serial killer in
mailman David Berkowitz. Sometime after the "Son of Sam" entered popular
demonology, the film *Seven* (1995) memorably ended with the postal delivery
of a severed head, while Lew McCreary's novel *The Minus Man* (1994) gave his
serial killer the means to drift through the country by moving from postal job to
postal job. The mail system now is more likely to evoke spree killing or the letter bombs of the Unabomber. Kevin Costner's 1997 film version of David Brin's
Postman (1985), in which mail delivery acts as an emblem of civilization in a
post-apocalyptic world, was a spectacular failure.

Womack incorporates the slang term into his jargon of the future and
makes anger a central thematic of his America. Interestingly, Butler and Wom-

ack include identical scenes in their texts, which give further density to the rages they depict. "Speech Sounds" opens with the sentence "There was trouble aboard the Washington Boulevard bus" (87) and describes a wordless fight between two men in the gangway of one of the few remaining buses traversing the city. An early sign of descent for Lola's family in *Random Acts* is having to use a collapsing bus service: "at 72nd a crazy man got on. . . . All of a sudden the crazy man started hitting a little old lady, she was sitting in one of the single seats" (48). This is not simply disdain for the proximity and inter-mixing of people forced to use public transport systems (a peculiarly Western terror, perhaps). These scenes explore one of the interfaces around which a discriminating typology of contemporary explosive affect has begun to emerge. Road rage, the frustration at gridlock that escalates to murderous attack, was sufficiently familiar (in England, at least) to become the title of both a best-selling single and a novel in 1997, following much public concern and newspaper coverage over a motorway murder in May 1996.[3] Air rage was coined in the wake of increasing midflight attacks on aircraft and flight attendants. Phone rage acts as an early symptom of the uncontrollable anger suffered by the lead character of Paul Sayer's 1998 novel, *Men in Rage*: "A few weeks ago, at work, he had made a call from the empty desk in front of his, then—how to justify this?—he had ripped the phone from its socket and, before anyone came, jammed it into his bag. And why? Simply because he had been put on hold" (19). This is also exemplary of "desk rage," coined to describe increasing stress-related violence in the office.[4]

Road rage and its correlates violently express the everyday frustrations engendered by a new postindustrial landscape, isolating enraging encounters at technological interfaces—freeway, airport, phone network—in the specific landscape of a technologically saturated world. They articulate a sense in which infrastructural supports are now felt to be determining, rather than instrumental. Gridlocked, left on hold, stuck in line: these are the results of "service" systems collapsing through overcomplexification and underinvestment. These technological systems devour taxes and no longer work to save time but infuriatingly extend it. Perhaps the most iconographic moment of the rage this induces is the figure of "D-FENS," in the much-discussed film *Falling Down* (1993), firing a bazooka at the roadworks that have gridlocked Los Angeles and thus launched him on his rampage across the city.

It has been science fiction, though, that has found service as a critical tool for theorizing these new urban terrains. Mike Davis's influential analysis of the "militarization of city life" and the "sadistic street environments" of Los Angeles, for instance, berates urban theorists for ignoring the incarcerating logic of city planning and turns to "Hollywood's pop apocalypses and pulp science fiction" for texts that engage with this new imaginary (*City of Quartz* 223). David Rieff comments that the visual iconography of the film *Blade Runner* became so resonant that, ten years after its release in 1982, "it had become a part of everyday speech in Los Angeles" (134). *Blade Runner* may look rusty, however, compared to the imagined *polis* constructed in the 1990s science fiction of authors like Butler and Womack. Octavia Butler's two novels of the 1990s, *Parable of the Sower* (1993) and *Parable of the Talents* (1998), owe much of their terrain—a California riven by utter social collapse, violence, and the return of economic and racial slavery—to "Speech Sounds." Butler's vision, as Jim Miller has observed, also has much in common with Mike Davis's political analysis (347–49). Womack's apocalyptic New York, meanwhile, has a topography of militarized sectors, drawn up to protect the last of American capital. Outside rove ruthless Russian and Japanese competitors and the abandoned Hispanic, black, and mutant populations of the ghettos.

If these ecologies of fear constitute phantasmatic dystopias of contemporary America, they are also examinations of psychical extremity, of the rages that mark out the limits of subjectivity. I want to explore the contention that science fiction can become a privileged space in popular culture for examining that peculiar late twentieth-century phenomenon of "going postal," and that it can do so because it tends to privilege the conjunctures that determine the irruptions of rage. One would suppose, in a culture so dedicated to confessional display, that the language of psychotherapy could articulate the matrix of affective relations and conflicts from which rages are generated. Yet contemporary rages so distend subjectivity that the discipline of psychology is at a loss as to where to put its anger, while popular science fiction texts put on spectacular demonstrations of rage, playing on the ambivalent conjuncture of anxiety at being the object of violent anger alongside the undoubted pleasures of fantasized subjective identification with the momentary liberations that "going postal" might offer. My example is the *ur*-text of representations of male rampage, *The Terminator* (1984).

Locating Rage

Mr. A, a 45-year-old white man, was an attorney who lived with his wife and three children. . . . He described a "short fuse," felt out of control very quickly, and had an explosive temper and "anger attacks.". . . He felt these episodes were alien to him and was concerned that he would lose his job as a result. (Fava et al. 867)

Who (or what) is subject to rage? Can a community or a nation become enraged? Anger has sometimes been located as *the* defining American affect in recent cultural commentary. Gavin Esler's *United States of Anger* explores the transformation of the Great Society into the Angry Society. Renée Curry and Terry L. Allison, the editors of *States of Rage*, argue that "rage appears to define the daily existence of some groups in the United States," adding in a footnote

that "in no way do we want to claim that people across different cultures experience, feel, or manifest their rage in similar ways" (1, 11). Carol Tavris similarly
emphasizes the specificity of American anger. Attacking "ventilationist" models, in which anger is "thought to be a healthy emotion that costs too much
when it is suppressed" (28), Tavris indicts American attitudes by invoking comparison to cultures where rage is ritualistically contained or dissipated through
negotiation.

   If ventilating anger is peculiarly American, then for cultural conservatives,
"going postal" might indicate a grotesque exemplification of the "culture of
narcissism." Christopher Lasch's jeremiad against contemporary America suggested that "Americans are overcome not by the sense of endless possibility
but by the banality of the social order they have erected against it" (*Culture of
Narcissism* 39). "They tend," he argued, "to be consumed with rage. . . .
[O]utwardly bland, submissive, and sociable, they seethe with an inner anger
for which a dense, overpopulated, bureaucratic society can devise few legiti-
mate outlets" (40). The narcissistic self, Lasch later amplified, is "a self uncertain of its own outlines, longing either to remake the world in its own image or
to merge into its environment in blissful union" (*Minimal Self* 19). Eruptive rage
marks further evidence of society's regression to primitive satisfactions in the
absence of deference. Paternal authority, it seems, once ensured discipline and
contained affect.

   Lasch lambastes the "therapeutic sensibility" of American culture as narcissistic, yet organizes his own conceptions of collective disorders through psy-
choanalysis. While it can make sense to understand rage as a psychic regression, psychic mechanisms need not map wholesale onto the cultural expressions of "infantilism" that Lasch identifies. There are other routes for locating
rage within the Freudian subject. In "Instincts and Their Vicissitudes," Freud
suggested that "hate, as a relation to objects, is older than love. It derives from
the narcissistic ego's primordial repudiation of the external world." Since this
narcissism "always remains in an intimate relation with the self-preservative
instincts" (137), Freud offered in these observations the basis for the notion,
later developed by Heinz Kohut, of "narcissistic rage." This state, Kohut proposes, is the response of a subject who has never built adequate defenses or a
sustaining "selfobject." Without this, the subject feels invaded, reacting in a
rage in which "there is utter disregard for reasonable limitations and a bound-
less wish to redress an injury and to obtain revenge" (380). Kohut encourages
mapping the psychic onto the social: would it be possible to develop an account
of rage in America as symptom of a series of injuries to a narcissistic "nation-
object"?

   In a way, though, contemporary rage is defined exactly by its exorbitance,
its dislocation of the taxonomic language of official psychology. Outside the
small sphere of influence of psychoanalytic theory, the institutions of psychia-

try have spent the last decade working either to expel or to displace anger, leading one group to note the "surprising lack of diagnostic attention" given to rage
states in psychiatric research in comparison to the detailed nosologies for
depression and anxiety (Eckhardt and Deffenbacher 28). The 1987 revised third
edition of the American Psychiatric Association's *Diagnostic and Statistical
Manual of Mental Disorders* (*DSM*) did not locate anger in the section on mood
disorders, but merely under "Impulse-control disorders not elsewhere classified." Located here is the one anger-identified illness, "Intermittent Explosive
Disorder," defined as "failure to resist an impulse, drive, or temptation to perform some act that is harmful to the person or others" and in which "the degree
of aggressiveness experienced during the episodes is grossly out of proportion
to any precipitating social stressors" (321).[5] The accompanying note indicates
that "many doubt the existence" of IED as a discrete syndrome (321). The fourth
edition of the *DSM* (1994) gives a little more detail but also notes that anger is
more likely to be contained under categories like "oppositional defiant disorder" or "antisocial personality disorder" (611). The notes to the *DSM-IV
Guidebook* are even more skeptical: IED remains "one of the most problematic
categories" for the whole *Manual* (Frances et al. 344, 346). The *Guidebook* com-
municates that this category should be excluded from subsequent editions. In
response, a group of researchers published *Anger Disorders*, which reacted to
the exclusion of rage states from official diagnostics. It aimed to develop a set
of symptoms of dysfunctional angers. The resulting taxonomy would
redescribe road rage, for instance, as "situational anger disorder," with or without aggression.[6] It also provides space for General Anger Disorder, for the
"chronically and pervasively angry," where anger is not a displaced symptom
of anxiety or depression (Eckhardt and Deffenbacher 43–44).

These struggles of the American Psychiatric Association over where to put
its anger are symptoms that it may not be the affect of rage so much as the dis-
ciplinary paradigm of subjectivity that is registering a shift. In *The War of Desire
and Technology*, Allucquère Rosanne Stone suggests that texts like the *DSM* operate as "location technologies" in which subjects are determined by grids of
power that fix selves into bodies as "fiduciary subjects" (39–40), the state
defining that subject as "a political, epistemological, and biological unit that is
not only measurable and quantifiable but also understood in an essential way
as being *in place*" (90). Stone suggests that these machineries are dislocated once
societies reach a "technosocial" saturation, in which "technology *is* nature"
(39). She is interested in what happens when selves become detached from bodies in cyberspace; she presents several science fictions about the effects on subjectivity that these technologies induce. The problem that the discipline of
psychology has in categorizing rage reflects the other side of these "technosocial" conditions. Where Stone explores the utopian possibilities of multiple
selves through these new technologies, rage marks out a different type of en-

counter with these conditions, in which subjectivity is experienced as radically under stress. The diagnostics of the APA have nothing to say about these, but slang expressions like "going postal" or "road rage" evoke exactly what the etiologies of Intermittent Explosive Disorder cannot: the impact on sense of selfhood in the transformation of the terrains of employment and domestic life in technosocial America.

The first exploration of workplace violence in 1992 found that the Post Office had a "high-pressured, authoritarian, and frequently hostile work environment" (Layden 45). Abusive managers were rewarded and complainants punished. "Post office managerial practices are described as paramilitary. Time clocks calibrated on military time measure attendance in hundredths of a second and dock employees for seconds of tardiness. Sometimes, employees have to ask permission to use the bathroom" (47). This is what individual pathologies risk obscuring and why the USPS wishes to displace a term that identifies its managerial practices as a condensation of the brutalizing effects of post-Fordist labor markets: a downsized, overstretched core workforce, with an attendant pool of casualized jobs for routinized, mechanical work. When postal worker Steven Brownlee was given psychiatric assessments after killing two coworkers, it was discovered that, after working 70- to 80-hour-a-week shifts, he was convinced that sorting machines were talking to him (Lasseter 43). The experience of the office workers in Jack Womack's novel *Ambient* (1987) seems all too possible: "all Dryco computer ops . . . worked in thirty-two hour shifts; on average, they received forty cents an hour after taxes as overtime pay. . . . The system had flaws; some employees went insane—they were fired—and some grew blind" (50). With a contracting structure of welfare support and declining standards of living for the majority, the reprimand or firing that produces explosive rage is more than what human resource managers call "career dissonance." Kirby Farrell suggests that "social death" might be more apposite: the prospect of an economic and social annihilation that can produce murderous or suicidal berserking (290).

The technologies that have displaced or deskilled the male subject are also perceived to have invaded and transformed the "feminine" space of domesticity. This is manifested in a diversity of cultural narratives. I have argued elsewhere that accounts of alien abduction circulate not least for their gothicization of new medical technologies and the magical animation of domestic technologies: the flashing zeros of video clocks and the disturbances in TVs spell out the secret of the "missing time" of abduction.[7] Tales of amnesiac gaps and eruptions of blind rage at the interfaces of mechanical systems are part of the same cluster of traumatic responses to highly technologized landscapes.

The science fiction genre, as Vivian Sobchack has observed, "has always taken as its distinctive generic task the cognitive mapping and poetic figuration of social relations as they are constituted and changed by new technological

modes of being-in-the-world" (*Screening Space* 224). Such a cognitive definition
might occlude the kind of *affective mapping* I have been tracking here. Because
anger evacuates the subject, I want to shift my analysis from literature to film,
from (in Ong's terms) the "interiority" of writing to the kinetic pleasures of visual media. The intermeshing of bodies and machines of the technosocial has its
"promising monsters" (Haraway, "Promises of Monsters" 321). It also produces
enraged responses to threatened borders, and science fiction cinema has presented us with some of the most enduring images of enactions of rage.

The Terminator's Rage

Critic Sean French defends *The Terminator* as "the most important and influential film of the 80s" (9) and this as its "greatest scene": "He wanders
through the police station blasting policeman after policeman. . . . It's a glorious
slapstick sequence, that makes you laugh out loud because of its excess and
flamboyance and lack of shame. Are we really allowed to enjoy all these cops
getting blown away?" (59). French's affirmation of the low, exploitation-genre
sf of the first film is equaled by his contempt for the Terminator of the absurdly
overcapitalized sequel: "any honest filmgoer preferred the homicidal cyborg
who murdered women and policemen" (54). The Terminator's unstoppable trajectory through the American landscape models the endless reiterations of male
rampage in Hollywood cinema over the last fifteen years. "Rage produces compelling images precisely because of our ambivalence about it," Sharon Willis
states in her analysis of contemporary American cinema: these images typically
oscillate between "frightening or ludicrous excesses with a certain gleeful, celebratory edge" (98). These ambivalences are what energize the spectatorial experience of *The Terminator*. The fluid movement of identification between
Terminator and target allows both phantasmatic release of rage at authorities
(the cops, complacent psychiatrists) or abjected social objects (street punks,
gun-shop owners) and the more masochistic pleasures of being the slashed and
wounded object of such implacable rage.

Released in 1984 at the midpoint of Ronald Reagan's presidency, the film's
extremes of sadomasochistic pleasure and the hysterical masculinities it portrays might appear to be tied too closely to a specific historical moment to be
immediately useful for any analysis of contemporary rage. The plot, developed
around the notion of defense computer systems becoming autonomous and
using nuclear arsenals to eliminate humans, speaks to a peak of nuclear proliferation, protest, and imaginations of disaster. Apocalyptic representations
carry very specific date stamps. Yet *The Terminator* has remained a template for
narratives of technological malevolence. Bill Joy, the cofounder of Sun Micro-
systems, opened the new millennium with predictions that "humans clearly

face extinction" through new technologies advancing toward autonomy (240). The vector might have changed—genetic and biotechnologies have replaced nuclear and biological weapon's systems—but Joy still envisions the future through texts like *The Terminator*.

But the low-budget "tech-noir" *mise en scène* of the film is now capable of articulating different technological concerns than the nuclear apocalypticism that drives it. Constance Penley has observed that the film's ambiguities focus on the technologies that "provide the texture and substance of the film: cars, trucks, motorcycles, radios, TVs, time clocks, phones, answering machines, beepers, hairdryers, Sony Walkmen, automated factory equipment" (118). Everyday technologies mark out alienated relations or fail their human owners: phone booths, answering machines, and call-holding systems threaten death or hint at malice. Penley is right to suggest that the film offers itself as a critical dystopia, "a dialogue with Americana that bespeaks the inevitable consequences of our current technological addictions" (123). The film is too incoherent, however, for a consistent critical logic to emerge: the audience is caught up in the exhilarating forward propulsion of the cyborg's programmed rage to terminate Sarah Connor, carrier of the hopes of human survival. Meanwhile, for Robert Arnold, the closing scenes of both *The Terminator* and its sequel, *Terminator 2: Judgment Day* (1991), are enacted in industrial sites that resonate after fifteen more years of deindustrialization. In the first film, the pursuit of the human targets culminates in the unlikely landscape of a *working* factory. This is a phantasmatic *mise en scène,* matched by the steelworks where both terminators meet their end in the sequel. Arnold suggests that Sarah Connor's termination of the cyborg, crushing it between steel plates on the assembly line, speaks to the catastrophic condition of industrial manufacture in the early Reagan era in the face of Japanese-identified computerized production. The scene offers the consolation of instrumental control over technology.[8] The sequel revenges itself even more graphically on the "flexible" skills required in a postindustrial terrain by annihilating the protean T1000 with ancient heavy industry. These spectacles re-secure human agency in a deskilled industrial landscape. In an important way, they shore up the integrity of unalloyed human subjectivity.

In another way, however, the human/machine hybridity of the cyborg figure, so populous in sf cinema of the 1980s and 1990s, is exactly concerned with working through the transformations of subjectivity promised by technosociality: *The Terminator* initiates a line of texts that rehearse this trauma. This is why Robert Arnold sees sf, with its foregrounded technologies, as a privileged contemporary cinema: it is "a partial means of integrating people who are violently subjected to the alienation effects of industrial capitalism into its social formation" (22). Mark Seltzer, in his book *Serial Killers*, proposes a model that explains how this subjection translates into images of the rage of rampaging machines. He argues that the rise of the serial killer coincides with the Second Industrial Revolution in the late nineteenth century with its technologies of inscription, recording, and collating (the typewriter, the phonograph, the statistical model). These technologies provided effective forms of controlling the masses and produced what Seltzer terms "the statistical person," the self experienced through norms and averages. The serial killer literalizes this experience of number in which "the unremitting flood of numbers, codes, and letters is popularly seen as replacing real bodies and real persons" (17)—hence an abstracted "murder by numbers." Seltzer argues that serial killing thematizes "the everyday intimacies with technology in machine culture" (69). No doubt thinking of the corpses littered behind the cyborg, Seltzer isolates the Terminator as "the very icon of the artifactual or constructed person as killing machine" (129).

Arnold Schwarzenegger's iconic status helps this representativity: the blurrings of star and role in *The Terminator* mean that this 'roid rage is perfectly balanced between "android" and "steroid," between machine murder and the violent instabilities that attend the gender confusions around the hypermasculine bodybuilder.[9] This matrix around the technologically inscribed and enraged subject could be taken as the unifying element of Schwarzenegger's career, one of constant image reprogramming. Albert Lui proposes that his corpus of films stands as "an ambitious prospectus of New Vocations for the Human Being," focused on "divided subjectivities," before wryly adding that "no one has established that there is a person *there* whose subjectivity could be damaged, constructed, or in any way altered" (105, 107).

In *Total Recall* (1990), this is built into Quaid/Schwarzenegger's apparent first encounter with technological implantations of memory: the doctors find only a "mess" of grafts and erasures of overlaid, inconsistent memory chains. Destabilizing them prompts an eruptive rage that leaves four men dead at Quaid's feet, a voracious paranoia, and the beginnings of a rampage. This interplay of body and machine inscription, memory, forgetting, and violence (the subject of another cyborg account, *RoboCop* [1987]) locks into the technologized conception of the subject of memory as well as theorizations of rage.[10] Quaid's explosion matches the description of Blind Rage Syndrome, where "physical violence is accompanied by amnesia, the period of 'blind rage'" (Simón 132). This framework continues to operate through the revision of the "hardbody" in the early 1990s toward "increasingly emotional displays of masculine sensitivities, traumas and burdens" (Jeffords 172). Schwarzenegger's "softened" roles in comedies like *Kindergarten Cop* (1990), in which rage is directed only at abusive fathers, and *Twins* (1998) can be read for their overelaborate psychological explanatory frames—another route into the traumatized subject. The "soldier male" body in *The Terminator* is rewritten as a machinelike carapace over a traumatic core, and the hardbody becomes an abused object of wound culture.[11]

"Hollywood routinely equivocates about berserking, often constructing it as a form of conversion experience—a fantasy of a new identity achieved by bursting inhibitions," Kirby Farrell suggests (297). The link between berserking and "futuristic" cinema, he goes on to argue, is clear because contemporary selves suffer "cybernetic subversion through cameras and robots" that threaten "to mechanize, numb, or attenuate subjectivity" (323). Schwarzenegger was propelled into stardom through the "I'll be back" scenes of release in *The Terminator*: for an audience pinned down by the technocracy of police and state and frozen by the threats of erasure by machines, the exhilaration of identification with berserking is in its rush, its feelings of temporary invulnerability, and its murderous revenge on authority. "The berserker feels like a god," Jonathan Shay, analyst of Vietnam veterans, has argued (qtd. in Farrell 347), and the infectious kinetics of spectacular sf cinema delivers this rush of rage against attenuations of the self.

Sean French delights in his identification with the Terminator of the first film. His disappointment with the sequel might, more symptomatically, concern the relocation of the violent spectacle of rage *away* from the figure of Schwarzenegger. Looking for an equivalent scene of rage in *Terminator 2: Judgment Day*, Sharon Willis pinpoints Sarah Connor's raid on the Cyberdyne computer designer, Miles Dyson: "even the narrative justification for Sarah Connor's murderous rage—that Dyson's single-minded scientific commitments will lead indirectly to nuclear apocalypse as a computer network takes over the world—cannot contain the political resonances of the image before us: an enraged white woman and her black victims. Finally, this scene condenses a variety of competing fantasies: the combative force of the woman warrior is directed at a middle-class African American man, who, just by the way, is ultimately responsible for the destruction of the world" (123) .

This is what a sole focus on the technological determinants of subjectivity may risk occluding from an account of contemporary rage. Willis brilliantly unpacks the apparently accidental figurations of race and gender in this and other male rampage films. *Terminator 2*, in its retelling from the cultural center of its marginal predecessor, anxiously tries to rewrite the first film's account of rage. Jonathan Goldberg has suggested that the first Terminator's leather-clad, body-built thrust is "the relentless refusal of heterosexual imperatives" (246), pathologically driven enough to kill not one but three potentially reproductive Sarah Connors. By 1991, the cyborg is retooled to prevent the Armageddon of the heterosexual subject and to reconstitute the family around the sacrificial authority of the father. This reassertion takes place because the hardbody has shifted onto the female form: it is Linda Hamilton's rebuilt muscularity that holds the attention now. Her survivalist maternal rage breaks down, however, as she stands over the cowering bodies of Dyson and his family: she is unable to terminate him. Even her shift to discursive rage ("Fucking men like you built the hydrogen bomb. . . . You think you're so creative. You don't know what it's like to really create something—to create a life") is cut short by her son. For Thomas

Byers, Sarah's rant "serves to identify the ideological underpinnings of her 'excessive' anger and to make feminism seem hysterical" (20). What this logic implies is a symptomatic location of distending American "states of rage" into the body of the feminist. Only the judicious exercise of *paternal* violence can avert the destruction of the American polity. Authority returns to the good father, the idealized cyborg, who, as Byers observes "is capable of the most extreme violence, but who *will not hurt us*" (23). The scene that Willis investigates for its image of the murderous female hardbody, however, is one overdetermined by race, and therefore puts in question the provenance of that "*us.*" If *Terminator 2* insists on the authority of the white father, then the film has to work against the insight of the first film's account of the pathologies of white rage.

Rage is often theorized as a psychic regression, and regression is marked in racial terms. "Berserking" derives from the "bare shirt" rituals of Viking marauding; "running amok" is borrowed from the "violent or furious assault of homicidal intensity . . . associated with the indigenous peoples of the Malay archipelago" (Carr and Tan 1295). Because of such primitivist associations, black violence in America is not regarded as anomalous but as inevitable, regressive violence. This conservative view is reinforced by cycles of economic exclusion, which leaves the subject of the murderous attention paid to young black bodies scandalously underreported.[12] The legitimacy of black and minoritarian *outrage* at this situation is registered in numerous studies that have tied "black" and "rage" together for over thirty years.[13]

Here is the final determinant for the popular fascination with spectacles of "going postal" and the recent attempts to locate rage within psychiatric taxonomies. These are symptoms of the apparent *anomaly of white rage* in contemporary America. "Homicidal people at the workplace generally are depicted as white males in their thirties and forties with migratory job histories," Layden suggests (38).[14] "Patients are primarily Caucasian males. They lead normal lives except for brief periods of intense violence. The patients' appearances are likewise outwardly unremarkable," Simón adds (132). All of Simón's case studies, like those of Fava, concern white anger, although the diagnostic importance of whiteness hovers uncertainly between "examined" and "unexamined" assumptions. One way of rejecting berserker films and their audiences is, as Farrell notes, to term both constituencies "wretched white trash" (citing Roger Ebert 320).

The most discussed representation of "going postal" is Joel Schumacher's film *Falling Down*, which aims for a "universal" assertion even as the rage to which it gives vent is raced as white (Schumacher has plaintively stated that "there have been several movies in the U.S. about anger in the street but they had all been by African Americans. Well, they're not the only angry people in the United States" [qtd. in Davies 214]). The film's protagonist, Bill Foster, so identifies with the defense industries he works for that his redundancy hollows him out. His defenses collapse and his sequence of violent encounters with others derives from the grandiose self of narcissistic rage and its urge to eradicate difference (whether Korean, Hispanic, or neo-Nazi white). As he trudges across the racial territories of Los Angeles, magically surviving a hail of Hispanic bullets, crushed off public buses by hordes of the African American poor, and refusing to be a compliant consumer, you can almost see the metallic cyborg sheen beneath his skin and experience a ghost of the sadomasochistic identifications called up by *The Terminator*.

The Terminator addresses the excoriation of subjectivity in the post-industrial landscape. This technosociality, in Allucquère Rosanne Stone's reading, promises possibilities of selves detached from bodies, multiplicity, new forms of desire. But in the tech-noir version of the future offered by *The Terminator*, these promises are boundary threats that produce exorbitant rage. In this last turn of the screw, this pathology of rage needs to be analyzed as a deadly logic of white male identity. Dana Nelson theorizes White Manhood (as an ideal impossible of attainment, not a description) as "a counterphobic ideal" against "kinds of social diversity" (33) and argues that it is "shadowed by revenant otherness," is "constantly haunted within . . . by its own violences towards others" (200). Richard Dyer's formative study, *White*, ends with a chapter on "White Death" in which the androids of *Alien* (1979) and *Blade Runner* (1982) constitute the ideal definition of whiteness: they are hollow, machinic, artifactual beings (213). And while Fred Pfeil discusses the rampagers of *Lethal Weapon* (1987) and *Die Hard* (1988) as white men played with "the resonance of skills discounted or dismissed in the new late-capitalist world" (28), it is the figure of Schwarzenegger that appears in his conclusion, functioning as a "figure of both past and future, by parodying the hard-working, industrious, compulsive white male worker" (31)—and embodying all the rages of that threatened subject-position. As *Terminator 2* ends with a sacrificial father restoring mother to son and reconstituting the family, the film asks its audience to forget the sacrifice of the other, black father, Dyson, and the orphaning of his son.

Fraternity is shattered by demographic transformation, by the disarticulation of masculine identification with work, and by the reinscription of subjectivity through technology. Yet American culture still sufficiently glorifies the model of redemption through violence, so that the temporary invulnerabilities of "going postal" might seem a gloriously simple solution to the complex transformations of the postindustrial terrain. Recently, there have been too many illustrations of this deathly logic. In late July 1999, Mark Barton murdered his family and shot nine people dead in a killing spree in Atlanta, Georgia. Barton's rage was intensified by the loss of his family savings through day-trading with an Internet account, a technology that democratizes access to Wall Street yet leaves individuals—unlike regulated stock-trading institutions—without protection from indifferent market forces. His last port of call was to a trading center named All-Tech Trading. Only ten days later, Buford Furrow, leading member of the racist Aryan Nations group, attempted to kill children at a Jewish daycare center in Los Angeles. Furrow's anger was calculated and ideological, rather than an explosive rage, and the only fatality was a gruesomely apposite figure: a Filipino postal worker.

These "postal" rages are annihilations of others; often they are also annihilations of self. I do not, however, want my analysis to be mistaken as repeating, at whatever distance, these violent acts of annihilation. Subjectivity is not at some catastrophic end, and I do not ascribe to American sf a purely dystopian role, one that rehearses again and again the infraction and destruction of selfhood. When the philosopher Jean-Luc Nancy invited a group of thinkers to respond to the puzzling question "Who comes after the subject?" he emphasized that this invitation was absolutely not part of a "widespread discourse of recent date [which] proclaimed the subject's simple liquidation" (5). Rather, the *who* of his question implied "a move forward toward someone—*some one*—else in its place" (5). Allowing a utopian possibility to lodge itself in an interstitial space of "the ends of the subject," it seems to me that Nancy could also be describing aspects of sf: presenting apocalyptic ends but also transformative possibilities. In Octavia Butler's *Parable of the Sower* and *Parable of the Talents*, for instance, there is, amid the uncanny returns to violently enforced economic slavery, systematic murder, and racial purity campaigns, an investigation of the redemptive possibilities of a resacralized utopian hope—a kind of reflexive ethics that avoids dogma and allows multiracial communities to explore possibilities of cooperation. These texts are, as Jim Miller puts it, "critical dystopias motivated out of a utopian pessimism in that they force us to confront the dystopian elements of postmodern culture so that we can work through them and begin again" (337). Almost as if in sync, Mike Davis's apocalyptic analyses of the incarcerating logic of the inner city have now shifted, in his recent study, *Magical Urbanism*, to the positive transformations effected by Latino communities on the inner city. Rages will continue to rip incoherently through the popular cultural fabric as the global flights of capital continue to uproot whatever anchors of identity the precarious stabilities of industrial culture allowed, but these deterritorializations are also different potentialities and promises. This is what the disciplines of psychology and psychotherapy may not be able to locate, but it is in this ambivalent and enraged interregnum that some of the most interesting contemporary American sf inheres.

Part Three

Reimagined Apocalypses and Exploded Communities

10

Apocalypse Coma

VERONICA HOLLINGER

On the Edge of the Future

The Year 2000 Has Already Happened
—Jean Baudrillard, 1985

Now that our seemingly interminable wait for the end of the millennium is finally over, it becomes interesting to review some perspectives on apocalypse that were developed in both speculative fiction and critical-theoretical discourse during the last decades of the last century.[1] In order to suggest at least some of these perspectives, as well as something of their critical and ideological implications, I want to construct a dialogue between two very different novels and to situate this dialogue within the context of some of the influential examinations of postmodernism that began to appear during the mid-1980s. This is the moment when William Gibson's *Neuromancer* (1984) was first published, a novel that presented itself as a virtual manifesto for cool antiapocalypticism, a hip refutation of apocalyptic anxieties. In contrast, Douglas Coupland's neoconservative salvation story, *Girlfriend in a Coma* (1998), is a late-1990s expression of apocalyptic wish fulfillment, a Generation-X fantasy of (re)creating the world. *Neuromancer* is one of the most widely read science fiction novels of the past fifty years and was almost single-handedly responsible for the 1990s turn toward postmodernism of science fiction theory and criticism.[2] Among its various challenges to the conventions of genre sf is its revision of some of the thematic implications of apocalyptic plot elements. Coupland's novel, published just before the turn of the millennium, is a postgeneric fiction (to recall a term used by both Gary K. Wolfe and Lance Olsen elsewhere in this collection), drawing freely on a variety of realist, science fictional, and supernatural fantasy plot elements to create a hybrid narrative that looks hardly anything at all like science fiction. In spite of this, it self-consciously recalls science fiction's Golden Age apocalypticism, specifically through its intertextual borrowings from Arthur C. Clarke's 1953 novel, *Childhood's End*.

Needless to say, the past twenty years or so have been an(other) extremely fertile period for the apocalyptic imagination. As culture critic Mark Dery wrote in 1999, a moment already on the far side of the millennial divide, "The belief that we are history's witnesses to extremes of social fragmentation and moral malaise, that we stand at critical junctures and teeter on the brink of momentous decisions, is part and parcel of the fin-de-siècle; the fin-de-millennium simply turns up the cultural volume tenfold" (*The Pyrotechnic Insanitarium* 31). A wide range of cultural discourses has enthusiastically contributed to increasing this "cultural volume," including those of critical theory and speculative fiction.[3] Both critical theory and sf undertake, in their various ways, to map features of the present, both its continuities with and discontinuities from previous sociocultural formations; and both have had recourse to the rhetoric of apocalypse—of endtimes, of radical transformations—in their representations of life in contemporary Western culture.[4] Encouraged by the confluence of a calendar system that situates us on a millennial cusp and by a series of apparently unprecedented epistemological and technological ruptures and transformations, the apocalypse has recurred obsessively in our cultural discourses, responding to our intimations that, whatever else it may be, the postmodern condition is certainly a critical condition.

To be postmodern is to sense that we have become separated from the past by the ruptures and crises of ever more quickly receding recent history and also to recognize that we do not yet have much of an idea about where we are headed. In the context of technoculture, it is the feeling that we now lead science fictional lives, that we have been precipitated into time-future before we were quite ready for it. And just as nineteenth-century *fin-de-siècle* anxiety encouraged the development of a body of science fiction that envisioned the outcomes of decadence and devolution, so a century later sf has provided fertile ground for exploring the postmodern sense of a precipitous present hovering on the edge of the future.

Antiapocalyptic

"Things aren't different. Things are things."
—William Gibson, *Neuromancer* 270

The mid-1980s generated a variety of critical-theoretical reports on the contemporary condition that, taken together, influenced most subsequent mappings of the postmodern as a more or less new, more or less different, more or less transformed moment in historical consciousness. Many of these reports from the edge were careful, however, to discourage any cultural investment in scenarios of radical catastrophe and transformation; for the most part, they argued strongly against the perceived seductions of apocalyptic logic and rhetoric. One exemplary statement is Jean-François Lyotard's by-now classic definition of postmodernism as "incredulity toward metanarratives" (xxiv), suggesting as it does an intellectual refusal of the logic of apocalypse, which is nothing if not the logic of a totalizing master narrative. Lyotard concludes *The Postmodern Condition* (translated into English in 1984) by calling, perhaps ironically, for "a war on totality" (82).

Equally discouraging of attempts to characterize the present in terms of apocalyptic endings and beginnings is Jacques Derrida's deconstructive (anti)philosophy, which challenges deep-seated anxieties about, and desires for, originary moments and revelatory closures in human history; deconstruction convincingly argues that the movements of history are more accurately characterized by terms like "free play" and "infinite deferral." In a reading of two of Derrida's well-known essays on the subject of apocalypse, Christopher Norris argues that Derrida is concerned to demonstrate the importance of participation in "the heritage of critical demystification" (239): "what Derrida seeks is a means to *comprehend* that [apocalyptic] rhetoric, to take full account of its 'performative' aspect, before it achieves the referential status of a discourse whose final guarantee would be catastrophe itself" (247).[5]

"Critical demystification" is also at work in Donna Haraway's "A Manifesto for Cyborgs: Science, Technology, and Socialist Feminism in the 1980s" (1985). Haraway develops her "Manifesto" around the cyborg—product of both science fiction and the military-industrial complex—as an imaginative figure generated *outside* the framework of the Judeo-Christian history of fall and redemption, a history that unfolds between the twin absolutes of Edenic origin and apocalyptic Last Judgment. Like Derrida, Haraway warns that (nuclear) apocalypse might, in fact, be the all-too-possible outcome of our desire for the resolution of historical time. Haraway too is wary of cultural discourses that privilege resolution, completion, and totality. She concludes "A Manifesto for Cyborgs" with the warning that "the production of universal, totalizing theory is a major mistake that misses most of reality, probably always, but certainly now" (204).

At this same moment in the mid-1980s, science fiction took one of its most significant generic turns with the publication of Gibson's first novel, *Neuromancer,* which almost single-handedly established cyberpunk as its own sf subgenre. *Neuromancer* simultaneously relies upon and dismisses genre sf's longstanding fascination with apocalyptic scenarios. After hundreds of pages of nonstop suspense and narrative action, its final scene appears to be an anticlimactic throwaway. The text here concentrates on Wintermute, a vastly powerful artificial intelligence (AI) which, through its union with the Neuromancer AI, is now integrated into a coherent subject/self of awesome proportions and power. As Wintermute announces to Gibson's protagonist, Case: "I'm the sum total of the works, the whole show." If any sf situation were ever set up for apocalyptic revelation, this would seem to be it, but when Case asks, in suitably world-weary hacker tones, "So what's the score? How are things different? You running the world now? You God?" the AI replies only, "Things aren't different. Things are things" (269–70). The AI also informs Case that it is now in communication with another vast intelligence like itself in the Centauri system; to this potentially world-shaking piece of interstellar news Case responds merely with, "Oh . . . Yeah? No shit?" "No shit," affirms the AI. "And then the screen was blank" (270).

For all intents and purposes, this is the concluding scene of *Neuromancer,* an action novel that provides its fair share of climactic moments but rarely fails to undercut them when their significance threatens to get out of hand. Neither

characters nor readers will get the satisfaction of apocalyptic resolution or revelation here. Although the text certainly mobilizes the imagery of apocalypse to
build narrative tension, it ultimately dismisses the apparent significance of
these images. The Rastafarian inhabitants of the Zion-habitat, for example, believe themselves to be living in "the Final Days" (110), engaged in an all-or-
nothing spiritual struggle with the forces of "Babylon." Like most of the central
human characters in *Neuromancer*, however, they have been recruited by the
Wintermute entity and they serve other than human interests. Wintermute itself is not without a sense of its own potential for apocalyptic transcendence,
but its self-representation remains offhand and ironic: after appearing to Case
as a human figure, for instance, it asks him: "You want I should come to you in
the matrix like a burning bush?" (169).

Keeping in mind that the apocalypse promises not only ending but also
revelation, it is significant that the final scenes in *Neuromancer* provide neither
conclusions nor disclosures. As Derrida explains in his exegesis on the meaning
of "apocalypse": "I disclose, I unveil, I reveal the thing that can be a part of the
body, the head or the eyes, a secret part, the genitals or whatever might be hidden, a secret, the thing to be dissembled, a thing that does not show itself or say
itself, that perhaps signifies itself but cannot or must not first be handed over to
its self-evidence" ("Of an Apocalyptic Tone" 64). Given *Neuromancer*'s lack of
investment in the very idea of such radical disclosure, it is crucial to the novel's
plot that Wintermute cannot know the "true name" which, when spoken, will
fuse Wintermute and Neuromancer into one vastly powerful virtual entity.
Here is how Gibson presents the climactic moment when Case hacks this information from the Villa Staylight's computers:

– *now*
and his voice the cry of a bird
unknown,
3Jane answering in song, three
notes, high and pure.
A true name. (262)

The moment of apocalyptic revelation remains "unspoken" in the text; consequently, the text is incapable of imparting the "secret, the thing to be dissembled," to its own readers.

Earlier in the novel, at the climax of its central action sequence—the Straylight run—an obviously much less world-weary Case has demanded the pass-
word that would unite the divided selves of the AI, and his demand is couched
in terms of a passionate desire for the radical transformation of his fictional
world: "'Give us the fucking code. . . . If you don't, what'll change? What'll ever
fucking change for you? . . . I got no idea at all what'll happen if Wintermute
wins, but it'll *change* something!' He was shaking, his teeth chattering" (260).

When Wintermute wins, it certainly does change *something*, but not for Case or for any of the other central human characters, whose lives remain untouched by either catastrophe or revelation. This is Case's "happy ending":

> He spent the bulk of his Swiss account on a new pancreas and liver, the rest on a new Ono-Sendai and a ticket back to the Sprawl.
> He found work.
> He found a girl who called herself Michael. (270)

In his 1986 preface to *Burning Chrome*, Gibson's first collection of short stories, editor Bruce Sterling, well known for his own fiery millennial prophecies about the death of old-guard science fiction, identifies an antiapocalyptic element in Gibson's writing that he associates (accurately or not) with cyberpunk sf as a whole:

> Gibson's extrapolations show, with exaggerated clarity, the hidden bulk of an iceberg of social change. This iceberg now glides with sinister majesty across the surface of the late twentieth century, but its proportions are vast and dark.
> Many SF authors, faced with this lurking monster, have flung their hands up and predicted shipwreck. . . . [Gibson] has avoided this easy out. This is another distinguishing mark of the emergent new school of Eighties SF [that is, of cyberpunk]: its boredom with the Apocalypse. (xi)

What Sterling identifies as "boredom" with (what amounts to) the aesthetics of apocalypse is also a preference for the logic of the anticlimax. Cyberpunk, at least in Gibson's original version, demonstrates a kind of postmodern ennui with the narrative conventions of earlier apocalyptic fictions—whether the "Golden Age" variety of the post-Hiroshima period, exemplified by classics such as Clarke's *Childhood's End* (1953), or the later New Wave variety of ironic disaster fictions such as Kurt Vonnegut, Jr.'s *Cat's Cradle* (1963) and J. G. Ballard's *Crystal World* (1966). While this is no doubt due, in part, to the dissipation of postwar nuclear anxieties, it may well also owe something to the sheerly anticlimactic nature of an overhyped end-of-the-millennium, an ending that we seemed poised to experience for most of the second half of the twentieth century.

Apocalyptic

> She closes her eyes and she sees things—images of blood and soil mixed together like the center of a Black Forest cake; Grand Canyons of silent office towers. Houses, coffins, babies, cars, brooms, and bottle caps all burning and draining into the sea and dissolving like candies. There's a reason for this, she's sure.
> —Douglas Coupland, *Girlfriend in a Coma* 202

The cool antiapocalypticism of cyberpunk not only challenged the deep-seated apocalyptic tendencies of genre sf as a whole but, as the official end of the millennium approached, served as a continuing site of resistance to the growing tide of eschatological sentiment in both genre fiction and mainstream cultural analyses. Not surprisingly, the dizzying lack of boundaries and the devastating disavowal of metaphysical significance embodied in the writings of Lyotard and Derrida on the one hand and cyberpunk on the other reflect only one side of the critical-historical coin. Even most theoretical reports from the edge have been less than completely successful in resisting the lure of apocalyptic rhetoric. As Norris explains in his study of Derrida's writings on apocalypse, "Apocalyptic pronouncements are common enough in the writing of recent *avant-garde* French intellectuals. They go along with that strain of theoretical anti-humanism which heralds an end to all traditional (anthropocentric) philosophies of language and interpretation" (227). Michel Foucault, for example, writes of "the death of the author" and "the end of man"; and Derrida examines at least the possibility of both "the end of representation" and "the end of metaphysics." And, of course, Jean Baudrillard's continuing assessment of the overtaking of the "real" by its "simulation" depends for its effectiveness, at least in part, on the unabashedly apocalyptic rhetoric and imagery he scatters throughout writings like "The Year 2000 Has Already Happened" (1985) and *The Illusion of the End* (1992). Baudrillard's apocalypticism may be sublimely ironic, but French irony cannot erase the sheer eschatological *affect* of his reports from the trenches of hyperreality. Even Haraway's cyborg, functioning as it does as a challenge to Judeo-Christian apocalypticism, constructs through its demolition of the liberal-humanist subject its own version of "the end of man."[6] The postmodern condition, after all, *is* a critical condition, and both theory and speculative fiction continue to be marked by anxiety about—as well as desire for—radical endings and transformations.[7]

Douglas Coupland's *Girlfriend in a Coma* enacts a precise repudiation of the Derridean universe of absolute futility and freedom and a particularly contemporary (re)turn to the anxious comforts of apocalyptic logic. In *Girlfriend* the end of the world provides a genuine salvation for disaffected characters who find themselves trapped in the unending and meaningless stream of time-in-technoculture. While the novel's plot is relatively unencumbered by the technologically inflected discourse of conventional science fiction, at the same time its focus is very specifically the anomie of Western technoculture in the two decades leading up to the end of the millennium. If *Neuromancer* was *the* speculative fiction for the mid-1980s, *Girlfriend in a Coma* demonstrates the distance between that moment of relative cultural confidence and its own moment in the late 1990s.

As has been frequently noted, Gibson's novel is populated by a wide variety of artificial intelligences and technologically enhanced humans: *Neuromancer* celebrates a posthumanist acceptance of the fusion of the human and the technological. In contrast, Coupland's novel constructs such a merging in terms of loss and dehumanization: when one character asks whether the new technologies have made human beings "new and improved and faster and better," another wearily tells her that "[y]ou'll get used to them. . . . It's not up for debate. We lost. Machines won" (143). While a defining feature of the central human characters in *Neuromancer* is their ability to adapt to a constantly changing technological environment, that same environment has rendered Coupland's Gen-Xers "stunted" and "lacking" (143).

Coupland's novel is set in the affluent middle-class suburbs of Vancouver, and his main characters are a group of childhood friends for whom the promise of the 1970s has been betrayed by the increasingly banal realities of the 1980s and 1990s. As adults they inhabit, in Coupland's terms, a wasteland of North American commodification and addiction: Richard sells real estate and drinks heavily; Pam and Hamilton, both of whom become addicted to heroin, work at Monster Machine, providing special effects for a variety of West Coast television series (one of which is clearly modeled on *The X-Files*); Wendy's life is overshadowed by her unremitting schedule as an emergency-room doctor; Linus, the most promising of them all, wastes his time on pointless road trips. These are the unlikely survivors of the end of their world. On November 28, 1999, every single human being in the world, except for these five friends (as well as Richard's girlfriend, Karen, and their teenaged daughter, Meaghan), falls into a deep sleep and dies. Human time and human history, which have become reduced to absurdist insignificance, simply stop—the world will remain asleep for a year, until these characters come to accept their roles as the neoapostles of a re-created reality. Unlike most recent apocalyptic scenarios, Coupland's end of the world is the result of neither nuclear war nor eco-catastrophe; it is as deliberately fantastic a way of wiping the slate clean and starting over as is the biblical Flood.

In *Girlfriend in a Coma*, characters hover between dreams of a golden past forever lost in time and a future that is at once banal and dreadful.[8] Reading the novel is like reading a fictional affirmation of Fredric Jameson's observation that contemporary Western culture can be defined, in part, through its loss of the sense of a viable future, concomitant with its loss of a sense of history. In "Postmodernism, or The Cultural Logic of Late Capitalism" (1984)—another extremely influential mid-1980s document that helped to map our theoretical ideas about postmodernity—Jameson opens by observing that "[t]he last few years have been marked by an inverted millenarianism, in which premonitions of the future, catastrophic or redemptive, have been replaced by senses of the end of this or that" (53). He goes on to argue that "we now inhabit the synchronic rather than the diachronic," contending that contemporary cultural expressions "are today dominated by categories of space rather than by categories of time" (64).[9] In Jameson's analysis, history has become transformed into nostalgia and the past has become reduced to a series of glossy images available to us only in endless circulation through electronic media; at the same time, the failure of the utopian imagination in the context of commodity capitalism spells the failure of our ability to imagine better futures, if indeed we can still imagine any futures at all.

In 1979, when *Girlfriend* opens, seventeen-year-old Karen Ann McNeil, the eponymous girlfriend, leaves a sealed letter with her boyfriend, Richard, and then proceeds to fall into a coma that lasts until 1997—prefiguring the sleep that will eventually overtake all of humanity. In her letter to Richard, Karen expresses her extreme anxiety about time-future:

I've been having these visions this week. . . . [T]hese voices are arguing while I get to see bits of (this sounds so bad) the Future!

It's dark there—in the Future, I mean. It's not a good place. Everybody looks so old and the neighborhood looks like shit (pardon my French!!)

I'm writing this note because I'm scared. . . . I feel like sleeping for a thousand years—that way I'll never have to be around for this weird new future. (28)

Significantly, the sign of her body's failure is its now utter dependence upon technology; as Richard notes, "The machinery of [Karen's] new life was fully set in motion—the IVs, respirator, tubes, and wave monitors" (29). In contrast to the conventions of cyberpunk and other technologically oriented speculative fictions, Karen's new cyborg body spells tragedy, not triumph. Contrast the comatose Karen with *Neuromancer*'s central female character, the razor-girl/bodyguard Molly Millions. Endowed by technology with more than human speed and strength, Molly too has experienced coma of a sort: the money for her technoenhancements has been earned by her work as a "meat puppet," a prostitute who remains unconscious of the work that her body is doing: "Renting the goods, is all. You aren't in, when it's all happening" (147).

While *Neuromancer* famously blurs the distinctions between categories such as authentic and inauthentic, organic and technological, *Girlfriend* is careful to maintain these distinctions. This is highlighted, for instance, in Richard's appalled reaction to the discovery that Pam and Hamilton have constructed a plastic dummy of Karen's body at Monster Machine; his immediate desire is "to see the real Karen, who only differed slightly from the plastic female replica" (91), but who, nevertheless, is *not* a replica, *not* a simulacrum, but the woman he loves.

While Karen hides out in her coma, Richard and his friends wander aimlessly through nearly two decades of enervated existence before being rescued by the end of the world. In Jameson's terms, history has become reduced to mere temporal sequence for these characters: they become more and more lost, more and more despairing, less and less capable of imagining a future that might be different from their meaningless present. Nostalgia for a more authentic and more meaningful world pervades *Girlfriend*, but the past (represented by the more innocent 1970s) is gone and there is no future, only the promise of more of the same. The only possible redemption from absolute insignificance is through the absolute destruction of things as they are. So, in Coupland's impossible fantasy of salvation, history comes to an end and his characters are transformed into "post-historic" (275) subjects who are then returned to the world in order to "clear the land for a new culture" (274). As Karen has suspected, there is indeed a reason for this particular end of the world; it is revealed to them through Jared, a friend who died young and who, as a ghost, narrates part of the story and helps to prepare them for their roles as the neoapostles of new-world salvation: "Grind questions onto the glass on photocopiers," he orders them. "Scrape challenges onto old auto parts and throw them off of bridges so that future people digging in the mud will question the world, too" (272).

Karen, who has awakened from her coma after eighteen years, provides the defamiliarizing perspective that damns the present: her devastating observations about what the world has become serve to demonstrate the loss of innocence and authenticity of this present world order: "People didn't evolve. I mean, the world became faster and smarter and in some ways cleaner. Like cars—cars didn't smell anymore. But people stayed the same. They actually— *wait*—what's the opposite of progressed?" (217).

Coupland's novel is neoconservative salvation history complete with ritual sacrifice. In her role as the novel's Christ figure, Karen must willingly return to her coma so that Richard and his friends can devote the rest of their lives to making the world a more meaningful place. The novel concludes with images of newfound truth, newfound hope, and the potential for a newly re-created world:

> Richard thinks about being alive at this particular juncture in history and he can only marvel—to be alive at this wondrous point—this jumping-off point toward further reaches. . . .
> You'll soon see us walking down your street [he thinks], our backs held proud, our eyes dilated with truth and power. . . . We'll draw our line in the sand and force the world to cross our line. Every cell in our body explodes with the truth. . . . We'll be adults who smash the tired, exhausted system. We'll crawl and chew and dig our way into a radical new world. We will change minds and souls from stone and plastic into linen and gold— that's what I believe. That's what I know. (284)

Coupland's rejection of the hip antiapocalypticism of texts like *Neuromancer* is emphasized by his novel's self-consciously intertextual (re)turn to the paradigmatic Golden Age apocalypticism of Arthur C. Clarke. Early in *Girlfriend*, considering his own dismal moment in time, Richard muses: "That month I had read a science fiction story, *Childhood's End*. In it, the children of Earth conglomerate to form a master race that dreams together, that collectively moves planets. This made me wonder, what if the children of Earth instead fragmented, checked out, had their dreams erased and became vacant? What if instead of unity, there was atomization and amnesia and comas?" (61).

Richard's ultimate vision of the achievement of a long-deferred adulthood rewrites Clarke's tale of the end of the human race. More accurately, *Childhood's End* describes the evolution of the *children* of the human race into a vast psychic organism that triumphantly sets out for the stars; in the process, older generations and Earth itself are destroyed. Clarke's final vision in *Childhood's End*, referred to by the one remaining human spectator as "the climax of all history" (214), is one of the most transcendent moments in genre sf: "There's a great burning column, like a tree of fire, reaching above the western horizon. It's a long way off, right round the world. I know where it springs from: *they're* on their way at last, to become part of the Overmind. Their probation is ended: they're leaving the last remnants of matter behind. . . . And—oh, this is hard to describe, but just then I felt a great wave of emotion sweep over me. It wasn't joy or sorrow; it was a sense of fulfillment, achievement" (215–16).

Coupland echoes Clarke's metaphorical appeal to images of infancy and maturity to dramatize the release of his characters from their long childhood within the stifling exigencies of commodity capitalism. Richard's final vision—"We'll be adults who smash the tired, exhausted system"—demonstrates that, at long last, Coupland's characters are on the verge of experiencing the as-yet-unknown freedoms of a new maturity, as the end of the world breaks up the unceasing flow of what Kermode has referred to as "simple chronicity," the meaningless passage of time (46). Coupland's narrative describes the transformation of "simple chronicity" into meaningful history.

Girlfriend in a Coma strongly supports Jameson's observations about the postmodern loss of the sense of a viable future. Although the novel ends on a note of radical desire, at a "jumping-off point toward further reaches," it nevertheless has nothing to say about the new world toward which it gestures. All it can assure its readers is that this new world is attainable; as Jared asks Richard: "haven't you always felt that you live forever on the brink of knowing a great truth? Well, that feeling is true. There *is* the truth. It does exist" (272).[10] Like a textual Moses, *Girlfriend* points us toward the Promised Land but cannot itself enter.

Such a lack of vision is, perhaps, inevitable. In its rejection of both postmodern irony and the "play" of infinite deferral, Coupland's novel is, in its own way, a determined repudiation of the posthuman values espoused by *Neuromancer*, more engaged in refusal than affirmation. From this perspective, *Girlfriend* is an expression of what I take Krishnan Kumar to be referring to when he complains, in his discussion of contemporary utopianism, that "we seem to be in the presence here of a debased millenarianism, without a compensating utopian vision." Like Jameson, Kumar sees expressed in contemporary apocalypticism only "endings without new beginnings" (212); in his view, "[w]e have, it seems, at the end of the second millennium achieved *the* millennium, the hoped-for state of peace and plenty. But it brings no pleasure, and promises no happiness. In this sense it seems not to make much difference whether we look with foreboding to a dismal future, or proclaim our good luck at the way things have turned out. Neither brings any comfort" (205).

In fact, both *Neuromancer* and *Girlfriend* fall silent as they approach the edge of apocalyptic revelation, although for very different reasons. *Neuromancer*'s silence is deliberate and ironic; it confirms that there is nothing to reveal, that "things aren't different. Things are things." It deemphasizes the potential for (political) change within the historical processes of an increasingly interconnected global order. *Girlfriend*'s silence—equally apolitical—is the text holding its breath on the edge of significance. Unlike *Neuromancer*'s characters, *Girlfriend*'s characters have awakened from their decades-long "coma" and the text leaves them—and its readers—poised for a revelation that is always to come at the end of human history.

Postapocalyptic

> And yet, unspeakable and portentous events have occurred, are occurring, as we were looking the other way, or even watching directly.
>
> —James Berger, *After the End* 217

What if, as Richard asks, "instead of unity, there was atomization and amnesia and comas?" (61). What if the characters in both *Neuromancer* and *Girlfriend in a Coma* have actually missed the (or at least *an*) apocalypse, "as [they] were looking the other way, or even watching directly"? (Berger 217). By shifting the interpretive perspective on these two novels only slightly, it is possible to apply Coupland's coma metaphor to Gibson's novel as well and to (re)read each novel from another (postapocalyptic) point of view. After all, there is a sense in which each fictional world is, in fact, (always already) postapocalyptic—for all *Neuromancer*'s antiapocalyptic skepticism and for all *Girlfriend*'s apocalyptic yearning. Such a rereading suggests something of the complex nature of the contemporary apocalyptic imagination, something of our own sense of history as a series of traumatic endings and beginnings.

As Claire Sponsler has astutely noted, the narrative worlds of cyberpunk are often constructed in familiar postapocalyptic terms (253). *Neuromancer*'s world, for example, has survived not only at least one nuclear war, but also a pandemic that seems to have destroyed most of the larger mammals. For *Neuromancer*'s characters, of course, pandemics and wars are just more events in the succession of events that shape human time; so is their technologically driven "post-humanization," characterized by Case as "a gradual and willing accommodation of the machine" (203). As Sponsler observes, "Cyberpunk . . . attaches zero value to its apocalypses: they are neither good nor evil, they simply *are* (or rather *have been*, since they invariably occur at some time before the story opens)" (253). While Gibson's characters demonstrate an appropriate level of "boredom with the apocalypse," however, *Neuromancer* itself seems to invite an active exploration of the nature and significance of historical transformation, self-consciously situating its characters on the other side of a series of historical traumas and limning the features of an ironically postapocalyptic fictional world.

As befits an action-oriented caper novel, characters in *Neuromancer* rarely stop hustling, and in their sheer breathless momentum they are very unlike *Girlfriend*'s apathetic Gen-Xers. All this activity remains focused on the frenetic present moment, however, on the adrenaline rush of wheeling and dealing, on the "intricate dance of desire and commerce" (11) that defines their world; they remain unconcerned by and, for the most part, unaware of, the historical events that have shaped that world, and equally unconcerned about the possibilities of the future. While their headlong momentum certainly drives the narrative, it is no accident that the text repeatedly calls attention precisely to their *lack* of attention—as in Case's last meeting with Wintermute. And it is no accident that so many characters experience repeated lapses in consciousness, suggesting as this does their failure to grasp the enormity of the social and technological upheavals that have marked their recent history and, as the conclusion of the novel suggests, will continue to do so.

I have already mentioned Molly's work as a "meat puppet." Then there are the members of the wealthy and powerful Tessier-Ashpool clan, who routinely spend much of their lives in cryogenic deep-freeze, each activated for a limited time to take individual control in the running of their commercial dynasty. After his death, the Dixie Flatline, hacker *par excellence*, has become a downloaded personality, a "data construct," that remains, for the most part, inactive; when recalled to consciousness, it has no memory of previous waking events. Armitage, the ostensible organizer of the Straylight run, is also a construct, a synthetic personality grafted onto the traumatized ruins of what used to be Colonel Gregory Corto.

Even Case, despite his being the point-of-view consciousness in the novel, suffers frequent lapses in awareness. His keenest pleasures are associated with the physical unconsciousness that accompanies his times spent in the virtualities of cyberspace. Moreover, he several times experiences extended periods of virtual existence when his consciousness is trapped in cyberspace by Wintermute and he subjectively lives for days and weeks while only minutes pass in the physical world. Gibson chillingly evokes the schizophrenic nature of Case's physical withdrawal during one of the scenes in which he shares Molly's physical perceptions through the technology of "simstim": he finds himself "staring down . . . at a white-faced, wasted figure, afloat in a loose fetal crouch, a cyberspace deck between its thighs, a band of silver trodes above closed, shadowed eyes. . . . He was looking at himself" (256).

Not so dissimilar to *Neuromancer*'s Case and Molly, *Girlfriend*'s characters also sleep through their lives, seduced by commodities and simulation. In spite of the fact that we last see them looking ahead to an unimaginable new world, *Girlfriend* first constructs them as unwitting survivors in a postapocalyptic world ineradicably marked by the division of time-present from time-past. Significantly, the text identifies comas as "a byproduct of modern living. . . . Comas are as modern as polyester, jet travel, and microchips" (63), as Linus points out, suggesting the aptness of the coma as a metaphor for the distractions of contemporary existence. While, unlike Gibson's characters, *Girlfriend*'s characters do gradually develop an awareness of how blank and meaningless their lives have become, such awareness only leaves them paralyzed, devoid of both energy and agency, until outside forces precipitate their involvement in renewal.

Before the miraculous intervention that literally stops the miserable course of human history in *Girlfriend*, the world has already been trapped within the eternal present of commodity culture, so that, for Linus, for example, "the future is only about changes [in] this world—fashion and machines and architecture" (92). And Hamilton explains his heroin addiction as the inevitable outcome of life in the capitalist utopia that surrounds them: "Don't you understand, Richard? There's nothing at the center of what we do. . . . No center. It doesn't exist. All of us—look at our lives: We have an acceptable level of affluence. We have entertainment. We have a relative freedom from fear. But there's nothing else" (95). These characters inhabit a postapocalyptic world of Baudrillardian simulation, living on in the cluttered and meaningless spaces of the hyperreal. Even before their world comes to a literal end (however temporarily), they have been irrevocably cut off from the innocence and authenticity of a past that lives on only in Karen, the one character who, thanks to her literal coma, has remained unmarked by the desperate banality of time-present. As Coupland writes of Karen, "She provided the idea that some frail essence from a now long-vanished era still existed, that the brutality and extremes of the modern world were not the way the world ought to be" (76). But the new world remains as "unspoken" in Coupland's text as does the "true name" that Gibson's text refuses to pronounce.

Both *Neuromancer* and *Girlfriend in a Coma* are exemplary representations of aspects of the postmodern condition. The same postapocalyptic sensibility has also been invoked in the rhetoric of critical-theoretical discourse, for instance in Foucault's "archaeological" examinations of epistemological ruptures, in Jameson's careful descriptions of a contemporary "inverted millenarianism," and in Baudrillard's ironic descriptions of the contemporary landscape of simulation and hyperreality. For Baudrillard, *philosophe* of simulation, the extreme event is precisely the overtaking of the real by the hyperreal and the disappearance of active desire into passive fascination. Thus, for him, postmodernity is clearly the result of an apocalyptic transformation that locates us on the other side of things, just as Gibson's and Coupland's characters find themselves on the other side of a variety of traumatic historical divides.[11]

In a recent interview that strikingly recalls Jameson's comments about "an inverted millenarianism," Gibson explains his sense of the ongoing nature of the postmodern apocalypse, suggesting how we might (re)read the apparently antiapocalyptic tenor of *Neuromancer*: "I do not usually deal in the capital-A Apocalypse. What I've said so far has to do with the ongoing, the daily, the little-a apocalypse, and I believe that each of us today is aware, to some degree, of some convulsive quality in contemporary existence which may actually be new in the experience of the species. There are too many first times today, too many last times" (qtd. in Clute, *The Book of Endtimes* xii).[12]

While the metaphors of apocalypse respond to our sense of the critical condition of the postmodern present, they are, of course, only metaphors, elements of stories devised by ourselves through which we represent and explain the "real" to ourselves. The postmodern apocalypse is not the end of history; rather, it is the apocalypse *within* history, our own particular apocalypse, and as such it is and is not singular, it is and is not absolute. The apocalypse is always situated somewhere in our fraught future; at the same time—to recall that paradigmatic deconstructive phrase—the apocalypse has always already occurred.

Both *Neuromancer* and *Girlfriend in a Coma* suggest that this has become the inevitable shape of human history, that "unspeakable and portentous events have occurred, [and] are occurring" while we remain caught up in our own present concerns, incapable of appreciating their import until long after the fact. These novels also suggest that time-present—postmodern time—is a kind of supplemental time, a time-after-the-end-of-time. While "post" binds us to the old world, the paradigms of modernity that previously provided strategies for negotiating the world can no longer necessarily be trusted. From this perspective, the cautionary "post" in "postmodern" is a complex construction: it demonstrates our sense of distance from an old-world modernism, our anxiety that we are, in fact, on the other side of irrevocable change—postmodernity as a kind of philosophical apocalypse—at the same time as it represents our hesitation in letting go of the past. The contemporary moment might certainly (and dramatically) be characterized as postapocalyptic, balanced between two different versions of the present moment: like Gibson's characters, our investment in the scenarios of absolute endings and beginnings tends to be an ironic one, at the same time as, like Coupland's characters, we find ourselves already on the other side of an implacable historical divide, nostalgically recalling more authentic and less complex modes of being-in-the-world.

11

Kairos

The Enchanted Loom

GWYNETH JONES

Apocalypse: The last book of the New Testament, any book purporting to reveal the future or last things, a revelation or disclosure (Gr. *Apokalypsis*, an uncovering)

The Second Law (and the Seventh Seal)

The world is coming to an end. John Gribbin, British astrophysicist and popular science writer, cites two striking pieces of evidence for this, in his study of the ultimate fate of the universe, *The Omega Point*. The first is that, if you drop an ice cube into a cup of hot coffee, the coffee will grow cold, whereas we never see ice cubes forming spontaneously out of cold liquid while the remaining liquid stays hot. Heat always tends to even out. The second is that at night the stars are bright in a dark sky. If the universe had existed for all eternity, with the same number of stars and galaxies distributed in the same way as we see now, the stars—pouring out their energy—would have filled up the spaces among themselves with light, and the whole sky would be ablaze. The stars haven't been there forever, and they aren't going to last forever either. Eventually all the energy in the known universe will be evened out to a flatline. The stars in the night sky prove that we are living in a place that changes. The darkness around them tells us the direction of that change. Though we inhabit a pocket of nonequilibrium, where the coffee and the ice cube have not reached lukewarm, motionless calm, our fate is inescapable. The universe as we know it was born, and it will die. The seventh seal will be broken; there will be silence in heaven.

Somehow that cup of cooling coffee, which always seems to turn up in descriptions of the second law of thermodynamics, fails to convince me. It's too culture bound. One has to be in the habit of drinking a hot liquid called coffee; one has to be in the habit of letting it grow cold. And the second clause is weak. "We never see this effect . . . ," meaning, strictly, that *we haven't seen it yet*. How can I be sure a defiant ice cube will not fight its way back through the entropy barrier one day if the scientists refuse to tell me for certain that that won't happen? Perhaps this childish resistance of mine is a reminder that cosmology itself is culturally bound. As John Gribbin also remarks, while introducing his readers to the Big Bang hypothesis version of the Last Things, wide acceptance of the idea that the universe has a beginning, a middle, and an end is relatively new to human thought (11). For most of our history, the majority of our cultures have favored either a cyclic universe, a continual creation, or an eternal stasis. The success of this novelty is perhaps a sign of the powerful connections between our dominant scientific culture and Judeo-Christian theology. Modern physicists may believe themselves to be secularists, but the founders of modern science were theologians, and their cultural tradition informs our scientific concepts. Whatever way you look at it, it surely isn't a coincidence that the Big

Bang itself bears a remarkable resemblance to the creation event of Genesis when suddenly, just on a whim (or a vacuum fluctuation), *God said, let there be light. . . .* We had better accept it. Jews, Greeks, Christians, Muslims: we are all of us, here in Europe, still engaged in sailing from Byzantium.[1]

We may also see the Big Bang hypothesis, and the onward-upward cosmic myth that lurks within it, as phenomena of population dynamics. When a critical threshold is passed in the growth and density of human population, either locally or globally, maybe stories of this kind are bound to become important. In "normal" human life, a child's experience is of moving onward and upward, physically and socially, but when adulthood is reached that drive slows down. Life settles into the immemorial cycle of the generations: marriage and bringing up children, putting down roots, growing old. It's only in special circumstances, of unusual success or unusual hardship, that the adult community has to start fragmenting and moving outward, *heading somewhere*. For us, in the modern era, the pace of population growth, which brings with it the idea of progress from a finite beginning to some unknown goal, is unceasing. Maybe that's why the Big Bang hypothesis has become the dominant Creation myth of our global culture. The universe can no longer be seen as a vast wheel, repeating the circle of the seasons on a hugely magnified scale, through cosmological eons. Trapped in permanent adolescence, we feel a Darwinian certainty that *something's got to give*, that every envelope of containment will be broken. We promise ourselves a day of doom, when we will break through the crystal spheres into unlimited heaven.

Escape Plans

This adolescent project of escaping from the human condition is generally supposed to be the chief business of science fiction, and, obediently, my first two novels were devoutly eschatological. The first, *Divine Endurance* (1984), was set in a far-future Southeast Asia, where I imagined the last scientific creation of mechanistic civilization reappearing from the past and mediating the final transition of the human race into a future of enlightened, peaceful, superpowered posthumanity. I followed the classic pattern, leading my far-future characters—the ultimate machine is one of the characters; she's a *metagenetic gynoid*, a living doll who can grant every wish of the human heart—through death, judgment, heaven, and hell, to childhood's end and the brink of a new-made world. *Divine Endurance* was an exercise in displacement. I set the book in a place far removed from my own "Western" world, and borrowed images from Hinduism, Buddhism, and Islam, because it's so much easier to write about big ideas in an alien language. You just don't have the vocabulary to tie yourself in knots. In the second book, *Escape Plans* (1986), I bravely decided to tackle the same subject using the iconography of my own Western, Roman-Greek, Judeo-Christian culture. In the early 1980s, when I was writing *Escape Plans*, I read a collection of articles on cosmology by Stephen Hawking.[2] I was much struck by the points of similarity between cutting-edge cosmological theory and Judeo-Christian theology, and, also, between such theory and the project of science fiction. I wrote about the way outer space can be mapped onto the sacred "other world" of heaven: how "our" culture, the international culture based on the riches of the United States, has (or had) developed an almost medieval idea of life on earth as merely a preparation for our real and much more wonderful future life, out there in the empyrean, where everything in the shining corridors is clean and bright, and nobody dies, nobody drops litter, nobody farts. I wanted to examine this mysterious convergence, whereby both science and religion were insisting that something inimical to human life—like death, or life in a hard vacuum—is certain to be the gateway to perfect freedom and happiness.

I set my story on a version of our earth where there had been no Christian-Era disruption. Classical civilization had continued into the Space Age, the shiny ships had been launched, but then the inhabitants of my earth had found that the way was blocked. Their solar system was sitting in the middle of a trapped region of spacetime (a Stephen Hawking bubble universe), without any possibility of access to the big beyond. They'd discovered that they were the only occupants of this region. No one and nothing from outside could get in, no one inside could get out . . . short of a miracle.

In the childhood of humanity we all believed that the world was ruled by great unseen presences called Death and Love and Chance and Harvest—personified but not controlled by us. There was another theory, almost as universal. Human beings looked up at the deathless stars and decided that we could be immortal too, if we could get up there. In one form or another, this myth was everywhere. Its memory lingered on in the human psyche, until people began to make accurate multidimensional models of spacetime. And whether our myths shaped our physics or the other way round, the vision of eternal youth and unbounded freedom was buried somewhere deep in the drive to space travel. So when we discovered that we are alone, we are trapped and we can never get out, that was the end of a very ancient hope, and also the end of exploration. . . . Not that we really believed that we were going to live forever "out there." But it has an insidious, enduring effect on morale, to know that you are living inside a Black Hole. (*Escape Plans* 39)

I gave my thwarted explorers a medieval universe: where the earth is at the center of things, yes, but that means (as people who talk of the Copernican "dethroning of Man" often forget) the lowest state of being. Then I presented them with the hope of rescue, a messenger from outside their event horizon. She told them that they couldn't beat the equations by building more powerful spaceships or by finding a way to mobilize ever more staggering amounts of energy. But if they would give up everything material, everything that bound them to human life: if they would strip themselves of everything physical, then they could achieve escape velocity. Few people really believed the savior's good news. The path to glory she offered was too difficult, too demanding. Naturally, the Space Age "Romans" of my alternate earth executed her. Needless to say there were rumors, impossible to substantiate, difficult to disprove, that she had survived the experience. I'm sure you know the story. It has been recycled in countless science fictions. Along with eschatology in general, it's one of the ur-narratives of the genre. This predicament of ours, with all its grief and evil, is a temporary problem. *Somebody* knows the way out. You haven't met her and neither have I, but a friend of a friend of mine actually saw the evidence . . .

Well, in the real world space travel is a cramped, ramshackle, and smelly business, and nobody seems to get very far. The heaven we were once promised is now firmly relegated to the land of make-believe. This rather spoils the point of *Escape Plans*, because I didn't want my story to be a fairy tale; I wanted it to make sense. I wanted my characters to be longing for redemption "from the body of this death" the way that people might long to escape from poverty or disease. The cosmology strand, however, was safe from the collapse of space-age futures. It was, it still is, as close to the hard science as I could get it. I put my alternate earth in a bubble universe, so that I'd be able to make sweeping statements about the desperate isolation. But in this great big expanding universe of our own, we are still, as far as we know, absolutely alone. Current cosmology says that the earth is at the center of a sphere, an envelope determined by the light that has reached us since the Big Bang. Supposing we manage to search that whole sphere and find nothing but hot gas and cold rocks, *which is not totally unlikely, on the present evidence*, it is logically, fundamentally impossible for us to break out any further. In the end, the predicament I described in *Escape Plans* could be the simple truth about our existence in this universe. We're in prison, alone, and we can never get out.

In Praise of Limited Solutions

The walls of our prison are high, but they're an awesomely long way off. In fact, as I noticed after a while, most science fiction is not apocalyptic. If science fiction is, as I have suggested, a response to a situation of population expansion, the solutions the genre offers are usually less extreme than mine. There's no need to resort to utter and absolute change to restore a sense of *lebensraum*. From ancient times, storytellers have simply cleared the ground with some disaster movie scenario such as Gilgamesh's and Noah's Flood—easily extrapolated from actual events. In the modern era global thermonuclear war served the same purpose for a generation of science fiction writers. In the postmodern era, we have an embarrassment of possibilities. We can crash the population with a killer virus; a decade or two of low-intensity warfare; the failure of a major food crop; a megasized pollution incident; an asteroid strike—not to mention plain old global warming, which can sink much of modern civilization in a watery grave.

More optimistic storytellers see no need for the line on the graph to plunge at all. By their reckoning we will neither fall nor leap into the unknown. We will simply find more and more efficient ways to harness the energy of the sun, until the least hospitable of the planets bows to the power of human territorial expansion, and finally the whole solar system is converted into a Dyson Sphere, with the sun in the center of a vast hive of entirely mundane (as it were) technological achievement. The vintage model for this antiapocalypse, according to which, instead of reaching the moment of uncovering, we just go on *spreading*, outward and outward forever, is probably Olaf Stapledon's *Last And First Men* (1930). Kim Stanley Robinson in his formidable Mars trilogy—*Red Mars* (1993), *Green Mars* (1994), and *Blue Mars* (1997)—has envisaged the expansionist future in extraordinary depth and detail, while Greg Egan of Australia has done the same job from a nonhumanist point of view, in his hard-science infotainment *Diaspora* (1997). The Mars trilogy and *Diaspora* are both important science fictions (with the caveat that *Diaspora* may not be comfortable reading, if trying to think in five dimensions alarms you). Both of them depict the apotheosis of the Industrial Revolution and the American Dream. Wave after wave of the brightest and the best, overcoming all obstacles, will build cities on the burning line between night and day on Mercury, swim like dolphins (with genetically engineered adaptation) in the methane seas of Titan, send digitized clones of themselves to explore the farthest distant quarters of the galaxy. Of course, the Second Law still gets us in the end. Heat will even out. But there is no need to envisage or to fear that dying fall. It will not happen to us, or to any imaginable seed of ours.

Before I go any further into my own apocalyptic progress, I want to acknowledge the value of limited solutions. Most science fiction is written for and by people unhappy with the idea of dying (immortality or indefinite longevity is phenomenally constant on the agenda) but otherwise broadly satisfied with things as they are. Like the poor in times of revolution, sf writers don't really want anything different, just *more* (and more and more) of the same. This is certainly a sensible approach. Progress has its price (too bad, in terms of those optimistic futures, for the billions who are *not* among the brightest and the best); but idealistic revolutions tend to have depressingly poor results. There's an awful symmetry, whereby the bid for freedom rebounds to a position more doctrinaire, repressive, and harsh than the situation it set out to cure.

But to return to my history. I wrote my first two books without realizing that my fiction was related to my life experience, except in the most banal sense. (I lived in Southeast Asia when I was writing *Divine Endurance*. *Escape Plans* was partly inspired by the Space Race, which I had followed as a child in the sixties.) Eventually it dawned on me that I was dreaming about the end of the world for personal reasons and that I was not alone. Whatever complex of familial, genetic, and historical factors had made me dissatisfied with the state of affairs that normal science fiction writers only want to see expanding forever, I had plenty of company in the mid-1980s. Social discomfort, and specifically sexual discomfort, seemed to be the secret force behind a different kind of apocalyptic discourse. I had never been interested in literary theory, but through feminism I started reading the texts, and I was deeply intrigued. I was especially impressed by Roland Barthes's landmark study *S/Z* (1974), which anatomizes (I first wrote *atomizes*, which may be a more accurate term) a story by Balzac, about a man who falls in love with an Italian singer, a castrato, a transvestite whom he believes to be a woman. In *S/Z*, Barthes blows away the cobwebs of period romance and recovers the utter *strangeness* of this tale, which challenges first the fixed nature of human sexual relations and then, as if the connection were inevitable, the fixed connection between words and things. Language itself, I learned, is a covering, an outer dress. It has hooks at the back: one can take it off. This was *very* interesting, because it was exactly what I was being told—and by the same sexual route—in feminist science fiction.

Autodeconstructionism

Now that it's all over, the project of feminist science fiction seems like some mad plan the CIA might have cooked up at the height of the cold war. Our mission was to infiltrate and destroy the archetype of male sexual adventure. For science fiction is nothing else. James Tiptree, Jr., legendary double agent in the sf gender wars, blew the cover on that in her series of superbly virile stories.[3] The chaste technological diaspora is a fake, says Tiptree. The whole fantasy empire of sf is nothing other than an orgy of cosmic impregnation. The optimism of the expansionists, even the most humane of them, is secretly based on the law of might-is-right, on the endemic abuse of power, which is justified (sometimes openly, sometimes cryptically) by recourse to the natural sexual drive of the human male.

It was fashionable at that time (we made it fashionable: one of our covert disinformation campaigns) for both men and women to complain bitterly about the inappropriately "sexist" cover art of sf, which kept people from taking the genre's sober, intelligent, futurist speculation seriously. But we knew very well (and so did the men, though most of them didn't dare say so), that the art—all those air-brushed spacegirls in the crotch-hugging suits; all those wispily clad or bronze-breasted females ravished (as far as public decency permitted) by monsters or spacemen—was telling the honest truth. Sf is an expansionist myth. It's about *reproductive success*. The gadgets and spaceships are all very fine and dandy, but what we're *always, really* talking about is how Man gets out there to the edge of the known, grabs hold of a chunk of that alien dark, and pumps it full of his seed.[4] We feminist fans and writers had decided that we did not like being cast as *the alien dark*. We set about to give ourselves a different costume and a little more variety. We proved, by fictional experiment, that men could be the ones who stayed at home, fit only for sexual pleasure and procreation, while the women made discoveries and had adventures. We replaced the void-piercing phallic engineering with an enveloping matrix of life sciences; we proved that the adventure story template would function under these conditions. We claimed that we simply wanted a piece of the action, a few strong female characters on the bridge of the *Enterprise*, but, yes, of course we wanted to take over. For a while, we sincerely believed that by deconstructing and reconstructing our genre, this reactionary stronghold of the imagination, we would have some effect on the real world.

If only we'd been satisfied with those strong female characters. But it wasn't enough. We found that we didn't want to write about male impersonators, "men with breasts" doing hero stuff. We wanted real women in our space adventures. But what, exactly, is a real woman? Now that's where our problems began. We tried to reverse the polarity of the myth, tried to make that female darkness the subject of the story and banish the male principle of light to the sidelines. In doing this, we ran up against the veil of language itself. How do you write an action-adventure where female-dark-passive equals win? It's difficult or impossible, because *win* is inexorably coded bright-active. Which (in the revised lexicon) ought to equal *lose*. We were trapped by an abstract system of differences to which we'd given moral weighting, and there seemed to be no way out. When articulate language itself is held to be an invention of the evil empire, how in hell do you write stories? When we realized what we'd done to ourselves, the movement splintered. Women, and other feminists, who were willing to burn a little incense at the shrine of *might is right*, simply became orthodox science fiction writers; and many of them prospered. Others found a modest niche for themselves writing virtuous, virtually adventure-free versions of the great adventure. The most rational and rigorous of the cadre simply gave up, laid their cards on the table, and walked away. The impasse that we had to reach had been predicted from an early stage. In an important story published in 1970, Joanna Russ,[5] the most assured polemicist of that feminist decade, describes precisely the predicament of a young woman who wants to be a science fiction writer. The story is called "The Second Inquisition." It's set in small-town Middle America (the period doesn't really matter). A young girl meets—or maybe fantasizes this role onto her parents' rather odd female lodger—a visitant from the future. The woman is everything a woman cannot be, in the stifling conventional society of this small town. She awakens the hope of escape, but her complicated and mysterious adventure cannot touch the real girl's real life of dress codes, peer pressure, social expectations. Two worlds collide, trying to occupy the same space, and the adventurer disappears, leaving the girl stranded with only the memory of a dream. Any girl can enjoy reading science fiction, as long as she's prepared to become a male impersonator, or at least a "tomboy" in her imagination. But when she tries to put *herself* into the dream, the adventure vanishes.

I say "us" and "we" when speaking of feminist science fiction in the seventies, out of solidarity. Most of it happened in the United States, and to me it might as well have been on Mars. Meanwhile the postwar economic boom that had been pumping through U.K. society in my childhood and adolescence had ground to a halt. I remember telling people, when I was an undergraduate, that I wasn't interested in scrabbling for wealth or position. I wanted to live the life of a socialist artist, doing as much needful labor as would keep me fed and having the rest of my life for my own work. In the Welfare State, that made perfect sense. In the 1980s, reality began to bite. We children of the dream had dismissed the whole idea of *taking power*, so there was nothing we could do to defend Utopia, the Good State of equality and liberty (free health and education for all!) that we'd thought was our native land. My friends and I had no faith in politics; there was no party we could join. Our only consolation was to fantasize (like so many dreamers before us) some kind of absolute change . . . a movement coming up from the streets, a violent overthrow that would somehow, this time, be good and innocent.

This was my situation when I began to write my third eschatological novel, *Kairos* (1988), equally uncompromising in theme but another step closer to home. In *Divine Endurance* I had written about the end of all things as a long-haul tourist. In *Escape Plans*, I told the tale of supernatural breakthrough in the imagery of a world I'd seen on television. In *Kairos* I set the scene in my own here and now: in the grungy, defeated margins of feminist and socialist protest, in 1980s Britain.

The story features a lesbian couple, Otto Murray and Sandy Brize. Otto, a middle-class radical, runs a shoestring socialist-feminist bookshop. Her partner, Sandy, is the clever working-class kid who bought the dream of escape but caught that disease in the virulent form that destroys all hope of material success. There's also Candide, Otto's ten-year-old son (my characters tend to come in threes, but that's another story). Sandy's life is in crisis. She's tired of being Otto's "wife"; she has no faith in Otto's politics. The relationship is falling apart, and Sandy seems to be having a serious breakdown. At this point Candide's pet dog disappears (the dog, by the way, is called Vera, which means "the true image"). Vera has been kidnapped by a sinister acquaintance of the couple who is now working for a cult organization called Breakthru. Candide starts to get small pieces of his dog delivered in the mail, along with threats of more to follow if he doesn't hand over a maguffin object that has fallen into his mother's hands. He knows his mother won't deal with right-wing terrorists. He enlists Sandy as his knight errant, and they set out to rescue the pet.

Sandy becomes the tomboy male-impersonator. Candide soon begins to suspect that she has the requisite powers to be a superhero. But poor child, his hero/ine is at an existential impasse: bright-active-positive on the outside, full of darkness and destruction within. Here's Sandy holding forth about the trouble with revolutions:

> "It's lucky normal criminal human nature takes over so quickly. If revolutionaries ever followed things through, where would it end? First you unmask your enemies, then you unmask your friends, then you unmask yourself. You think you've got the world naked, free of bias, and then you see a little rough edge somewhere, and you start picking at it. That's what's happened to me. Scritch, scratch, another mask comes off: and another and another. It hurts worse than anything. But it is such fun to see the stuff coming away. You start off with politics, then you do it to sex and money. Before you know it, you're right through the skin of things. Unmask the street, unmask the trees. . . ." (*Kairos* 162)

This is an *apocalypse* indeed, making sense of the term but making the project extremely alarming. When we *uncover* what's going on inside a science fiction story, we come up against a truth that's exasperating for all feminists, and indeed for all political radicals, or even for all heterodox thought. Limited revolution is no revolution at all. James Tiptree, Jr., put it succinctly: "*It'll never change unless you change the whole world . . .*" ("Women Men Don't See" 154; emphasis added). But where's the change going to stop? What if you follow those rubs and inconsistencies, the parts of the world that don't fit, what if you track them down, through history, biology, ecology, and on and on, until you reach the fundamental supports of reality itself? What if you find that establishing gender equality in the workplace is going to interfere with whatever makes the sun come up in the morning, or water run downhill (which is, after all, exactly what outraged conservatives have expected us to believe, over the years). Well then, what then? If it's up to you, what's your choice? What are you going to do?

Angels and Aliens

At the risk of trespassing onto biblical territory, I'd like to examine, briefly, the technical difference between apocalyptic writing and prophecy. According to the biblical commentaries, prophets speak about their own world and in their own voices, whereas apocalypts describe future events and typically disguise their identities, adopting the handle of some previous visionary. Thus, the "John" of Revelation isn't claiming to be the same person as "John" the New Testament Evangelist; "he" is merely establishing his credentials. The prophet's career may be recorded by someone else, but he or she is ordered by God to speak: *go and tell them in Nineveh*; while the apocalypt is told by the angel to write: *write it in a book*. Wise advice. The prophet's news is humanly, personally convincing (*you've been wicked and you have to repent*). The apocalyptic message is only credible if its origin is supernatural; and on Judgment Day itself, repentance isn't exactly irrelevant, but it isn't going to make any difference to the main program. The heavens are still going to be stripped bare of stars, the sea will be no more, the world is still going to be rolled up like a scroll. Science fiction also comes in these two sizes. In my first two books I'd stayed (just about) on the prophecy side of the line. Now I was going to tackle the real, no-kidding, cosmic derailment, the day when, in the twinkling of an eye, *everything* changes. I needed to think about angels and about the end of time.

In our present millennial era, supernatural agents bearing messages from the beyond are called aliens, but it's fairly clear that the physical phenomena giving rise to these reports have been the same throughout human history. Eyewitness accounts of the spectacular celestial displays at Fatima, Portugal, at the beginning of the last century would certainly pass equally well as descriptions of ufo activity.[6] As a skeptic, I'm bemused by the way modern ufologists blithely embrace this continuity as confirmation of their own beliefs. See! The aliens have been visiting for hundreds of years! What is it that stops them from dropping the other shoe and accepting that these lights people see in the sky— the glowing shapes, the whirling wheels—have always been *strange lights in the sky* and that the supernatural scolding (which is such an essential part of the ufo myth) has been added after the fact, dressed to the taste of the times. The bottom line seems to be that signs and wonders simply aren't thrilling unless there's a human interest element. Personally I deplore this attitude. I'm prepared to be awed by a meteor shower or an aurora borealis show that doesn't care (so to speak) if I live or die. But what's really strange, when you look at the idea closely, is the way both the alien-hunters and the religious visionaries are so determined that their Small Gray sightings and their close encounters with the Virgin Mary have to be *material* experiences. How does that confirm the validity of the vision? Material like what? Like thought? Like neutrinos? Like quarks?

I suppose that if there have been strange lights in the sky from time to time throughout human history, it may indeed be because the angels, or the aliens, have always been warning us that the end is nigh. If a thousand ages in their sight is but a moment gone, they probably have a different idea of what "nigh" means. Or perhaps they are talking to us in our own language—telling us that the end of the world is coming *real soon now*, in a very human sense: *this project will remain incomplete for the indefinite future*. But what does hard science have to say about the actual arrival of Judgment Day, and related phenomena? At first, the raw material looks unpromising. According to the currently most favored theory of the Second Law, there will be no spectacular End of All Things, no matter how unimaginably distant, just an inexorable fade-out. Happily, there are other choices on the menu. There's the Dark Matter theory, which holds that there has to be far more mass in the universe than can be accounted for. If there is enough of this mysterious Dark Matter, most of which has yet to be identified (Gribbon 29–149), then instead of expanding vapidly to heat-death, the universe will reach a maximum and start to contract. At that point of involution, all the fundamental laws will collapse. The cosmos will start folding over on itself like an orange being unpeeled, and time will run backward (whatever that means) toward the Big Crunch. I think we can safely envisage some very strange phenomena, a whole Book of Revelation of special effects, around that turning point . . . with the slight problem, for the apocalyptic storyteller, that Planet Earth and all things human will have been interstellar dust for eons by then.

Definitive, final solutions in cosmology come and go. As I revise this essay (in the autumn of the year 2000) the Steady State universe (where nothing changes) is looking strong, while the whole Big Bang paradigm, with all its ramifications, is looking shaky.[7] But to return to the Big Crunch, which was fashionable when I was writing *Kairos*, there is a simple solution to the problem of the intractable timescale. If all bets are off, if time ceases, and every fundamental law is undone—which is what the science *says* (and this science, remember, is describing the behavior of the fundamental particles that make up my body and my brain, as well as the gas clouds between the stars)—then the Apocalypse Experience (although, er, of course, it's really happening already, or all the time, *sub species aeternitas*) can start happening for us any time. We can be the observers that make it happen. (There are many scientists who claim to believe that the universe only exists insofar as we observe it. The slow attrition of heat-death is something we observe all the time in everything around us and in our own mortality: so heat-death is safe. It makes science fictional sense to assume that the End of the World also needs to be validated in this way.) The Crunch could start tomorrow. And if it does, I think I can safely predict that we'll be having some weird neurological experiences, to go with the (objective?) lights in the sky. So what will the end of all things be like, experienced as a human event, dressed in the language and the desires of the human mind? That's what I tried to imagine: and here's Sandy again, a little farther along the road:

"Oh, I see it. . . . This is what it is, it's a mind flying apart. If someone tries to dismantle their mind, there comes a level of incredible resistance. And then the sun bursts open. Flying apart, flying apart! And I said, '*I want what is not.*' I stepped out of the middle dimensions, into the other world, the other side of things. And I carried everything that I touched with me." She held up her hands, grubby and gray, with the white skin showing blue veins through the grime.

"Look, look. These aren't hands anymore. They are words now. And soon, and soon. . . ." The dead angel had vanished. . . . Sandy went on covering the old factory floor with exploding universes: trees and dreams and chairs and memories—all breaking, all spinning, all returning through the channel of her mind to the unnamable, the undivided. (*Kairos* 204)

Wings That Can't Be Broken

Apocalyptic writing is called "gospel"—that means good news—"for bad times." The current proliferation of ufo sightings, alien abductions, and bleeding statues too, seems—broadly speaking—to be the province of the fundamentalist Right, my natural enemies. If those folk are feeling hard-pressed, and taking refuge in daydreams about winding up the whole shebang, this should be good news for me (not to mention for all of life on this small planet). Alas, no. People repent for prophets. Apocalyptic warnings don't tend to alter anyone's moral behavior (one is either blessed or done for, so why worry?); and, anyway, I'm afraid the aliens can't be trusted any better than the angels of the Lord. They are not going to turn up and whisk the abductees and the chat-show hosts away to some Seventh Heaven or better planet. No, Sandy's dream is not going to come true. In the real world, I have no faith in signs and wonders.

Once, I saw the Holy Spirit. It (or rather, She, since I understand Santa Sophia may be regarded as female, in the same sense as the Father and Son are regarded as male) appeared as a patch of glittery, scratchy golden light, hanging in the air in the bathroom, above the toilet cistern. I was three. I think my vision had something to do with sandpaper, a pleasing phenomenon that I'd recently met for the first time. Once, when I was nine, my mother reported telepathic contact. She had heard my voice saying in her mind, "*Mummy*," with such strange clarity of internal locution that she investigated, and we established that it could have happened at the very moment when I, in Woolworth's in Barrow-in-Furness (a town in Cumbria, not far from the United Kingdom's most notorious nuclear power plant; that probably had something to do with it), that afternoon had spied a bin full of nougat, her favorite candy, and decided to buy some for her.

Luckily for me, there are no further incidents to report. I was in no danger of getting caught up, like the three children of Fatima, in the tidal forces of adult need, which might have transformed my strange moments into a huge, helpless edifice of lies. But I remember also, and better than either of those barely-there brushes with the paranormal, that once I dreamed, with unearthly sweetness, that my father was teaching me to walk on air. It was in the back yard of the house where I grew up. He was standing on the path, in his shirt sleeves, encouraging me by lifting his hand in time. I was stepping easily, like climbing upstairs, about a meter above the damp patch of turf we called our "lawn." My father, the storyteller, taught me to tell stories. He taught me how to free myself (really, truly) from the prison of the middle dimensions, from the body of this death.

In the Middle of a Dark Wood

The Greek word *kairos* means opportunity: the critical moment, right proportion, or due measure. It was adopted in the first centuries after Christ by early millenarians, as a term to describe Christ's Second Coming, which they believed to be imminent. The kairos isn't death, judgment, heaven, or hell. It is the moment of discontinuity: it is *change itself*. In my third and last eschatological novel, kairos is first described as "a reality changing drug." Designer drugs were much talked about at the time, so it seemed a suitable disguise. As the concept gradually unpacks itself through the plot, this "drug" turns out to be an event. In the world up to the kairos, all the normal rules apply. When the change begins there's political and social chaos, accompanied by the traditional range of wonders. After it, everything seems normal again, except that in strange small ways it is evident that different fundamental laws apply. Things which were once utterly impossible, like ghosts, magic, social justice, gender equality, are quietly on the increase. *Kairos* is a punning game, a cosmological play on words, and a version of the Gospel for Hard Times adapted for the consolation of those people—such as feminist science fiction writers—whose habitat is fixed, for as long as the laws of this world endure, between a rock and a hard place. But there is something else.

I have a great deal of sympathy with the apocalyptic writers. I don't feel obliged to convince my readers that an angel came and told me the plot. Yet we clearly share a hunger for the truly extraordinary and a need to express outsize ideas in bizarre, gaudy imagery. We are frequently told, by people who want to believe in religion and yet appear rational (modern cosmologists never seem to be worried about the second bit) that we are not to take those lakes of fire and so on literally: it's *all in the mind*. In *Kairos* I tried to take that idea itself "literally." Everything is in the mind. As Sandy, in possession of the substance that changes reality, approaches her goal, the dead rise, the stones speak, angels walk among men. What's happening (in Sandy's view and mine) is that the relationship between mind and matter is being turned inside out. Ideas have become material; *things* are falling apart.

No kind of realist fiction (including no kind of rational sf) can contain the wild landscapes that thought weaves on the loom of the mind. Maybe all the stories we tell ourselves about the supernatural, and all our dreams of escape, can be traced back to our impatience with the gulf between the limited world we *perceive out there* and the unconstrained freedoms of the mind where time can run backward and distance is no object, where we can easily visit the future or speak to the dead. The first book in which I tackled this intimate discontinuity was *Escape Plans*, where ALIC, my neo-Roman protagonist, has to grapple with the notion of a kind of redemption through interstellar quantum physics. In a sense the same thing is happening in *Kairos*. Strip the special effects out of the narrative, and you will find my characters (who have either lost or never possessed the soothing distractions of material comfort and power) struggling to come to terms with the contradiction of being human. Nothing more than that. Is there anywhere, in any state of being, a world that measures up to the magic of consciousness itself? Is there a native land for us, exiles stranded in this extraordinary separation from every other animal, vegetable, rock, or gas? Well, maybe there is.

In the late twentieth century, modern physics and cosmology were startlingly open to the romantic interpretation of writers like Frijof Capra, whose *Tao of Physics* (1976) fascinated me. It seems (or seemed; there is no guarantee that postmodern science will tell the same story) that the conditions of *mind* are mysteriously reproduced in the world of the very small. Where did the color and charm and strangeness of the quantum world come from? Did we invent it because we can't do without the supernatural, or are we constrained to invent such ideas, because these bizarre conditions are indeed the truth about reality? Perhaps there's no answer to that. Ancient theologies have shaped modern science; the design of an experiment defines the results. As quantum physicists are fond of saying when cornered, some events are inextricably entangled. But wherever it came from, the weirdness doesn't go away. It just gets folded down (whatever that means) into the chinks, along with the other eleven or so dimensions that share the cosmos with the four we know. To put it another way, maybe there's no need to search the skies for messages from the kingdom of heaven. The freedom from limitations is within us.

Kairos: The Enchanted Loom

Science fiction takes us to the brink of a new creation—but no further, because it wouldn't be any fun. When I wrote *Divine Endurance*, I described the death (after a long decline) of mechanistic culture. I cautiously did not attempt to describe the new age of gentler, organic, female rule. The moment of change is portentous; the reality of change is going to be a world just like this one, except for some novel technology or a new kind of income tax. When William Gibson conjured up cyberspace in *Neuromancer* (1984), the global data network gave birth to a divine intelligence. In our world we have the Internet. Even the aliens won't be supernatural anymore, the day they actually arrive. As I've explained, my fictional eschatologies are obedient to this law. The special effects look dangerous, but the brave new world is only this one, with a bow to the strange conditions of quantum reality. But there is always that moment . . .

Kairos means opportunity, but *kairos* are also the loops that hold a piece of weaving to the loom. This double meaning at once suggests (it did to me, anyway) the famous and prescient metaphor of human consciousness as an "enchanted loom";[8] and I had that metaphor in mind when I was writing. Just as in a piece of weaving, where no single thread tells you anything about the picture, our selfhood is the experience of a system of differences: the single, coherent picture is an illusion. I wanted to reach a point (an imaginary point) of reconciliation between the restless, magical human mind and this stubborn world of ours, which wears its bizarre magic only on the inside. But I also wanted to describe the state of someone willing to risk everything: willing to cut those threads that hold our existence in shape, no matter what should follow.

When you were a child, sometimes, maybe, you wished there could really be witches on broomsticks, talking animals, spirits in the forests. Maybe, on one of those cold dusky evenings at the beginning of winter, with the stars coming out, you dreamed that you had the strangest powers. Now that you are grown and you know how much it would cost, do you really want to change the world, to reverse the vital polarity between light and darkness, male and female, real and unreal? Are you sure?

It occurred to her, last of all, that the ghost was real to her. "You wanted something different?" it said, in silent intolerable progress towards her and the child. "Well, here I am. How do you like me?"

Sandy stood up. She forgot that she was afraid, though her body was still howling that this was worse than death. Since she had given up on normal life, she had penetrated a few layers of self-deceit, that was all. She was no better off now than she had been as a political activist, waving banners and marching. She only saw more clearly how she was trapped: up against the wall of the world. It was nothing circumstantial that was making her suffer, it was *things as they are*. What I want is what is not, she thought. And this, as I told myself a little while ago, is one of those. And here it comes.

She did not abandon the rational position she had outlined to Candide a few minutes ago. Let this be a dream or a delusion, that made no difference to its meaning in the world of Sandy. Or to the meaning of what Sandy chose to do, on being confronted with her heart's desire. "Welcome," she said. "Do what you like to me, I don't care. I am glad that you're here." (*Kairos* 158–59)

Welcome, to all the powers of darkness . . .

Does anybody feel any different? No? Well, it was worth trying.

Maybe it takes a little time . . .

12

Dead Letters and Their Inheritors

Ecospasmic Crashes and the Postmortal

Condition in Brian Stableford's Histories of

the Future

BRIAN STABLEFORD

Ruin is the destruction toward which all men rush, each pursuing his own best interest in a society that believes in the freedom of the commons. Freedom in a commons brings ruin to all.
                    —Garrett Hardin, "The Tragedy of the Commons" 1244

Science fiction, even at the popular level, should always be exploratory and it should always be ironic; it should celebrate the process of scientific discovery and enlightenment, and it should brutally examine any and all idols of contemporary thought in the cynical hope of finding feet of clay.

Science fiction should never lend its inventive energy to the cause of day-dream wish-fulfillment, although its most precious inventions will inevitably be plundered wholesale for exactly that purpose; its plots should never be populated with straw men whose narrative function it is to be blown away, and its heroes should never be content to become rich or to achieve the kinds of sexual success that are stereotypical of romantic fiction or pornography.

In every science fiction story the question ought to be raised as to whether the hero might be utterly misguided in everything he believes and is trying to achieve; every time a problem is solved, and every time a conclusion is arrived at, a cunning and skeptical observer should start pointing out the new problems which have thereby been created and the new conflicts which have been opened up.

Any science fiction story which does not annoy at least half its readers ought to be reckoned a failure; any science fiction reader who ends a story feeling comfortable and satisfied ought to throw it away and go looking for something that will mock, insult and disturb him—not in the way that a conventional horror story disturbs him, by assuming that any disruption of the everyday world is *ipso facto* evil, but in the authentic sciencefictional way, which is to suggest that there is nothing more ridiculous, degrading and unworthy of the commitment of an intelligent person than normality—except, of course, for a conventional eucatastrophe.
                    —Brian Stableford, "How Should a Science Fiction Story End?" 15

* * *

The notion that the present world order is bound to be devastated in the relatively near future by an all-encompassing ecocatastrophe has been a fundamental assumption of Brian Stableford's science fiction since the very beginning. Almost all of his Earth-set novels deal with the aftermath of some such crisis. Their main focus is, however, on processes of postcatastrophic reconstruction whose architects are intent on avoiding any repetition of disaster. This usually involves the emergence of a posthuman condition whose central feature is extreme longevity—a condition that he describes, following the example of Al Silverstein, as emortality. ("Immortality" is here construed as providing total immunity against death, while mere "emortals," although free of the ravages of age and disease, remain perennially vulnerable to violent annihilation.)

The basic future-historical template of Stableford's emortality stories was first set out in a futurological "coffee-table book," *The Third Millennium: A History of the World, AD 2000–3000* (1985), whose text he wrote in collaboration with David Langford. This describes in some detail the ecospasmic Crash, which puts a grim end to the world's population explosion in the twenty-first century, then outlines in a more languid fashion the salvation of humanity by the careful application of sophisticated biotechnologies. Although the book was an item of hackwork, whose well-intentioned text was rudely butchered by its packager, Stableford continued to use its vision of the future, and simple variants thereof, as a template for many of the short stories he began to write when he returned to sf writing in 1986 after a five-year absence. As time went by, the tacit histories backgrounding these stories diverged considerably from one another and from their original, partly by virtue of the attention Stableford paid to current developments in biotechnology and partly by virtue of purely idiosyncratic additions.

Ten years after the publication of *The Third Millennium*, Stableford prepared an outline for a series of six novels that would constitute a revised and updated historical template. Although all six volumes were to be based on preexistent works whose backgrounds were only loosely related (one of which had not been published and three of which had only been published in abridged form), the prospectus promised to revise the stories in question to make their settings fully consistent. Because the series failed to find a publisher in the U.K. and its eventual U.S. publisher cautiously insisted on commissioning one volume at a time—beginning with the one that he considered to be the most commercial rather than the earliest-set—the bibliography of the series has become slightly confused. The sequence as originally envisaged began with the novel now titled *The Cassandra Complex* (2001) and continued with *Inherit the Earth* (1998), *Architects of Emortality* (1999), *Dark Ararat* (planned for publication in 2002), *The Fountains of Youth* (2000), and *The Omega Expedition* (planned for publication in 2003). Given that none of the books so far published has appeared under the titles on the manuscripts, the titles of the unpublished books must be regarded as speculative.

A detailed account of the situation of this series of novels within Stableford's massive literary output or its significance within his long and checkered career would be far too tedious for readers of a volume such as this to bear, but it would be impossible to present a competent analysis of their manner and method without saying something about the exceedingly peculiar situation of biotechnology within the general field of science fiction—something of which Stableford, who has made a few slight contributions to the mapping of the genre's history, is obviously aware.

The first notable example of speculative fiction in which biotechnology plays a crucial role is *Mizora*, published in 1890 under the pseudonym of Princess Vera Zaronovitch. In *Mizora*, the male of the species is extinct, having been made redundant by new reproductive technologies. Related technologies have freed the Mizorans from dependence on crop plants and animal husbandry, all food being synthetic. Advanced medical technology has resulted in the conquest of disease and the extension of the human lifespan. Princess Zaronovitch takes it for granted that all these advances are implicitly good: perfect foundation stones for a utopian society. Within the course of the next hundred years, however, she proved to be in a minority so tiny that its enumeration does not require all the fingers of a single hand.

Tissue culture experiments carried out by Alexis Carrel and others in the early part of the twentieth century prompted J. B. S. Haldane to produce *Daedalus; or, Science and the Future*, a lecture read at Cambridge University on 4 February 1923 and reprinted as a pamphlet. Haldane proposes that the technologies that will remake human society in the second half of the twentieth century will be "biological inventions," the most important of which will be synthetic food. He declares that advances in the understanding of basic biological processes will produce many technological applications of which the world stands in dire need but sounds a cautionary note about the manner in which they are likely to be received by the public. After offering a list of the great biological inventions of the past, he observes that "[t]he chemical or physical inventor is always a Prometheus. There is no great invention, from fire to flying, which has not been hailed as an insult to some god. But if every physical and chemical invention is a blasphemy, every biological invention is a perversion. There is hardly one which, on first being brought to the notice of an observer from any nation which has not previously heard of their existence, would not appear to him as indecent and unnatural" (Haldane 44). This passage—which Stableford is exceedingly fond of quoting—recognizes and calls attention to the great irony of biotechnological progress that has comprehensively blighted all but a few examples of speculative fiction dealing with such innovations. Everything that we think of as "human nature"—and, indeed, almost everything we nowadays think of as "nature"—is in fact the product of biotechnological invention. Everything that we think of as good and every worthwhile human achievement owes its existence to biotechnology, and yet—paradoxical as it may seem—the grateful awe with which we cling to the products of the biotechnological discoveries of the past has as its flip side a deep suspicion of all further biotechnological discoveries.

Haldane's close friend Julian Huxley extrapolated the ideas contained in *Daedalus* in a satirical parable set in darkest Africa, "The Tissue-Culture King" (1926), but Julian left it to his younger brother Aldous to bring the message home in *Brave New World* (1932). The most eloquent testimony to the accuracy and force of Haldane's argument is that during the next half century this magnificently cynical and brutally sarcastic comedy was never supplemented, let alone surpassed, by any similarly comprehensive account of a biotechnologically sophisticated society. There seems to have been a tacit admission by almost all subsequent writers that this one novel had said all that needs to be said on the subject. In 1951, when James Blish published an essay, "The Biological Story," in the May issue of *Science Fiction Quarterly*, he had to begin with the lament that he had only been able to find one solitary example of a sensible application of biotechnology; this was Norman L. Knight's novella "Crisis in Utopia" (1940).

The real subject matter of "Crisis in Utopia" is not, in fact, the "tectogenetics" on which the future Utopia of the forty-second century is based but the extreme prejudice of the Utopians against the use of such technologies on the human genome. Blish points out that other pulp sf stories extrapolating biological ideas had routinely played upon the same anxiety in more brutal fashion; they were, almost without exception, exercises in teratology. Nothing changed in the next thirty years; the vast majority of sf stories about biotechnology continued to take the form of Frankensteinian fables in which the products of induced mutation and other interventions, however well intended, run amok and have to be destroyed. Even stories about such seemingly benign innovations as the conquest of disease and aging routinely insisted on finding some crucial fly in the ointment. Blish made a conscientious attempt to oppose this trend in his own work and was not the only sf writer to side with Norman Knight in the 1950s and 1960s, offering objections to a prejudice whose enormous strength was taken for granted, but such attempts received a massive setback when Gordon Rattray Taylor published *The Biological Time-Bomb* in 1968, launching an orgy of alarmism that was imported into the United States by Vance Packard's best-selling *People Shapers* (1978).

Everything that has happened in the field of biotechnology since the genetic code was cracked in the 1960s, up to and including the current controversies regarding cloning and genetically modified foods, provides conclusive evidence that Haldane was a far better prophet than he could possibly have wished. The vast majority of civilized human beings, who are in every respect the products of biotechnology and who consider the biotechnologies of the past to be entirely and definitively natural, seemingly cannot contemplate the biotechnologies of the present—let alone those of the future—without suffering a reflexive tidal wave of neurotic anxiety and blind, unreasoning terror. This is the context in which Stableford's work has to be read, not merely as the reality surrounding it but as an appalling circumstance against which he has continually tried—albeit ineffectually and well-nigh invisibly—to excite justified moral outrage.

We can, of course, only speculate as to the extent to which the longstanding unpopularity of Stableford's work is due to its mere incompetence rather than his insistence on swimming against what he knows too well to be an irresistible ideological tide, but it would only be kind to assume that the latter factor plays some small part. By the same token, we have no way of knowing what awful hidden perversity compels him to such madness, and it is probably kinder not to speculate. The simple fact is, however, that providing what opposition he can to the irrational follies of a sick society is what he has chosen to do—and the horrid history of similar exercises in public outrage goes at least some way toward explaining the slightly bizarre manner in which he chooses to do it. One must presume that every time Stableford sees TV news footage of posturing idiots uprooting test crops of genetically modified plants or hears moral imbeciles railing against the mere idea of cloning or the practice of harvesting stem cells from early embryos, he is consumed by a righteous anger that has no other vent but literary work that (as he surely knows full well) is unlikely to sell and highly likely to fall by the generic wayside even if it does.

* * *

The Cassandra Complex is the only book in the emortality series that is set before the Crash that will put an end to the population explosion, although all of its leading characters know that the Crash is inevitable. This knowledge is, of course, what qualifies them as victims of the Cassandra complex, named for the Trojan prophetess whose true anticipations were rendered impotent by the refusal of their hearers to act upon them. Stableford has also written stories that make much of the equally ironic Oedipus effect, which describes the capacity that both true and false prophecies have to pervert the future if they do provoke action, however slight. There is a sense in which this series of novels, and the entire corpus of which it is a part, may be regarded as the desperate effort of a self-diagnosed sufferer from the Cassandra complex to exert an Oedipus effect.

The plot of *The Cassandra Complex*, whose elements are borrowed from the short story "The Magic Bullet" (1989), is superficially disguised as an exercise in futuristic crime fiction, although the mystery of why a once-famous but conspicuously unsuccessful biotechnologist has been kidnapped is merely a peg on which to hang a series of philosophical discussions. The first four novels in the projected series are all cast in the same mock-criminous mold, although the crimes and the processes of their detection become increasingly tokenistic and increasingly absurd until the formula reaches a breaking point in the nakedly preposterous black comedy of *Architects of Emortality*.

The main characters of *The Cassandra Complex* are somewhat older than is usual in crime stories, all of them being in their sixties or seventies. This enables them to look back as well as forward over considerable historical spectra whose patterns display technology-driven social changes. As technologies of longevity become more effective in each volume of the series, these spectra are gradually elongated and elaborated, mimicking the geometrical shift of changing time-scales of the four parts of *The Third Millennium* (a literary device borrowed from Olaf Stapledon's *Last and First Men*). The central character of *The Cassandra Complex*, the kidnapped biologist Morgan Miller, is conspicuous by his absence until the climax, when he is allowed on stage to explain everything. This too is a recurring device; the central characters of *Inherit the Earth* and *Architects of Emortality*, Conrad Helier and Jafri Biasiolo, never appear on stage at all, and all five of the preparatory volumes refer more or less obliquely to the absence of Adam Zimmerman, who is the true progenitor of the series in two separate but closely related senses.

Within the series Zimmerman is the facilitator of the economic coup that delivers Earth into the tender care of the "Hardinist Cabal." In a wider context, the first story Stableford wrote when he returned to sf writing in 1986 (after having given it up as a futile exercise in 1981) was ". . . And He Not Busy Being Born," which is an account of Zimmerman's remarkable biography. If the final volume of the projected series is ever published, it will incorporate a heavily revised version of this biography and will bring Zimmerman onto the stage at last. Even as a true progenitor, however, Zimmerman is not the character whose absence from center stage is most crucially important, as *The Fountains of Youth* makes abundantly clear. Although Mortimer Gray is the first-person narrator of that text, its central character—unsurpassably conspicuous by his remarkable absence—is Death. The narrative purpose served by all these absent characters is that missing persons prompt searches, the most important of which are searches for understanding.

The plot of *The Cassandra Complex* revolves around a tangled knot of misconceptions. Morgan Miller's kidnappers appear to believe that he made a highly significant discovery forty years before, but his long-time acquaintance Lisa Friemann—whose status as a forensic scientist allows her to hover in the margins of three separate investigations mounted by the police, the Ministry of Defense, and a powerful business consortium known by various nicknames, including the Hardinist Cabal—cannot believe that he would not have confided in her had he done so. Lisa's faith in Miller is gradually weakened as evidence accumulates that he may indeed have discovered a technology of emortality, about which he kept scrupulously silent because it could only work on premenopausal women (a category into which she no longer fits). It might not be worth calling attention to the fact that this ironic pattern is repeated in later volumes in the series, because it might be regarded as trivial. After all, if there were no misconceptions entangling a plot, where would the dramatic tension come from? At the very least, though, it is worth pointing out that none of the texts relies to any extent whatsoever on threats of imminent death overhanging the active characters. From the very outset, Death really is conspicuous as a force that is in the process of losing its sting. Then again, misconceptions are like missing persons, and the searches they prompt are even more narrowly focused into searches for understanding. There is one important respect in which *The Cassandra Complex* is solidly set in the mainstream of the literary tradition summarized by Stableford's entries on "Immortality" in the two editions of *The Encyclopedia of Science Fiction* (1979; 1993). The twist in the tale's tail reveals that the biotechnology of longevity on which the plot pivots has a direly unfortunate side-effect, which places all the holders of the secret—whose numbers increase by leaps and bounds in the final phases of the novel—on the horns of a moral dilemma that some of them find acutely uncomfortable. All the other volumes in the series do likewise—but each new technology, even in falling short of a hoped-for perfection, remains powerful enough to be a tangible force in prompting progress toward a posthuman utopia from which the perennial prospect of disaster that blights our own world has been conclusively removed. The novel and the series, therefore, adopt the formula in order to undermine it, to expose its imaginative pusillanimity, and to demand further searches for understanding.

In sum, *The Cassandra Complex* sets in place an elaborate pattern of motifs, methods, and mannerisms that is carried forward and gradually transmuted by the later volumes in the series (although its process of development has, of course, been somewhat obscured by the publisher's insistence on issuing the volumes out of sequence).

* * *

The people of the post-Crash world featured in *Inherit the Earth* (expanded from the similarly titled novella) have shelved the biotechnological line of approach to technologies of emortality favored by Morgan Miller in favor of nanotechnological processes of repair that currently promise lifespans in the region of 150 to 200 years. It is widely believed, however, that there will be an "escalator effect" by which the beneficiaries of the present generation of repair technologies will be preserved long enough to obtain a further boost from the next generation, which will in turn enable them to reap further benefits as ever more sophisticated nanotechnologies enter the public domain.

The kidnappee in *Inherit the Earth* is Silas Arnett, a member of a group of biotechnologists who pioneered the use of what J. B. S. Haldane called "ectogenesis"—the growth of human embryos in artificial wombs—in response to a plague of sterilizing viruses which might or might not have been the final phase of the "plague wars" whose first phase had just begun in *The Cassandra Complex*. The character put under the greatest pressure by the kidnapping, Damon Hart, is the disaffected son of the leader of the group, Conrad Helier, rumors of whose death are thought by the kidnappers to have been greatly exaggerated. The movers of the plot ultimately turn out to be the descendants of the Hardinist Cabal, whose stranglehold on the world economy has been further increased by their effective monopoly on the deployment of nanotechnology— a stranglehold that they intend to make absolutely secure by reining in any rogue biotechnologists capable of upsetting their applecart. As in *The Cassandra Complex*, the technology of which the world's secret masters are slightly afraid turns out in *Inherit the Earth* to have more ramifications than are immediately obvious, although their potential is not spelled out in any detail until they are integrated, explicitly but unobtrusively, into the background of *Architects of Emortality* (expanded from a novella entitled "Les Fleurs du Mal," which was an abridgment of a similarly titled unpublished novel).

The novel envisaged as the third volume of the projected series, *Dark Ararat*, was always conceived as a sidestep, in that it will describe the landfall of the only survivor of a group of interstellar "Arks" launched at the height of the Crash, when the more anxious members of the Hardinist Cabal became convinced that the world was doomed. It was placed third in the original sequence, although news of the landfall does not reach Earth until partway through *The Fountains of Youth*, because its key characters are awakened from suspended animation with memories of a world historically located between the worlds of *The Cassandra Complex* and *Inherit the Earth*, and it is therefore more closely associated with those novels than with the later triad, which deals with societies that are much more technologically advanced.

As the final version of *Dark Ararat* has not yet been written and the unpublished manuscript on which it will be based will require very considerable modification, it is probably best to pass over it quickly, without saying too much about the mystery that serves as a plot except that—as in the succeeding volume—it involves a murderous crime of passion rather than a strategically designed kidnapping. (Given the absurdly relaxed time schedule on which books like the one containing this essay work, the novel will hopefully have been in print for some time before anyone other than editors and referees actually has the opportunity to read these words, so the addressees of this paragraph may, ironically, already be far better equipped than the present author to see exactly how *Dark Ararat* fits into the series.)

While the first three novels were always conceived by the author as mock-thrillers, the final three were always conceived as comedies. For bridging purposes, however, *Architects of Emortality* retains a calculatedly absurd murder-mystery framework in which Oscar Wilde, a genetic engineer specializing in flower design, lends his expertise as an aesthetic theorist to the investigation by Charlotte Holmes and Hal Watson of a series of murders signed (pseudonymously) "Rappaccini." The fact that some American reviewers—and, indeed, at least one of the editors involved in the novel's progress from typescript to print—somehow failed to notice that the story is a sarcastic joke is not entirely surprising, given that *Brave New World* has always suffered from the same problem. As in *The Cassandra Complex*, the investigation of the crime that moves the plot of *Architects of Emortality* is carefully monitored by the descendants of the Hardinist Cabal, whose front organizations are now popularly known as the MegaMall. Oscar Wilde is here the only character sufficiently cursed by the Cassandra complex to realize exactly how unlucky he is to have been born at the tail end of humankind's abortive alliance with repair nanotechnology. The old people of this world can no longer take comfort in the illusory escalator effect, and they are already making way for a new breed of biotechnologically created emortals, here called "naturals."

The seemingly final conquest of death that is visible to the characters of *Architects of Emortality* is fully realized in *The Fountains of Youth*, whose central character is Mortimer Gray, the first man to set out to write a comprehensive history of death, and hence the first to provide a truly enlightened analysis of the significance of its newly minimized role in human affairs—which is, of course, by no means a total elimination. The novel is an expansion of the novella "Mortimer Gray's History of Death," which was itself expanded from an earlier unpublished novella.

The author's hope must have been that the mock-thriller elements of the series would have built an audience whose curiosity was sufficient not merely to see them through the carefully hybridized comedy of *Architects of Emortality* but also to encourage them to tolerate the fact that the final two volumes in the series constitute an extraordinarily elaborated and blatantly comic bildungsroman devoid of all the conventional melodramatic props of popular fiction. It is, of course, difficult to set exciting stories in any utopia, and a utopia of emortals is even less hospitable to urgent dramatic tension. Stableford presumably knew that this problem further compounded the one mapped out by Haldane, that the redoubled difficulty made the publication of an account of a biotechnologically sophisticated utopia into the greatest challenge available to a contemporary writer, and that even if he ever contrived to get some such work into print he would get no medals for it, but he went ahead anyway. Some critics might consider him brave—although none, to date, has actually said so—but the cynics who think him merely stubborn to the point of perversity are probably more accurate judges of character.

Mortimer Gray is scheduled to return as one of the central characters of *The Omega Expedition*, so that his bildungsroman can continue to provide a narrative frame of sorts. As a historian, he will be fascinated to meet up with Adam Zimmerman, whose appearance—if the final volume ever reaches print—will permit the establishment of a useful bridge across the entire timespan of the series. A secondary bridge will be established to *Inherit the Earth*. As all this is purely speculative at the time of writing, however, it is probably best to say no more and to pass swiftly on to a loftier analytical overview of the series and the many short stories loosely associated with it.

* * *

The various versions of the Crash that feature in Stableford's stories all have one thing in common: no one is uniquely responsible for them. They are never the work of scapegoatable "villains" but the inevitable collective result of perfectly ordinary people following their individual self-interest. The eco-spasms in Stableford's science fiction always work out on a global scale the logic of Garrett Hardin's classic essay, "The Tragedy of the Commons," invariably taking for granted the statement that appeared as the article's summary blurb in *Science*: "The population problem has no technical solution; it requires a fundamental extension in morality." Many of Stableford's stories deal with individuals who feel obliged to conceal actions taken to oppose or ameliorate the effects of ecocatastrophe because they rightly fear being perceived, in terms of an obsolete morality, as "villains" by those whose individual interests they are subverting. The most obvious example of a character of this kind is Conrad Helier, who is remembered in *Inherit the Earth* as a hero only because he has taken great care to conceal the fact that he helped to spread the plague of sterility that put a stop to the population explosion before perfecting the artificial wombs that forced the business of reproduction to become subject to collective planning. Others include the members of the Hardinist Cabal, who obtained that name by virtue of applying the remedy implicit in the argument of "The Tragedy of the Commons," establishing themselves as effective owners—and therefore interested protectors—of Earth's surface.

Stableford is careful in his depiction of these characters not to represent them as authentically heroic; he usually suggests that their contributions to the public good arise out of the desire for self-glorification or personal enrichment rather than genuine altruism. The character who precipitates by far the most extravagant change for the better envisaged by any of his stories, Giovanni Casanova in "A Career in Sexual Chemistry," does so entirely by accident while pursuing his own base agenda. The character who does most to help the world to recover rapidly from the most extreme of all Stableford's imagined Crashes, Cade Carlyle Maclaine in "Hidden Agendas" (1999), is generally considered—not altogether unjustly—to be a war criminal. The central character of "Ashes and Tombstones" (1999), a direct sequel to "Hidden Agendas" set in the aftermath of the same almost-terminal Crash, lives in similar fashion as a recluse, clinging hard to the secret of exactly what he did at the height of the crisis, and why. The vague patterns formed by the Malthusian checks in Stableford's various retrospective accounts of ecospasmic Crash usually give due credit to famine but tend to assume that the principal destructive role has been played by genetically engineered diseases. Oddly enough, however, his characterization of "plague wars" actually emphasizes the lack of individual accountability for the Crash, because none of the wars in question is ever formally declared and none of the plagues is ever conclusively traced to its source. Reference is frequently made to speculations about the first plague war being a campaign waged against the poor by the rich—an attempt to clear away unproductive and troublesome "underclasses"—and the second being a retaliatory strike that inevitably rebounded, but the fundamental assumption is always that the people of the future will never have anyone to blame for the birth pangs of their new order.

Even the assiduous historian of death in all its aspects, Mortimer Gray, dismisses the question as irrelevant as well as unanswerable in *The Fountains of Youth*. Mortimer Gray belongs to a set of characters quite distinct from that comprising the likes of Conrad Helier and Cade Carlyle Maclaine. He is neither hero nor villain, either in objective terms or in terms of his reputation. He is frequently accused of being a fool, and although he resents such accusations far more than does Oscar Wilde in *Architects of Emortality*—who casually reinterprets the word to transform it into a compliment—there is some justice in it. He is a very earnest jester, but his principal reason for being is to remind the world of emortals of their extraordinary good fortune in not having to die. Similar "wise fools" occupy center stage in such tales as "Cinderella's Sisters" (1989), "Skin Deep" (1991), and "The Cure for Love" (1993), although—like the inquisitive children in "What Can Chloë Want?" (1994), "The Age of Innocence" (1995), and "The Pipes of Pan" (1998), and the young Emily Marchant in *The Fountains of Youth*—they might perhaps be more kindly described as "clever innocents." All stories dealing with exotic worlds-within-texts find innocents abroad useful as characters, because they can ask the questions whose answers the reader needs to know, but Stableford's use of such characters goes beyond mere matters of narrative convenience. His inquisitive innocents are figures who mirror both the negligence that can cause Crashes and the hopeful optimism that might prevent them, not merely alloyed but oddly allied.

The most exaggerated adult example of this kind of character, apart from Mortimer Gray, is Adam Zimmerman. All the Stablefordian characters cast in this peculiar mold are tentatively but boldly engaged in the problematic business of trying to contrive a Hardinesque "fundamental extension in morality." In effect, they are learning to be posthuman without the benefit of preexistent role models. They frequently make a mess of it, but they always stick to their guns, because they take it for granted that the first and foremost virtue a posthuman will require is stubbornness. How could it be otherwise, if the key to posthumanity is postmortality? All these characters find themselves adrift in a historical moment caught between a disaster-laden past and a hopefully utopian future, knowing—however vaguely—that they are the people who will have to discover the moral compass that future generations will use to guide them through a world of infinite opportunity. All but the youngest are also aware—dimly, at least—that if they fail, then Pandora's box is likely to be unlocked again. They are not heroes, because their role is an essentially unheroic one. The most fundamental premise of the overarching project of which their individual tales are but a part is that, if worldwide disaster is the collective result of vast numbers of mostly insignificant individuals rationally and doggedly pursuing their own interests, then any recipe for the salvation of the world must involve vast numbers of mostly insignificant individuals whose equally dogged and equally rational pursuit of their own interests must yield an arithmetical sum, within a new and fundamentally different moral context.

* * *

Stableford's fascination with Haldane's *Daedalus* and its distorted reflections in "The Tissue-Culture King" and *Brave New World* has often prompted
him to try to redeem the imagery of the last-named work from its horrific connotations. The most telling of those images is contained in its first chapter,
which introduces the "hatchery" in which the children of the future are produced in clonal batches from artificial wombs. *Inherit the Earth* follows *The Third
Millennium* in arguing that the removal of the privileges of fertility from natural
wombs is highly desirable, because the one thing that must be brought under
strict political control in a world of long-lived people is the dynamics of its population. This proved, not unexpectedly, to be the most controversial contention
of both books, and Stableford has tried hard in other stories—especially "The
Invisible Worm" (1991), "The Age of Innocence," and *The Fountains of Youth*—to
offer sympathetic accounts of alternatives to the nuclear family. "The Pipes of
Pan" considers the other side of the coin, describing an absurd situation resulting from a stubborn determination to hold on to the nuclear family in the world
of emortals. "The Invisible Worm" and *The Fountains of Youth* both assume that,
in order to protect the right to found a family that is currently guaranteed by
the United Nations and European charters of human rights, it will be desirable
in a world of emortals for the normal exercise of that right to be posthumous.
Stableford's stories take it for granted that children will routinely be raised in
aggregate households formed by groups of between eight and twelve adults for
that specific purpose. Although "The Invisible Worm" suggests that an outcome of this kind might be achieved by the voluntary exercise of political will,
the future history series assumes that this would be impossible, and for this reason the role of the Crash in that series is somewhat ambiguous. The plague
wars, which contrive the relatively sudden reduction of the human population,
provide cover for the deployment of a "plague of sterility," which facilitates the
evolution of a population whose numbers are much more easily controllable.

A different apologetic case is made out in "Hidden Agendas" and "Ashes
and Tombstones," which are set in a future where the Crash is far more drastic,
almost causing the extinction of the human and many other species. In this future, ectogenesis and cloning technologies become enormously valuable assets
in contriving a rapid, multispecific "repopulation" of Earth, whose ironic "heroes" are genetically engineered cockroaches. Even here, though, the Crash is
slightly ambiguous; although it is certainly a disaster of epic proportions, it
does clear the way for the development of a more careful—and hence more sus-
tainable—relationship between human beings and reproductive technologies.

Such ambiguities as this have long been a major feature of genre science
fiction, where every disastrous cloud that stops short of total annihilation (if
only by a whisker) usually turns out to have a silver lining—and it is perhaps
just as well, given that the destructive imagery of sf would otherwise seem ni-
hilistic or pornographic. Stableford's knowledge of this fact is probably one of

the factors that has made him so cautious in his handling of the idea of a population Crash that he has never attempted to describe it in any detail. He does, however, take the trouble to point out in the summary of the relevant chapter of Mortimer Gray's History of Death that the everyday work of natural mortality produced Crash-like casualty figures on a regular basis throughout the twentieth century, with only moderate aid from murderous malice—and Mortimer Gray is in no doubt as to which ought to be reckoned the greater tragedy. It is not altogether surprising, therefore, that even the leading characters in *The Cassandra Complex*—who know that they will have to live through the impending Crash or die trying—ultimately take the view that they have some reason to be cheerful on account of the brief and intrinsically frustrating glimpse of the possibility of emortality that has been vouchsafed to them. Stableford presumably hopes that his audience will eventually come to a similar conclusion, although he is unlikely to be holding his breath in the meantime.

* * *

Stableford's fiftieth novel, *Year Zero* (2000), might be regarded as a brief holiday from the serious business of the future-history series. It is by far the broadest of all his comedies, features by far the cleverest of all his innocent protagonists, and its plot climaxes (on 31 December 2000) in by far the most extravagant of all his imagined apocalypses. Along the way it "reveals" that the alien grays whose UFOs are currently haunting the world are trying to pick up a few existential tips from humankind before deciding how to restart the evolutionary process in their homeworld, which they have unfortunately ruined. Their ecospasm, irredeemable even by heroic cockroaches, has reduced a rich and strange biosphere to the "cyanobacterial slime" from which it began. Ours will follow suit unless the hapless heroine can find a way to thwart the Devil—who is not only alive and well but up close and personal—although she knows full well that he is only a phantom of the cerebral cortex, a mere projection of the human desire for moral order. Similar themes, dressed in equally gaudy costumes, recur in many of the "dark fantasies" that Stableford has written alongside his science fiction. If his science fiction is primarily devoted to his dreams of world salvation, his fantasies can easily be seen as their nightmarish flip side: the Gothic suspicion that human decadence may indeed be irredeemable and that postmortality is a phantom of the cerebral cortex, a mere projection of the personal desire for moral order. The Crash, however, is inevitable, as real as real can be even though it has not yet happened. If there are two things of which we can all be absolutely certain, one is that the ecosphere will soon go postal and the other is that the current leaseholders of Earth will all die soon. The question that remains to be answered is whether our descendants will be deliverable thereafter. Brian Stableford hopes that they will but does not imagine that it will be easy.

13

Utopia, Genocide, and the Other

JOAN GORDON

When one teaches both science fiction and literature of the Holocaust, each subject begins to interrogate the other, sometimes in unexpected ways. My readings of alien contact novels, previously informed by postcolonialist and utopian criticism, have thus become increasingly disrupted by echoes of the historical Holocaust. In many recent alien contact novels, I have found impulses toward both genocide and utopia, impulses that are linked rather than in opposition.

The recent novels *Celestis*, by Paul Park (1995), and *The Sparrow* (1996) and *Children of God* (1998), by Mary Doria Russell, are three among the many contemporary novels of alien contact that explore this sensitive dependency among utopia, genocide, and the alien Other.[1] These works form a particularly illuminating juxtaposition because, while *Celestis* describes the worst sort of ethnocentric and imperialist colonization, *The Sparrow* shows colonization at its most sensitive, empathetic, and culturally considerate. In both *Celestis* and *The Sparrow* (and its sequel *Children of God*), however, the utopian impulse, when expressed through the colonization of an alien culture, results in genocide. In this chapter I struggle to understand why genocide seems so inevitably the result of movement between cultures. Paul Park and Mary Doria Russell suggest that genocide is a utopian project.

In a recent essay in *Granta*, Michael Ignatieff usefully defines genocide as "any systematic attempt to exterminate a people or its culture and way of life" (123). It is at first hard to imagine how such violence could be associated with utopia, but Ignatieff makes a convincing case: "What could be more like paradise on earth than to live in a community without enemies? To create a world with no more need for borders. . . . A world safe from the deadly contaminations and temptations of the other tribe? What could be more beautiful than to live in a community with people who resemble each other in every particular? . . . What could be more seductive than to kill in order to put an end to all killing? This utopia is so alluring that it is a wonder the human race has been able to survive at all" (125). In the novels I have named, and in many others, this deadly allure is shown, illustrating not only postcolonialist issues but post-Holocaust (i.e., post-Shoah) ones as well.

In novels of alien contact, as in the history of colonization, the first impulse of human confrontation with the alien, the Other, is to annihilate it. This annihilation may occur through familiarization: by assimilating or by "passing," by absorbing or being absorbed by the dominant culture. That is the peaceful method. Or the annihilation may occur through erasure: by expulsion or killing.[2] Peaceful or violent, through familiarization or erasure, these are impulses toward genocide, "any systematic attempt to exterminate a people or its culture and way of life." So the aliens, however frightening, do not themselves evoke the monstrous in these novels; the terrifying impulse toward genocide does.

We call Adolf Hitler a monster, though he was quite human, because of his genocidal project. No wonder, then, that the contemporary German relationship to this familiar monster is, as we say, problematic. Consider the example of Anselm Kiefer, a contemporary German artist who confronts, appropriates, and interrogates his parents' generation—and, by association, his own—for their participation in the Nazi regime. Kiefer is best known for monumentally (monstrously?) scaled works: canvases that cover vast wall spaces, huge lead books, fields of broken glass.

A 1998 exhibit at the Metropolitan Museum of Art concentrated on his smaller works on paper.[3] One watercolor succinctly illustrates the problem of Hitler's utopian project. Called "Everyone Stands Under His Own Dome of Heaven" (1970), it shows a fallow field with a small figure a bit off-center, one arm raised in the Nazi salute, the figure surrounded by a transparent blue dome. The Nazi has his vision of heaven, of utopia, and it is for him, and his kind, alone. As with every conventional utopia, it is in stasis, like the fallow field; it is isolated, its dome like the trench that isolates More's paradigmatic Utopia from the rest of the world; it is exclusionary, since the ideal world must exclude any who are unworthy of it.[4] Kiefer's painting illustrates the grim truth that Hitler's genocidal project was a utopian one, meant to bring about an ideal world that contained only ideal people. Kiefer's response to Hitler's project is post-Holocaust art in its self-conscious ironization: post-Holocaust, first of all and most simply, because it is art about the historical Holocaust, created after the event, and second, because it is art that uses such postmodern artistic techniques as appropriation and self-conscious reference to do so.

As the eyewitnesses and survivors of that specific Holocaust reach old age, more and more second-hand witnesses and descendants of survivors tell their stories; in Art Spiegelman's *Maus* (1986, 1991), Jane Yolen's *Devil's Arithmetic* (1988), and Bernhard Schlink's *Reader* (1995), we read of the second- or even third-generation echoes. Presumably, this is post-Holocaust literature in the same way that Anselm Kiefer's productions are post-Holocaust art, concerned not so much with the event itself as with its aftershocks: historically and stylistically "post."

But that is not what I mean by postholocaust in science fiction.[5] I understand the term *postholocaust sf* to refer to something quite different, to works that follow humankind after a nuclear, ecological, or other cataclysmic disaster. Also called postapocalyptic, it is a huge subgenre of science fiction: from Mary Shelley's *Last Man* (1826) through Walter M. Miller's *A Canticle for Leibowitz* (1960) to Elizabeth Hand's *Winterlong* (1990). Evolution, survival, transformation, and, yes, utopianism, often inform these novels, but genocide only very rarely. Unlike postholocaust sf, however, the other post-Holocaust literature, grounded in the historical calamity, is compelled to confront issues of totalitarianism, racism, and genocide in a way that postholocaust sf tends not to do.[6]

There is another, smaller subgenre of sf that one might think would confront these issues, even if postholocaust sf does not—what *The Encyclopedia of Science Fiction* calls "Hitler Wins" sf. John Clute's entry in the category lists, among others, Philip K. Dick's *Man in the High Castle* (1962), Norman Spinrad's *Iron Dream* (1972), and James P. Hogan's *Proteus Operation* (1985) ("Hitler Wins" 573). While these works commonly examine Hitler's warped utopian totalitarianism within a projected German victory in World War II, the racism and genocide that were among its defining characteristics figure only in the background. The Jewish protagonist of *The Man in the High Castle*, for example, knows he is better off in the Japanese-controlled western United States rather than in the German-controlled eastern, though this fact is not central to the novel at all. Nevertheless, these works might also be called post-Holocaust literature.

I do not wish to claim that either of these sf subgenres *should* deal with the racism and genocide of the historical Holocaust, but the more I think about it, the more curious I find the omission. Why does postholocaust sf not invoke reference to the historical Holocaust, to the Shoah? In popular culture, invocations of the word *Holocaust* or associated pictorial images signify seriousness and horror with a very specific historical reference. Indeed, simply to utter the word is to conjure up the iconic images of locked boxcars, skeletal figures, and mass graves. Yet in sf that iconic association does not occur. Instead, postholocaust sf novels deal with nuclear devastation, meteors, ecological disaster, disease, anything but deliberate genocide.

Since both nuclear destruction and the Final Solution are intentional technological horrors, both should encourage scientific as well as ethical speculation. Does the discrepancy of examination have to do with attitudes toward each of these horrors? Many people believe that employing the atomic bomb was morally justified; and it was employed by the victors, so it gained that moral cachet as well. As we know, morality, like history, is determined by the victors. Perhaps it is easier to found a story of evolution, renewal, improvement, or even simply survival upon an event that can, to some extent, be justified; there can be no justification for the Final Solution. Also, people may have felt that once the camps were liberated, that particular threat was over, whereas nuclear threat lingered through the cold war—though, as current events constantly remind us, racism and genocide neither began nor ended with the Nazis. And to build a utopia, one of the projects of the postholocaust sf novel, on the corpses of a genocide after Hitler's precedent would be hideous.

Yet isn't it odd that the "Hitler Wins" subgenre also generally avoids the ugly realities of Hitler's genocidal policies, concentrating instead on how totalitarianism affects those allowed to *live* under its sway? Why is that? Such a concentration permits the exciting Gothic rhythm of capture and escape rather than the more hopeless scenario of the Final Solution. I wonder, too, if the sense of hallowed solemnity that understandably surrounds the literature of the Holocaust, and the insistence upon the event's unique place in history, render its subject inappropriate for this often satiric subgenre, as well as for any other kind of fantastic displacement.

James Berger, in *After the End: Representations of Post-Apocalypse* (1999), implies another explanation for the evocative absence of genocidal content in these two forms of post-Holocaust sf in his discussion of "the Shoah's 'second generation,'" all those who grew up after the Holocaust. He describes their world as "a condition of silence, hints, ellipses; of enormous, inarticulable wounds whose features must be imagined" (66). Citing scholars from Theodor Adorno to Jean-François Lyotard to show how "the Holocaust has been regarded as apocalyptic," he describes "an event in history whose traumatic impact seems to annihilate, along with a physical population, all previous ways of thinking and that transforms the world that follows so as to make it incommensurable with what went before" (60–61). Certainly, this describes the visionary project of the best postholocaust/postapocalyptic sf. It also suggests that such sf, in avoiding reference to the Shoah, may nevertheless refer to it by its very ellipses, turning it into a metaphor whose tenor has been obliterated and "whose features must be imagined." Berger goes on to observe that, for "the Shoah's 'second generation,' whether or not its members are actually children of survivors, . . . [w]hat is most noteworthy during this period is that the cultural fascination was with Nazis, not with Jews" (66). The Nazis, though defeated, nevertheless represent figures of power over "the absent shapes of the shamed, unspeaking Jews" (66). Again, one can consider the "Hitler Wins" subgenre as an expression of the elliptical world of the Shoah's second generation, drawn to the figures of power and turning away from "the absent shapes" of the victims.

Finally, however, I believe it is the force of literalized metaphor that best explains the seeming anomaly of underrepresentation. In the genre where saying "he was alone in the world" means something much stranger than in, say, the stories of Willa Cather, it also always retains its metaphorical meaning as well.[7] Postholocaust sf is metaphorically suited to themes of isolation, survival, and rebirth, for instance; "Hitler Wins" sf is suited to the themes of fascism and rebellion. By that token, then, confronting the nonhuman Other literalizes the metaphorical dehumanization of racism. Therefore, the sf trope that most frequently lends itself to issues of racism and genocide, and has done so for years, is alien contact. Ever since H. G. Wells made the connection between the British genocide of indigenous Tasmanians and the Martian invasion of England in *The War of the Worlds* (1898), the confrontation of humankind with the alien Other has served as an analogy for the confrontation between different human cultures. The novel of alien contact is, thus, suited metaphorically to use our xenophobic notions of the ethnically monstrous to explore what is, instead, ethically monstrous, and, in so doing, it confronts the genocidal tendencies of utopian fiction.

Building the trench between the ideal world and the flawed mundane one has always been problematic for utopian novels. Usually they employ geographical isolation to avoid more unpleasant ways of setting up the necessary conditions of exclusivity. To set up the isolated, exclusive society, however, the author sometimes kills off the offending parties—as when, for instance, James Tiptree, Jr., uses epidemic disease to kill off the men in "Houston, Houston, Do You Read?" (1976). In Mary E. Bradley Lane's 1889 pre-Holocaust utopian novel, *Mizora: A Prophecy*, genocide is more frankly evoked; when someone asks, "what became of the dark complexions?" the Aryan Mizorans say, "We eliminated them" (92). After all, "what could be more seductive than to kill in order to put an end to killing?"

It has become more and more difficult, however, to write a utopian novel that ignores the cost of building a version of More's trench, thanks, I would argue, to the insights of postcolonial studies. The insights of Frantz Fanon and Terry Goldie, among others, have exposed the monstrous social implications of the utopian vision. Postcolonial studies has made it difficult to write a utopian novel because it forces us to confront the human cost of setting up the utopian community. Postcolonial studies has also elucidated how important it remains to examine the implications of confrontations with alien social structures, and thus to speculate about the potentially utopian, neither ignoring the corpses of those who fall into the isolating trench nor sinking into the stasis of complacency, the other danger of utopia. The alien contact novel provides a particular type of "cognitive estrangement," to use Darko Suvin's famous definition of science fiction, in which we can examine the ways in which colonizers deal with what are, to them, alien cultures. If colonizers attempt to absorb an alien culture by familiarizing it, the alien contact novel foregrounds the alien culture's estrangement from the colonizers. Concomitantly, if colonizers attempt to erase the alien culture in an act of genocide, the alien contact novel insists upon "cognition," recognition of the violence and injustice of the act. By placing the reader on the borderland between the familiar and the alien, the writer of the alien contact novel provides what Brooks Landon calls a "zone of possibility" in his discussion of science fiction (*Science Fiction After 1900* 17) and what Frantz Fanon calls, in his landmark essay, "National Culture," a "zone of occult instability" where learning and change can take place.

Fanon describes the zone of occult instability as an area of potential for change created by processes of decolonization. In this zone meanings are indeterminate, flexible though still meaningful, sometimes paradoxical. Postcolonial studies is concerned with the hegemonic colonization of one culture by another and with the process of decolonization, which occurs as the colonized culture works to break away. The colonizer can exploit the zone of instability in order to retain control through neocolonial institutions, but this zone is also the site of rebellion against the colonizer.

Paul Park's novel *Celestis* provides one such zone of occult instability. The planet Celestis, with two intelligent native humanoid species, is subjected to a human colonization as oppressive as the nineteenth-century European colonization of Africa or the specifically British colonization of India. As the human character Simon puts it: "An immaculate new world . . . and on it they had resurrected all of the most shameful and most boring aspects of the bad old days. How had they managed it? Out of bad books and bad films—nothing like this had existed on Earth for hundreds of years" (46). The human utopian vision here is of "an immaculate new world," but so characterized only for the colonizers, who find the native species beneath acknowledgment: no wonder they resurrect the "bad old days." In the attempt to reach that immaculate utopia they must annihilate the native beings, and they do so through both familiarization and erasure.

On Park's planet, the two humanoid species have a symbiotic relationship and communicate telepathically. One species, small and seemingly tractable, the colonists call Aborigines and treat as servants or "special pets" (13). In their attempts to assimilate, to be accepted as equals, or even simply to appear less repellant to the dominating colonizers, the Aborigines undergo extensive surgical alterations and take drugs that submerge their telepathic, rejuvenative, and sensory powers. The other species, tall, silent, with similarly acute sensory and telepathic powers and described as having faces "midway between a vulture, a python, and a wolf" (126), is perceived as threatening and labeled as "Demons"; these have been hunted almost to the point of extinction. The novel traces the story of a human, Simon, and his Aborigine lover, Katherine, as they are kidnapped by Aborigine rebels.

Here assimilation of the Aborigines annihilates the culture of the colonized species without violence, through familiarization: the natives collaborate so as to look and behave like their colonizers rather than be left out of the imposed colonial economy. Taking on the characteristics of their colonizers, they attempt to become more familiar to them, to provide referents; "otherwise, communication would be too difficult" (31), since the colonizers make no attempt to understand the "alien" culture. This attempt at acculturation is no more benign than were American efforts to assimilate Native Americans by sending them to boarding schools to unlearn their culture or Australian programs to remove Aboriginal children, the "Lost Generations," from their families and place them with white families for similar reasons. It is as troubling and futile as efforts by the Indians under the Raj to become so familiar to colonizers that they would be indistinguishable from them. The utopianist colonizer first seeks to annihilate the contamination of difference in this way, by dismissing the value of the Other and refusing to allow that difference expression. If any trace of difference remains, the alien cannot become familiar enough to cross the trench into utopia. The "paradise on earth . . . safe from the deadly contaminations and temptations of the other tribe" cannot be achieved. Familiarization (and its inevitable failure) leads to erasure just as racism leads to genocide.

The Demons, perceived by the human colonists as more threatening, are literally demonized, and they are violently erased, annihilated as surely as were the Tasmanian Aboriginals or as Hitler wished for the Jews and the Gypsies. The colonizers succumb to the allure of genocide. What cannot be familiarized must be erased through violence, on Celestis as it is on Earth.

In both cases, the human utopian agenda requires a static master/servant society, so stagnant it echoes myths of India at the height of the Raj. This is no accidental reference; Simon, the main human character in the novel, who is of Indian ancestry, makes the connection, saying, "I feel I can talk about these things. . . . For many years my own race was a subject one, conquered and colonized by what you call the Europeans" (52). It is apparent as the novel begins that any thought of utopia is gone in this grim colonial outpost abandoned by its home planet. The treatment of both Aborigines and Demons reveals how the static ideal has been exposed as nostalgia for a rigid and barren imperialism, which reinscribes the familiar tools of this utopian project: brutal suppression and genocide.

As the novel ends, however, the assimilationist Aborigines, along with the few remaining Demons, have begun a revolution and are returning to their original forms. By doing so, they become able to perceive the universe in a way utterly beyond human understanding. Rather than attempting to enter the barren human Dome of Heaven, the stagnant, exclusionary utopia, they estrange themselves from all things human. They shed human ways of knowing as well—to insist upon their own ways—and demonstrate the true cognitive estrangement of decolonization. Here is how Park describes an Aborigine woman's reemerging alien perceptions: "She could perceive above her a net without a center or circumference. A net of stars joined by fragile threads, and there was no pattern, no design, for these things were formed out of perception, out of individual creation, which had no place in this new sky. Human beings had it backward with their world of facts, their heaven of hypotheses. . . . The soul's clarity. Its permanence. The infinite net of fragile threads that linked all creatures except humankind" (260). Spurning the controlled and controlling human utopia, "their heaven of hypotheses," which had attempted to annihilate alien difference, the woman perceives something like an antiutopia: not a better or ideal world, formed out of isolation and exclusion, but a nonworld "without a center or circumference," without any pattern or design that might form an exclusive Dome of Heaven. Its only exclusion is the one group that rejects, that cannot see, the "fragile threads that linked all creatures."

The vision of chaos that marks the Aborigine woman's rejection of human assimilation sounds very much like Fanon's zone of occult instability. A net with no pattern or design: this is a vision of instability and indeterminacy, meaningful, and so decentered that the idea of a center becomes meaningless. The aliens of Celestis estrange themselves from their colonizers through both violent rebellion and a return to alien perceptions—estranged cognition. The intellectual rebellion of their alien perceptions—that is, their reversion to their original native perceptions—provides the impetus for rebellion against the colonizer.

If utopia here requires the genocide of the alien, what then does the escape from another's utopian project require? This novel allows only troubling answers—violent rebellion and another vision of exclusion. While Celestis explores a postcolonial understanding of why utopia must be rejected, it hardly offers a comforting substitute. As the novel ends, Simon has escaped from the rebels, saving the life of Katherine (or wresting her from her recovered Aborigine consciousness). Because we do not learn if the rebellion succeeds or fails, we are invited to speculate on the aftermath. We might wish that the revolution would succeed and that the Aborigines and Demons, and maybe even the humans, now humbled, would live in harmony. It is much more likely, however, that the result of the rebellion would be the destruction of the humans (another genocide), the extinction of the already endangered Demons, rebellion having come too late to hope for the survival of their species, and the eventual extinction of the Aborigines who cannot reproduce without the Demons. Instead of any comforting resolution, Celestis and many other alien contact novels make clear how postcolonialist critique exposes the connection between utopia and genocide. Living in the zone of occult instability, however, may be almost as dangerous.

In Celestis the colonizers do everything wrong. The Sparrow shows colonizers doing everything right, but the result, especially as it is played out in the sequel, Children of God, is the same—genocide. The Sparrow, like Celestis, provides a zone of occult instability, where utopian possibility occurs, not through colonization or rebellion, but in a zone of mutual cooperation where boundaries blur in free exchange of language, ideas, and material goods. The colonizers do their best to avoid hegemony, to colonize without dominating, to teach and to learn from the natives. Each group is transformed by the other. But this empathetic feedback loop, which seems like a postcolonial utopia, works no better in the long run than the worst encounters of nineteenth- and twentieth-century imperialism. The Sparrow and Children of God suggest that complacency is as dangerous as trench-building, may in fact lead to the trenches.

The Sparrow's chronological story begins as radio-astronomers detect evidence of life beyond our solar system in the form of "other-worldly" music. An expeditionary force of Jesuit priests and laypeople, all of whom feel the guiding hand of God in the discovery and the expedition, then travel to make first contact. Upon landfall on the planet Rakhat, they find a compatible ecosphere and two sentient species; just as in Celestis, however, the arrival of a third sentient species forces the narrative beyond more easily resolved binary conflicts. Un-like the colonizers in *Celestis*, the humans in this novel make contact, make friends, share knowledge without intruding, learn the native languages, and develop theories about the natives' social structures. The human mission seems to have come upon, and contributed to, a Garden of Eden, a trope made in-evitable by their sense of divine propulsion.

Russell takes pains to establish how good the expeditionary force is—how generous, ethical, compassionate, witty, smart, sincere, well trained, even di-vinely inspired. They fall in love with each other, the readers fall in love with them, and we all fall in love with the alien Runa, with whom they first make contact, beings who are gentle, playful, social vegetarians with no word for edge: "they have no concept of borders, such as separate our nations" (233). Such a world-view makes unlikely any dangerous border skirmishes in the zone of occult instability. The only way the humans interfere is to teach basic gardening techniques to the Runa, who thrive on the increased food supply.

When we meet the other alien species, the Jana'ata, we like them too, though not as much: they are aggressive traders who look down on the less cul-tured and less technologically advanced Runa. Nevertheless, they are very bright, eager to interact and trade, and are the producers of the beautiful, seem-ingly spiritual music that led to the human discovery of the first intelligent life beyond our home planet. How can we not like a species that reminds us so of ourselves: capitalistic, technological, even artistic? We might worry, given these reminders, that the Jana'ata would be prone to imperialism, yet they deal fairly with the Runa, who do, indeed, seem a bit dim, and the Jana'ata do not infringe upon Runa camps.

Perhaps, we think, this planet might be a postcolonial utopia, a place where societies with different levels of technology and different world-views might coexist in harmony, without either hegemonic colonialism or the vicious ultra-nationalism that sometimes replaces the colonialist presence. Perhaps the oddly familiar Runa represent developing countries and the similarly familiar Jana'ata industrialized ones. Perhaps trade, both financial and cultural, pro-vides a peaceful zone where instability implies only growth.

Or perhaps we are being set up, our complacency as readers making us a bit dim ourselves. The gap between the story of the mission to the planet Rakhat and the story of Father Emilio Sandoz, the mission's only returned sur-vivor, assures us that this is the case. Father Sandoz's story, which takes place upon his return, is cross-cut with the story of the mission, and the novel's sus-pense, which is considerable, lies in our wondering how the Garden of Eden could have so devolved as to contain the torture and abuse that Sandoz has clearly experienced and the monstrous behavior of one native species toward the other that he has clearly witnessed. Only in the novel's last pages do we learn how the two stories make their horrific reconciliation. There we discover that the relationship between the two alien species is that of predator (the Jana'ata) to prey (the Runa) and that the human beings have disturbed the population balance between the species by introducing gardening to the Runa and interfering with the Jana'ata as they cull the Runa population explosion in what looks like cannibalism to the humans. There too we learn that the "heavenly" music of the Jana'ata is really pornographic and that Father Sandoz has been maimed by the Jana'ata to live as a sex slave. The colonizers, with the best intentions in *their* world, had dangerously familiarized the world of Rakhat.

As terrible as the volume's conclusion is, the second volume, *Children of God*, goes further, showing how the human mission's open-minded and considerate interchange with two equally open-minded and considerate species leads to the suicidal guilt of one species and a war between the two species whose goal is genocide. Because of human interference, the Jana'ata see themselves as predatory colonizers (like the humans in *Celestis*) with monstrous cannibalistic appetites and disintegrate into self-loathing, while the Runa learn to see themselves as outraged victims of the Jana'ata and institute a bloody war to destroy their oppressors. In these novels, as with those "ordinary Germans" who supported Hitler's program, companionable human complacency in the perception of the Other leads to genocide as surely as does the ghastly isolationist trench-building of *Celestis*. Familiarization rapidly descends into violent erasure.

Terry Goldie observes that the colonizing narrator ultimately engages in self-description, and that is what the human colonists of Russell's novels do. In *Fear and Temptation*, Goldie examines the ways in which colonizers have portrayed indigenous peoples, emphasizing the "white failure to penetrate the indigene episteme" (9). "Our image of the indigene," he says, "has functioned then as a constant source for semiotic reproduction in which each textual image refers back to those offered before" (6). The colonizer's awareness is contained within a semiotic that precedes the expedition, giving form and expectation to the encounter. This engagement in self-description, this seeing the self in the Other, leads away from estrangement into a dangerously complacent familiarization.

For *The Sparrow*, postcolonial assumptions seem to work comfortably in the encounter with the two sentient species. Believing they have learned from terrestrial history, Russell's humans arrive without intentions of commerce or conversion. The assumed purity of their mission, however, blinds them to the larger paradox of the novel: the humans may represent an ideal group, but every concept they bring to the mission, including the "prime directive" to avoid interference, remains necessarily contained within the realm of human thought. Like computers programmed in a particular operating language, they simply cannot have a thought outside their own grammar. The human colonists believe, for instance, that God has sent them to this planet. And we readers, however sophisticated, share these limitations, since we read within that same grammar.

Blinded by self-description, by the metaphorical aptness of the alien species, by the very literalization of metaphor central to sf, we, like *The Sparrow*'s main characters, see only the similarities between the alien species and ourselves and cannot estrange ourselves from Rakhat. Thus we cannot see how the Runa gender roles differ fundamentally from ours, how an agrarian economy would prove disastrous for population control on Rakhat, how the relationship between the Runa and the Jana'ata, two different species, is profoundly different from the difference between two different cultures within the same species, as is the case of any human encounter on Earth. The human characters believe they understand and believe they are acting morally, but this is so only within the grammar of their now-alien belief system. By complacently familiarizing the Other, they have unwittingly (not systematically) attempted to absorb the Other. But because the alien world truly is Other, it cannot be absorbed, as we learned in *Celestis*. At the novel's close, Father Sandoz, his confessors, and the readers join in an epiphany of cognitive estrangement, smack dab in the zone of occult instability: "in our own despair, against our will, comes wisdom through the awful grace of God" (Aeschylus, qtd. in Russell, *Sparrow* 404). Such wisdom comes at great cost, too great a cost to permit any of the characters to live in a complacent utopia.

The novel's sequel, *Children of God*, imagining a return to Rakhat, first restates the epiphany of *The Sparrow* in more specific terms: "First contact—by definition—takes place in a state of radical ignorance, where nothing is known about the ecology, biology, languages, culture, and economy of the other" (*Children* 21). In this second volume, Emilio Sandoz moves from a position of radical ignorance to one of knowing witness to genocide.

In the first volume it became clear that neither the garden of a balanced ecosystem, which greeted the humans, nor the garden of agrarian reform, which they introduced in their radical ignorance and self-reflexive blindness, can produce a utopia, though they imagined one when they arrived and hoped for one as they settled in. In the second volume, it is the Runa who dream of utopia, a dream made possible because they now understand all too well the notion of borders. If we remember Michael Ignatieff's remarks that opened this essay, we understand the danger of this acquired knowledge: "To create a world with no more need for borders. . . . This utopia is so alluring that it is a wonder the human [or any] race has been able to survive at all" (125). We are not surprised when the Runa decide how to form their utopia—"Kill them, one by one—until they trouble us no longer" (239)—as they try to annihilate the Jana'ata. Further well-meant and disastrous meddling occurs as the human Native American missionary identifies the Plains Indian culture with the Jana'ata, again demonstrating how familiarizing absorption invites the possibility of trench-building erasure. Russell's novels demonstrate another disheartening connection between utopia and genocide: postcolonial concepts of the zone of occult instability and the colonizer's unavoidable self-describing blinders expose this connection.

Questions remain. Is familiarization, which seems intuitively empathetic, like a sharing of cultures, like a fulfillment of E. M. Forster's exhortation to "only connect," really a kind of destruction of the Other, an unwitting genocide? More generally, if genocide is a utopian project, is utopia inevitably a genocidal project? Until or unless this question can be answered no, it will be hard to write a utopian novel. The Nazis linked utopia, eugenics, and genocide in what we now call the Holocaust. Postcolonialist criticism reminds us that these links remain culturally forged, and it provides a forum in which to examine and detach these links. Science fiction, in its defamiliarizing transformations, provides the form for such an examination. Specifically, alien contact novels such as Celestis, The Sparrow, and Children of God will enable sf to work through complex issues of cultural encounter, exploring topics of ethical monstrosity, which they share with other post-Holocaust art.

14

Dis-Imagined Communities

Science Fiction and the Future of Nations

ISTVAN CSICSERY-RONAY, JR.

Science Fiction and the Postnational Turn

Readers expect science fiction to conduct thought experiments about the future of human institutions. These projections are variously plausible and implausible; they may include not only rational extrapolations from current historical trends but also alternate universes, counterfactual histories, and futures revalued by the recovery of archaic pasts. Given the exuberance and excess of the science fictional imagination, it would be significant if some powerful contemporary institutions were ignored or excluded from the sf megatext.[1] In this essay I investigate just such an exclusion: the concept of nation. This concept, with its complex history and implications, is so rarely explored in sf's thought experiments that one might conclude that it has been rejected as something that *cannot* exist in *any* future. More surely than even more fantastic social formations, like utopia or the recrudescence of premodern societies, the role of nationality appears unimaginable in sf's futures.

To paraphrase Nietzsche, we explain the future only by what is most powerful in the present. If we are to conclude from the representations of sf, then we should assume that nations and nationality are not sufficiently powerful to be involved in sf's imaginary future solutions to dilemmas posed in the present. I argue in this essay that sf has traditionally viewed itself as a genre that transcends nationality and nationalism and has thus enjoyed the post-1960s development of globalism, which it predicted for most of the twentieth century. I also argue that this globalizing imaginary is based on a notion of history and historical innovation that systematically, though unconsciously, ignores the role of nationality in the development of individual consciousness, to the extent that sf cannot imagine a future society in which nationality has any significance. This "postnationalist"—or antinational—orientation forms the basis for some of the most powerful world-construction models in the genre's treasury, models that disavow national particularity and bypass the cultural tensions that might emerge in the relationships of self-distinguishing national cultures in the future. Although fully in harmony with globalist theory, which perceives the withering away of the nation-state in the age of transnational economic and cultural flows, denationalizing sf, I contend, is based less on a purely rational perception of the logic of history than on the political perspective of the dominant technopowers, for whom national cultural identity represents an obstacle to political-economic rationalization, the foundation upon which their hegemony is based.

James Gunn, a noted science fiction writer and scholar, has offered an elegant definition of the genre that justifies sf's antinational leanings:

Science fiction is the branch of literature that deals with the effects of change on people in the real world as it can be projected into the past, the future, or to distant places. It often concerns itself with scientific or technological change, and it usually involves matters whose importance is greater than the individual or the community; often civilization or the race itself is in danger. . . .

. . . [S]cience fiction could not be written until people began to think in unaccustomed ways. They had, first of all, to think of themselves as a race—not as a tribe or a people or even a nation. Science fiction may contain unconscious cultural or political biases, but there is little tribalism, little rejoicing in the victory over another human group, but rather an implied or overt criticism of the act of war, and there is even less nationalism. (1–2)

It is not difficult to see why sf would consider nations to be undesirably alien social models. However we define nations and nationality (which I attempt later), they are unambiguously linked with a kind of collective memory that owes little to scientific rationalization. National solidarity has deeply nonrational sources: language, genealogy and kinship codes, customs and mythic charters, religion, traditional arts, and historical links to specific lands. To feel like part of a nation, one must idealize the arbitrary facts of one's birthplace and parentage, revere the mysterious knowledge of one's national language, religion, and mythology, and, above all, accept and enjoy distinctive and irreducible differences among human groups. Science fiction's favored models, by contrast, are fundamentally rationalistic: utopia and dystopia, both of them models striving for universal validity (the one the fully rationalized society, the other the excessively rationalized society); technoscience (the application of scientific discovery to social life by replacing irrational traditions with rationalized practices); the reduction of human motives to universal abstractions (ingenuity, heroism, evil, curiosity; race, gender, class, degree of development); social evolution (reason in history, the dynamic historical transformation of social life through scientific principles drawn from natural processes); convergent worlds (the tendency of all worlds to meet and interflow because they follow the same evolutionary principles); and the tendency to reduce phenomena to the most rational explanation. Even the most sublime dimension of science fiction, the sense of wonder, is predicated on the potential of rational technohistorical or natural processes to exceed the wildest expectations and experiences of human beings. Clearly, the premises of national identity do not easily find a niche in such an antiparticularist universe of discourse.

This antipathy to nationality is in step with the leading contemporary globalist and world-system theories. Best articulated by Benedict Anderson's *Imagined Communities* and the works of Ernest Gellner, most discussions about nations and nationality in the West treat nations as historical epiphenomena of recent provenance, conjured into existence by modernization.[2] For Anderson, nations in their modern political forms are the products of bourgeois literary elites who constructed imaginary communities through journalism, novelistic fiction, language reforms, and cultural policy.[3] Nations in this view are the ideological constructions of nation-states; they are the imaginary *goals* of nationalism rather than their primordial origins.

Globalist theory extends this view. For better or worse, the legitimacy of nation-states has been undermined to an unprecedented degree by the driving institutions of the postmodern world. The Internet, global capital markets, multinational corporations, the commodification of all cultural practices in global market terms, and social movements sophisticated in communications technologies have vitiated most of the attractive energies of national identification. Although nation-states still exert enormous influence on the world system, their elites and their economies increasingly depend on transnational capital flow. Diasporas, the flows of populations moving either voluntarily or by force across international borders, have irreversibly weakened the conception of a nation as a homogeneous population residing in a defined territory administered by the national state. Mediating these processes are the cultural flows that remove national styles and traditions from their historical contexts.[4]

It should be clear that this postmodern evolute of modernization theory surmises, even when it does not explicitly affirm it, that the forces controlling the means of global communication and the circulation of information (which now encompass the world financial system) are transforming the world's particular societies into provinces in a world system that legitimates the global influence of the Great Technological Powers, who are by and large the heirs of the Great Imperialist Powers of old. Yet when viewed from Chechnya, East Timor, Palestine, and Israel, from the perspective of the Lakota, the Maori, and the Inuit, the story of the Wired World-Without-Nations seems less compelling. In general, globalist theory does not imagine that the complex loyalties and histories that inspire national consciousness can still have a significant effect on human history—a view currently shared equally by the Left's internationalism and the Right's multinationalism. Both view nations as obstacles to progress, and critical theory on the Left is particularly apt to condemn national identity for its putative complicity in the racism, gender oppression, genocides, and wars of the past two centuries.[5]

Opposed to this equation of national consciousness with ideology is the view that there is more to a nation than the cynical control of a population by a bourgeois elite. For these theorists, national cultures create a flexible and tenacious form of human identity. Nations are associations of solidarity that have existed in many political forms, not only the modern nation-state, and have demonstrably served powerful affective and cognitive needs of human beings. Nationalist projects derive from, and depend on, a collective sense of shared experiences, values, and languages that have continued over several generations. National feeling has power because it "assures collective dignity . . . for populations excluded, neglected or suppressed in the distribution of values and opportunities," and it provides a way to understand and preserve identity in the face of annihilation, by transferring cultural values and practices to posterity (Smith 182). In this view, nations existed in complex forms before they became the main legitimizing concept of the modern state.[6]

Nationality—and I must emphasize that I distinguish nations from nation-states, and national consciousness from nationalism—is a difficult concept to manage because of a duality inherent in the concept. The nationalism-nation relation is "perceived very differently by different people, since several obscure questions underlie it: Is nationalist ideology the (necessary or circumstantial) reflection of the existence of nations? Or do nations constitute themselves out of nationalist ideologies (though it may mean that these latter, having attained their 'goal,' are subsequently transformed?). Must the 'nation' itself—and naturally this question is not independent of the preceding ones—be considered as a 'state' or as a 'society' (a social formation)?" (Balibar and Wallerstein 46).

Nations have been extremely varied in their historical instances, yet they maintain certain forms of continuity and identity throughout their mutations (and these may also change over time). Among these elements of continuity are the extension of the analogy of the kinship group to a larger population that may include members who are not biologically related[7] and the further assumption that this is the basis for claims of some form of sovereignty vis-à-vis other populations. The kinship analogy with family creates deep conceptual problems, for people may be well aware of the analogical character of nations, yet what the analogy means can be different for different cultures at different historical moments. By the same token, political sovereignty is determined by historical tradition and the synchronic possibilities of the present. For all that, individuals who identify themselves as members of a nation consider themselves continuous with earlier generations who may have enjoyed more or less sovereignty and cultural distinctiveness than they do. (It is important here to distinguish nationality from ethnicity. For this context, nationality is essentially defined by the group itself, and it includes a claim to sovereignty, which may be prospective or retrospective. Ethnicity is attributed to others by a dominant national group or state, as a term to limit sovereignty. The dominant nation is "the people"; ethnic groups are always *a* people.)

Although the mutability of the concept of nation is an obstacle to the sort of clear historical taxonomy desired by social theory, one would think it should offer rich possibilities for the political imagination of science fiction. Why then has science fiction—which has been fascinated by the future influence of other aspects of social identity, like gender, race, sexual culture, class, consensus, and domination—shown so little interest in the future of nationality?

It was not always so. In the heyday of the nation-state at the end of the nineteenth century, European science fiction generally treated nations as elemental social entities, impossible to dis-imagine. Future-war fiction, in particular, routinely depicted collisions between major imperial powers, a model that easily expanded into Social Darwinian fantasies of race wars, like the fashionable Yellow Peril stories.[8] But war was not required. National identity was considered as significant an element of character as class, gender, and profession. Jules Verne's protagonists, for example, are almost always identified by their various countries of origin, and national stereotypes provided him with a good deal of his character motivation.

The conventions changed with H. G. Wells. He consistently bypassed the problem of concrete representation of national identity through two formative innovations. The first was to depict the shock of the novum on the intimate, everyday social existence of English people, emphasizing the catastrophic transformations of familiar national and regional conditions rather than a global perspective. By depicting the effect of the Martian invasion on a recognizable part of the English countryside, for example, Wells represented the shock as it might be felt by a typical English reader, whose unreflective provincialism, true to the precepts of literary realism, was the best proving ground for universal humanism. Everyday conditions in the south of England stood in for the human condition. Since the invading aliens of *The War of the Worlds* (1898) do not make national distinctions among humans, humans do so at their peril.

Wells's other major innovation was to displace the novum into the future, where evolutionary processes are sure to produce enormous changes in human institutions. Thus the extravagantly hyperbolized "two nations" of *The Time Machine* (1895) are not in any politically useful way still English. Time and their own historical problems have transformed them into something so different that it is their very humanity that is questioned, not their national identity. With this move, too, Wells made his English nation into a universal model for the future of the human species. By perfecting a way of representing familiar social life either in, or impinged upon by, the future, Wells stayed loyal to the devices of circumstantial realism and evaded the potential contradictions that might arise among a universalist humanism, socialism, and the deep English national feeling.

After Wells, one finds in science fiction mainly assumptions of national naturalness (that is, the use of the author's and public's nation as the unreflective natural scene of the action) or the expectation that historical evolution will eventually make nations obsolete. Most decisively, the future of nations was much less a burden for the U.S. science fiction emerging from the pulps than for European writers. The United States had largely resolved its national question with the expulsion of the European colonials from its territories, the near-extermination of its aboriginal population, and the establishment of economic hegemony over Latin America. Free of the anxiety about foreign invasions that marked English futuristic writing from 1871 on[9] and enjoying the steady expansion of its territory, sf from the Gernsback era on displays a barely conscious American triumphalism.

After World War II and especially after the 1960s, science fiction began to imagine, as did much social theory, alternatives not only to nation-states (with which it was never comfortable) but also to world governments. Most striking of all, writers began to imagine the deterioration of their own societies, which disqualified even their own milieus as potential models for national futures. This spirit of political negation inspired the dramatic turn of sf everywhere: the dark visions of the English New Wave, the countercultural critiques of U.S. fiction, the *samizdat* bitterness of Soviet science fiction, Japanese catastrophism, and eventually cyberpunk's slum globe. Science fiction's future worlds were still divided into competing polities, but existing nations or historical models were generally expunged from the megatext. Where political communities continued to operate, they were replaced by fantastic communities based on abstract principles rather than histories: Male Lands and Female Lands, utopian settlements and the capitalist multinations, Third World worlds, cultures of desire and cultures of repression.

Varieties of Dis-Imagining

For most of the twentieth century and into the twenty-first, sf has absented nations from future history—not only the possible heirs of our present's nations but any imaginary variant of a community with a claim to cultural distinctiveness and political sovereignty in a system of related communities. The tactic does not always work, however. World-construction models are also world reductions; complex cultural and political social relations may be strategically excluded from science fictional worlds, but the unconscious dimensions of identity usually make their presence felt even in reduced designs.

Science fiction removes nations as agents or subjects of future history, and national cultures as historical forces, through five basic strategies of displacement, world models in which national identity is disavowed: *transgalacticism/transglobalism, corporate globalization, apocalyptic winnowing, biological displacement,* and *archaicization.*

1. Transgalacticism. The staple of space opera is the image of galactic or global political entities so vast that national differences disappear into triviality. Constructing conflicts between abstract superpowers, empires, and federations, or between a hegemonic state and its abstract population, avoids the need to represent cultural specificity and national politics and transforms history into a contest of political power justified by a superadded morality or ideology. The galactic space opera, moreover, usually converts problems of cultural variety and social evolution (two areas in which nations have played an especially important role) into matters of charismatic individual leadership.

Isaac Asimov's original Foundation trilogy (1951–53), for example, plays out a galactic history of several hundred years over millions of inhabited worlds.[10] Although the action involves several different planets and planetary clusters, Asimov never presents them as concrete societies, only as political structures (prefectures, kingdoms, confederations, empires, etc.) whose political leaders and diplomatic legates make all their decisions without reference to cultural identity, tradition, or communal solidarity. These worlds are abstract counters in the unfolding historical game between the galactic plan of the Foundation and its various dialectical antagonists. For the Asimovian galactic history, cultural or national specificity is irrelevant. Only the abstract historical stages of social progress matter for the Plan, and only the individual agents who emerge to facilitate or to block the Plan matter for the plot. In Asimov's galactic system, national cultures and identity are, as God was for Laplace, unnecessary hypotheses.

In the 1960s and after, space operas became much more interested in cultural differences among worlds. Yet even here the cultures were embodiments of abstract principles rather than complex historical societies. New mutations of the space opera have recently appeared that share not only a deep suspicion of Western conceptions of culture but also ambivalence about the legitimacy of *any* culture's values.

Dan Simmons's *Hyperion* (1989) is especially interesting in this context. Simmons consciously models his transgalactic polity as a dispersed replay of earthly human history. The galaxy is replete with colonies and protectorates linked by several kinds of matter-transmission technology, under the umbrella of the galactic government that is explicitly named the Hegemony. Each colony has a dominant culture characteristic of a historical human community: there is Hebron, a planet for the Jews; there is Barnard's World, an academic corn-desert imitating the nineteenth-century American Midwest; there is Qom-Riyadh, the home of the New Order Shiites; and so on. Human collectives are descended from terrestrial communities that once migrated from the now-defunct Old Earth.

So close are the lines of descent that Simmons actually invokes the anachronistic problems of *national* identity. For example, one of the central protagonists, Fedmahn Kassad, is the child of the star-crossed earthly people known as Palestinians: "[H]e and his family lived in the slums of Tharsis, human testimony to the bitter legacy of the terminally dispossessed. Every Palestinian in the Worldweb and beyond carried the cultural memory of a century of struggle capped by a month of nationalist triumph before the Nuclear Jihad of 2038 wiped it all away. Then came their Second Diaspora, this one lasting five centuries and leading to dead-end desert worlds like Mars, their dream buried with the death of Old Earth" (116). The Palestinians suffer from homelessness, deserts, refugee camps, slums—the same historical stalemate after 2538 (the date of the novel's action) as in 1989 (when it was first published).

Simmons's transgalactic order is a deliberate pastiche of human history;

each commune, each person, each military campaign, each brand of beer, is merely an evocation of now-mythic earthly history. Surprising and grotesque combinations occur—like Zen Gnosticism and New Order Shia—but these are merely combinations of ancient elements. By the novel's end, the Consul, most attractive of the protagonists, admits that he has joined the hated enemies of the Hegemony, the Ousters, who have been able to create new things only because they have escaped the cultural system of the Hegemony.

Hyperion is a premier example of the classic space opera's postmodern mutation.[11] Its theme is space opera itself, and the difficulty of imagining histories and cultures different from our own. Versions of our present nations appear five centuries from now because the Hegemony's population is incapable of beginning anything new. Yet, ironically, in this novel about the tiredness of the idea of nations and traditional groups, Simmons creates an image of something he doubts: an imaginary nation. One of his worlds, Maui-Covenant, is in some ways merely a simulated Polynesian island, whose original charter was to "save the dolphins" from extinction on Earth. Simmons transforms this New Age cliché into a rich culture in which humans, dolphins, and "motile isles"—living islands that move themselves with "treesails" and gather nutriments from the oceans with enormous root systems—have formed a "Covenant of Life." The Maui-Covenanters invent new technologies to integrate themselves more deeply into their conscious, common ecosphere.

Perhaps unintentionally, Simmons populates Maui-Covenant with exactly the kinds of social, political, and ecological factors that lead to a collective awareness of distinctiveness and sovereignty. It is telling that it is the destruction of this culture by the Hegemony, after years of resistance struggles, that inspires the Consul to betray his system and to side with the Ousters. Couched deep in Simmons's glib and showy science fiction is a threnody for an imaginary national culture.

2. Corporate Globalization. In the world system dear to cyberpunk and technoir the powers of the state have been usurped by profit-driven corporations, while the functions of communal solidarity have been reduced to the level of weak local and professional groups—gangs, squatters, hackers, blackmarketeers, indentured laborers, and so on. In space-based futures, the newly colonized planets, asteroids, and space stations are owned and run as industries by private monopolies in dark partnerships with world governments.

In cyberpunk, especially, the concept of nation, with its implication of some historical homogeneity through time, has been made obsolete by the dramatic heterogeneity of human, primarily urban, society. There is no national community to legitimize a state, nor is there a state that might consolidate a national constituency. The privileged setting for all significant action in the future is the postmodern metropolis, which behaves as a self-operating city-state, rather than a national center.[12]

In the corporatized world, legitimacy and identity themselves are made dramatically problematic, since the source of the global corporations' power is their technological manipulation of consciousness and physical integrity. The body politic seems to dissolve as the human physical body is constantly desta-bilized. Solidarity with others is extremely tentative and limited, since personal identity—that is, solidarity with oneself—becomes unmanageably fluid. On the corporate globe, self-identification with a territory becomes problematic when physical space becomes virtualized; with religion, when states of consciousness can be artificially induced; and with history, when memory and perception can be manipulated in the brain. The global corporations thus trade in the destruc-tion of traditions and cultures, as well as of all those feelings of continuity and solidarity that require a sense of integration with a society larger than one's mortal self. Where space opera was particularly congenial for the displacement of superpower relations, the virtualized metropolis of cyberpunk aptly dis-places contemporary globalization.

For cyberpunk writers, the problem of imagining a role for nations in the future is more difficult than for space-operators or archaicizers. Cyberpunk aims to depict the deterioration of the conditions of the present, and nation-states are exemplary forms of human community (and one might say of histor-ical complacency, ripe for attack) in the present. This concern has inspired some unusually respectful responses to nationality. As the near-future of corporate globalization becomes realized, nations and nation-states come to represent bases for resistance. It is in this vein that William Gibson, in an afterword writ-ten for the Hungarian translation of *Neuromancer* (and alluded to in the Ace hardback anniversary edition in English [1994]), seemed to apologize to the peoples of Eastern Europe for not prophesying the collapse of the Soviet Union.[13]

3. Apocalyptic winnowing. In the apocalyptic catastrophe subgenre, a small fraction of humanity survives the near-annihilation of the species. The sur-vivors are deprived of the conditions of civilization—mainly other people with whom they might cooperate and reestablish complex social relationships and institutions. Typically, they degenerate into tribes. The genre often treats this reduction of human civilization as a form of historical purification, or at least an opportunity to begin the civilizing process again from scratch. This genre seems to have a particular affinity with the West Coast of the United States, where ties to European and Asian historical traditions are loose and where a certain mythology of ecotopian harmony embodied in extinct aboriginal Native Amer-ican cultures has popular currency. Perhaps the most important exemplar of apocalyptic winnowing is Ursula K. Le Guin's *Always Coming Home* (1985).

Always Coming Home is an ambitious metafictional experiment. Le Guin braids many different genres of telling, from the committedly antinarrative an-thologization of the Kesh people's folktales and songs to an elegant and straightforward first-person narrative of a mixed-nation girl, Stone Telling. As she grows, Stone Telling moves through the society of her mother, the pastoral Kesh of the Na Valley, to the tribe of her father, the patriarchal and hierarchical warrior society of the Condor people, ultimately to return to the Kesh with a full appreciation of their peaceable culture. The novel is set in a future California that has been completely reconfigured by geological cataclysms. Millions perished at the time, but the survivors reinvented social structures and cultures and have now passed their traditions down for generations. The Na Valley culture is based on a composite of certain aboriginal Native American cultures; the people are organized in a complex of clans and voluntary associations, they are agricultural, they celebrate seasonal festivals and perform customary rituals, and for the most part they communicate only with other valley towns.

Opposite the pastoralists are the warlike Dayao, the People of the Condor. Where the Kesh are tolerant and anarchistic pagans, with no gender or political hierarchies, the Condor people are exaggeratedly monotheistic, violently patriarchal, and organized in slave-holding warrior societies that oppress women of all classes. While the Kesh are generally literate, the Dayao restrict literacy to the male elite. The Kesh live in a loose association of villages and cultivate their cultures locally, while the Dayao centralize every aspect of their culture: in their leader (the Condor himself), their state, and their central capital City.

In terms of our discussion, Le Guin not only pits two diametrically opposed cultures against each other, clearly favoring the pastoralists over the warriors. She also pits a people who share loose kinship associations and cultural practices against a group that has organized itself into an abstract state. The Dayao have identified with their totem rather than their region, and they have codified all their cultural practices. They have become identified with the City, engineering, and the war machine. While the Kesh are glad to be without history (they speak of the historical period of humanity as the time "when they lived outside the world" [152]), the Condor men are establishing their one true transcendental narrative.

The book is self-consciously utopian in many ways—and Le Guin plays with contradictions openly, occasionally with irony. Yet at the heart of *Always Coming Home* is an ideological antagonism that is simplistic even in the utopian tradition: between the localistic, clan-based Kesh society, where power is distributed in myriad ways and which is essentially peaceful, harmonious, skillful in managing conflict, and jealous of its smallness; and a hierarchical, patriarchal, racist, militaristic, monotheistic society representing the zero degree of the modern, scientific state. In terms of the future of nations, *Always Coming Home* presents the simplest possible view: there are immanentist, ecofriendly communes, which do not permit themselves to even think of themselves as distinct political entities, and there are centralizing, transcendentalist, self-aggrandizing protonational states.

4. Biological displacement. With biological displacement, science fiction elides the distinction between national culture and race and allows the political-cultural problems of nationality and ethnicity to slip into the context of racial difference. It does this through the depiction of the alien.

The alien is one of science fiction's most important contributions to mythopoeisis. It is the nexus of the science fictional societies' barely avowed, and often wholly disavowed, feelings about human relationships that deviate from cultural norms. Yet for all the freedom the alien provides the science fiction writer, it is constrained by a fundamental ambivalence in almost all its manifestations. The alien is ontologically Other only by virtue of its being *biologically* Other.

Sf most often depicts aliens' biological relations to humans as a nebulous kind of species difference, thereby constructing alien-human difference as analogous to terrestrial racial difference. In both cases, this construction permits much the same imaginary sleight-of-hand as the concept of race. It permits the dominant members of a culture to see aspects of themselves objectified in Others while also disavowing them, by placing the Others beyond a nonnegotiable, *essential* line of separation. As a result, human national-political, ethnic, class, and gender differences are distanced beyond mediating human institutions. Rapprochement is only possible accompanied by the anxiety that differences may prove to be intractable and even dangerous; or at the risk of violating a taboo about which the central protagonists are deeply ambivalent and the audience is ontologically confused. Is the difference between an alien and a human being a fundamental one that prevents interbreeding, as in animal biology, and, by analogy, the exchange of desires and projects? Are the human institutions that have to do with relations across biological generations—family, clan, gender, nation—biologically exclusive or merely culturally circumscribed?

Race insinuates the model of species difference into relations among members of the human species. It purports to name qualities deeper than expression, and consequently deeper than culture and politics. Race implies forces that cannot be examined in oneself and yet that may manifest themselves at any time. The insidiousness of race lies precisely in this precondition for its being imagined at all, lying beneath all conscious articulations, all sharing of premises, all decisions. When race is in play, it implies that nature supersedes culture.

Anxiety over sexual power and purity underlies most articulations of alien-human contacts, as it does most conceptions of race. Aliens permit the anxiety to be exaggerated or refined in fantastic displacements. From the Bug-Eyed Monsters absconding with Anglo blondes on the covers of the pulps and C. L. Moore's Medusa-like alien lover in "Shambleau" (1933), to the incarnations of erotic repression, the Phi-creatures, of Lem's *Solaris* (1961; trans. 1970), to the cosmos-inseminating monoliths of Clarke's and Kubrick's *2001: A Space Odys-*

sey (1968), the alien has always disturbed the deep-lying connection between biology and human culture. Popular forms of sf are often explicit about it. The various *Star Trek* series, for example, have taken this anxiety and ambivalence as an overarching theme, since their medium permits them to revisit alien contacts in many forms. *Star Trek* is particularly concerned with the ambivalence of transspecies—and by analogy, transnational and transracial—erotic desire. Over the years the series have depicted hundreds of alien-human romances and flirtations. Alien-human relations are central to *Star Trek*, but it lacks any definition of alienness. Many important characters are the offspring of mixed-species unions. If the morphological and physiological differences between alien species do not prevent physical union and communication with humans, are the aliens actually analogies for different *nations*, whose alienness is a matter of culture and history? The biological differences between aliens and humans appear to be significant, but there is no telling *how* significant. While *Star Trek* attempts to figure tolerance by displacing racial difference onto alien-human difference, it reproduces the very confusion that inspires confusion about race among real humans, conflating cultural difference with putative natural difference.[14]

Eleanor Arnason's *Ring of Swords* (1993) represents an original subversion of this complex of ambiguities. Arnason brings humans, expanding through the galaxy much like Federation units from *Star Trek*, into collision with an alien warrior species, known as the *hwarhath*, who are doing much the same thing. The *hwarhath* are so familiar from the sf megatext that their first appearance seems faintly parodistic. They are tall, fur-covered males, with flat faces, blue eyes, and bar-pupils—traits that combine elements of *Star Wars*'s wookies, future simians from *Planet of the Apes*, and highly evolved goats. They also adhere to a complex code of warrior honor and are strictly homosexual. In this, too, they bear an almost too-close resemblance to terrestrial warrior societies, especially samurai and the Freikorps. They are similar enough to be distorted mirror images of the human, like almost any television extraterrestrial, but with a twist.

The narrative seduces the reader into assuming that the *hwarhath* are less complex than humans because they have excluded women, and presumably families, from their culture—and not incidentally, the zone of intergender contact where anxieties about race come to the fore. At first, we assume that the aliens probably reproduce themselves artificially or through the enslavement of women, as in the various Manlands of feminist dystopian fiction. The sexual element of alien-human contact comes unusually quickly to the foreground, however, in the relationship between Nick Sanders, a human "traitor," and Etin Gwarha, a *hwarhath* general. To complicate matters, Sanders had no homosexual history before his liaison with Gwarha, and so cannot be considered somehow "naturally" drawn to the *hwarhath* sexual culture. This twist also skews the conventional subtext of alien-human erotic connections. The contact (with its displaced referent of cultural interaction and communication) is deviant by both terrestrial and *hwarhath* standards (the latter have not accorded full onto-logical status to human beings); consequently, the connection remains marginal and cannot be turned to either species' advantage. Since no reproduction is in-volved, there is no contest about *power to control reproduction*. The contact be-tween the species must apparently be defined either in terms of competing forms of biological male dominance behavior (complicated by the evident lack of *hwarhath* females to dominate) or explicitly as *cultural difference*.

The sexual connection between Nick and Gwarha excludes the vexed fe-male term from the relationship between species. Anna, the human female who acts as the reader's surrogate in the action, at first appears to be the potential ro-mantic center (one of Arnason's many deft manipulations of the reader's expec-tations) and gradually comes to be seen as the outsider, barred from the culture/biology ambivalence by the femaleness that would normally in science fiction put her in the middle of it. As the action progresses, readers realize that instead of suppressing the female, Arnason's situation frees Anna to act as a cultural go-between with the *hwarhath* women, who, it turns out, are the central governors of moral-cultural values of the aliens, and their human enemies. Through Anna and the *hwarhath* women, the aliens are shown to be diverse in traditions, regional histories, dialects, and interpretations of the dominant codes. Arnason thus subverts the traditional hierarchy of values associated with nationality, that is, a norm-enforcing patriarchy (or fratriarchy) dominat-ing the reproductive power of women like Le Guin's Condor people. Among the *hwarhath*, cultural consciousness is of such a high order that it guides the morality of its members—and it is the women who control physical reproduc-tion and the politics of sexual union (determining which male's sperm they will use for the continuation of their kinship lines), as well as the strategic, prophy-lactic separation of the genders. The *hwarhath* women ensure the species sur-vival of their own nations, and not incidentally that of human beings.

By playing with the expectations of sexual ambivalence and the racializa-tion of aliens, Arnason shows she is aware of the confusion that biological dis-placement brings to questions of contact between cultures. Although in *Ring of Swords* the concept of nation and national culture has been displaced onto a bi-ologically different species, Arnason prevents the association of aliens with race, bringing to the fore the question of communication among conscious, self-defining traditional cultures with claims to both political and personal auton-omy.

5. Archaicization. In its long tradition of archaicization, science fiction repre-sents tightly integrated social groups organized in anachronistic structures.

Some of these groups have maintained their structures against historical change through physical isolation (consciously, as in the Mennonites of Leigh Brackett's *Long Tomorrow* [1973], or by accidents of history, like the benighted planet Arkanar in the Strugatskys's *Hard to Be a God* [1964]); others have adopted archaic forms in reaction to modernity or its collapse. This category sometimes overlaps with apocalyptic winnowing, for the human remainder in the latter category more often than not is depicted returning to archaic, usually tribal, social forms.

Arguably, settled societies in the age of space travel, mass diasporas, and technologies of identity must be archaic to some degree, because their interactions are too slow and local to have any effect on the pace and scope of the fiction's dominant world. Science fiction is fond of societies that operate by rules associated with primitive cultures—from lost races (isolated in the past as well as in space), quasi-Native Americans and frontier space stations, toga-clad utopians and Amazons in military societies, all the way to contemporary science fiction's fascination with aboriginal cultures and the voodoo deities that populate Gibson's cyberspace. Archaicized science fiction societies are not usually intentional allegories for nationality; they function mainly to limn the contours of the imaginary modernity of most science fiction.

One of science fiction's very rare experiments in linking the future of nationality to archaic societies is Mike Resnick's *Kirinyaga* (1998). In a series of linked stories, *Kirinyaga* depicts the settling and eventual decline of a premodern East African culture, the Kikuyu, in the artificial environment of a biospheric satellite. The Kirinyaga colony's spiritual leader, the *mundumugu* (shaman) Koriba, is a Western-educated intellectual who has repudiated both modernity and the "artificial tribe known only as Kenyans" (21). Koriba maintains cultural purity by insisting that only premodern practices be followed, even when comfort, health, and personal dignity suffer. The *mundumugu* recounts the hopes and gradual dissolution of the experiment in elegant moral fables.

Kirinyaga is striking not so much for its emulation of African storytelling style in the context of science fiction as for the original way it reproduces the contradictions that have characterized the depiction of utopias since Thomas More. At the outset, the Kirinyaga colony attempts to reestablish a traditional culture by simulating its territorial conditions on an Earth-orbiting satellite. Not only is the pure Kikuyu culture protected from modernity by the hypermodernity of "Maintenance," the meta-utopian administration of the satellite; but also the Kikuyu culture, with its myths and fables intimately associated with Kenyan geography and its desire "to live as one with the land" (93–94), is reproduced in physically deterritorialized form, floating in space.

The fundamental problem for the Kirinyagan Kikuyu is that their culture is a simulation far more artificial than the supposed artificiality of the multiethnic modern nation-state of Kenya. They are attempting to preserve their traditions and sovereignty in isolation from the very history in which their original national culture developed. To achieve its sovereignty, Kirinyaga has to accept conditions of dependency far greater than Kenya's. Land, weather, seasons, and all other natural forces that influence the concrete material culture are simulated by Maintenance. Moreover, the desire for cultural purity is in bad faith, since the *mundumugu* is the sole possessor, not only of Kikuyu lore, but of the programming code that allows him to communicate with Maintenance and to administer the weather. The culture therefore becomes an emanation of a single individual's will, rather than the adaptive, organic evolution of communal practices. The *mundumugu* pretends to administer magically, but in fact he depends on the technocenter's cooperation with him. Not even the language of Kirinyaga is authentic, since Koriba makes no attempt to impose the use of Kikuyu, which he considers a dead language. Swahili is used instead—a language whose status as the lingua franca of East Africa is arguably just as artificial as the modern nation-state.

Kirinyaga, in sum, is more dependent on the powers that operate Maintenance than the Kikuyu ever were on the British. In fact, if there is a utopia in *Kirinyaga*, it is the invisible society that is willing to create the conditions for a social experiment on such a scale, and for so little evident reward. If the world were truly sufficiently corrupt to warrant the restoration of Kikuyu cultural purity, it would long ago have used the Kirinyaga biosphere for more corrupt economic and political purposes.

Resnick wishes to show his respect for the Kikuyu culture, and *Kirinyaga* is an attempt to construct an elegy for such organic cultures in the medium of sf—an unprecedented attempt at synthesizing the archaic and the hypermodern. These premodern nations are noble, he seems to say, but not viable. There is a conscious moral: every nation that withdraws from the world system will eventually want to rejoin it at the expense of its historical traditions, and it will not create a new culture of its own. Nations are necessarily doomed. But there are unconscious morals as well: national consciousness is the work of powerful individuals who act in bad faith; nationality deprived of territory is a matter of empty symbols only; traditional culture is always pure, and purity cannot survive under modern conditions.

The pleasure in reading the depiction of Kirinyaga's nobly doomed Kikuyu derives from the *containment* of the archaic, the spiritual, and the cultural, within the narrative and the story just as in the satellite. Our sympathies are very much with the narrator, despite his acts of bad faith and his rigidity, because the modern world is already a failed experiment. The reader is left with the feeling of noble spectatorship, as a dignified experiment in removing oneself from the pettiness of bourgeois Western history fails. One almost hesitates to ask why Maintenance, so generous with its satellite biospheres, seems to have done nothing to improve Earth.

Kirinyaga is unique in its careful focus on an archaic nation's imaginary point of view. But it is of a piece with those metropolitan science fictions that idealize archaic societies at the moment that they describe the conditions that ensure their destruction. Missing from both is the concept of a nation that is collectively committed to sovereignty and also creatively impure.

The Japanese Future

Although works and writers have emerged that at least wonder about the dis-imagining of nationality, the general trend in recent years has been in the opposite direction. The collapse of Communist governments brought with it the collapse of state-subsidized noncommercial science fiction in Eastern Europe. Translations of American pulp science fiction have inundated the markets, bringing with them the image of American-inspired multinational capitalist hegemony. It has become so difficult to sell science fiction written by nationals that in Hungary, for instance, the most successful Hungarian writers feel compelled to use English-sounding pen names.[15]

In Japan, this denationalization of science fiction has perhaps gone furthest. It is well known that *manga* and *anime*, of which science fiction is a primary genre, traditionally downplay specifically Japanese features and employ highly exaggerated stylizations of European, especially Anglo-American, elements. Characters' faces and bodies bear little trace of Asian appearance, and settings are usually urban spaces in which English street and shop signs are at least as common as Japanese.[16] The sf stories usually have no concrete connection with Japanese history or contemporary social life; in science fiction genres of *anime*, conflicts are always in some transglobal nonplace with no specificity, combining elements of Asian and U.S. metropolises.

Similarly, Japanese science fiction employs cyborgs with obsessive regularity. Central protagonists are often robots or cyborgs, and the futuristic cities they inhabit are so wired that they are cyborgized in their own right. Japanese science fiction rarely presents the cyborg state as inherently negative; it may inspire ambivalence but rarely condemnation. For every bad cyborg, there is a surplus of good ones. The cyborg is, as Donna Haraway has written, not a creature of nature. Its origin is always in question, and whatever its first state was, it was never purely biological. By the same token, it does not reproduce itself biologically. It does not provide origins. Cyborgs are by definition not linked to traditions, to families and clans, or to traditional nations. They are separated from any organic community (for their membership can only be virtual and artificial), and the proliferation of positive cyborgs in Japanese *anime* marks not only a fascination with high technology but also an attempt to imagine what personal identity might be like after the full deconstruction of traditional communal loyalties.

Many, if not most, of sf-anime's cyborg protagonists are beautiful women (also with stylized non-Japanese features) who are invariably displayed with exaggerated sexual allure. Inevitably, these female cyborgs become concerned about romance and reproduction, which would also reproduce traditional quasi-biological communities. In some cases, as in *Armitage III: Poly-Matrix* (1997), the most advanced female-form cyborg series is endowed with the ability to mate with human males. In *Ghost in the Shell* (1996), however, the cyborg heroine is "impregnated" by another cyborg, raising the prospect of the displacement of human cultural and social reproduction onto a cyborg nation.

Japanese science fiction is characterized by a marrow-deep ambivalence about postmodernity. Japan is, in a sense, in a unique position in the current world system: it is one of the most recently colonized postcolonial nations and was also, by the end of World War II, the most advanced premodern one. The contemporary Japanese state, for all its global economic power, is inherited from the structure imposed on the Japanese by the American victors after World War II. Masao Miyoshi has argued that the Japanese nation-state constructed by the colonizers was a counterfeit, "having neither a discrete history nor logic that would convince the newly independent citizens of its legitimacy or authenticity" (80). In the case of Japan, American "nation building" imposed what Westerners considered to be the culmination of political evolution on a society whose historical logic was completely different and of no less ancient pedigree. Defeated into Western modernity, the Japanese were forced to imagine a future that was not truly theirs, yet that they would have to embody.

In Miyoshi's terms, after independence the Japanese "had to renegotiate the conditions of the nation state in which they were to reside thereafter" (81). The renegotiating occurred in a fairly secure manner, at least as far as the political sphere was concerned, largely because Japan was forbidden by the victors to maintain armed forces or to to intervene militarily on foreign soil. The substitution of a Western nation-state for an organic Japanese nation was reflected in Japanese science fiction, the caretaker of the popular images of the future, through a pervasive sense of destruction. The *Godzilla* films' regular destruction of modern Japanese cities was one side of it;[17] another side was the most popular Japanese science fiction novel of the 1970s, Sakyo Komatsu's *Japan Sinks* (1973), which tells of the destruction of the Japanese islands in a precisely rendered volcanic cataclysm. From this perspective, the denationalization of characters and settings in *manga* might be taken as another depiction of the destruction of national identity.

An interesting turn may be taking place, however, in Japanese science fiction, to reclaim, if not Japanese nationalism, then a sense of national identity as a theme in science fiction. Two, perhaps unlikely, examples of this national turn, are Masato Harada's *Gunhed* (1996), a rare live-action version of a popular science fiction *manga* of the same name, and *Patlabor II* (1995), an *anime* made by Mamoru Oshii just before *Ghost in the Shell*.

Gunhed is in most respects a derivative cyberpunk entertainment, imitating tech-noir action films like James Cameron's *Aliens* (1986). A crew of professional scavengers composed of Japanese and American roughnecks who speak Japglish with each other flies to an artificial Pacific island, where a rogue computer, Kyron 5, has linked up with other megacomputers elsewhere to take control of the world and eliminate humanity. The crusty scavengers are picked off one at a time by gruesome cyberweapons until only a Japanese protagonist, paradoxically called Brooklyn, and a sultry *gaijin* Texas Ranger, Tex, are left intact. It becomes Brooklyn's job to rebuild a demolished AI-enhanced transformer-tank, a Gunhed, and to fight his way with it past the robotic defense systems to the Kyron 5 core. Although most of the action follows the ritualized episodic pattern of *mecha* (sf-*anime* that fetishizes robotic weapons systems), Brooklyn's role is unusual. Even though he is handsome and athletic, his manliness is in doubt. He can't drive a tank or a fly a plane at the outset, he pops cheroots of carrot between his lips instead of cigarettes like his macho cohort, and he is regularly mocked for his wimpiness by the beautiful Tex, who wears black leather and a dominatrix's smirk. Left with no more support than one of the skillful and agile child companions found on the artificial island, Brooklyn is encouraged by the increasingly chatty Gunhed to take command of the tank. Before revving up, Brooklyn dons a Japanese World War II pilot's helmet and wears it until his victory, which is decided when he takes possession of the phallic control crystal of the Kyron 5. In the final scene, as they fly off escaping the exploding island, the now kittenish Tex asks, "do you want to drive?" and puts Brooklyn in the driver's seat.

Though there is little to praise in the plot, Brooklyn's character development is an allegory worthy of attention. The sole true Japanese male in the film begins as a decidedly unmacho vegetarian, with a non-Japanese name and with no phallic control at all. By the end, after taking control of the Gunhed (an over-the-top Freudian redundancy if there ever was one) and affecting the style of the last modern Japanese warrior, he is rewarded by the *gaijin* dominatrix with the flight controls, while she relaxes into feminine passivity for him. In the final shot, Brooklyn pops another carotin cheroot between his lips, signifying that for all his newfound spunk, he is still a vegetarian.

Camped up as it is, *Gunhed* nonetheless tells a tale of the social unconscious. Japanese machismo was utterly stifled by the externally imposed proscription against establishing armed forces. Brooklyn, whose identity is American-derived, comes into his own when he takes responsibility for his technology and uses force to defend the world. His American anima, who may have only been encouraging him with her prickly irony and seductive style, gladly gives him back his power—which, we know, a carrot eater will not abuse.

In more artistic and serious form, this same tale is retold in Oshii's *Patlabor II*. Like the Gunhed, a Patlabor is an AI-enhanced robot warrior, used by the Japanese police forces of the near-future. The Patlabors and their creators are impressed into an unusual police action after Tokyo comes under attack by unknown forces. At first it appears Americans are responsible; even when this is disproved, the American forces make clear that they will intervene if social order is not restored in Japan. Under this threat to sovereignty from the former occupiers, and to internal peace by the unidentified terrorists, the Patlabor crew discovers that the true source is Tsuge, the designer of the Patlabors and a former, highly honored Japanese officer who was forced to watch his unit of Patlabors destroyed during a UN peacekeeping mission, when he was forbidden by the UN commander to engage in combat.

As Michael Fisch writes in his important article, "Nation, War, and Japan's Future in the Science Fiction Anime Film *Patlabor II*," Oshii's film intervened in a national debate about the proper role of the Japanese military following the Gulf War. Oshii makes clear visual allusions to Japan's quandary: should it continue the disarmed, wealthy, and contented status quo, in which it is prevented from taking responsibility for its international role by an externally imposed constitutional prohibition, or is there a possible need to discard the neocolonial arrangement and to "renegotiate" participation in world government? Particularly striking in *Patlabor II* is the subtle and gradual transformation of the graphic imagery in the film. As the police heroine, Nagumo, who was once the antagonist's favorite student and lover, approaches his headquarters on an abandoned platform in Tokyo Bay, her appearance becomes less and less *gaijin*, and the public inscriptions and signs are all in Japanese. As she approaches the provoker of Japanese national consciousness, whom she respects despite his violence, the art itself becomes more markedly Japanese. In the final scene, as Nagumo handcuffs Tsuge, he grasps her black gloved hands in his white gloved ones, in an image of Asian complementarity of opposites: white hands holding black, simultaneously manacled and clasped in friendship. As Fisch notes, the ending is disturbingly ambivalent. But graphically, the message is clearer: the national element is affirmed.

Who Imagines the Future?

It is difficult to imagine something that one does not care about. It is safe to say that science fiction writers living in the major nations, the vanguards of technohistory, have little interest in the future of smaller and less central nations. Similarly, the elites of the latter nations will have less and less interest in preserving their nations' autonomy, seeing themselves as potential internationals or singleton multinationals. It is also safe to say that tens of millions of people will move across borders of nation-states and find their loyalties divided, their vision of the future clouded. More and more it will seem that only the technohistorical center will have a future. It is unclear whether the writers and readers of the less central nations, with languages that do not have the ear of power, and histories locked in those languages, will wish to use the tools of science fiction—which are perhaps precisely the tools of hegemony—to imagine worlds in which their descendants will have a role. So far we have seen only the science fiction futures of the nations that think they are empires. We must wait to see whether the nations who think they are nations will imagine different futures.

Notes

1. The situation in England was somewhat different. There was, to be sure, a substantial tradition of post-Wells "scientific romances," ably documented by Brian Stableford in *The Scientific Romance in England, 1890–1950*. But as Stableford notes, this tradition never really cohered as a popular market (only a handful of titles made their way into the Penguin line, which dominated British paperbacks until the postwar years) and essentially disappeared as a separate tradition when Americanized science fiction began to appear. Nor were British readers immune to the attractions of the American pulps: British fan societies existed on the model of the Americans, at least one British pulp (*Tales of Wonder*) began publishing in 1937, and more than one British reader from that era remembers the excitement of finding cheap copies of American pulps, which had been imported after being used as ship ballast during the war years.

2. The term *supergenre* is employed by Eric S. Rabkin in *The Fantastic in Literature* and, in a somewhat broader sense, by R. D. Mullen in "Books in Review: Supernatural, Pseudonatural, and Sociocultural Fantasy."

3. In the horror field, an argument could be made that similar canon-defining anthologies include Dorothy Sayers's three volumes of *Great Short Stories of Detection, Mystery and Horror* (1929–1934; retitled as *The Omnibus of Crime* series in the United States, with somewhat different contents) and Herbert Wise and Phyllis Fraser's *Great Tales of Terror and the Supernatural* (1944). The Sayers anthologies, with their substantial content of supernatural fiction in the "Mystery and Horror" sections, were almost certainly among the first respectable twentieth-century anthologies in England to identify horror as a distinct literary tradition, while the Wise and Fraser omnibus shared with Healy and McCo-

mas's *Adventures in Time and Space* the distinction of being reprinted by Random House's Modern Library, which meant that the books would remain widely available and in print for decades, thus influencing generations of readers.

4. Admittedly, this choice of key figures is supposed to be somewhat provocative but not entirely arbitrary; though a case could be made for Isaac Asimov in science fiction and Poe in horror fiction, it seems to me that Heinlein and Lovecraft more directly set the terms of ideological debate for the writers who followed in their wake.

5. Lessing's forays into science fiction include not only the well-known Canopus in Argos series of philosophical novels (1979–83), but substantial elements of other novels such as *The Four-Gated City* (1969), *The Fifth Child* (1988)—which is also viewed by some readers as a horror novel—*Memoirs of a Survivor* (1981), and *Mara and Dann* (1999). Piercy's best-known works in the field are *Woman on the Edge of Time* (1976) and *He, She, and It* (1991). Theroux's most familiar title is *O-Zone* (1986), and Updike's is *Toward the End of Time* (1997).

6. Charles Fort (1874-1932) was an American journalist who specialized in popular compilations of mysterious or inexplicable phenomena, which he consistently employed to tweak scientists and the scientific world-view. The Fortean Society, founded in 1931, included Ben Hecht, Theodore Dreiser, and Alexander Woollcott, but Fort's most direct influence in fiction is to be found in the stories of Russell and other contributors to *Unknown* and to a lesser extent *Astounding Science Fiction*. Science fiction writer Damon Knight published a biography of Fort in 1970, and a magazine, *The Fortean Times*, continues to be published.

7. One of Dick's earliest novels, *Time out of Joint* (1959), bears resemblances to the film *The Truman Show*, in that both begin with characters unaware that their entire community is a sham constructed for their benefit, but Dick quickly moved on to more complex and sophisticated versions of alternate reality, including *The Man in the High Castle* (1962), in which a world where the Nazis won is shown to be a sham—but in which the "real" world is not ours, either; *The Three Stigmata of Palmer Eldritch* (1965) and *A Scanner Darkly* (1977), both of which explore the alternate realities of hallucinogenic drugs; *Ubik* (1969), which examines the notion of reality as perceived by a consciousness preserved in a machine; and *Do Androids Dream of Electric Sheep?* (1968), in which androids may be indistinguishable from humans even to themselves.

8. Two of the more insightful discussions of science fantasy as a subgenre may be found in Carl D. Malmgren's *Worlds Apart: Narratology of Science Fiction* and Brian Attebery's *Strategies of Fantasy*.

9. Lethem's first novel, *Gun, With Occasional Music* (1994), mixed elements of fantasy, dystopia, surrealism, and the hard-boiled detective novel, and his 1995 collection *The Wall of the Sky, the Wall of the Eye* is a veritable sampler of the free appropriation of multigenre materials. Carroll initially gained popularity among horror readers, though his complex first novel, *The Land of Laughs* (1980) borrows at least as much from fantasy. More recent novels like *The Marriage of Sticks* (1999) and *The Wooden Sea* add elements of science fiction. Auster's New York Trilogy (*City of Glass* [1985], *Ghosts* [1986], *The Locked Room* [1986]) manipulates the conventions of the detective story to create metaphysical puzzles of identity with overtones of supernatural and horror fiction. Di Filippo's *Steampunk Trilogy* (1995) is a collection of three tales which draw on conventions of fantasy, science fiction, and horror ("steampunk" is a term sometimes used to refer to alternate-world sf

based on or in nineteenth-century science, but this is only marginally the case with di Filippo's tales, one of which, for example, imagines a fantasy-world love affair between Walt Whitman and Emily Dickinson). Stepan Chapman's *Troika* (1998) begins as a surrealistic fable set in an apparent dreamscape but increasingly invokes genre tropes to destabilize our initial impression by offering hints of more traditional science fiction and fantasy. Hand, in the loosely connected narratives of *Waking the Moon* (1995), *Black Light* (1999), and the title story of the collection, *Last Summer at Mars Hill* (1998), draws upon conventions of fantasy, horror, and the more limited subgenre of occult fiction.

10. "The enormous pressure to become a reliable cash cow has resulted in a big portion of bookstore shelf space being taken up by franchise work, reinforcing wish-fulfillment fantasies of people in search of an entertaining escape from reality," wrote Kim Stanley Robinson in a symposium of comments in *Nebula Awards 33* (255). The annual Nebula Awards anthologies have for several years included such "symposia" in which various writers and editors comment upon the state of the field, and Robinson's comment expresses succinctly one of the most persistently recurring themes in these annual assessments.

11. As an example, the science fiction newsmagazine *Locus* compiles an annual list of recommended books in each of several categories—novels, collections, anthologies, etc. In the category of single-author story collections (not including British or Australian publications), the recommended list for the year 2000 included twenty-three titles, only seven of which (30.4%) were published by large commercial publishers. The same list for the year 1990 yielded eighteen titles, eleven (or 61.1%) published by commercial presses.

3. Omniphage: Rock 'n' Roll and Avant-Pop Science Fiction

1. Although Barthelme did not expand on the notion, I take him to mean that many modern painters from, say, the impressionists forward felt the sometimes conscious and sometimes unconscious urge to reevaluate their aesthetic relationship to external reality in the face of a new technology that captured that external reality flawlessly. Their reevaluation took the form of an increasing turn inward that no longer emphasized the "accurate" portrayal of the world *out there* but rather initially an "accurate" portrayal of the world *out there* deliberately filtered through a subjective consciousness, and then an "accurate" "portrayal" of the "world" *in here*.

2. This is Di Filippo's term, which he defines in "Ribofunk: The Manifesto" as a speculative mode that combines an emphasis, not on cyberpunk's cybernetic realm, but on the realm of the cell and funk's mutational forms.

3. Claude E. Shannon was the mathematician whose 1938 paper on the isomorphism of Boolean algebra and certain types of switching circuits inspired research into the Electrical Logic Machine, or computer, and whose 1948 paper on a mathematical theory of communication informs much of Di Filippo's novel.

4. I did recruit rock 'n' roll into *Live from Earth*, by the way, but only as a kind of very distant backbeat by dropping into nearly every page made-up song titles, weird band names, and musical allusions (to, among others, John Lennon's post-Beatles output), but the book had as its core other things in mind.

5. Staying with the Body: Narratives of the Posthuman in Contemporary Science Fiction

This chapter was written while I was on a period of research leave supported by the University of Lincolnshire and Humberside.

1. Research within the field of artificial intelligence and robotics is already exploring the possibility that consciousness can be downloaded and stored as data. Hans Moravec has been particularly instrumental in the development of these ideas; see his *Mind Children: The Future of Robot and Human Intelligence*.

2. See Haraway's "The Promises of Monsters: A Regenerative Politics for Inappropriate/d Others." There are many such promising monsters in science fiction. The following novels provide some fascinating examples: Octavia Butler's *Dawn* (1987), *Adulthood Rites* (1988), and *Imago* (1989); Emma Bull's *Bone Dance* (1991); Elizabeth Hand's *Winterlong* (1990) and *Aestival Tide* (1992); Lisa Mason's *Arachne* (1990) and *Cyberweb* (1995); and Laura Mixon's *Proxies* (1998).

3. David A. Kirby points out that the film is "virtually alone among recent popular-culture narratives in its rejection of the genetic-determinist ideology" (212).

4. The phrase *spectacular body* is taken from Yvonne Tasker's book *Spectacular Bodies*. In her discussion of action cinema, she cogently argues that "the range of images and experiences on offer within this form, which have been characterized by many critics and commentators as both *simple* and *obvious*, are both rich and ambiguous" (166). I hope it is clear from my discussion of *The Matrix* that I agree with her.

5. Kay Schaffer uses the term *cyberform* to describe the character of Circuit Boy in *All New Gen*, a computer-art installation by VNS Matrix.

6. The term *paradoxical space* is used by Gillian Rose to describe the space associated with the "emergent subject of feminism," which occupies a contradictory position both inside and outside the hegemonic discourses of masculinism.

7. The phrase *inappropriate/d others* was originally used by Trinh Minh-ha as the title of a special issue of *Discourse*, in the context of a critique of postcolonialism.

7. Sex/uality and the Figure of the Hermaphrodite in Science Fiction; or, The Revenge of Herculine Barbin

1. See, for example, Money's discussion of social constructionism and the need for surgical intervention in the first chapter of *Sex Errors of the Body and Related Syndromes*. With regard to the number of sexes, Money argues that prior to "contemporary medical interventions, many children with a birth defect of the sex organs were condemned to grow up as they were born, stigmatized and traumatized. It simply does not make sense to talk of a third sex, or of a fourth or fifth, when the phylogenetic scheme of things is two sexes. Those who are genitally neither male nor female but incomplete are not a third sex. They are a mixed sex or an in-between sex. To advocate medical nonintervention is irresponsible" (6).

2. I use the term *intersex* to refer to real people but use *hermaphrodite* to emphasize the metonymic quality of the figure in sf. In a somewhat similar vein, I also adopt the pre-

dominant personal pronoun used in the sf works themselves to refer to hermaphroditic characters.

3. For example, Suzanne Kessler's 1990 article, "The Medical Construction of Gender: Case Management of Intersexed Infants," focuses primarily on revealing "the ways in which the physicians' discourse and practice both construct two sexes and maintain that only two sexes really exist" (Hausman 73).

4. See Thomas Laqueur's *Making Sex* for an examination of just how relatively recent the ideology of sexual dimorphism is in Western cultures.

5. While "herm" is an obvious abbreviation of hermaphrodite, "ferm" and "merm" are neologisms.

6. Alfred Kinsey, Wardell B. Pomeroy, and Clyde E. Morton's *Sexual Behavior in the Human Male* was published in 1948 and was followed, in 1953, by a companion volume, *Sexual Behavior in the Human Female.*

7. My point here is purely about familiarity for the reader floundering in an apparently anti-intuitive world (two sexes being taken so thoroughly for granted in our own culture). It is interesting to note that, when Fausto-Sterling revisited her original article in 2000, she rejected the idea of even a five-sex schema, preferring to argue that "male and female, masculine and feminine, cannot be parsed as some kind of continuum. Rather, sex and gender are best conceptualized as points in a multidimensional space" ("The Five Sexes, Revisited").

8. The pronoun problem is a well-known issue in what is perhaps the most famous sf novel dealing with hermaphrodites, Ursula Le Guin's *Left Hand of Darkness* (1969). I examine this novel later in this chapter.

9. "Di" is the Concord term for someone attracted to both "opposite" sexes. See the novel's glossary for definitions of the nine sexual orientations recognized in the Concord.

10. The Haran desire to excise the excess is revealed most clearly in the novel when Haliday, another herm, is injured, and Warreven and Tatian have to have "him" transferred to an off-world hospital in order to ensure that the Haran doctors don't castrate "him." When this is explained to Tatian, he thinks, "It was one thing not to know how to treat herms' complex bodies, entirely another to surgically alter them to conform to Haran prejudice—but then, on a world that didn't admit herms existed, there would always be the temptation to 'correct' the 'defect' rather than go to the effort to restore Haliday to 3er natural condition" (246)

11. See, for example, Anne Fausto-Sterling's *Sexing the Body: Gender Politics and the Construction of Sexuality*; see also the Website for the Intersex Society of North America at http://www.isna.org.

12. Some, like the racial dimorphisms of "black" and "white," are more obviously "apparent" than others; sex and gender still retain at least some degree of scientific credibility to reinforce their place within the dominant discourse.

13. See specifically Lamb and Veith's "Again, *The Left Hand of Darkness*: Androgyny or Homophobia?" for a discussion of this issue.

14. On the material basis of this need to interpret through sex, see also Judith Butler's *Bodies That Matter.*

8. Mutant Youth: Posthuman Fantasies and High-Tech Consumption in 1990s Science Fiction

1. In his enthusiastic brief for the manifold pleasures of "interactive tactile telepresence" (or, in his more infamous coinage, "teledildonics"), Howard Rheingold admits the immense technical difficulty of producing functional "smart skin" owing to "the extremely powerful computers needed to perform the enormous number of added calculations required to monitor and control hundreds of thousands of sensors and effectors. Every nook and protuberance, every plane and valley and knob of your body's surface, will require its own processor" (347).

2. Nick Dyer-Witheford uses the Marxist term "general intellect" to describe the "polycentric, communicatively connected, collective intelligence" of the Internet at its best moments, though capitalist industry is persistently seeking to "forc[e] its traffic into the commodified pathways of video-on-demand, teleshopping, telegambling, and personalized advertising" (228).

3. *Dead Girls* (1992), *Dead Boys* (1994), and *Dead Things* (1997).

4. See, for example, John Holt's *Escape from Childhood: The Needs and Rights of Children.*

9. "Going Postal": Rage, Science Fiction, and the Ends of the American Subject

1. To read *Random Acts* is at least partly to be inducted into Womack's street slang or patois of the future. In this, Womack's novel is indebted to Anthony Burgess's *A Clockwork Orange* (1962), which also links innovative language and exorbitant violence. See also Veronica Hollinger's "'A Language of the Future': Discursive Constructions of the Subject in *A Clockwork Orange* and *Random Acts of Senseless Violence.*"

2. "The Disgruntled Postal Worker Zone," True Stories section, <www.wco.com/~schwa/zone/true.html>.

3. Catatonia, "Road Rage" (Warner Brothers Music, 1997); Ruth Rendell, *Road Rage* (London: Hutchinson, 1997).

4. See Seumas Milne's "Rising Stress Brings 'Desk Rage' at Work."

5. The third edition (1984; rev. 1987) carried a separate diagnosis, "*Isolated* Explosive Disorder," but this has been dropped from subsequent editions.

6. Without aggression: "an individual who is angry primarily in traffic situations, even after relatively minor driving hassles, but only curses internally at the offense." With aggression: "the individual not only becomes angry in traffic when cut off, but also does things such as drives menacingly up behind the other driver, shouts a string of epithets, makes visible obscene gestures, or forces the offending driver off the road" (Eckhardt and Deffenbacher 43).

7. See Luckhurst, "The Science-Fictionalization of Trauma: Remarks on Narratives of Alien Abduction."

8. Arnold's article, "Termination or Transformation," details the loss of 200,000 manufacturing jobs in the auto industry alone between 1978 and 1980 and recalls the pervasive economic scares in the early 1980s that robotics would replace three million American jobs by the end of the century.

9. For a reading that suggests that the "cinema of musculinity" [*sic*] offers a simulta-

neous excess of masculinity with a "feminized" display of the built body, see Yvonne Tasker's *Spectacular Bodies: Gender, Genre and the Action Cinema*.

10. Mikkel Borch-Jacobsen, writing about multiple personality, notes that "it is difficult to avoid the comparison with technology: patients are 'switched' like television channels; elements of trauma are decomposed and recomposed as easily as 'processing' words on a computer; and the patient's past is brought back as easily as 'rewinding' a video cassette" (52).

11. See Klaus Theweleit's "Ego of the Soldier Male."

12. For statistics and a reading of this disavowal, see Sara Knox's *Murder: A Tale of American Life*.

13. Claire Kahane considers "outrage" the discursive, politicized articulation that arrives after affective rage. "Rage . . . wipes out the subject; outrage is expressed in voice *by* the subject" ("The Aesthetics of Rage" 127). Contemporary African American articulations of outrage might begin with William Grier and Price Cobbs's *Black Rage* (1969) and culminate with bell hooks's *Killing Rage: Ending Racism* (1995), although these would only be bookends for a large literature.

14. The crucial term in the citation is "depicted." Although there are cases of African American postal workers "going postal," the *cultural representation*, as it is for the serial killer, is that of the white male. Carla Freccero has helpfully proposed that the figure of the white serial killer works as a "fetish in public culture," "a condensation of the violence of American historicity into a singular subject who performs discrete, singular injurious acts" ("Historical Violence" 48–49). The white male rampager offers a similar containing function.

10. Apocalypse Coma

1. This discussion owes much to Frank Kermode's landmark study, *The Sense of an Ending: Studies in the Theory of Fiction* (1966). As David Seed has observed in his introduction to *Imagining Apocalypse: Studies in Cultural Crisis*, "What made [Kermode's] work so useful, as witness its countless citations in apocalypse theory, was its central insight that apocalypse was a narrative, one of the fictions which we employ to make sense of our present" (11).

2. I am not suggesting here that *Neuromancer* is either the first or even the most successful example of the "postmodernization" of literary science fiction. Joanna Russ's *Female Man* (1975) and Samuel R. Delany's *Stars in My Pocket Like Grains of Sand* (1984), to take only two examples, both suggest otherwise. Gibson's novel was a huge bestseller, however, and it was the resulting "cult of cyberpunk" that turned the attention of many critics and theorists to the postmodern possibilities of science fiction.

3. Studies that consider nineteenth-century *fin-de-siècle* apocalypticism include Elaine Showalter's *Sexual Anarchy* (1990) and Richard Dellamora's *Apocalyptic Overtures* (1994); more generalized cultural studies include Mark Kingwell's *Dreams of Millennium* (1996), Mark Dery's *Pyrotechnic Insanitarium* (1999), and David Seed's edited collection, *Imagining Apocalypse* (2000). Theoretically oriented critical studies include Jean Baudrillard's *Illusion of the End* (1992), Lee Quinby's *Anti-Apocalypse* (1994), Dellamora's edited collection, *Post-*

modern Apocalypse (1995), and Malcolm Bull's edited collection, *Apocalypse Theory and the Ends of the World* (1995). Science fiction has been a particularly fertile fictional genre for narratives of natural and technological catastrophe since at least the middle of the nineteenth century. This has been explored in studies ranging from Susan Sontag's early "Imagination of Disaster" (1965) to David Ketterer's *New Worlds for Old* (1974), and from W. Warren Wagar's *Terminal Visions* (1982) to Scott Bukatman's *Terminal Identity* (1993).

4. Carl Freedman's recent study, *Critical Theory and Science Fiction* (2000), makes a convincing argument for the critically historicizing work of estrangement undertaken—at least *in potentia*—by these two very different discourses (see, particularly, his chapter, "Articulations" [24-93]). Although Freedman concentrates, for the most part, on critical theory developed in the context of (a modernist) historical materialism (Marx, Lukács, Althusser, for example), his arguments remain valid for later poststructuralist and postmodernist theoretical constructions. See also Istvan Csicsery-Ronay, Jr., "The SF of Theory: Baudrillard and Haraway" (1991).

5. The two essays in question are "Of an Apocalyptic Tone Recently Adopted in Philosophy" and "No Apocalypse, Not Now (full speed ahead, seven missiles, seven missives)," translated into English in 1982 and 1984, respectively. A science fiction version of Derridean free play might look something like Bruce Sterling's cyberpunk novel, *Schismatrix* (1985). In its far-future universe of radical human self-fashioning, Sterling's protagonist considers "the blindness of men, who thought that the Kosmos had rules and limits that would shelter them from their own freedom. There were no shelters. There were no final purposes. Futility, and freedom, were Absolute" (273).

6. See Lee Quinby's discussion of apocalyptic and antiapocalyptic tendencies in a range of feminist theoretical positions (34–39). As her title, *Anti-Apocalypse*, indicates, Quinby's analyses of the truth claims of apocalyptic systems of whatever kind tend to be decidedly critical, although she makes a strong case for the inherently different emphases of feminist (as opposed to masculinist) apocalypticisms. She argues that feminism "will by definition always be implicated in apocalyptic desires for the end of (masculinist) time and the transcendence of (masculinist) space, including the space of the innately gendered body. Feminism can be, however (and often is these days), *anti*-apocalyptic insofar as it is anti-essentialist, anti-universalist, and anti-eschatological" (36).

7. Cyberpunk's antiapocalypticism did not, after all, greatly disrupt the millennialist tendencies of most popular genre fiction of the last two decades. Apocalyptic scenarios have been a mainstay of twentieth-century sf especially since the end of World War II; the major shift has tended to occur in modes of destruction—for example, from the nuclear devastation of novels such as Walter M. Miller's *Canticle for Leibowitz* (1955) to the epidemiological and environmental catastrophes of novels such as Elizabeth Hand's *Glimmering* (1997).

8. In this, Coupland's characters strikingly resemble conservative historian Francis Fukuyama's decadent "last man," his "post-historic" subject of an unchanging world order defined by the triumph of global capitalism. See Fukuyama's *End of History and the Last Man* (1992).

9. Jameson bases this observation upon "the hypothesis of some radical break or *coupure*, generally traced back to the end of the 1950s or the early 1960s" (53). He offers an even more detailed critique of "our incapacity to imagine the future" in "Progress Versus

Utopia; or, Can We Imagine the Future?" (1982). Here Jameson suggests that the conventional technologically driven future visions of sf "are now historical and dated" and that sf's present inability to imagine the future "might at best signal a transformation in the historical function of present-day science fiction" (244).

10. Given that passages such as this one are not intended to be taken as ironic (if they are, that irony is certainly well concealed), Coupland's novel takes on the "apocalyptic tone" identified by Derrida: "Whoever takes on the apocalyptic tone comes to signify to, if not tell you, something. What? The truth, of course, and to signify to you that it reveals the truth to you: the tone is the revelator of some unveiling in process" ("Of an Apocalyptic Tone" 84).

11. In his recent study of apocalypticism in contemporary cultural discourses, James Berger convincingly argues that such imagery responds to the postmodern sense that we are indeed living on "after the end." Berger makes a strong case that the twentieth century's historical Holocaust is the apocalyptic event shaping much of post–World War II cultural sensibility, the unrepresentable event dividing us from everything in history that predates it, a trauma requiring constant, collective, neurotic working through.

12. These "first times" and "last times" continue to appear in Gibson's later fiction. The plot of his most recent novel, *All Tomorrow's Parties* (1999), for example, is constructed on a foundation of apocalyptic expectation, the certainty that, as one of the central characters states: "It's all going to change. . . . We're coming up on the mother of all nodal points. I can see it, now. It's *all* going to change" (4). As in *Neuromancer*, however, most of the characters remain unaware of the events that are in the process of radically transforming their own historical moment.

11. *Kairos*: The Enchanted Loom

The original version of this paper was read at KUTU4, a seminar celebrating the Apocalypse held at the University of Oulu, Department of the Humanities, Finland, 30–31 October 1997. If you are reading this, then maybe the ritual failed, but maybe not. The end of the world can be a subtle explosion.

1. *The golden smithies of the Emperor! | Marbles of the dancing floor | Break bitter furies of complexity, | Those images that yet | Fresh images beget . . .* (W. B. Yeats, "Byzantium" [1933]).

2. Notably "The Edge of Space Time." A more recent book, *Black Holes and Baby Universes* (1993), gives an updated overview of these ideas.

3. An overview of the work of James Tiptree, Jr., pseudonym of Alice Sheldon, can be found in Sarah Lefanu's *In the Chinks of the World Machine* (105–29).

4. This is most clearly spelled out in Tiptree's "And I Awoke and Found Me Here on the Cold Hill's Side" (1971).

5. Joanna Russ, an extraordinarily influential figure in feminist sf, is nowadays far too little read outside academic circles, and far too much perceived as "only" a polemicist. Her science fiction ideas, along with Tiptree's, may truly be said to have paved the way for the cyberpunk revolution of the 1980s, but at what a cost. We feminists of sf read the dazzling *Neuromancer* perhaps with much the same feelings as those unfortunate elvensmiths in *The Lord of the Rings*, when the Dark Lord unveiled his new creation. We knew

that the One Ring had been forged, and there wasn't a thing we could do to save ourselves, and what's more, *we had helped him to do it.*

6. From the account of A. Garrett, a professor from the University of Coimbra who witnessed the events of 13 October 1917: "The sun, a few moments before, had pierced the thick clouds that held it hidden so that it shone out clearly and strongly. . . . It looked like a burnished wheel cut out of mother-of-pearl. . . . This disc span dizzily round; . . . it whirled round upon itself with mad rapidity . . . then, preserving the celerity of its rotation, detached itself from the firmament and advanced, blood-red, towards the earth, threatening to crush us with the weight of its vast and fiery mass" (C. C. Martindale, S.J., *The Message of Fatima,* 77–78).

7. To bring the situation right up to date, Marcus Chown reports, in an article called "Double or Quits," on British physicist Humphrey Maris's current claim to have split the electron. If that's true, then the whole edifice of modern physics theory, from quantum mechanics to the Big Bang, is in serious trouble.

8. The "enchanted loom" metaphor was first used by Sir Charles Sherrington, English neurologist, in the Gifford lectures series, "Man and His Nature" (1942).

13. Utopia, Genocide, and the Other

1. A by no means exhaustive list of novellas and novels drawn from the last fifteen years that explore this conjunction would include, in alphabetical order by author: Eleanor Arnason's *Ring of Swords* (1993), Derrick Bell's "Space Trader" (1992), Octavia Butler's Xenogenesis trilogy (1987–89), Orson Scott Card's *Ender's Game* (1985), Suzy McKee Charnas's "Listening to Brahms" (1989), C. J. Cherryh's *Foreigner* (1993), Elizabeth Moon's *Remnant Population* (1996), Susan Shwartz's *Heritage of Flight* (1989), Joan Slonczewski's *Children Star* (1998) and *Brain Plague* (2000), and Sheri S. Tepper's *Six Moon Dance* (1998).

2. Native Americans, for instance, upon becoming the alien Other in their homeland, endured efforts at both kinds of annihilation by their colonizers: familiarization into the mainstream culture through such measures as the prohibition against speaking native languages in school and erasure in the Trail of Tears and the Indian Wars.

3. See Nan Rosenthal's *Anselm Kiefer: Works on Paper in the Metropolitan Museum of Art.*

4. Fredric Jameson's critical essay on Louis Martin's *Utopiques: Jeux D'Espaces* concludes with a brief and cogent discussion of the trench in utopian narratives. Jameson observes that trench cutting is an operation "not only of disjunction but . . . exclusion as well" (20) and that this act "is also the source of everything problematical about [utopias]" ("Of Islands and Trenches" 21).

5. Throughout this essay, I employ uppercase Holocaust and post-Holocaust when referring to the historical calamity also called Shoah. I use the lowercase holocaust and postholocaust when referring to apocalyptic imaginings not connected to the historical event.

6. Suzy McKee Charnas's Holdfast novels (1974–99), Sheri Tepper's *Gate To Women's Country* (1988), and James Morrow's *This Is the Way the World Ends* (1986), all of which

show utopian impulses toward genocide not only leading to apocalypse but arising from it, are important exceptions. Indeed, Charnas has said that knowledge of the historical Holocaust has informed much of her work (see Gordon, "Closed Systems Kill: An Interview with Suzy McKee Charnas").

7. Brooks Landon offers a concise overview of the literalization of metaphor, citing Samuel R. Delany, Brian Attebery, and Ursula K. Le Guin in his *Science Fiction After 1900: From the Steam Man to the Stars* (8–9). Landon, citing Delany, says that "[w]hat is different in SF . . . is its level of 'subjunctivity,' the tension between the words of an SF story and their referents." Landon offers several illustrative examples of this literalization of metaphor in sf, including Le Guin's "I'm just not human until I've had my coffee"; a metaphor in mundane conversation may become a description of a startling transformation in an sf story (8).

14. Dis-Imagined Communities: Science Fiction and the Future of Nations

1. Damien Broderick uses the term *sf megatext* for the network of intertextual connections that link the devices and themes of sf works with each other (*Reading by Starlight* 57–63). Sf contrasts with most genres in the extensiveness of these cross-references.

2. Gellner's main statement is *Nations and Nationalism* (1983).

3. See, especially, Anderson's chapter, "The Origins of National Consciousness" (37–46).

4. Arjun Appadurai's *Modernity at Large* is the most engaging and influential text on transnational flows and the erosion of the nation-state.

5. See Mike Featherstone's "Localism, Globalism, and Cultural Identity"; Eric Hobsbawm's *Nations and Nationalism Since 1780*; Russell R. Berman's cogent critique in "Beyond Localism and Universalism: Nationhood and Solidarity" and his contributions to the discussion in "Nationhood, Nationalism and Identity: A Symposium" in the same issue of *Telos* (77–111); and Anne McClintock's "'No Longer in Future Heaven': Gender, Race, and Nationalism."

6. William G. McCoughlin draws a distinction between "ethnic nations" and nation-states (10); John H. Moore speaks of "tribal nations" (8, 321–23). In an 1831 decision, the U.S. Supreme Court affirmed that the political relationship between the Indian nations and the U.S. government was predicated on "peculiar and cardinal distinctions" that Indian nations are sovereign nations within a sovereign nation (Gonzalez and Cook-Lynn xlii). Treaties between the U.S. government and Indian tribes were made formally between nations. See Moore also on the emergence of a national language among the Cheyenne (9).

7. Many Native American nations, like the Iroquois, depended heavily on adoptions and "naturalizations" to replace casualties to the population incurred in their many wars (Jennings 37). The Cheyenne also recommended exogamy: "the Cheyenne nation was predicated not on *preserving* the biological separateness of the population, but on *extending* and *hybridizing* the nation with other groups" (Moore 8).

8. See I. F. Clarke's "Future-War Fiction: The First Main Phase, 1871–1900."

9. See Brian Stableford's *Scientific Romance in Britain 1890–1950* (33).

10. The three novels of the original Foundation series are *Foundation* (1952), *Foundation and Empire* (1952), and *Second Foundation* (1953).

11. See Christopher Palmer's "Galactic Empires and the Contemporary Extravaganza: Dan Simmons and Iain M. Banks."

12. There are almost too many of these teeming, culturally polyglot metropolises to list, from the Los Angeles of 2019 in *Blade Runner* (1982) to the indeterminately Asian city of *Ghost in the Shell* (1996). See Wong Kin Yuen's "On the Edge of Spaces: *Blade Runner*, *Ghost in the Shell*, and Hong Kong's Cityscape," in which Wong argues that the cyberpunk/tech-noir cities of recent sf films are based on former colonial cities, especially Hong Kong.

13. *Nearománc*, trans. Örkény Ajtay (Budapest: Valhalla Páholy, 1992), 345–46.

14. See Leah R. Vande Berg's "Worf as Metonymic Signifier of Racial, Cultural, and National Differences."

15. See Anikó Sohár's *Cultural Transfer of Science Fiction and Fantasy in Hungary, 1989–1995*, especially Chapter 3, "Hungarian Books as Translations, or the Strange World of Pseudotranslations" (175–254).

16. See Frederick L. Schodt's *Dreamland Japan*, especially 59–62.

17. See Ken Hollings's "Tokyo Must Be Destroyed."

Bibliography

Acker, Kathy. *Empire of the Senseless*. London: Picador, 1988.

A.I. Website. 2001. 21 April 2001 < http://aimovie.warnerbros.com/>.

American Psychiatric Association. *Diagnostic and Statistical Manual of Mental Disorders*. Washington, D.C.: APA. Rev. 3rd ed., 1987; 4th ed., 1994.

Anderson, Benedict. *Imagined Communities*. London: Verso, 1991.

Anderson, Laurie. "Language Is a Virus." *Home of the Brave*. Warner, 1987.

———. "O Superman." *Big Science*. Warner, 1987.

Appadurai, Arjun. *Modernity at Large: Cultural Dimensions of Globalization*. Minneapolis: University of Minnesota Press, 1996.

Arnold, Robert. "Termination or Transformation? The *Terminator* Films and Recent Changes in the U.S. Auto-Industry." *Film Quarterly* 52 (Spring 1998): 20–30.

Atlantis Falling Website. September 2000. 21 April 2001 <http://www.atlantisfalling.com/>.

Attebery, Brian. *Strategies of Fantasy*. Bloomington: Indiana University Press, 1992.

Aylett, Steve. *Slaughtermatic*. New York: Four Walls Eight Windows, 1998.

Badler, Norman I. "Virtual Human Web Pointers." 15 March 2001. 21 April 2001 <http://www.cis.upenn.edu/~badler/vhlist.html>.

Balibar, Etienne, and Immanuel Wallerstein. *Race, Nation, Class: Ambiguous Identities*. Trans. Chris Turner. London: Verso, 1991.

Balsamo, Anne. *Technologies of the Gendered Body: Reading Cyborg Women*. Durham, N.C.: Duke University Press, 1996.

Bangalore University Website (fictitious). 21 April 2001 <http://bangaloreworlduin.co.nz/index.html>.

Barthelme, Donald. "Symposium on Fiction." *Shenandoah* 27, 2 (1976): 3–31.

Barthes, Roland. "The Death of the Author." *Image/Music/Text*. Trans. Stephen Heath. New York: Hill and Wang, 1977. 142–48.

———. *S/Z*. Trans. Richard Miller. New York: Hill and Wang, 1974.

Baudrillard, Jean. "The Ecstasy of Communication." Trans. John Johnston. *The Anti-Aesthetic: Essays in Postmodern Culture*, ed. Hal Foster. Port Townsend, Wash.: Bay Press, 1983. 126–33.

——. *The Illusion of the End.* 1992. Trans. Chris Turner. Stanford, Calif.: Stanford University Press, 1994.

——. "The Precession of Simulacra." Trans. Paul Foss, Paul Patton, and Philip Beitchman. *A Postmodern Reader*, ed. Joseph Natoli and Linda Hutcheon. Albany: SUNY Press, 1993. 342–75.

——. "Simulacra and Science Fiction." Trans. Arthur B. Evans. *Science Fiction Studies* 18 (November 1991): 309–13.

——. "The Virtual Illusion: Or the Automatic Writing of the World." *Theory, Culture, and Society* 12, 4 (1995): 97–107.

——. "The Year 2000 Has Already Happened." *Body Invaders: Panic Sex in America*, ed. Arthur Kroker and Marilouise Kroker. Trans. Nai-Fei Ding and Kuan Hsing Chen. Montréal: New World Perspectives, 1987. 35–44.

Beard, Joseph J. "Virtual Actors Create Real IP Headaches." *New York Law Journal* (10 April, 17 April 1998). 21 April 2001 <http://www.ljx.com/practice/sports/0417virtual.html>.

The Beatles. *Sgt. Pepper's Lonely Hearts Club Band.* EMI, 1967.

Beebe, Roger Warren. "After Arnold: Narratives of the Posthuman Cinema." *Meta-Morphing: Visual Transformation and the Culture of Quick-Change*, ed. Vivian Sobchack. Minneapolis: University of Minnesota Press, 2000. 159–79.

Benford, Gregory. *Artifact.* New York: Tor, 1985.

——. *Cosm.* New York: Avon Eos, 1998.

——. *Eater.* New York: Avon Eos, 2000.

Berger, James. *After the End: Representations of Post-Apocalypse.* Minneapolis: University of Minnesota Press, 1999.

Berman, Russell R. "Beyond Localism and Universalism: Nationhood and Solidarity." *Telos* 105 (Fall 1995): 43–56.

Bingo Website. 21 April 2001 < http://scifi.ign.com/media/bingo.mpg>.

Blish, James. "The Biological Story." *Science Fiction Quarterly* (May 1951): 89–91.

Borch-Jacobsen, Mikkel. "Who's Who? Introducing Multiple Personality." *Supposing the Subject*, ed. Joan Copjek. New York: Verso, 1994. 45–63.

Bowie, David. *Diamond Dogs.* RCA, 1974.

Bowie, Lester. *Avant Pop.* ECM, 1986.

Brande, David. "The Business of Cyberpunk: Symbolic Economy and Ideology in William Gibson." *Virtual Realities and Their Discontents*, ed. Robert Markley. Baltimore: Johns Hopkins University Press, 1996. 79–106.

Broderick, Damien. *Reading by Starlight: Postmodern Science Fiction.* London: Routledge, 1995.

Brooker, Will. "Internet Fandom and the Continuing Narratives of *Star Wars*, *Blade Runner*, and *Alien*." *Alien Zone II: The Spaces of Science Fiction Cinema*, ed. Annette Kuhn. New York: Verso, 1999. 50–72.

Bukatman, Scott. *Blade Runner.* BFI Modern Classics. London: British Film Institute, 1997.

——. "Taking Shape: Morphing and the Performance of Self." *Meta-Morphing: Visual*

Transformation and the Culture of Quick-Change, ed. Vivian Sobchack. Minneapolis: University of Minnesota Press, 2000. 225–49.

———. *Terminal Identity: The Virtual Subject in Postmodern Science Fiction.* Durham, N.C.: Duke University Press, 1993.

———. "The Ultimate Trip: Special Effects and Kaleidoscopic Perception." *Iris* 25 (Spring 1998): 75–97.

Bull, Malcolm, ed. *Apocalypse Theory and the Ends of the World.* Oxford: Blackwell, 1995.

Burroughs, William S. *Nova Express.* New York: Grove, 1964.

———. *The Soft Machine.* New York: Grove, 1961.

———. *The Ticket That Exploded.* New York: Grove, 1962.

Butler, Judith. *Bodies That Matter: On The Discursive Limits of "Sex."* New York: Routledge, 1993.

Butler, Octavia E. *Parable of the Sower.* New York: Warner, 1993.

———. *Parable of the Talents.* New York: Seven Stories Press, 1998.

———. "Speech Sounds." 1983. *"Bloodchild" and Other Stories.* New York: Four Walls Eight Windows, 1995. 87–110.

Byers, Thomas. "Terminating the Postmodern: Masculinity and Pomophobia." *Modern Fiction Studies* 41 (Spring 1995): 5–35.

Cadigan, Pat. "Pretty Boy Crossover." 1986. *Patterns.* Kansas City, Mo.: Ursus, 1989. 129–38.

———. *Tea from an Empty Cup.* New York: Tor, 1998.

Cadora, Karen. "Feminist Cyberpunk." *Science Fiction Studies* 22 (November 1995): 357–72.

Calder, Richard. *Cythera.* New York: St. Martin's, 1998.

Carr, John, and Eng Kong Tan. "In Search of the True Amok: Amok as Viewed Within the Malay Culture." *American Journal of Psychiatry* 133 (November 1976): 1295–98.

Cawelti, John G. *Adventure, Mystery, and Romance: Formula Stories as Art and Popular Culture.* Chicago: University of Chicago Press, 1976.

Chown, Marcus. "Double or Quits." *New Scientist* 168 (14 October 2000): 24–27.

Clarke, Arthur C. *Childhood's End.* 1953. New York: Ballantine, 1979.

Clarke, I. F. "Future-War Fiction: The First Main Phase, 1871–1900." *Science Fiction Studies* 24 (November 1997): 387–412.

Clute, John. *The Book of Endtimes: Grappling with the Millennium.* New York: HarperCollins, 1999.

———. "Hitler Wins." *The Encyclopedia of Science Fiction.* 2nd ed., ed. John Clute and Peter Nicholls. New York: St. Martin's, 1993. 572–73.

———. Introduction. *Interzone: The Second Anthology,* ed. John Clute, David Pringle, and Simon Ounsley. London: Simon and Schuster, 1987. vii–x.

Clute, John, and John Grant, eds. *The Encyclopedia of Fantasy.* New York: St. Martin's, 1997.

Coalition for Robotic Freedom Website (fictitious). 21 April 2001 <http://www.inourimage.org/home.html>.

Connor, Steven. *Postmodernist Culture: An Introduction to Theories of the Contemporary.* 2nd ed. Cambridge: Blackwell, 1997.

Coupland, Douglas. *Girlfriend in a Coma.* New York: HarperCollins, 1998.

Cox, F. Brett. "The Brute Facticity of the Corpse: James Morrow, Science Fiction Writer." *Paradoxa* 5, 12 (1999): 16–24.

Csicsery-Ronay, Istvan, Jr. "Cyberpunk and Neuromanticism." 1988. *Storming the Reality Studio: A Casebook of Cyberpunk and Postmodern Fiction*, ed. Larry McCaffery. Durham, N.C.: Duke University Press, 1991. 182–93.

——. "The SF of Theory: Baudrillard and Haraway." *Science Fiction Studies* 18 (November 1991): 387–404.

Cubitt, Sean. *Digital Aesthetics*. Thousand Oaks, Calif.: Sage, 1998.

Curry, Renée, and Terry L. Allison, eds. *States of Rage: Emotional Eruption, Violence, and Social Change*. New York: New York University Press, 1996.

Dark City Website. 1998. 21 April 2001 < http://www.darkcity.com/index.html>.

Davies, Jude. "Gender, Ethnicity and Cultural Crisis in *Falling Down* and *Groundhog Day*." *Screen* 36 (Fall 1995): 214–32.

Davis, Kenneth C. *Two-Bit Culture: The Paperbacking of America*. Boston: Houghton Mifflin, 1984.

Davis, Mike. *City of Quartz*. London: Vintage, 1995.

——. *Magical Urbanism*. London: Verso, 2000.

Delany, Samuel R. *Dhalgren*. 1975. New York: Wesleyan University Press, 1996.

——. "*Paradoxa* Interview with James Morrow: Blinded by the Enlightenment." *Paradoxa* 5, 12 (1999): 132–49.

——. *Starboard Wine: More Notes on the Language of Science Fiction*. Pleasantville, N.Y.: Dragon, 1984.

Dellamora, Richard. *Apocalyptic Overtures: Sexual Politics and the Sense of an Ending*. New Brunswick, N.J.: Rutgers University Press, 1994.

——, ed. *Postmodern Apocalypse: Theory and Cultural Practice at the End*. Philadelphia: University of Pennsylvania Press, 1995.

Denby, David. "Dazzled: Mutants and the Human Problem." *New Yorker* 24 July 2000: 86–87.

Derrida, Jacques. "No Apocalypse, Not Now (full speed ahead, seven missiles, seven missives)." Trans. Catherine Porter and Philip Lewis. *Diacritics* 14 (Summer 1984): 20–31.

——. "Of an Apocalyptic Tone Recently Adopted in Philosophy." Trans. John P. Leavey, Jr. *Semeia* 23 (1982): 63–97.

——. *Of Grammatology*. Trans. Gayatri Chakravorty Spivak. 1967. Baltimore: Johns Hopkins University Press, 1976.

Dery, Mark. *Escape Velocity: Cyberculture at the End of the Century*. New York: Grove, 1996.

——. *The Pyrotechnic Insanitarium: American Culture on the Brink*. New York: Grove, 1999.

Dettmar, Kevin J. H. "An Introduction to Postmodernism: Just Let Them Hear Some of That Rock 'n' Roll Music." *Chronicle of Higher Education* 25 September 1998: B4–5.

Di Filippo, Paul. *Ciphers*. San Francisco: Cambrian, 1997.

——. "Ribofunk: The Manifesto." 26 February 2000 <http://www.streettech.com/bcp/BCPtext/Manifestos/Ribofunk.html>.

Digital Domain Website. 21 April 2001 <http://digitaldomain.com/index2.html>.

Doane, Mary Ann. "Technophilia: Technology, Representation, and the Feminine."
    Body/Politics, ed. Mary Jacobus et al. New York: Routledge, 1990. 163–76.
Dyer, Richard. *White*. New York: Routledge, 1997.
Dyer-Witheford, Nick. *Cyber-Marx: Cycles and Circuits of Struggle in High-Technology Capi-
    talism*. Urbana: University of Illinois Press, 1999.
Eckhardt, Christopher, and Jeffrey L. Deffenbacher. "Diagnosing Anger Disorders."
    Anger Disorders: Definition, Diagnosis, and Treatment, ed. Howard Kassinove. Wash-
    ington, D.C.: Taylor and Francis, 1995. 27–47.
Edwards, John. "The Planet of Perpetual Night." *Amazing Stories* (February 1937): 15–57.
Esler, Gavin. *The United States of Anger: The People and the American Dream*. Har-
    mondsworth: Penguin, 1998.
Eugeni, Ruggero. "*Myst*: Multimedia Hypertexts and Film Semiotics." *Iris* 25 (Spring
    1998): 9–26.
Ewen, Stuart, and Elizabeth Ewen. *Channels of Desire: Mass Images and the Shaping of
    American Consciousness*. New York: McGraw-Hill, 1982.
Exposure Website. 21 April 2001 < http://www.scifi.com/exposure/>.
Falling Down. Dir. Joel Schumacher. Warner Home Video, 1993.
Fanon, Frantz. "National Culture." 1961. Trans. Constance Farrington. *The Post-Colonial
    Studies Reader*, ed. Bill Ashcroft, Gareth Griffiths, and Helen Tiffin. New York: Rout-
    ledge, 1995. 153–57.
Farrell, Kirby. *Post-Traumatic Culture: Injury and Interpretation in the Nineties*. Baltimore:
    Johns Hopkins University Press, 1998.
Fausto-Sterling, Anne. "The Five Sexes: Why Male and Female Are Not Enough." *Sci-
    ences* (March/April 1993): 20–25. 11 April 2000 <http://www.neiu.edu/~ls-
    fuller/fivesexes.html>.
———. "The Five Sexes, Revisited." *Sciences* (July/August 2000). 11 April 2000
    <http://www.nyas.org/membersonly/sciences/sci0007/fausto_body.html>.
———. *Sexing the Body: Gender Politics and the Construction of Sexuality*. New York: Basic,
    2000.
Fava, Maurizio, Keith Anderson, and Jerrold F. Rosenbaum. "'Anger Attacks': Possible
    Variants of Panic and Major Depressive Disorders." *American Journal of Psychiatry*
    147 (July 1990): 867–70.
Featherstone, Mike. "Localism, Globalism, and Cultural Identity." *Global/Local: Cultural
    Production and the Transnational Imaginary*, ed. Rob Wilson and Wimal Dissanayake.
    46–77. Durham, N.C.: Duke University Press, 1996.
Federman, Raymond. "Critifiction: Imagination as Plagiarism." 1976. *Critifiction: Post-
    modern Essays*. Albany: SUNY Press, 1993. 48–64.
Final Fantasy Website. 2000. 15 August 2001 <http://www.movies.go.com/movies/F/
    finalfantasythemovie_2001/index.html>.
Fisch, Michael. "Nation, War, and Japan's Future in the Science Fiction *Anime* Film *Patla-
    bor II*." *Science Fiction Studies* 27 (March 2000): 49–68.
Fisher, Kevin. "Tracing the Tesseract: A Conceptual Prehistory of the Morph." *Meta-
    Morphing: Visual Transformation and the Culture of Quick-Change*, ed. Vivian
    Sobchack. Minneapolis: University of Minnesota Press, 2000. 103–29.
Foucault, Michel. Introduction. *Herculine Barbin, Being the Recently Discovered Memoirs of*

a Nineteenth-Century French Hermaphrodite, ed. Michel Foucault. Trans. Richard Mc-
Dougall. 1978. New York: Pantheon, 1980. vii–xvii.

Frances, Allen, Michael B. First, and Harold Alan Pincus. *DSM–IV Guidebook: The Essential Companion to the DSM, Fourth Edition.* Washington, D.C.: American Psychiatric
Association, 1995.

Freccero, Carla. "Historical Violence, Censorship, and the Serial Killer: The Case of
American Psycho." *Diacritics* 27 (Summer 1997): 44–58.

Freedman, Carl. *Critical Theory and Science Fiction.* Hanover, N.H.: Wesleyan University
Press, 2000.

French, Sean. *The Terminator.* BFI Modern Classics. London: British Film Institute, 1996.

Freud, Sigmund. "Instincts and Their Vicissitudes." 1915. *Pelican Freud Library.* Vol. 11.
Harmondsworth: Penguin, 1984. 103–38.

Fukuyama, Francis. *The End of History and the Last Man.* New York: Free Press, 1992.

GATTACA. Dir. Andrew Niccol. Sony Pictures, 1997.

Gellner, Ernest. *Nations and Nationalism.* Ithaca, N.Y.: Cornell University Press, 1983.

Ghost in the Shell. Dir. Mamoru Oshii. Manga Entertainment, 1996.

Gibson, William. *All Tomorrow's Parties.* New York: Putnam, 1999.

———. *Idoru.* New York: Putnam, 1996.

———. *Neuromancer.* New York: Ace, 1984.

———. *Virtual Light.* New York: Bantam, 1993.

Glide Project Website. 21 April 2001 <http://www.academy.rpi.edu/glide/
testbed/overview.html>.

Goldberg, Jonathan. "Recalling Totalities: The Mirror Stages of Arnold Schwarzenegger." *The Cyborg Handbook,* ed. Chris Hables Gray. New York: Routledge, 1996.
233–54.

Goldie, Terry. *Fear and Temptation: The Image of the Indigene in Canadian, Australian, and
New Zealand Literatures.* Kingston, Ont.: McGill-Queen's University Press, 1989.

Gonzalez, Mario, and Elizabeth Cook-Lynn. *The Politics of Hallowed Ground: Wounded
Knee and the Struggle for Indian Sovereignty.* Urbana: University of Illinois Press, 1999.

Goonan, Kathleen Ann. *Queen City Jazz.* New York: Tor, 1994.

Gordon, Joan. "Closed Systems Kill: An Interview with Suzy McKee Charnas." *Science
Fiction Studies* 26 (November 1999): 447–68.

Gribbin, John. *The Omega Point: The Search for the Missing Mass and the Fate of the Universe.*
London: Heinemann, 1987.

Grier, William, and Price Cobbs. *Black Rage.* London: Jonathan Cape, 1969.

Grosz, Elizabeth. *Volatile Bodies.* Bloomington: Indiana University Press, 1994.

Gunhed. Dir. Masato Harada. Sunrise, 1996.

Gunn, James. Introduction. *The Road to Science Fiction: From Gilgamesh to Wells,* ed. James
Gunn. New York: Mentor, 1977. 1–14.

Halberstam, Judith. *Skin Shows: Gothic Horror and the Technology of Monsters.* Durham,
N.C.: Duke University Press, 1995.

Halberstam, Judith, and Ira Livingston, eds. *Posthuman Bodies.* Bloomington: Indiana
University Press, 1995.

Haldane, J. B. S. *Daedalus; or, Science and the Future.* London: Kegan Paul, Trench and
Trubner, 1923.

Haraway, Donna. "A Manifesto for Cyborgs: Science, Technology, and Socialist Feminism in the 1980s." 1985. *Coming to Terms: Feminism, Theory, Politics,* ed. Elizabeth Weed. New York: Routledge, 1989. 173–204.

———. "The Promises of Monsters: A Regenerative Politics for Inappropriate/d Others." *Cultural Studies,* ed. Lawrence Grossberg, Cary Nelson, and Paula Treichler. New York: Routledge, 1992. 295–337.

Hardin, Garrett. "The Tragedy of the Commons." *Science* 162 (1968): 1243–48.

Hausman, Bernice L. *Changing Sex: Transsexualism, Technology, and the Idea of Gender.* Durham, N.C.: Duke University Press, 1995.

Hawking, Stephen. *Black Holes and Baby Universes.* New York: Bantam, 1993.

Hayles, N. Katherine. *Chaos Bound: Orderly Disorder in Contemporary Literature and Science.* Ithaca, N.Y.: Cornell University Press, 1990.

———. "Flickering Connectivities in Shelley Jackson's *Patchwork Girl*: The Importance of Media-Specific Analysis." *Postmodern Culture* 10, 2 (2000) <http://muse.jhu.edu/journals/postmodern_culture/toc/pmc10.2.html>.

———. *How We Became Posthuman: Virtual Bodies in Cybernetics, Literature, and Informatics.* Chicago: University of Chicago Press, 1999.

Heim, Michael. "The Design of Virtual Reality." *Cyberspace/Cyberbodies/Cyberpunk: Cultures of Technological Embodiment,* ed. Mike Featherstone and Roger Burrows. Thousand Oaks, Calif.: Sage, 1995. 65–77.

Hobsbawm, Eric. *Nations and Nationalism Since 1780.* Cambridge: Cambridge University Press, 1990.

Hollinger, Veronica. "'A Language of the Future': Discursive Constructions of the Subject in *A Clockwork Orange* and *Random Acts of Senseless Violence.*" *Speaking Science Fiction: Dialogues and Interpretations,* ed. Andy Sawyer and David Seed. Liverpool: Liverpool University Press, 2000. 82–95.

———. "(Re)reading Queerly: Science Fiction, Feminism, and the Defamiliarization of Gender." *Science Fiction Studies* 26 (March 1999): 23–40.

Hollings, Ken. "Tokyo Must Be Destroyed." *Digital Delirium,* ed. Arthur Kroker and Marilouise Kroker. New York: St. Martin's, 1997. 241–52.

Hollow Man Website. 2000. 21 April 2001 <http://www.spe.sony.com/movies/hollow-man/>.

Holmes, Morgan. "Queer Cut Bodies." *Queer Frontiers: Millennial Geographies, Genders, and Generations,* ed. Joseph A. Boone et al. Madison: University of Wisconsin Press, 2000. 84–110.

Holt, John. *Escape from Childhood: The Needs and Rights of Children.* Harmondsworth: Penguin, 1975.

hooks, bell. *Killing Rage: Ending Racism.* London: Holt, 1995.

Huxley, Aldous. *Brave New World.* London: Chatto and Windus, 1932.

Huxley, Julian. "The Tissue-Culture King." *Amazing Stories* (August 1927): 451–59.

Ignatieff, Michael. "The Scene of the Crime." *Granta* 63 (Autumn 1998): 121–28.

Jackson, Shelley. *Patchwork Girl (Hyperfiction).* Watertown, Mass.: Eastgate, 1995.

Jameson, Fredric. "Of Islands and Trenches: Naturalization and the Production of Utopian Discourse." *Diacritics* (June 1977): 2–21.

———. "Postmodernism, or the Cultural Logic of Late Capitalism." *New Left Review* 146 (July/August 1984): 53–94.

———. *Postmodernism, or, The Cultural Logic of Late Capitalism.* Durham, N.C.: Duke University Press, 1991.

———. "Progress Versus Utopia; or, Can We Imagine the Future?" 1982. *Art After Modernism: Rethinking Representation*, ed. Brian Wallis. New York: New Museum of Contemporary Art, 1984. 239–52.

Jeanine Salla Website (fictitious). 21 April 2001 <http://www.familiasalla-es.ro/>.

Jeffords, Susan. *Hard Bodies: Hollywood Masculinity in the Reagan Era*. New Brunswick, N.J.: Rutgers University Press, 1994.

Jennings, Francis. *The Ambiguous Iroquois Empire: The Covenant Chain Confederation of Indian Tribes with English Colonies from Its Beginning to the Lancaster Treaty of 1744*. Boston: Norton, 1984.

Johnson, Mark. *The Body in the Mind: The Bodily Basis of Meaning, Imagination, and Reason*. Chicago: University of Chicago Press, 1987.

Jones, Gwyneth. *Deconstructing the Starships: Science, Fiction, and Reality*. Liverpool: Liverpool University Press, 1999.

———. *Divine Endurance*. London: Allen and Unwin, 1984.

———. *Escape Plans*. London: Unwin, 1986.

———. *Kairos*. London: Unwin Hyman, 1988.

———. *North Wind*. London: Gollancz, 1994.

———. *Phoenix Café*. 1997. Rev. ed. New York: Tor, 1998.

———. *White Queen*. 1991. New York: Tor, 1994.

Joy, Bill. "Why the Future Doesn't Need Us." *Wired* (April 2000): 238–62.

Kahane, Claire. "The Aesthetic Politics of Rage." *States of Rage: Emotional Eruption, Violence, and Social Change*, ed. Renée Curry and Terry L. Allison. New York: New York University Press, 1996. 126–45.

Keller, Evelyn Fox. *Reflections on Gender and Science*. New Haven, Conn.: Yale University Press, 1985.

Kelly, Kevin, and Paula Parisi. "Beyond *Star Wars*." *Wired* 5, 02 (1997): 1–11 <http://hotwired.lycos.com/collections/film_special_effects/5.02_lucas1.html>.

Kermode, Frank. *The Sense of an Ending: Studies in the Theory of Fiction*. New York: Oxford University Press, 1966.

Kessler, Suzanne J. "The Medical Construction of Gender: Case Management of Intersexual Infants." *Signs: Journal of Women in Culture and Society* 16, 1 (1990): 3–26.

Ketterer, David. *New Worlds for Old: The Apocalyptic Imagination, Science Fiction, and American Literature*. Bloomington: Indiana University Press, 1974.

Keyes, Daniel. *Algernon, Charlie, and I: A Writer's Journey*. Boca Raton, Fla.: Challcrest Press, 1999.

King, Stephen. *Danse Macabre*. New York: Berkley, 1982.

Kingwell, Mark. *Dreams of Millennium: Report from a Culture on the Brink*. New York: Viking, 1996.

Kirby, David A. "The New Eugenics in Cinema: Genetic Determinism and Gene Therapy in *GATTACA*." *Science Fiction Studies* 27 (July 2000): 193–215.

Knight, Norman L. "Crisis in Utopia." *Astounding Science-Fiction* (July, August 1940): 9–38, 126–54.

Knox, Sara. *Murder: A Tale of American Life*. Durham, N.C.: Duke University Press, 1998.

Kohut, Heinz. "Thoughts on Narcissism and Narcissistic Rage." *Psychoanalytic Study of the Child* 27 (1972): 360–400.

Komatsu, Sakyo. *Japan Sinks.* 1973. Trans. Michael Gallagher. Tokyo: Kodansha International, 1995.

Kroker, Arthur. *Spasm: Virtual Reality, Android Music and Electric Flesh.* New York: St. Martin's, 1993.

Kroker, Arthur, and Michael A. Weinstein. *Data Trash: The Theory of the Virtual Class.* Montréal: New World Perspectives; New York: St. Martin's, 1994.

Kuhn, Annette, ed. *Alien Zone: Cultural Theory and Contemporary Science Fiction Cinema.* London, Verso, 1990.

Kuhn, Annette, ed. *Alien Zone II: The Spaces of Science Fiction Cinema.* New York: Verso, 1999.

Kumar, Krishnan. "Apocalypse, Millennium and Utopia Today." *Apocalypse Theory and the Ends of the World,* ed. Malcolm Bull. Oxford: Blackwell, 1995. 200–24.

Laidlaw, Marc. *Kalifornia.* New York: St. Martin's, 1993.

Lakoff, George, and Mark Johnson. *Philosophy in the Flesh: The Embodied Mind and Its Challenge to Western Thought.* New York: Basic, 1999.

Lakoff, George, and Mark Turner. *More Than Cool Reason: A Field Guide to Poetic Metaphor.* Chicago: University of Chicago Press, 1989.

Lamb, Patricia Frazer, and Diane L. Veith. "Again, *The Left Hand of Darkness*: Androgyny or Homophobia?" *Erotic Universe: Sexuality and Fantastic Literature,* ed. Donald Palumbo. Westport, Conn.: Greenwood, 1986. 221–31.

Landon, Brooks. *The Aesthetics of Ambivalence: Rethinking Science Fiction Film in the Age of Electronic Reproduction.* Westport, Conn.: Greenwood, 1992.

———. "Diegetic or Digital? The Convergence of Science-Fiction Literature and Science-Fiction Film in Hypermedia." *Alien Zone II: The Spaces of Science Fiction Cinema,* ed. Annette Kuhn. New York: Verso, 1999. 31–49.

———. "Not Your Father's Olds: Subverting the Semblance in the Age of the Avant-Pop." *Paradoxa* 4, 11 (1998): 539–55.

———. *Science Fiction After 1900: From the Steam Man to the Stars.* New York: Twayne, 1997.

Lane, Mary E. Bradley. *Mizora: A Prophecy. A Manuscript Found Among the Private Papers of Princess Vera.* 1889. Boston: Gregg, 1975.

Laqueur, Thomas. *Making Sex: Body and Gender from the Greeks to Freud.* Cambridge, Mass.: Harvard University Press, 1990.

Lasch, Christopher. *The Culture of Narcissism: American Life in an Age of Diminishing Expectations.* New York: Warner, 1979.

———. *The Minimal Self: Psychic Survival in Troubled Times.* New York: Norton, 1984.

Lasseter, Don. *Going Postal: Madness and Mass Murder in America's Post Offices.* New York: Pinnacle, 1997.

Lawrence, D. H. "Fenimore Cooper's Leatherstocking Novels." *Studies in Classic American Literature.* New York: Doubleday, 1951. 55–73.

Layden, Dianne R. "Violence, the Emotionally Enraged Employee, and the Workplace: Managerial Considerations." *States of Rage: Emotional Eruption, Violence, and Social Change,* ed. Renée Curry and Terry L. Allison. New York: New York University Press, 1996. 35–61.

Lefanu, Sarah. *In the Chinks of the World Machine: Feminism and Science Fiction*. London: Women's Press, 1988.

Le Guin, Ursula K. *Always Coming Home*. New York: Harper and Row, 1985.

———. Introduction to "Nine Lives." *Those Who Can: A Science Fiction Reader*, ed. Robin Scott Wilson. New York: Mentor, 1973. 204–6.

———. "Is Gender Necessary?" 1976. *The Language of the Night: Essays on Fantasy and Science Fiction*. New York: Pedigree, 1979. 161–69.

———. "Is Gender Necessary? Redux." 1987. *Dancing at the Edge of the World*. New York: Harper and Row, 1989. 7–16.

———. *The Left Hand of Darkness*. New York: Ace, 1969.

Leigh, Stephen. *Dark Water's Embrace*. New York: Avon Eos, 1998.

Leyner, Mark. *Et Tu, Babe*. New York: Harmony, 1992.

———. *My Cousin, My Gastroenterologist*. New York: Harmony, 1990.

Loyer, Erik. *Chroma* (motion graphic narrative) Website. 21 April 2001 <http://www.marrowmonkey.com/>.

Luckhurst, Roger. "The Science-Fictionalization of Trauma: Remarks on Narratives of Alien Abduction." *Science Fiction Studies* 25 (March 1998): 29–53.

Lui, Albert. "The Last Days of Arnold Schwarzenegger." *Genders* 18 (Winter 1993): 102–12.

Lykke, Nina, and Rosi Braidotti. Postface. *Between Monsters, Goddesses and Cyborgs: Feminist Confrontations with Science, Medicine and Cyberspace*, ed. Nina Lykke and Rosi Braidotti. London: Zed Books, 1996. 242–49.

Lyotard, Jean-François. *The Postmodern Condition: A Report on Knowledge*. 1979. Trans. Geoff Bennington and Brian Massumi. Minneapolis: University of Minnesota Press, 1984.

Malmgren, Carl D. *Worlds Apart: Narratology of Science Fiction*. Bloomington: Indiana University Press, 1991.

Marilyn Project Website. 21 April 2001 <http://ligwww.epfl.ch/~thalmann/research.html>.

Martindale, C. C. *The Message of Fatima*. London: Burns and Oates, 1950.

The Matrix. Dir. Wachowski Brothers. Warner, 1999.

The Matrix Website. 21 April 2001 <http://www.whatisthematrix.com/>.

McCaffery, Larry. "Avant-Pop: Still Life After Yesterday's Crash." *After Yesterday's Crash: The Avant-Pop Anthology*, ed. Larry McCaffery. New York: Penguin, 1995. xi–xxxi.

———. "Cutting Up: Cyberpunk, Punk Music, and Urban Decontextualization." *Storming the Reality Studio: A Casebook of Cyberpunk and Postmodern Fiction*, ed. Larry McCaffery. Durham, N.C.: Duke University Press, 1991. 286–307.

McClintock, Anne. "'No Longer in Future Heaven': Gender, Race, and Nationalism." *Dangerous Liaisons: Gender, Nation, and Postcolonial Perspectives*, ed. Anne McClintock, Aamir Mufti, and Ella Shohat. Minneapolis: University of Minnesota Press, 1997. 89–112.

McCoughlin, William G. *Cherokee Renascence in the New Republic*. Princeton, N.J.: Princeton University Press, 1986.

McCreary, Lew. *The Minus Man*. Harmondsworth: Penguin, 1994.

McFadden, Tim. "Notes on the Structure of Cyberspace and the Ballistic Actors Model." *Cyberspace: First Steps*, ed. Michael Benedikt. Cambridge, Mass.: MIT Press, 1991. 335–62.

McHale, Brian. "POSTcyberMODERNpunkISM." *Constructing Postmodernism*. New York: Routledge, 1992. 225–42.

———. *Postmodernist Fiction*. New York: Methuen, 1987.

Merrick, Helen. "Posthumanity—The Only Game in Town? The Material Girl Strikes Back." *Foundation* 29 (Spring 2000): 95–97.

Michelson, Annette. "Bodies in Space: Film as 'Carnal Knowledge'." *Artforum* (February 1969): 56–63.

Miklitsch, Robert. "Rock 'n' Theory: Autobiography, Cultural Studies, and the 'Dream of Rock.'" *Postmodern Culture* 9, 2 (1999) <http://jefferson.village.edu/pmc/text-only/issue.199/9.2miklitsch.txt>.

Miller, Jim. "Post-Apocalyptic Hoping: Octavia Butler's Dystopian/Utopian Vision." *Science Fiction Studies* 25 (July 1998): 336–60.

Milne, Seumas. "Rising Stress Brings 'Desk Rage' at Work." *Guardian* (2 September 1999): 6.

Minh-ha, Trinh T., ed. Special Issue on Postcolonialist Theory: "She: The Inappropriate/d Other." *Discourse* 8 (1986/87).

Mission to Mars Website. 2000. 21 April 2001 <http://video.go.com/m2m/index.html>.

Miyoshi, Masao. "A Borderless World? From Colonialism to Transnationalism and the Decline of the Nation State." *Global/Local: Cultural Production and the Transnational Imaginary*, ed. Rob Wilson and Wimal Dissanayake. Durham, N.C.: Duke University Press, 1996. 78–106.

Modleski, Tania. *Feminism Without Women*. New York: Routledge, 1991.

Money, John. *Sex Errors of the Body and Related Syndromes: A Guide to Counseling Children, Adolescents, and Their Families*. 2nd ed. Baltimore: Brookes, 1994.

Moore, John H. *The Cheyenne Nation: A Social and Demographic History*. Lincoln: University of Nebraska Press, 1987.

Moravec, Hans. *Mind Children: The Future of Robot and Human Intelligence*. Cambridge, Mass.: Harvard University Press, 1988.

Morrow, James. *Blameless in Abaddon*. New York: Harcourt, 1996.

———. *The Eternal Footman*. New York: Harcourt, 1999.

———. *Towing Jehovah*. New York: Harcourt, 1994.

Mullen, R. D. "Books in Review: Supernatural, Pseudonatural, and Sociocultural Fantasy." *Science-Fiction Studies* 5 (November 1978): 291–98.

Murray, Janet H. *Hamlet on the Holodeck: The Future of Narrative in Cyberspace*. New York: Free Press, 1997.

Nancy, Jean-Luc. Introduction. *Who Comes After the Subject?* ed. Eduardo Cadava, Peter Connor, and Jean-Luc Nancy. London: Routledge, 1991. 1–9.

Nelson, Dana. *National Manhood: Capitalist Citizenship and the Imagined Fraternity of White Men*. Durham, N.C.: Duke University Press, 1998.

Nicholls, Peter, ed. *The Encyclopedia of Science Fiction*. London: Granada, 1979. 2nd ed., ed. John Clute and Peter Nicholls. New York: St. Martin's, 1993.

Norris, Christopher. "Versions of Apocalypse: Kant, Derrida, Foucault." *Apocalypse The-*

ory and the Ends of the World, ed. Malcolm Bull. Oxford: Blackwell, 1995. 227–49.

Olsen, Lance. *Burnt.* La Grande, Ore.: Wordcraft, 1996.

——. *Ellipse of Uncertainty: An Introduction to Postmodern Fantasy.* Westport, Conn.: Greenwood Press, 1987.

——. *Freaknest.* La Grande, Ore.: Wordcraft, 2000.

——. *Live from Earth.* New York: Ballantine / Available, 1991.

——. *Time Famine.* San Francisco: Permeable, 1996.

——. *Tonguing the Zeitgeist.* San Francisco: Permeable, 1994.

Ong, Walter J. *Orality and Literacy: The Technologizing of the Word.* London: Methuen, 1982.

Palmer, Christopher. "Galactic Empires and the Contemporary Extravaganza: Dan Simmons and Iain M. Banks." *Science Fiction Studies* 26 (March 1999): 73–90.

Parisi, Paula. "The New Hollywood." *Wired* 3, 12 (1995): 1–11 <http://hotwired.lycos.com/collections/film_special_effects/3.12_new_hollywood1.html>.

——. "Shot by an Outlaw." *Wired* 4, 9 (1996): 1–6 <http://hotwired.lycos.com/collections/film_special_effects/4.09_billups1.html>.

Park, Paul. *Celestis.* New York: Tor, 1995.

Patlabor II. Dir. Mamoru Oshii. Manga Video, 1989.

Penley, Constance. "Time Travel, the Primal Scene, and Critical Dystopia." *Alien Zone: Cultural Theory and Contemporary Science Fiction*, ed. Annette Kuhn. London: Verso, 1990. 116–27.

Pfeil, Fred. *White Guys: Studies in Postmodern Domination and Difference.* New York: Verso, 1995.

Pierson, Michele. "Welcome to Basementwood: Computer Generated Special Effects and *Wired* Magazine." *Postmodern Culture* 8, 3 (1998) <http://muse.jhu.edu/journals/postmodern_culture/toc/pmc8.3.html>.

Pixar Website. 21 April 2001 <http://www.pixar.com/>.

Plant, Sadie. "The Virtual Complexity of Culture." *Future Natural: Nature, Science, Culture*, ed. George Robertson et al. New York: Routledge, 1996. 203–17.

Prince, Stephen. "True Lies: Perceptual Realism, Digital Images, and Film Theory." *Film Quarterly* 49, 3 (1996): 27–37.

Prometheus Factor Project Website <http://www.incitegraphics.com.au/movieproj/home.html>.

Quinby, Lee. *Anti-Apocalypse: Exercises in Genealogical Criticism.* Minneapolis: University of Minnesota Press, 1994.

Rabinovitz, Lauren. Introduction. *Iris* 25 (Spring 1998): 3–8.

Rabkin, Eric S. *The Fantastic in Literature.* Princeton, N.J.: Princeton University Press, 1976.

Race for Atlantis Website 21 April 2001. <http://www.imax.com/raceforatlantis/>.

Resnick, Mike. *Kirinyaga: A Fable of Utopia.* New York: Random House, 1998.

Reynolds, Craig. "Characters, Improvisation, and . . . " Website. 30 October 2000. 21 April 2001 <http://www.red3d.com/cwr/characters.html>.

Rheingold, Howard. *Virtual Reality.* New York: Simon and Schuster, 1991.

Rieff, David. *Los Angeles: Capital of the Third World.* New York: Simon and Schuster, 1991.

Robinson, Kim Stanley et al. "Alive and Well: Messages from the Edge (Almost) of the Millennium." *Nebula Awards 33: The Year's Best SF and Fantasy Chosen by the Science-Fiction and Fantasy Writers of America,* ed. Connie Willis. New York: Harcourt, 1999. 245–57.

Romney, Jonathan. Review of *GATTACA. Sight and Sound* 8 (March 1998): 48–49.

Rose, Gillian. *Feminism and Geography: The Limits of Geographical Knowledge.* Cambridge: Polity Press, 1993.

Rosenthal, Nan. *Anselm Kiefer: Works on Paper in the Metropolitan Museum of Art.* New York: Abrams, 1998.

Russ, Joanna. "The Second Inquisition." 1970. *The Adventures of Alyx.* London: Women's Press, 1985. 165–92.

Russell, Mary Doria. *Children of God.* New York: Villard, 1998.

———. *The Sparrow.* New York: Ballantine, 1996.

Sayer, Paul. *Men in Rage.* London: Bloomsbury Press, 1998.

Schaffer, Kay. "The Game Girls of VNS Matrix: Challenging Gendered Identities in Cyberspace." *Virtual Gender: Fantasies of Subjectivity and Embodiment,* ed. Mary Ann O'Farrell and Lynne Villain. Ann Arbor: University of Michigan Press, 1999. 147–68.

Schodt, Frederick L. *Dreamland Japan: Writings on Modern Manga.* Berkeley, Calif.: Stone Bridge Press, 1996.

Scott, Melissa. "Shadow Man." 11 April 2000 <http://www.rscs.net/~ms001/shadowm.html>.

———. *Shadow Man.* New York: Tor, 1995.

Seed, David. "Introduction: Aspects of Apocalypse." *Imagining Apocalypse: Studies in Cultural Crisis,* ed. David Seed. New York: St. Martin's, 2000. 1–14.

Seltzer, Mark. *Serial Killers: Death and Life in America's Wound Culture.* London: Routledge, 1998.

Shaviro, Steven. *The Cinematic Body.* Minneapolis: University of Minnesota Press, 1993.

Sheehan, Bill. *At the Foot of the Story Tree: An Inquiry into the Fiction of Peter Straub.* Burton, Mich.: Subterranean Press, 2000.

Showalter, Elaine. *Sexual Anarchy: Gender and Culture at the Fin de Siècle.* New York: Viking Penguin, 1990.

Simmons, Dan. *Hyperion.* 1989. *Hyperion Cantos.* New York: Guild America Books, 1990. 1–416.

Simón, Armando. "The Berserker/Blind Rage Syndrome as a Potentially New Diagnostic Category for the *DSM-III.*" *Psychological Reports* 60 (February-June 1987): 131–35.

Sirius, R. U. "A User's Guide to Using This Guide." *Mondo 2000: A User's Guide to the New Edge,* ed. Rudy Rucker, R. U. Sirius, and Queen Mu. New York: HarperPerennial, 1992. 14–17.

Smith, Anthony D. "Toward a Global Culture." *Global Culture: Nationalism, Globalization, and Modernity,* ed. Mike Featherstone. London: Sage, 1990. 171–91.

Sobchack, Vivian. "'At the Still Point of the Turning World': Meta-Morphing and Meta-Stasis." *Meta-Morphing: Visual Transformation and the Culture of Quick-Change,* ed. Vivian Sobchack. Minneapolis: University of Minnesota Press, 2000. 131–58.

———. "New Age Mutant Ninja Hackers." *Flame Wars: The Discourse of Cyberculture,* ed. Mark Dery. Durham, N.C.: Duke University Press, 1994. 11–28.

———. *Screening Space: The American Science Fiction Film*. 2nd ed. New York: Ungar, 1987.

Sobchack, Vivian, ed. *Meta-Morphing: Visual Transformation and the Culture of Quick-Change*. Minneapolis: University of Minnesota Press, 2000.

Sohár, Anikó. *The Cultural Transfer of Science Fiction and Fantasy in Hungary, 1989–1995*. Frankfurt am Main: Peter Lang, 1999.

Sonic Youth. "The Sprawl." *Daydream Nation*. Enigma, 1988.

Sontag, Susan. "The Imagination of Disaster." 1965. *"Against Interpretation" and Other Essays*. New York: Farrar, Straus, and Giroux, 1986. 209–25.

Sponsler, Claire. "Beyond the Ruins: The Geopolitics of Urban Decay and Cybernetic Play." *Science Fiction Studies* 20 (July 1993): 251–65.

Stableford, Brian. "The Age of Innocence." *Asimov's Science Fiction* (June 1995): 88–100.

———. ". . . And He Not Busy Being Born." *Interzone* 16 (Summer 1986): 3–8.

———. *The Architects of Emortality*. New York: Tor, 1999 (expanded from "Les Fleurs du Mal," *Asimov's Science Fiction* [October 1994]: 104–61).

———. "Ashes and Tombstones." *Moon Shots*, ed. Peter Crowther and Martin N. Greenberg. New York: DAW, 1999. 38–56.

———. *The Cassandra Complex*. New York: Tor, 2001 (expanded from "The Magic Bullet," *Interzone* 29 [May-June 1989]: 51–59).

———. "Cinderella's Sisters." *The Gate* 1 (May 1989): 9–27.

———. "The Cure for Love." *Asimov's Science Fiction* (December 1993): 8–30.

———. *The Fountains of Youth*. New York: Tor, 2000 (expanded from "Mortimer Gray's History of Death," *Asimov's Science Fiction* [April 1995]: 254–305).

———. "Hidden Agendas." *Asimov's Science Fiction* (September 1999): 70–98.

———. "How Should a Science Fiction Story End?" *New York Review of Science Fiction* 78 (February 1995): 1, 8–15.

———. *Inherit the Earth*. New York: Tor, 1998 (expanded from "Inherit the Earth," *Analog* [July 1995]: 12–175).

———. "The Invisible Worm." *Magazine of Fantasy and Science Fiction* (September 1991): 10–38.

———. "The Pipes of Pan." *Magazine of Fantasy and Science Fiction* (June 1997): 69–91.

———. *The Scientific Romance in England, 1890–1950*. New York: St. Martin's, 1985.

———. "Sexual Chemistry." *Interzone* 20 (Summer 1987): 27–34. Rpt. as "A Career in Sexual Chemistry." *Sexual Chemistry: Sardonic Tales of the Genetic Revolution*. New York: Simon and Schuster, 1991. 21–41.

———. "Skin Deep." *Amazing Stories* (October 1991): 9–16.

———. "What Can Chloë Want?" *Asimov's Science Fiction* (March 1994): 74–82.

———. *Year Zero*. Mountain Ash: Sarob Press, 2000.

Stableford, Brian, with David Langford. *The Third Millennium: A History of the World, AD 2000–3000*. London: Sidgwick and Jackson, 1985.

Star Wars Website. 21 April 2001 <http://www.starwars.com/>.

Sterling, Bruce. "Catscan 5: Slipstream." *Science Fiction Eye* 1 (July 1989): 77–80. *Frontier Publications Archives: Bruce Sterling—Catscan Columns*, May 2001 <http://www.eff.org/pub/Publications/Bruce_Sterling/Catscan_columns/catscan.05>.

———. "Lifelike Characters." Speech at the 1995 Lifelike Computer Characters Confer-

ence. 29 September 1995. 21 April 2001
  <http://www.research.microsoft.com/ui/oldlcc/lcc95/sterling.html>.

———. Preface. *Burning Chrome*. By William Gibson. 1986. New York: Ace, 1987. ix–xii.

———. *Schismatrix*. 1985. New York: Ace, 1986.

Stewart, Garrett. *Between Film and Screen: Modernism's Photo Synthesis*. Chicago: University of Chicago Press, 1999.

———. "Body Snatching: Science Fiction's Photographic Trace." *Alien Zone II: The Spaces of Science Fiction Cinema*, ed. Annette Kuhn. New York: Verso, 1999. 226–48.

———. "Kubrick's *Odyssey* as Filmic Epiphany." *Moments of Moment: Aspects of the Literary Epiphany*, ed. Wim Tigges. Leiden: University of Leiden Press, 1999. 401–19.

———. "The Photographic Ontology of Science Fiction Film." *Iris* 25 (Spring 1998): 99–132.

———. "The 'Videology' of Science Fiction." *Shadows of the Magic Lamp: Fantasy and Science Fiction in Film*, ed. George Slusser and Eric S. Rabkin. Carbondale: Southern Illinois University Press, 1985. 159–207.

Stone, Allucquère Rosanne. *The War of Desire and Technology at the Close of the Mechanical Age*. Cambridge, Mass.: MIT Press, 1996.

Straub, Peter. *Mr. X*. New York: Random House, 1999.

Tasker, Yvonne. *Spectacular Bodies: Gender, Genre, and the Action Cinema*. New York: Routledge, 1993.

Tavris, Carol. *Anger: The Misunderstood Emotion*. Rev. ed. New York: Touchstone, 1989.

Taylor, Gordon Rattray. *The Biological Time-Bomb*. London: Thames and Hudson, 1968.

Tepper, Sheri. *A Plague of Angels*. New York: Bantam Spectra, 1993.

Terminator, The. Dir. James Cameron. Orion, 1984.

Terminator 2: Judgment Day. Dir. James Cameron. Artisan Entertainment, 1991.

Theweleit, Klaus. "The Ego of the Soldier Male." *Male Bodies: Psychoanalyzing the White Terror*. Vol. 2 of *Male Fantasies*. Trans. Erica Carter and Chris Turner. Minneapolis: University of Minnesota Press, 1987. 206–51.

Tiedemann, Mark W. "Hybrids." *New York Review of Science Fiction* 12, 10 (2000): 15–17.

Tiptree, James, Jr. (Alice Sheldon). "And I Awoke and Found Me Here on the Cold Hill's Side." 1971. *Ten Thousand Light-Years from Home*. New York: Ace, 1973. 1–13.

———. "The Women Men Don't See." 1973. *Warm Worlds and Otherwise*. New York: Ballantine, 1975. 131–64.

Titan A.E. Website. 2000. 21 April 2001
  <http://www.afterearth.com/movies/titan_med.mov>.

Vande Berg, Leah R. "Worf as Metonymic Signifier of Racial, Cultural, and National Differences." *Enterprise Zones: Critical Positions on* Star Trek, ed. Taylor Harrison, Sarah Projansky, Kent A. Ono, and Elyce Rae Helford. Boulder, Colo.: Westview Press, 1996. 51–68.

Wagar, W. Warren. *Terminal Visions: The Literature of Last Things*. Bloomington: Indiana University Press, 1982.

Walser, Randal. "The Emerging Technology of Cyberspace." *Virtual Reality: Theory, Practice, and Promise*, ed. S. K. Helsel and J. P. Roth. Westport, Conn.: Meckler, 1991. 35–40.

Waxweb Website. 4 April 1995. 21 April 2001

<http:/www.village.virginia.edu/wax/wax.html>.

Weiland, Scott. "Barbarella." *12 Bar Blues*. Atlantic, 1998.

Wells, H. G. *The War of the Worlds*. 1898. New York: Bantam, 1988.

Wertheim, Margaret. *Pythagoras's Trousers: God, Physics, and the Gender Wars*. New York: New York Times Books, 1995.

Wiener, Norbert. *The Human Use of Human Beings: Cybernetics and Society*. Boston: Houghton Mifflin, 1954.

Willis, Sharon. *High Contrast: Race and Gender in Contemporary Hollywood Film*. Durham, N.C.: Duke University Press, 1997.

Wilson, Rob, and Wimal Dissanayake, eds. *Global/Local: Cultural Production and the Transnational Imaginary*. Durham, N.C.: Duke University Press, 1996.

Wollheim, Donald, ed. *The Pocket Book of Science Fiction*. New York: Pocket Books, 1943.

Womack, Jack. *Ambient*. New York: Grove, 1987.

———. *Random Acts of Senseless Violence*. London: HarperCollins, 1993.

Wong, Kin Yuen. "On the Edge of Spaces: *Blade Runner, Ghost in the Shell*, and Hong Kong's Cityscape." *Science Fiction Studies* 27 (March 2000): 1–21.

X-Men Website. 2000. 21 April 2001 <http://www.x-men-the-movie.com/>.

Contributors

BRIAN ATTEBERY's scholarly interests range from fantasy and science fiction to metafiction and theories of interdisciplinarity. He is the author of *Strategies of Fantasy* (1992) and, with Ursula K. Le Guin and Karen Joy Fowler, co-editor of *The Norton Book of Science Fiction* (1993). His latest book, *Decoding Gender in Science Fiction*, will be pubished by Routledge in 2002. He directs the Graduate Program in English at Idaho State University, where he sometimes doubles as Adjunct Instructor in cello.

ISTVAN CSICSERY-RONAY, JR., is Professor of History and World Literature at De-Pauw University in Indiana and a co-editor of *Science Fiction Studies*. His essays on sf, cybertheory, and postmodernism have been published widely in several languages. He is currently completing a book on sf theory entitled "The Seven Beauties of Science Fiction."

JOAN GORDON is Associate Professor of English at Nassau Community College in New York and Reviews Editor for *Science Fiction Studies*. She is the co-editor of *Blood Read: The Vampire as Metaphor in Contemporary Culture* (University of Pennsylvania Press, 1997) with Veronica Hollinger and is a past president of the Science Fiction Research Association. She has published widely on science fiction, including Starmont Readers' Guides to Joe W. Haldeman and Gene Wolfe.

VERONICA HOLLINGER is Associate Professor of Cultural Studies at Trent University in Ontario. She co-edits *Science Fiction Studies* and, with Joan Gordon, is co-editor of *Blood Read: The Vampire as Metaphor in Contemporary Culture* (1997). She has published widely on science fiction and is a past winner of the Science Fiction Research Association's Pioneer Award for scholarship.

GWYNETH JONES's essays and reviews have appeared in *Foundation, Interzone,* and *The New York Review of Science Fiction;* her collection of critical essays, *Deconstructing the Starships,* was published by Liverpool University Press in 1999. Her novels, typically exploring gender roles in hard science fiction, have been nominated four times for the Arthur C. Clarke Award, the fourth time for *North Wind* (1994). *White Queen,* the first novel in the Aleutian series, was co-winner of the James Tiptree Award in 1991. She is also a winner of two World Fantasy Awards. A new utopian novel, *Bold As Love,* is forthcoming from Gollancz UK.

BROOKS LANDON is Professor and Chair of the English Department at the University of Iowa. He has written widely on science fiction and science fiction film, including *The Aesthetics of Ambivalence: Rethinking Science Fiction Film in the Age of Electronic (Re)Production* (1992) and *Science Fiction After 1900: From the Steam Man to the Stars* (1997). In 2001 he won the International Association for the Fantastic in the Arts' Distinguished Scholarship Award.

ROB LATHAM is Associate Professor of English and American Studies at the University of Iowa, where he also directs the Sexuality Studies program. A co-editor of *Science Fiction Studies,* he has recently finished a book entitled *Consuming Youth: Vampires, Cyborgs, and the Culture of Consumption,* due from the University of Chicago Press in 2002.

ROGER LUCKHURST lectures in literature at Birkbeck College, University of London. He is the author of *"The Angle Between Two Walls": The Fiction of J. G. Ballard* (1997) and *The Invention of Telepathy, 1870–1901* (2002).

LANCE OLSEN is the author of more than a dozen books of and about cutting-edge fiction, including the first book-length study of William Gibson. He lives biologically in the mountains of central Idaho, and digitally at <www.cafezeitgeist.com>.

WENDY PEARSON is currently a Ph.D. student in English Studies at the University of Wollongong in New South Wales, Australia. Previously, she taught for fifteen years in Cultural Studies and English at Trent University in Ontario. Her article "Alien Cryptographies: The View from Queer" won the Science Fiction Research Association's Pioneer Award in 2000 for the best critical article of the year.

BRIAN STABLEFORD has published more than fifty novels, most recently a future history series so far consisting of *Inherit the Earth* (1998), *Architects of Emortality* (1999), *The Fountains of Youth* (2000), and *The Cassandra Complex* (2001). It will continue with *Dark Ararat* in 2002 and conclude with *The Omega Expedition* in 2003. His recent nonfiction includes a flagrantly propagandistic article on "Biotechnology and Utopia," reprinted in *The Philosophy of Utopia*, edited by Barbara Goodwin (2001). He also currently teaches an M.A. course, "Writing for Children," at King Alfred's College, Winchester.

GARY K. WOLFE is Professor of Humanities and English at Roosevelt University in Chicago. His *The Known and the Unknown: The Iconography of Science Fiction* (1979) received the Eaton Award, and he has subsequently received the Science Fiction Research Association's Pilgrim Award and the International Association for the Fantastic in the Arts' Distinguished Scholarship Award. He is currently a contributing editor and reviewer for *Locus* magazine and, with Ellen Weil, the author of a new study of Harlan Ellison.

JENNY WOLMARK lectures in critical and cultural theory at the University of Lincoln. She is the author of *Aliens and Others: Science Fiction, Feminism and Postmodernism* (1994) and editor of *Cybersexualities: A Reader on Feminist Theory, Cyborgs and Cyberspace* (1999). She is co-editor of the *Journal of Gender Studies*.

Index

Acknowledgments

We would like to express our ongoing gratitude to our friends and colleagues in the Science Fiction Research Association and the International Association for the Fantastic in the Arts. They are our ideal academy. We also thank Daniel Bernardi, John Digby, Jane Donawerth, John Scheckter, and Patricia Smith for wise advice and supportive gestures along the way and Trent University and Nassau Community College for the institutional support which is the *sine qua non* of projects like this. Finally, we are most grateful to the scholars and writers who contributed their work to make this project possible—graceful colleagues and graceful thinkers all.

Rob Latham's "Mutant Youth: Posthuman Fantasies and High-Tech Consumption in 1990s Science Fiction" is excerpted from *Consuming Youth: Vampires, Cyborgs, and the Culture of Consumption* (University of Chicago Press, 2002). We are grateful to the University of Chicago Press for permission to reprint this material.